Wake Tech
English 111 Reader

Rawpixel.com/Shutterstock.com

Editors

Wayde Vickrey
Monique Harris
Sarah M. Boone
Laura W. Ingram
Deborah Maness
Melanie Leah Bussi Morgan
Cynthia Booth Neighbors
Melody Owens
David C. Phillips
Tonisha Smith

Contributors

Don Ball
Julie Fenton-Glass
Lesley Greybeal
Laura W. Ingram
Beth Keeley
Deborah Maness
Joe Marohl
Win Neagle
Cynthia Booth Neighbors
Jim Neilson
Faye V. Stall
Jenifer Wolkowski

hayden-mcneil
Macmillan Learning

Macmillan Learning Curriculum Solutions
14903 Pilot Drive
Plymouth, MI 48170
www.macmillanlearning.com

Vickrey 2302-8 F20

Sustainability

Hayden-McNeil/Macmillan Learning Curriculum Solutions is proud to be a part of the larger sustainability initiative of Macmillan, our parent company. Macmillan has a goal to reduce its carbon emissions by 65% by 2020 from our 2010 baseline. Additionally, paper purchased must adhere to the Macmillan USA Paper Sourcing and Use Policy.

Hayden-McNeil partners with printers that use paper that is consistent with the environmental goals and values of Macmillan USA. This includes using paper certified by the Forest Stewardship Council (FSC), Sustainable Forestry Initiative (SFI), and/or the Programme for the Endorsement of Forest Certification (PEFC). We also offer paper with varying percentages of post-consumer waste as well as a 100% recycled stock. Additionally, Hayden-McNeil Custom Digital provides authors with the opportunity to convert print products to a digital format to use no paper at all. Visit http://sustainability.macmillan.com to learn more.

WELCOME!

Welcome to Wake Tech's custom English 111 reader. In our experience, good writers learn to write well by reading good writing. The good writings included in this reader were chosen by Wake Tech's English faculty and represent a broad selection of classical to modern readings.

To the instructor:

Readings are divided overall into some "Reading and Writing Strategies" on page 1 from Wake Tech instructors, and general "Readings (Alphabetical by author)" on page 35. Each of the general readings has a short collection of questions for guided reading at the end.

We have included three Tables of Contents (ToC). The first is a simple Alphabetical ToC arranged by author's last name. The second is a Thematic ToC beginning on page x for faculty who organize their classes in a thematic manner. And the third is a Rhetorical Mode ToC beginning on page xvi for faculty who use a modal organization in their classes. In addition to this Rhetorical ToC, each reading includes a brief list of abbreviated Rhetorical Modes for which the reading might be used. The key to these abbreviated modes can be found in the "Readings" on page v.

In addition, there is an "Index of Authors and Titles" (on page 343) for when you know the author or the title, but you just cannot find the reading. Those codes are found on page v.

To the student:

First, review the Reading and Writing Strategies from Wake Tech instructors; these writings are included because they can help you be a better writing student.

Second, plan to participate in your English 111 class by doing your readings as assigned (doing the readings is the beginning of your success in this class) and by participating in class. Student involvement is a key to student success.

Third, please note that success in a college class is more than simply doing the assigned reading. Success in college does require that you read the readings, but it also requires that you think about what you have read. Internalize the ideas. Make them yours whether you agree with them or not. Consider why your instructor assigned a given reading. What is in it for you? What does your instructor expect you to take away from that reading? How will it help you be a better student? A better thinker? A better writer?

Someone may have told you that you get out of life what you put into it, and that saying is never more true than in a college classroom. So get reading, get learning, get thinking, and get writing.

RHETORICAL MODE KEY

- **A** Analogy

- **AP** Argument and Persuasion

- **CC** Compare and Contrast

- **CE** Cause and Effect

- **CD** Classification and Division

- **DEF** Definition

- **DES** Description

- **IE** Illustration and Exemplification

- **N** Narration

- **PA** Process Analysis

TABLE OF CONTENTS

 READING AND WRITING STRATEGIES

Critical Reading 1
Dr. Joe Marohl

The Writing Process 5
Deborah Maness
Faye V. Stall

Making Meaning: An Introduction to Rhetoric 9
Dr. Lesley Graybeal

Writing Fluid Sentences and Cohesive Paragraphs 11
Dr. Jim Neilson

The Art of Summary in Academic Writing 15
Cynthia Booth Neighbors
Laura W. Ingram

Writing Introductions and Conclusions 20
Dr. Jenifer Wolkowski

Writing Effective Thesis Statements and Topic Sentences 23
Julie Fenton-Glass

Writing the Narrative-Descriptive Essay 25
Win Neagle

Writing the Definition Essay 26
Beth Keeley

Writing the Causal Analysis Essay 28
Win Neagle

Writing the Comparison and Contrast Essay 30
Julie Fenton-Glass

Writing the Exemplification Essay 33
Dr. Don Ball

 READINGS (ALPHABETICAL BY AUTHOR)

How to Mark a Book 35
Mortimer Adler

I Want to Be Miss America 40
Julia Alvarez

Is Google Making Us Stupid? 46
Nicholas Carr

You Left Out the Part About 57
Ta-Nehisi Coates

Learning to Read and Write 60
Frederick Douglass

Nickel and Dimed: On (Not) Getting By in America 66
Barbara Ehrenreich

Freewriting 93
Peter Elbow

Supersaturation, or, The Media Torrent and Disposable Feeling 97
Todd Gitlin

Salvation 104
Langston Hughes

When Bright Girls Decide that Math Is "a Waste of Time" 107
Susan Jacoby

My Creature from the Black Lagoon 111
Stephen King

Letter from Birmingham Jail 120
Martin Luther King Jr.

Stone Soup 136
Barbara Kingsolver

The Death of Horatio Alger 144
Paul Krugman

The College Dropout Boom 148
David Leonhardt

Being Country 160
Bobbie Ann Mason

Designer Genes..164
Bill McKibben

The Way to Rainy Mountain 176
N. Scott Momaday

The Maker's Eye: Revising Your Own Manuscripts 182
Donald M. Murray

Shooting an Elephant 188
George Orwell

A Note to Young Immigrants 195
Mitali Perkins

The Allegory of the Cave..198
Plato

Sex Ed..206
Anna Quindlen

Why the Rich Are Getting Richer, and the Poor, Poorer............................209
Robert B. Reich

Family Values 223
Richard Rodriguez

The Lonely, Good Company of Books... 231
Richard Rodriguez

Black and White in Shades of Gray.. 236
Reihan Salam

Under the Influence 242
Scott Russell Sanders

Wonder Woman...255
Gloria Steinem

Mother Tongue.. 265
Amy Tan

Sex, Lies and Conversation: Why Is It So Hard for Men and Women to Talk to
        Each Other?..271
Deborah Tannen

Where I Lived, And What I Lived For... 278
Henry David Thoreau

"This Is the End of the World": The Black Death...291
Barbara Tuchman

How Computers Change the Way We Think...301
Sherry Turkle

Everyday Use..308
Alice Walker

Once More to the Lake 317
E. B. White

Professions for Women 324
Virginia Woolf

Learning to Read..330
Malcolm X

Credits 339

Index of Authors and Titles...343

THEMATIC
TABLE OF CONTENTS

COMMUNICATION AND LANGUAGE

How to Mark a Book 35
Mortimer Adler

Learning to Read and Write 60
Frederick Douglass

Freewriting 93
Peter Elbow

The Maker's Eye: Revising Your Own Manuscripts 182
Donald M. Murray

The Lonely, Good Company of Books 231
Richard Rodriguez

Mother Tongue 265
Amy Tan

Sex, Lies and Conversation: Why Is It So Hard for Men and Women
    to Talk to Each Other? 271
Deborah Tannen

Learning to Read 330
Malcolm X

EDUCATION

Learning to Read and Write 60
Frederick Douglass

When Bright Girls Decide that Math Is "a Waste of Time" 107
Susan Jacoby

The College Dropout Boom 148
David Leonhardt

Sex Ed 206
Anna Quindlen

The Lonely, Good Company of Books 231
Richard Rodriguez

Mother Tongue 265
Amy Tan

How Computers Change the Way We Think 301
Sherry Turkle

Learning to Read 330
Malcolm X

GENDER AND SEXUALITY

I Want to Be Miss America 40
Julia Alvarez

When Bright Girls Decide that Math Is "a Waste of Time" 107
Susan Jacoby

Sex Ed 206
Anna Quindlen

Family Values 223
Richard Rodriguez

Wonder Woman 255
Gloria Steinem

Sex, Lies and Conversation: Why Is It So Hard for Men and Women
    to Talk to Each Other? 271
Deborah Tannen

Professions for Women 324
Virginia Woolf

FAMILY

I Want to Be Miss America 40
Julia Alvarez

You Left Out the Part About 57
Ta-Nehisi Coates

Stone Soup 136
Barbara Kingsolver

Being Country 160
Bobbie Ann Mason

The Way to Rainy Mountain 176
N. Scott Momaday

Family Values 223
Richard Rodriguez

Under the Influence 242
Scott Russell Sanders

Mother Tongue 265
Amy Tan

Everyday Use 308
Alice Walker

Once More to the Lake 317
E. B. White

TECHNOLOGY AND SCIENCE

Is Google Making Us Stupid? 46
Nicholas Carr

You Left Out the Part About 57
Ta-Nehisi Coates

Supersaturation, or, The Media Torrent and Disposable Feeling..................................97
Todd Gitlin

Designer Genes...164
Bill McKibben

The Allegory of the Cave...198
Plato

How Computers Change the Way We Think...301
Sherry Turkle

MEDIA AND POP CULTURE

I Want to Be Miss America 40
Julia Alvarez

Is Google Making Us Stupid?..46
Nicholas Carr

You Left Out the Part About...57
Ta-Nehisi Coates

Supersaturation, or, The Media Torrent and Disposable Feeling..................................97
Todd Gitlin

My Creature from the Black Lagoon...111
Stephen King

A Note to Young Immigrants...195
Mitali Perkins

Wonder Woman..255
Gloria Steinem

How Computers Change the Way We Think...301
Sherry Turkle

WORK AND CLASS

Nickel and Dimed: On (Not) Getting By in America...66
Barbara Ehrenreich

Supersaturation, or, The Media Torrent and Disposable Feeling..................................97
Todd Gitlin

The Death of Horatio Alger 144
Paul Krugman

The College Dropout Boom..148
David Leonhardt

Shooting an Elephant..188
George Orwell

Why the Rich Are Getting Richer, and the Poor, Poorer.....................................209
Robert B. Reich

Black and White in Shades of Gray..236
Reihan Salam

Everyday Use..308
Alice Walker

PHILOSOPHY AND RELIGION

Salvation..104
Langston Hughes

The Allegory of the Cave..198
Plato

Where I Lived, And What I Lived For...278
Henry David Thoreau

Learning to Read..330
Malcolm X

HEALTH AND MEDICINE

Designer Genes..164
Bill McKibben

Sex Ed...206
Anna Quindlen

Under the Influence 242
Scott Russell Sanders

"This Is the End of the World": The Black Death....................................291
Barbara Tuchman

POLITICS AND HISTORY

Nickel and Dimed: On (Not) Getting By in America...............................66
Barbara Ehrenreich

Letter from Birmingham Jail...120
Martin Luther King Jr.

The Death of Horatio Alger 144
Paul Krugman

The Way to Rainy Mountain...176
N. Scott Momaday

Shooting an Elephant...188
George Orwell

Black and White in Shades of Gray..236
Reihan Salam

"This Is the End of the World": The Black Death....................................291
Barbara Tuchman

Once More to the Lake 317
E. B. White

Learning to Read 330
Malcolm X

ETHICS AND MORALITY

You Left Out the Part About 57
Ta-Nehisi Coates

Salvation 104
Langston Hughes

Letter from Birmingham Jail 120
Martin Luther King Jr.

Stone Soup 136
Barbara Kingsolver

Designer Genes 164
Bill McKibben

Shooting an Elephant 188
George Orwell

IDENTITY

I Want to Be Miss America 40
Julia Alvarez

You Left Out the Part About 57
Ta-Nehisi Coates

Learning to Read and Write 60
Frederick Douglass

My Creature from the Black Lagoon 111
Stephen King

Being Country 160
Bobbie Ann Mason

The Way to Rainy Mountain 176
N. Scott Momaday

A Note to Young Immigrants 195
Mitali Perkins

Family Values 223
Richard Rodriguez

The Lonely, Good Company of Books 231
Richard Rodriguez

Under the Influence 242
Scott Russell Sanders

Wonder Woman 255
Gloria Steinem

Mother Tongue 265
Amy Tan

Where I Lived, And What I Lived For...278
Henry David Thoreau

Everyday Use..308
Alice Walker

Once More to the Lake 317
E. B. White

Learning to Read..330
Malcolm X

RACE AND CULTURE

I Want to Be Miss America 40
Julia Alvarez

You Left Out the Part About..57
Ta-Nehisi Coates

Nickel and Dimed: On (Not) Getting By in America.......................................66
Barbara Ehrenreich

Salvation 104
Langston Hughes

Letter from Birmingham Jail...120
Martin Luther King Jr.

The College Dropout Boom...148
David Leonhardt

Being Country..160
Bobbie Ann Mason

The Way to Rainy Mountain...176
N. Scott Momaday

A Note to Young Immigrants..195
Mitali Perkins

Sex Ed..206
Anna Quindlen

Why the Rich Are Getting Richer, and the Poor, Poorer...............................209
Robert B. Reich

Family Values...223
Richard Rodriguez

The Lonely, Good Company of Books...231
Richard Rodriguez

Black and White in Shades of Gray...236
Reihan Salam

Under the Influence 242
Scott Russell Sanders

Mother Tongue...265
Amy Tan

Everyday Use..308
Alice Walker

Learning to Read..330
Malcolm X

RHETORICAL MODE TABLE OF CONTENTS

NARRATION

I Want to Be Miss America 40
Julia Alvarez

You Left Out the Part About 57
Ta-Nehisi Coates

Learning to Read and Write 60
Frederick Douglass

Nickel and Dimed: On (Not) Getting By in America 66
Barbara Ehrenreich

Salvation 104
Langston Hughes

My Creature from the Black Lagoon 111
Stephen King

The Death of Horatio Alger 144
Paul Krugman

Being Country 160
Bobbie Ann Mason

The Way to Rainy Mountain 176
N. Scott Momaday

Shooting an Elephant 188
George Orwell

Family Values 223
Richard Rodriguez

The Lonely, Good Company of Books 231
Richard Rodriguez

Under the Influence 242
Scott Russell Sanders

Wonder Woman 255
Gloria Steinem

Mother Tongue 265
Amy Tan

Where I Lived, And What I Lived For 278
Henry David Thoreau

"This Is the End of the World": The Black Death 291
Barbara Tuchman

Everyday Use 308
Alice Walker

Once More to the Lake 317
E. B. White

Learning to Read 330
Malcolm X

DESCRIPTION

I Want to Be Miss America 40
Julia Alvarez

You Left Out the Part About 57
Ta-Nehisi Coates

Nickel and Dimed: On (Not) Getting By in America 66
Barbara Ehrenreich

Supersaturation, or, The Media Torrent and Disposable Feeling 97
Todd Gitlin

Salvation 104
Langston Hughes

The Way to Rainy Mountain 176
N. Scott Momaday

Shooting an Elephant 188
George Orwell

A Note to Young Immigrants 195
Mitali Perkins

"This Is the End of the World": The Black Death 291
Barbara Tuchman

Once More to the Lake 317
E. B. White

Learning to Read 330
Malcolm X

ILLUSTRATION AND EXEMPLIFICATION

I Want to Be Miss America 40
Julia Alvarez

How to Mark a Book 35
Mortimer Adler

You Left Out the Part About 57
Ta-Nehisi Coates

Nickel and Dimed: On (Not) Getting By in America 66
Barbara Ehrenreich

Freewriting 93
Peter Elbow

Letter from Birmingham Jail 120
Martin Luther King Jr.

Being Country 160
Bobble Ann Mason

Designer Genes 164
Bill McKibben

The Maker's Eye: Revising Your Own Manuscripts 182
Donald M. Murray

Shooting an Elephant 188
George Orwell

A Note to Young Immigrants 195
Mitali Perkins

The Allegory of the Cave 198
Plato

Sex Ed 206
Anna Quindlen

Why the Rich Are Getting Richer, and the Poor, Poorer 209
Robert B. Reich

The Lonely, Good Company of Books 231
Richard Rodriguez

Black and White in Shades of Gray 236
Reihan Salam

Sex, Lies and Conversation: Why Is It So Hard for Men and Women
    to Talk to Each Other? 271
Deborah Tannen

Where I Lived, And What I Lived For 278
Henry David Thoreau

How Computers Change the Way We Think 301
Sherry Turkle

Once More to the Lake 317
E. B. White

Learning to Read 330
Malcolm X

COMPARE AND CONTRAST

I Want to Be Miss America 40
Julia Alvarez

You Left Out the Part About 57
Ta-Nehisi Coates

Nickel and Dimed: On (Not) Getting By in America 66
Barbara Ehrenreich

Supersaturation, or, The Media Torrent and Disposable Feeling 97
Todd Gitlin

My Creature from the Black Lagoon 111
Stephen King

Letter from Birmingham Jail 120
Martin Luther King Jr.

Stone Soup 136
Barbara Kingsolver

Being Country 160
Bobbie Ann Mason

The Allegory of the Cave 198
Plato

Why the Rich Are Getting Richer, and the Poor, Poorer 209
Robert B. Reich

Black and White in Shades of Gray 236
Reihan Salam

Under the Influence 242
Scott Russell Sanders

Sex, Lies and Conversation: Why Is It So Hard for Men and Women
    to Talk to Each Other? 271
Deborah Tannen

Where I Lived, And What I Lived For 278
Henry David Thoreau

How Computers Change the Way We Think 301
Sherry Turkle

Everyday Use 308
Alice Walker

Once More to the Lake 317
E. B. White

Learning to Read 330
Malcolm X

DEFINITION

I Want to Be Miss America 40
Julia Alvarez

Supersaturation, or, The Media Torrent and Disposable Feeling 97
Todd Gitlin

Salvation 104
Langston Hughes

Letter from Birmingham Jail 120
Martin Luther King Jr.

Being Country 160
Bobbie Ann Mason

The Way to Rainy Mountain 176
N. Scott Momaday

A Note to Young Immigrants 195
Mitali Perkins

Sex Ed 206
Anna Quindlen

Family Values 223
Richard Rodriguez

Under the Influence 242
Scott Russell Sanders

Everyday Use 308
Alice Walker

CLASSIFICATION AND DIVISION

How to Mark a Book 35
Mortimer Adler

The Maker's Eye: Revising Your Own Manuscript 182
Donald M. Murray

Why the Rich Are Getting Richer, and the Poor, Poorer 209
Robert B. Reich

Family Values 223
Richard Rodriguez

Black and White in Shades of Gray 236
Reihan Salam

Mother Tongue 265
Amy Tan

ARGUMENT AND PERSUASION

Is Google Making Us Stupid? 46
Nicholas Carr

You Left Out the Part About 57
Ta-Nehisi Coates

When Bright Girls Decide that Math Is "a Waste of Time" 107
Susan Jacoby

Letter from Birmingham Jail 120
Martin Luther King Jr.

Stone Soup 136
Barbara Kingsolver

Designer Genes 164
Bill McKibben

Shooting an Elephant 188
George Orwell

A Note to Young Immigrants 195
Mitali Perkins

The Allegory of the Cave 198
Plato

Black and White in Shades of Gray 236
Reihan Salam

Sex Ed 206
Anna Quindlen

Why the Rich Are Getting Richer, and the Poor, Poorer 209
Robert B. Reich

Family Values 223
Richard Rodriguez

Wonder Woman 255
Gloria Steinem

Sex, Lies and Conversation: Why Is It So Hard for Men and Women
   to Talk to Each Other?..271
Deborah Tannen

Where I Lived, And What I Lived For..278
Henry David Thoreau

How Computers Change the Way We Think..301
Sherry Turkle

Professions for Women 324
Virginia Woolf

PROCESS ANALYSIS

I Want to Be Miss America...40
Julia Alvarez

How to Mark a Book..35
Mortimer Adler

Learning to Read and Write 60
Frederick Douglass

Nickel and Dimed: On (Not) Getting By in America.............................66
Barbara Ehrenreich

Freewriting 93
Peter Elbow

The Death of Horatio Alger 144
Paul Krugman

The College Dropout Boom...148
David Leonhardt

The Maker's Eye: Revising Your Own Manuscripts 182
Donald M. Murray

Why the Rich Are Getting Richer, and the Poor, Poorer........................209
Robert B. Reich

Under the Influence 242
Scott Russell Sanders

"This Is the End of the World": The Black Death...................................291
Barbara Tuchman

How Computers Change the Way We Think..301
Sherry Turkle

Learning to Read...330
Malcolm X

CAUSE AND EFFECT

Is Google Making Us Stupid?...46
Nicholas Carr

Supersaturation, or, The Media Torrent and Disposable Feeling..................97
Todd Gitlin

When Bright Girls Decide that "Math Is a Waste of Time"........................107
Susan Jacoby

The College Dropout Boom 148
David Leonhardt

Designer Genes 164
Bill McKibben

A Note to Young Immigrants 195
Mitali Perkins

The Allegory of the Cave 198
Plato

Sex Ed 206
Anna Quindlen

Family Values 223
Richard Rodriguez

Black and White in Shades of Gray 236
Reihan Salam

Under the Influence 242
Scott Russell Sanders

Wonder Woman 255
Gloria Steinem

Sex, Lies and Conversation: Why Is It So Hard for Men and Women
    to Talk to Each Other? 271
Deborah Tannen

Where I Lived, And What I Lived For 278
Henry David Thoreau

How Computers Change the Way We Think 301
Sherry Turkle

Learning to Read 330
Malcolm X

ANALOGY

How to Mark a Book 35
Mortimer Adler

The Maker's Eye: Revising Your Own Manuscripts 182
Donald M. Murray

The Allegory of the Cave 198
Plato

Professions for Women 324
Virginia Woolf

CRITICAL READING

Dr. Joe Marohl
Professor

Wake Technical Community College

1   Reading for college involves more than simply "reading over" assigned pages in textbooks. Even students who are diligent in keeping up with a course's reading requirements often forget what they read just a few days earlier. Reading to remember or, more importantly, to *learn* the material for later application at work and in life requires more than a quick read-through. Furthermore, beyond memorization of key facts, definitions, and data, professors expect students to demonstrate critical thinking skills. Critical thinking means the ability to process information and other people's opinions and come up with ideas, insights, and solutions of our own. It involves four distinct skills: analysis, synthesis, interpretation, and evaluation.

2   Careful readers must be able to methodically separate details and understand the ways these details contribute to the idea the author is trying to communicate. This skill is called analysis. For instance, in watching a film, an informed and critical viewer can distinguish different elements that contribute to the film's overall effectiveness: the quality of the dialogue and acting, the use of lighting and color, the variety of camera angles, and the pace of the editing, among others. In reading a chapter of a history textbook, the analytical student can separate the content into categories, like key personalities, an era's significant conflicts in beliefs and values, and causes and effects of specific events. Analysis also involves imagination. It's important to develop the habit of asking imaginative questions about texts, such as "How might this film be different with a different cast of actors?" or "What might have happened if the United States had decided to distance itself from the two world wars of the twentieth century?" The goal of analysis and all critical thinking is to form personal opinions on the subject. For college professors, a student's ability to develop well-informed but personal positions is more important than a student's ability to simply repeat information from readings and class lectures.

3   Another important critical thinking skill is synthesis. Synthesis is the ability to discover important connections between two separate ideas or among a larger number of ideas. Comparison and contrast are simple forms of synthesis. One goal of liberal arts education is to encourage students to detect important differences in things that people usually perceive as similar, such as differences between slavery in ancient Rome and slavery in the antebellum American South. Just as important, students should explore typically unnoticed resemblances, such as the similarities in storyline between two Hollywood films, like 1943's *Lassie Come Home* and 1982's *E.T. the Extra-Extraterrestrial* (which both contain themes like discovery, relationship-building, loss, and reunion). Over time, college students should begin to see connections even among the varied disciplines required for graduation, like how sentence grammar relates to mathematical logic and how geology helped shape American history. The goal is not simply to make unusual connections for their own sake, but to use them as a means of acquiring a point of view of one's own.

4   Besides analysis and synthesis, critical reading should involve interpretation. Interpretation is "reading between the lines" and "putting two and two together." When students interpret what they read, they are looking for the insinuations and implications of the author's choice of words, examples, and even pictorial illustrations. There's usually more to a written work than the words on the page. In some cases, such as a literature course, students may need to read a work for its tone, that is, the implied but never directly stated attitude of the author. Students should be able to detect when a writer is being ironic or sarcastic or playful or serious. Students should be able to make an educated guess about a writer's values and beliefs based on details that seem to support the assumption. The goals of interpretation are insight, understanding, and judgment, by which students can process the same information others have, yet come up with an original point of view that is consistent with logic and the facts.

5   Evaluation is the fourth skill involved in critical reading and critical thinking. Evaluation is an important aspect of college-level research. The authorities and experts we consult through research do not always agree with one another. Therefore, it's necessary to apply the three other skills (analysis, synthesis, and interpretation) to determine which source has the greater value in answering our research question. We must ask ourselves questions to confirm each expert's authority and credibility. Which authority is the most highly esteemed by other writers? Which

expert provides the most factual support for her or his opinion? Which writer draws the most valid conclusions from the existing information on the subject? Which writer shows the greatest respect for other points of view? Which point of view is the most consistent with itself? Which expert avoids emotionally charged and manipulative language? Which authority has the least to gain personally in holding the right opinion on the issue? Careful evaluation determines the weight we are willing to give something in the formulation of our own opinions on a subject. It is important for forming a personal stance that is not excessively influenced by emotion, cherished belief, prejudice, or need.

6   Obviously, these four skills cannot be exercised in one rushed reading. Critical reading involves at least three steps. The first of these steps is a quick glance over the material. The title, chapter headings, illustrations, and even the length of the work create certain expectations of what the writer intends to communicate and how, in much the same way that a movie trailer or poster prepares ticket-buyers for a particular film. Audiences go to a romantic comedy with expectations, which the filmmakers may then play with, either by meeting them or by modifying them through a series of surprise twists. Similarly, it's good to come to a reading assignment with expectations about what a writer might have to say, to be primed to engage actively with the material. Next, a fast-paced word-for-word reading fills in some of the details. At this point, we are reading for fun and discovery only, without stopping or pausing. This step should raise questions, though, inspired by critical thinking skills, and we will attempt to answer these questions in the next reading. The third step is to read the material slowly, taking notes, asking ourselves more questions about the ideas and the ways they are communicated, attempting answers to those questions, looking up unfamiliar words, and making judgments of our own. Slow and minutely focused reading is the key to understanding and retention; it sets the stage for our making discoveries of our own. An especially challenging work may require a greater number of readings, but the three-step process is a good place to start.

- Critical reading includes
    - Analysis
    - Synthesis
    - Interpretation
    - Evaluation
- A three-step process for critical reading includes
    - Skimming the material for overall topic and structure
    - Reading quickly for key questions and issues
    - Reading slowly and carefully for understanding

THE WRITING PROCESS

Deborah Maness
Associate Professor

Faye V. Stall
Associate Professor

Wake Technical Community College

What Is the Writing Process?

1   Writers have different strategies for getting words on paper. Some writers begin by jotting down everything they know about a topic. Some writers write a topic in the middle of a page and create a graphic organizer consisting of a web of ideas surrounding the topic to develop into separate paragraphs. Others research a topic before writing a word. Many professional writers are disciplined about scheduling time to write a specific number of pages daily. Creating a plan for a paper is important to create cohesive structure and a logical organization of ideas. No matter how a writer begins, there are specific steps that all writers should follow. The Writing Process includes structured steps to guide writers to a better product. The Writing Process includes pre-writing, drafting, revising and editing.

Pre-Writing

2   The first step in the writing process is choosing a topic and deciding how to present this topic in writing. Pre-writing allows the writer to explore different aspects of a topic and narrow down specific points. Pre-writing is any writing completed in preparation for a paper. It may include free writing, which is uninterrupted continuous writing. Pre-writing also includes outlining. An outline may be informal or formal. Informal outlines may be visual, like a web or shapes with ideas, or just lists of points to be included. A formal outline is more organized in phrases or complete sentences with a specific topic, thesis, topic sentences, supporting details, and resources. Pre-writing is an excellent beginning for writing for the writer to evaluate ideas and judge whether or not they have enough information and knowledge to write a thorough detailed paper.

Drafting

3   Once a writer decides on a topic that he or she feels can be fully developed into the required paper, the writing begins. Drafting is taking the ideas from the pre-writing and developing a good working thesis, topic sentences with paragraphs of support and elaboration, and in-text citations, if required. Drafting can begin at any point of the paper. Some students begin papers with the introduction and write in order of the body paragraphs to the conclusion. Often, it is better to write the thesis and body paragraphs before the introduction and conclusion. Sometimes students begin with an introduction, but as the paper is developed, it takes a different direction than first expected, and the previously written introduction no longer works well. Some writers find it easier to write the body paragraphs first, then the introduction and conclusion.

4   Writing can begin at any point in the paper. The most important strategy to remember is to fully develop all parts of the paper and not forget any parts: introduction, body paragraphs, and conclusion. To fully develop a body paragraph, think of the writing as a sandwich. The topic sentence and the concluding sentence are the pieces of bread. The meat, cheese, lettuce, and condiments are the supporting details. Supporting details give information that support the main point or idea; these details can be made up of examples, facts, statistics, and citations to give the paragraph elaboration.

5   When writing an introduction, remember to lead with a hook statement that captures the audience's attention and is relevant to the topic of the paper. Make sure that any background information is discussed. End the introduction with a thesis statement. The thesis provides the framework for the body paragraphs. A thesis should be multilayered and usually contains two to three directions of the topic the writer intends to discuss within the body paragraphs. A thesis should never be a question.

6   The conclusion restates the thesis using different wording and ends leaving the reader with a final thought to consider on the topic. Do not begin discussing anything new in the conclusion. The conclusion reviews the writing and brings finality to the essay. After writing a paper, it is wise to leave it for a period of time. Returning to a paper after a day, or at least a few hours, will help the writer read the paper more objectively to identify any points of weakness that need revision.

Revising

7   After a paper is written, the real writing begins to make the paper better. The paper needs to be read carefully to see if all points are explained thoroughly and are organized in the most logical order. A first step in revision is to read the thesis and topic sentences. Evaluate if the topic sentences are supporting the thesis and explaining the topic. A second step is to evaluate each paragraph. Each paragraph should be fully developed with details that make the points clear to the reader. The support in the paper must explain the topic and points in the paper. The support should be both adequate and comprehensive. This is how the length of the paper is achieved, providing details. This support often includes quotes from experts. These experts can be introduced so the reader understands their relevance. When citations are required, it is best to begin with a sentence that establishes credibility by providing the author's name and title of the text being used and providing context for the citation. Insert the citation, then follow the citation explaining why this quote is being used for support. Do not just drop in a citation.

8   Revision includes changing words, sentences, and even paragraphs of the paper to make it better. It also involves adding more information if needed, deleting information that is repetitive or not necessary, and moving words and sentences around to achieve cohesiveness to make the writing strong and unified. Another beneficial strategy that assists with cohesion and unity of the writing is to read the writing out loud. Some writers benefit from reading aloud themselves or to have someone else read it out loud to listen. Another technique is to read each sentence starting with the last sentence and moving backwards. Read each sentence to make sure each one is a complete thought and can stand alone. After the words of the paper are clear, proof for any errors in spelling, punctuation, and grammar, edit.

Editing

9   After a writer is pleased with the wording and organization of a paper, there are a few more details to review. Some scholars believe that revision and editing cannot be done at the same time. The human brain cannot do both activities synchronously because different skill sets are required. To begin editing, check the MLA formatting. A page number

header is inserted in the top right preceded by the student/writer's last name. Lines one through four in the top left identify the student/writer's name, instructor's name, course, and date written as day month year. Ensure there is a centered original title and all paragraphs are indented. All font must be consistent for the entire essay, including the header and Works Cited. Identify any problems notated by Microsoft Word. Often, spelling, grammar, and punctuation errors are marked with red, blue, or green lines under each word for the writer to correct. Confirm all sentences are punctuated. Review commas and correct comma splices. A comma splice is when a comma is used incorrectly to join two independent clauses. Look at the subject-verb agreement of each sentence. Review any pronouns used in the writing. Only third person pronouns are allowed in academic writing (he, his, him, she, her, hers, it, its, they, them, and their). Check to be sure a pronoun matches the subject, which is pronoun-antecedent agreement. Lastly, review the Works Cited citations and refer to correct examples. Editing improves the presentation of the essay.

Summary

10   The writing process provides a structure to begin a paper and develop a piece of writing to be the best possible. Writing is much like a painting, dance, or piece of music. Improvement is always possible. Using the Writing Process will provide writers with a guide to strengthen one's writing skills from the beginning to the end of an essay.

The Writing Process Steps

- Pre-writing
- Drafting
- Revising
- Editing

MAKING MEANING:
AN INTRODUCTION TO RHETORIC

Dr. Lesley Graybeal

Central University of Arkansas

1   When we study rhetoric, we participate in an intellectual tradition that dates back to ancient Greece, which was home to thinkers like Plato and Aristotle who first noticed the relationship between the communication and participation in a democracy. As we can still see today, individuals who wish to maximize their voices in a democratic society must be able not only to vote, but also to articulate grievances at town hall meetings, write letters to their elected officials, and engage in critical dialogue with fellow citizens. While the first *rhetors* were primarily concerned with oral communication, we now include both written and spoken communication in the study of rhetoric, and college students who take courses in both writing and speech will likely notice some overlap between the two. Regardless of the method of delivery, all rhetoric must have an audience and a purpose. In college-level rhetoric, we typically assume that we have a college-level audience with some exposure to our topic, and, depending on our purpose, we have a number of rhetorical modes at our disposal.

2   Rhetorical modes are tools for organizing expression—they provide some standard structures for writers to follow, like templates for communicating certain types of ideas. While most college-level essays will have an introductory paragraph at the beginning and a concluding paragraph at the end, how we organize our ideas between the introduction and the conclusion depends upon the rhetorical mode. A comparison and contrast essay, for instance, might be organized by point of comparison, while a process analysis essay might be organized step-by-step. Each rhetorical mode comes with certain expectations for the content and structure that an essay should have, and these expectations help us ensure that we accomplish our purpose in writing. Rhetorical modes help us frame how we think about our topic, and any given topic can be viewed from multiple angles and thus discussed using multiple modes. A writer interested in poverty, for example, might choose the rhetorical mode of definition to explore what conditions define poverty in the United States,

causal analysis to investigate the causes or effects of poverty, and narration to describe one person's lived experience in poverty. Each rhetorical mode would require the writer to take a slightly different perspective and would provide readers with different insights. While we may not always choose the rhetorical mode for a particular writing assignment, understanding the purpose of each rhetorical mode is the first step in becoming successful *rhetors* in the classroom and beyond.

- Rhetoric is a millennia-old intellectual tradition created to empower citizens to participate in a democratic society
- All rhetoric has an author and a purpose
- Rhetorical modes provide different ways to approach a topic in writing
- Different rhetorical modes use different structures to accomplish their purpose

WRITING FLUID SENTENCES AND COHESIVE PARAGRAPHS

Dr. Jim Neilson
Professor

Wake Technical Community College

1   When asked what makes a good paragraph, students often say, "it flows." But writing a good, coherent paragraph does not happen through a natural and spontaneous overflowing of linked sentences. Such writing requires hard work. And this work begins by learning and implementing a few basic strategies.

Something Old/Something New

2   Flowing suggests movement. And that's what good writing does— each sentence is connected to a previous sentence. Rather than a flowing stream, we might think of sentences as Legos. Each Lego block fits into another. If it doesn't, the Lego structure will have gaps. With enough gaps, the structure will collapse, just as a paragraph falls apart when its sentences aren't properly connected.

3   So how do we connect sentences like Legos? Each sentence should refer to something in the previous sentence (the old) and should add something (the new). Here's an example of two disconnected sentences from an essay analyzing Jonathan Swift's *Gulliver's Travels*:

Swift is a misanthrope, a man who is disgusted with and hates his fellow human beings. A striking example can be seen in descriptions of men and women.

4   The connection between these sentences is unclear. Here's a revision that better connects them:

Swift is a misanthrope, a man who is disgusted with and hates his fellow human beings. A striking example of *misanthropy* can be seen in *his* descriptions of men and women.

5   We now have two sentences that are connected. The second sentence refers back to the old of the previous sentence (*misanthropy—misanthrope, his—Swift*). And it adds something new (descriptions of men and women). This pattern—something old + something new—is the basic formula for connecting sentences.

Pronouns

6   Besides the something old/something new pattern, several parts of speech help connect sentences. For instance, in the example above "descriptions" was changed to "his descriptions." "His" is a pronoun that refers back to "Swift." Because pronouns always refer back to a noun, they can be used to connect sentences.

Repetition of Keywords

7   Another way to connect sentences is to repeat keywords. In the example above, the word "misanthrope" is used in the first sentence, "misanthropy" in the second. Students often seek synonyms to avoid this kind of repetition and often end up writing a sentence like this:

> Swift is a misanthrope, a man who is disgusted with and hates his fellow human beings. A striking example of this cynical malcontentedness can be seen in his descriptions of men and women.

8   This revision may eliminate repetition, but it also makes the connection between these sentences far less clear. We encourage students to risk being repetitive if doing so helps connect sentences.

Transitions

9   The proper use of transitional words and phrases is essential for showing connections between sentences. Transitions include coordinating conjunctions (for, and, nor, but, or, yet, so); conjunctive adverbs like "however" and "therefore"; and commonly used transitional expressions like "for example" and "in other words."

10   Transitions do more than connect sentences; they establish the relationship between sentences:

> Swift is a misanthrope, a man who is disgusted with and hates his fellow human beings. *For example,* misanthropy can be seen in his descriptions of men and women.

11   The transitional phrase "for example" signals the relationship between these sentences. The first makes an assertion, while the second gives an example of what has just been asserted. Clearly marking the relationships between sentences in this way helps readers understand how sentences are connected.

12   We encourage the frequent use of transitional words and phrases. These words, however, can become boring and repetitive if always placed at the beginning of a sentence. It's useful to remember, therefore, that

these transitions can appear elsewhere in a sentence—as in this sentence and the previous one, or as can be seen here:

> Swift is a misanthrope, a man who is disgusted with and hates his fellow human beings. Misanthropy, for example, can be seen in his descriptions of men and women.

Demonstrative Adjectives

13   A final part of speech that connects sentences is demonstrative adjectives: this, that, these, those, such. These words point to something that's already been said (just as in this sentence "these words" refers to the demonstrative adjectives identified in the preceding sentence).

14   However, it's important to use these words as adjectives, not pronouns.

> **CORRECT** ("This" as adjective):
>
> Swift is a misanthrope, a man who is disgusted with and hates his fellow human beings. *This misanthropy* for example, can be seen in his descriptions of men and women.
>
> **INCORRECT** ("This" as pronoun):
>
> Swift is a misanthrope, a man who is disgusted with and hates his fellow human beings. *This*, for example, can be seen in his descriptions of men and women.

15   When used as a pronoun, "this" is almost always too vague. To avoid such vagueness, "this" should be used as an adjective connected to a noun. Often, this noun will be a keyword.

16   Here's another example of the vague use of "this":

> Gulliver presents a far greater problem for the Lilliputians, who must be sure every morning "that [his] offensive matter should be carried off in wheelbarrows" (2051). *This* suggests a hatred of human nature at its most basic level.

17   The use of "this" as a pronoun here is vague. Does "this" refer to Gulliver's presenting a problem for the Lilliputians? To the Lilliputians' making sure that his offensive matter is carried off? To the fact that wheelbarrows are needed to do so?

18   Demonstrative adjectives linked to nouns or phrases, on the other hand, can be quite specific. They are especially useful when discussing evidence:

Gulliver presents a far greater problem for the Lilliputians, who must be sure every morning "that [his] offensive matter should be carried off in wheelbarrows" (2051). *This focus on the grossest aspects of human biology* suggests a hatred of human nature at its most basic level.

19   Here "this" is not left alone but is connected to a phrase that identifies the central point of this quote: "this focus on the grossest aspects of human biology." Thus, more than merely connecting sentences, demonstrative adjectives when used well can help explain the significance of evidence, one of the most consistent and important goals of academic writing.

- The following techniques and tools can be used to make writing "flow":
  - The combination of something old and something new
  - Pronouns referring to an antecedent in the previous sentence
  - Repetition of keywords
  - Transitional words and phrases, including conjunctions (like "and" and "but"), conjunctive adverbs (like "however" and "therefore"), and transitional expressions (like "for example")
  - Demonstrative adjectives (like "this" and "these") used as adjectives, *not pronouns*
  - Should expand the essay's focus to consider the broader implications

THE ART OF SUMMARY IN ACADEMIC WRITING

Cynthia Booth Neighbors
Professor

Laura W. Ingram
Assistant Professor

Wake Technical Community College

Introduction

1   Summary is a writing tool that allows scholars to demonstrate their comprehension and understanding of a published work through restatement of its main points. At the college level, students will often be asked to complete such a task. An instructor may direct a student to summarize an assigned article as a formal writing assignment, or the student may be asked to summarize the main points of a speech on a history exam. In addition, college students will at some point be called upon to provide summation of published sources to validate and support points in research essays.

2   So, what is meant when an instructor asks a student to summarize? What are the steps in completing the summary? And how does a formal guided summary differ from a summary of researched data?

What Is Summary?

3   A formal academic summary, as indicated in the introduction, is a restatement of the main points of a published work. A guided summary provides a restatement of each main point in order of presentation in the original. A more condensed summary may only focus on the overall point made in the work or on just one detail necessary to cite evidence or information in a research paper.

4   Summarizing often presents a dilemma to students because the first inclination they have is to respond to the text and to add in details. It is quite difficult to fight that urge to offer opinion or response rather than to simply repeat back what is stated in the article. It is also necessary when summarizing to refrain from repeating what was read word for word. Restating the information from the original article in a way that demonstrates comprehension of the text is the trick to writing an effective summary.

5   Remembering the **GIST** method of summary—or **Give Information Stated in the Text**—can help students adhere to the rules of summary. When summarizing, one should abide by the following:

1. Restate only the main points in the article/essay being summarized: Refrain from including any minor details, examples, names, numbers, incidents, etc. shared by the author to underscore or support the overall idea.
2. Restate in the summarizer's own words: Do not repeat verbatim what the author says in his/her work. Rather, the summation should re-tell in the student's words what the author has said.
3. Do not Respond: No added responses should be included in the summary.
4. Include consistent attribution to the author: Make sure that the author is credited as the source of the information stated.

6   Keep in mind also that the summary should be half the length (or less) of the original work. A paragraph should be summarized in one sentence. A three-page article should be summarized in about a page. Always follow the guidelines provided in the assignment being completed.

What Is the Process of Summarizing?

7   Reading and writing are two activities that are inherently linked: the ability to *write* well depends on one's ability to *read* well, and both apply to summarizing. Reading well is the first step in writing an effective summary; it requires careful and deliberate interaction with the text. Good readers do not simply identify words on a page; they ask questions, make inferences, and look for connections as they read, often making notes and highlighting important passages as they move through a text.

8   **Good readers begin by previewing the assigned text.** They might examine the title and skim through the text to look for any headings and subheadings that might provide clues to the topic of the text.

9   **Next, readers skim through the text looking only for the "big picture."** Rather than focusing on details, they focus only on the main idea, or the overall message that the author is attempting to convey to his or her audience. This is often a difficult step, as some authors may only imply a claim rather than directly stating it.

10   Once readers can determine the author's argument, they **read the text again**, writing down questions, marking significant points that connect directly to the author's thesis, and using a dictionary to look up

unfamiliar words. Bottom line: Reading well takes time. It requires a commitment to learn even when a text is not particularly interesting.

11   **In the planning phase, students should review the guidelines of the summary assignment.** Once students have carefully read the text, usually multiple times, they are still often not ready to write the summary. Successful writing requires careful planning. While some instructors may require only a paragraph of summary, others may require a few pages. Because a summary is a condensed version of a text, knowing what the assignment requires will help students decide which details should be included and which ones should not. This planning phase also gives students time to organize their thoughts and think about how to best present the author's argument before beginning a draft.

12   **In the planning phase, a student should also create an outline—** even if it's just a list of bullet points from the reading—that is focused on the author's argument and moves through the major supporting points presented in the text. If the outlining process is difficult, then the student is not ready to outline and should instead re-read the text.

13   **When an effective outline has been achieved, students may begin drafting the summary.** However, if the drafting process is difficult, then the outline may need more work. The summary must be unified around the author's thesis. Therefore, a successful summary usually begins with a paraphrase of the author's thesis. Then, the major points from the text must be presented and explained without quoting the text directly, making sure to mention the author periodically so that readers know that the ideas belong to the author of the text and not the student.

14   Note that the summary should not merely contain a list of major points from the text. "List" summaries fail to provide readers a complete picture of how the points from the text are related, and they typically reveal that the student lacks a deep and comprehensive understanding of the text. Thus, a successful summary must include transition sentences that guide readers through the information showing them how the points from the text are related to each other and, most importantly, how they are related to the author's thesis. An effective summary will not only demonstrate the student's exemplary reading comprehension skills, but will also provide readers with a good understanding of an author's claim, even without reading the text themselves.

15   In short, the process of summary entails the following steps: **previewing the text, skimming the text, re-reading the text, and creating an outline before finally drafting the completed summary.** Following

this process will ensure that the summary is comprehensive in covering all the main points and that it fully conveys the author's purpose in the original text.

How Is a Guided Summary Different from Summation of Research?

16   When writing research papers, students will be called upon to provide evidence and verification for points made in their drafts. In order to do so, it will be important to draw from published articles, reports, or studies that help them substantiate their arguments or define the issues being examined in their papers. Summary, along with direct quotes and paraphrase, is one of the methods used to present researched information within a student's paper.

17   Summarizing a researched source allows a student to focus on the pertinent information given that supports his or her argument. It allows the student to extract just the information from the researched work that is relevant to the point being made or the issue being defined. Think of it as the juice from the orange rather than the whole fruit.

18   Summary should be used when the wording is not distinctive, necessitating a precise direct quote, and when only a loose overall restatement is needed to support a point made. Summary works best when highlighting points from a lengthy researched article. For example, restating in a direct quote all processes and findings of a research study may be tedious and unnecessary: bottom lining the findings of the study in summation will be much more useful and expedient. Likewise, pasting in an image of a table or chart that provides statistical data may not be appropriate for a formal research essay: summarizing the findings and pinpointing just the information useful for the matter at hand is a better strategy, allowing the student to focus on the details from the table or chart that are pertinent and useful to the overall goal of the paper.

19   When restating information in a new way, students should adhere to two rules:
1.   Make sure that the restatement factually presents the meaning of the original. Do not exaggerate the findings or add in information that is not there.
2.   Make sure that the source of the information is clear. The author/source of the information should be presented clearly with a lead-in that includes the author/source's name.

Conclusion

20   Learning how to summarize effectively is a valuable tool. Students who master the art of summary will find this skill useful not only in writing papers for English classes, but also in effectively completing essay exams and reports for other disciplines. Summation is the first step to the more critical steps of analysis and evaluation, so it is a crucial aspect of any assignment in any discipline. Learning to summarize is also an effective study tool to help students digest what they read and retain the information. Being able to re-tell the main ideas provides a stronger comprehension of the material, certainly leading to better retention and recall. Summary is a definite key to academic success.

WRITING INTRODUCTIONS AND CONCLUSIONS

Dr. Jenifer Wolkowski
Associate Professor

Wake Technical Community College

Introductions

1   Students often get confused and anxious about introductions. Some of that anxiety comes from trying to force an introduction first. The good news, however, is that we don't *need* to write introductions first if we don't want to. Sometimes, introductions are best left until we get a better sense of what we are writing or we are more comfortable with the material. Sometimes, the head of intellectual steam we build up by writing the body of a paper helps to clarify what we really want to say in an introduction. Some writers even write their introductions last.

2   If it helps, we might think of an essay like a martini glass. The introduction is the top part of the glass. It starts with the broadest part, then tapers logically to the thesis (the olive!).

3   When we start an introduction, we might want to *think* in terms of "in today's modern society" or "today many people believe." Those actual  phrases are too vague to be of assistance in our final draft, but can be used as thinking tools. We might try to model our introductions on the very best educational documentary. Such films catch viewers' attention from the very first sentence! As we taper from the broadest observation to more specific ones, we encounter a rough patch: the sentence right before the thesis. The thesis usually ends the introduction, and the space just before it can be a wonderful moment of fluid brilliance or a jarring jump that confuses the reader for a split second. The best writers use this space as an opportunity to refine their thoughts and transition into the topic of their essay as a specific example of what they have been explaining.

Rose-Marie Henriksson/Shutterstock.com

Here are a few strategies for successful introductions:

- Offer history

- Offer background

- Cite a provocative statistic

- Correct a misunderstanding or incorrect assumption

Depending on the assignment, we might also want to

- Use a quotation

- Offer a striking example

- Share an engaging anecdote

Strategies to avoid in collegiate paper introductions include

- Announcing the essay directly ("This paper will discuss" or "In this paper I will discuss")

- Starting the paper with empty expressions, like "In today's society"

- Starting the paper with overly broad claims, like "Throughout history"

4   Introductions are the best way to convey passion and interest in a topic, hook our reader, and guide him or her confidently to our paper's ideas.

Conclusions

5   Let's return to the image of the martini glass to discuss the base of the glass: our conclusion. As we can see from the image, conclusions don't have to be giant or even the same size as other paragraphs—they just have to wrap things up well and stabilize the entire essay.

6   Just as introductions don't have to be written first, conclusions don't have to be written last. When conclusions are written as an afterthought, they are often dry, boring, disappointing paragraphs that leave the reader wishing the paper had ended almost any other way.

7   We might model our conclusions on the ending of a favorite movie. Such closing scenes often leave viewers feeling a sense of completeness, satisfaction, and delight. That may be a tall order for an essay's conclusion, but it's the very best set of goals.

8   When we start a conclusion, we might want to *think* in terms of "why should the reader care about this at all?" As a matter of fact, some of the

STRATEGIES

best conclusions start with the writing *thinking* "Everyone should care about this because..." and then writing the rest of that sentence!

9   College students should avoid repeating the exact words of the thesis unless directly told to do so by an instructor. With some lengthy and complicated assignments, revisiting the thesis is a nice way of reminding the reader of the main points. More often than not, however, if the essay has a strong main idea and an organized execution, it will feel redundant and boring to repeat the thesis in the conclusion.

Here are a few strategies for successful conclusions:

- Look ahead to a future where this issue is addressed or ignored

- Make a recommendation or call the reader to action

- Discuss broader implications (go the opposite way from your introduction—from the specific to the most general!)

Depending on the assignment, we also might want to
- Conclude with a fact, quotation, example, or anecdote

Strategies to avoid in collegiate paper conclusions include
- Starting the conclusion with empty expressions, like "In conclusion"

- Restating the thesis word-for-word

- Referring to the essay directly ("As previously stated...")

- Making a brand new point

10   Conclusions are the best way to convey passion and interest in a topic, leave our reader with a sense of satisfaction and shared interest, and end the paper with a flourish.

- Introductions
    - Should start broadly (but not too broadly) and narrow to the essay's specific focus
    - Should establish the inherent value and interest of the essay's topic
    - Don't have to be written first
- Conclusions
    - Should expand the essay's focus to consider the broader implications
    - Should reinforce the inherent value and interest of the essay's topic, without repeating the thesis word-for-word
    - Don't have to be written last

WRITING EFFECTIVE THESIS STATEMENTS AND TOPIC SENTENCES

Julie Fenton-Glass
Professor

Wake Technical Community College

1   Thesis statements and topic sentences are arguably the most important sentences of any student essay. As we write, we need to indicate to our readers where we are going with our thoughts and invite them to come along. Good thesis statements and topic sentences do both.

2   The thesis statement of any essay is the promise the writer makes to the reader. In other words, the thesis announces the topic of the paper and the particular parameters the writer will follow in discussing that topic; thus, the thesis statement should be carefully considered because of the importance of this promise. It should promise exactly what the writer plans for the essay to deliver. It is rather like a fence around a field, keeping the ideas within its boundaries without including more ideas than those expressed in the body paragraphs.

3   A key feature of both thesis statements and topic sentences is that they are *ideas,* not facts, that promote discussion and explanation in order to fully illuminate that idea to readers. A thesis statement or topic sentence that is a flat statement of fact encourages no further discussion, making the essay challenging to write and uninteresting to read.

4   Another significant characteristic of an effective and powerful thesis statement is that it should be unique to the essay in which it appears. It is a customized sentence, useful only to the individual writer who composed it. No one should be able to borrow it to write another essay, even if the general topic is the same. To its essay, a strong thesis statement is like a tailor-made suit of clothes that fits only the person for whom it was made.

5   Interestingly, we should always be ready for this important sentence to change as we explore our topic; as our thinking expands, so may our treatment of our topic, and so must our thesis. A thesis is flexible during the drafting stage and becomes fixed only when our ideas are fully expressed. Returning to the thesis to revise it after composing a complete draft of the essay can help us ensure that the essay fulfills the thesis's promise.

6   Topic sentences fulfill the same function on a paragraph level as the thesis statement does for the entire essay. While the thesis statement appears in the introduction (usually as the final sentence of that paragraph), topic sentences take their places at the beginning of body paragraphs and indicate the directions in which their individual paragraphs will go to support the thesis statement. Just like the thesis statement, topic sentences are unique; they shouldn't look like anyone else's or each other. Each paragraph has a specific purpose, a particular way in which it will explain or support the thesis idea, and each topic sentence needs to reflect this specific purpose. Additionally, the topic sentence is also a promise that a supporting idea will be discussed, no more and no less than the topic sentence indicates.

7   Strong writers work and rework thesis statements and topic sentences, as they function as the signposts that lead readers through the writers' thought processes. When effectively composed, these sentences focus our thinking and make our writing process more smooth and successful; as a result, we will be rewarded with stronger and more powerful essays.

- Thesis statements
  - Are a fence that establishes the boundaries of an essay
  - Are a promise to the reader about what an essay will deliver
  - Promote discussion, expressing claims rather than stating facts
  - May need to be revised and refined as the essay develops
- Topic sentences fulfill the same purpose as the thesis statement, but on an individual paragraph level

WRITING THE NARRATIVE-DESCRIPTIVE ESSAY

Win Neagle
Professor

Wake Technical Community College

1   Experience is a gifted teacher. Therefore, sharing our experiences in a vivid and captivating manner has the potential to elucidate meaningful ideas for our readers. When writing the narrative-descriptive essay, we must always be aware that we do so for the benefit of the reader, not for our own self-aggrandizement. In fact, some of the most powerful narrative work is crafted at the expense of the ego of the writer who is willing to share hurtful or embarrassing experiences so that others might avoid less than desirable paths or feel comforted if they have endured similar experiences.

2   One of the keys to making the narrative most impactful is to use descriptive writing that allows the reader to enter the world of the story. A common error to avoid regarding description is the overuse of adjectives and adverbs. While we think of these modifiers as descriptors, we should use them sparingly and only when concrete verbs and nouns won't get the job done by themselves. For instance, "Darius was upset" is not nearly as descriptive as "Darius hung his head and tried to hide his tears."

3   If we put the work into selecting meaningful events and conveying our stories vividly, our readers will be delighted at our generosity in sharing genuine pieces of ourselves.

- Narration and Description
  - Share personal experience in order to communicate an insight to the reader
  - Should immerse the reader in the world of the story
  - Should rely on concrete, specific verbs and nouns, not an overabundance of adjectives and adverbs

WRITING THE DEFINITION ESSAY

Beth Keeley
Associate Professor

Wake Technical Community College

1   When writing a definition essay, we are asked to provide an extended explanation of a word or a phrase that can be defined in a variety of ways. The definition is based on the writer's personal perspective and illustrated using specific examples.

2   Initially, when assigned to write a definition essay, it may occur to us as a simple process: "How hard can writing a definition be?" In contrast, the reference of such an assignment may present us with unspeakable anxiety: "How am I going to fill up three to five pages with a definition when Webster's dictionary defines it in fewer than two lines!" Before relenting to one extreme or the other, keep in mind that defining abstract ideas is not uncommon in our daily lives. Coaches often define what a *team player* is during practices and games. Parents explain the term *respect* to their children, and what a person defines as *success* is frequently based solely on personal views.

3   Although concrete words such as *paper, desk,* and *pencil* are not subject to argument, abstract ideas such as *discipline* can cause significant discussion and debate. Some Americans might define *patriotism* as defending the country through military service, while others would define it as questioning the country's elected officials through free speech. The primary idea is that the definition is based on the writer's opinion.

Choosing a Topic

4   The topic for a definition essay doesn't have to be a single word. Phrases can also represent ideas that are subject to abstract definition. The important concept is to choose something familiar.

Gathering Ideas

5   During the brainstorming process, we should consider our experiences and how they have shaped our understanding of the word or phrase

we are attempting to define. Examples that illustrate the definition will provide our reader with specific details.

6   We can take a variety of approaches to defining the term:

- **Analyze** it by thinking about the different parts of the word and how they relate to one another. How might others define it differently?

- **Compare/Contrast** the word. What is it similar to and how is it different from similar ideas?

- **Describe** a process that provides details for the definition.

- **Employ details** that are important to sharing a writer's perspective with the reader.

- **Use examples** in illustrating a writer's perspective.

- **Include narration** to share a relevant experience.

- **Avoid** using the dictionary to define your word; instead, **critique** the definition in the dictionary. What details is the dictionary definition missing? What personal perspectives does the dictionary definition lack?

Writing a Working Thesis Statement

7   The thesis of a definition essay introduces the word or phrase to be defined and perhaps offers a high-level definition. As in any other rhetorical mode, the thesis should include the topic of the paper and the purpose. A thesis statement for a definition essay might say, "A 'team player' is someone who makes individual sacrifices for the good of the entire group."

8   The purpose of a definition expository essay is to communicate a clear understanding of the writer's definition. We are not only sharing our viewpoint with the reader; we may even have the opportunity to broaden the reader's own assessment of the term we are defining.

- Definition
  - Should provide an extended, personal explanation of a term or idea
  - Should utilize examples and illustrations to explain what a term or idea means to the writer
  - May draw upon a dictionary for brainstorming, but should not be limited to the dictionary definition

STRATEGIES

WRITING THE CAUSAL ANALYSIS ESSAY

Win Neagle
Professor

Wake Technical Community College

1   Our brains are designed to identify patterns. In fact, we are so good at seeking out patterns that we sometimes see causal relationships that do not actually exist. Consider the birth of superstitions. One only needs to turn a baseball cap inside out for one or two come-from-behind innings to believe in the power of "rally caps." On the other hand, we also sometimes fail to see connections that are real. Some causal relationships are so complex and subtle that they might be invisible to all but the best informed and most astute. For instance, disease impacted human lives for thousands of years before we came to understand the relationship between germs and sickness. Because understanding causal relationships is at the heart of our ability to have an accurate and useful perception of the world around us, causal analysis is among the most rewarding types of text for both writers and readers.

2   When constructing a causal analysis, we will usually want to begin at one end of a causal chain and work towards the other. Our thesis statement might include a phrase like "resulted from" or "led to." These phrases signal specific and opposing directions of exploration. We might explore the effects of the catastrophic property damage of hurricane Katrina, or we might explore the causes that led to such damage. If we wanted to explore the larger chain, both the causes and effects of the damage, then what we might actually be exploring is how lax maintenance of public safety structures in New Orleans led to an increase in rent in Dallas (due to a high influx of displaced people). This type of unidirectional investigation is more interesting to readers than an unfocused listing of "the causes and effects of hurricane Katrina."

3   When searching for a topic for a causal analysis, keep in mind that we will want to avoid the obvious. For instance, discussing how the Civil Rights Act of 1964 put an end to many major forms of discrimination might not offer our readers much in the way of new knowledge. However, if we provide a close examination of how the tragic assassination of

President Kennedy resulted in a change in the political environment of America, setting the stage for a series of political maneuvers that led to the success of the measure, we might be offering readers something they had not previously considered. We might entice our readers with a thesis that reads something like this: "Had the secret service not decided to remove the protective bubble from the convertible that carried President Kennedy in a Dallas motorcade, the passage of the Civil Rights Act might have been delayed by several years."

4   Another strategy for locating a meaningful topic for causal analysis might be to consider common misconceptions. For instance, many doubters of evolution like to scoff at the notion that "humans evolved from monkeys." Providing an analysis of how *Homo sapiens* are thought to have descended from a common ancestor shared with monkeys, *Sahelanthropus tchadensis*, might offer clarification.

5   Whether we deliver new insights or correct erroneous thinking, causal analysis provides wonderful opportunities to give value to our readers.

- Causal Analysis
  - Typically investigates either causes or effects, rather than both
  - Should identify interesting patterns rather than the obvious ones
  - May correct common misconceptions

STRATEGIES

WRITING THE COMPARISON AND CONTRAST ESSAY

Julie Fenton-Glass
Professor

Wake Technical Community College

1   Comparison and contrast is a strategy we use on a daily basis to make choices, persuade ourselves or others, or to clarify understanding. A comparative study is one in which we seek likenesses in topics which may *not* seem very similar, while a study in contrasts allows us to highlight differences in topics that may seem *quite* similar. In most relatively short comparison and contrast essays (three or four pages), we usually don't focus on both comparisons and contrasts; instead, we acknowledge the presence of the differences very briefly in the introduction, then concentrate our body paragraph discussions on the similarities, or do the reverse: mention the similarities quickly and focus the remainder of the essay on the differences.

2   A successful comparison and contrast essay begins with a careful topic choice and focus. Typically, the two subjects being explored are from the same general class so that an exploration (either comparison, contrast, or both, depending on the assignment requirements) of their individual features yields some new and meaningful understanding: for example, an instructor might ask students to compare or contrast two of the essays in this book. Rather than pick randomly, a successful writer would pair essays that have some commonality. For instance, a discussion that brings together two essays on human behavior will yield interesting and worthwhile observations while one that tries to pair an essay about technology in the classroom with one about immigration issues will be cumbersome to construct, difficult for the reader to comprehend, and, more than likely, not worth the trouble for either the writer or the reader.

3   If permitted to choose topics outside of the reader, we still need to follow the same thinking, finding subjects that belong to that same general class. However, we will want to avoid subjects that have almost everything in common as no one will want to read an essay in which only obvious points are made. A comparison and contrast essay should always illuminate the two subjects in a new and rich way.

4   As in any essay, organization of a comparison and contrast essay is key to its success. Good writers want to avoid merely listing a random, jumbled assortment of features of the two subjects and instead give them similar treatment. Generally, two patterns of organization are useful in comparison and contrast essays: the point-by-point method and the block-by-block method.

5   In the point-by-point method, the essay is organized around the particular features the writer wishes to highlight of the two subjects. The following outlines illustrate the organization:

I. Feature 1	I. Intellectual foundations
a. Subject A	a. Being a nerd
b. Subject B	b. Being a snob
II. Feature 2	II. Effect on self-esteem
a. Subject A	a. Being a nerd
b. Subject B	b. Being a snob
III. Feature 3	III. Social consequences
a. Subject A	a. Being a nerd
b. Subject B	b. Being a snob

6   Notice how each section is ordered in the same way; Subject A is discussed first, followed by a discussion of Subject B. This organization pattern allows the reader to follow the writer's thinking closely, especially if the information is very specific or technical. A potential problem with this pattern is that the discussion might seem to flip flop back and forth and may encourage an overabundance of transitions in the process. A careful and thorough treatment of the topic should prevent these potential problems.

7   In the block-by-block organizational method, the writer's thinking is organized around the two subjects, as follows:

I. Subject A	I. Being a nerd
a. Feature 1	a. Intellectual foundations
b. Feature 2	b. Effect on self-esteem
c. Feature 3	c. Social consequences
II. Subject B	II. Being a snob
a. Feature 1	a. Intellectual foundations
b. Feature 2	b. Effect on self-esteem
c. Feature 3	c. Social consequences

STRATEGIES

8   Again, the sections are identically patterned; the same features are presented in the same order in each of the two sections. The advantage of the block-by-block method is that the writer can provide complete and thorough information about the first subject before moving on to the second. This organization pattern allows the reader to understand a subject as a whole, especially if the features are interrelated and difficult to separate. A danger of this pattern is that the discussion of the second subject may seem repetitious; again, thoughtful treatment will help the writer avert this problem.

9   A discussion of a carefully chosen topic constructed in a clear, logical, and organized way will be a successful beginning to a rich, meaningful, and illuminating comparison and contrast essay.

- Comparison and Contrast
    - May investigate similarities, differences, or both
    - Should arrive at new insights by focusing primarily on the key differences between two subjects that *seem* similar or on the key similarities between two subjects that *seem* different
    - Should be organized in a point-by-point or block-by-block structure

WRITING THE EXEMPLIFICATION ESSAY

Dr. Don Ball
Professor

Wake Technical Community College

1   *Exemplification* is a fancy word for using examples to explain a general truth. People who don't understand an issue need a writer to clarify it with examples. To illustrate, Robert Reich, a professor of economics and former Secretary of Labor under President Clinton, shares general and specific examples of the deteriorating economic landscape for American workers in his article "Why the Rich Are Getting Richer and the Poor, Poorer." He describes the instance of AT&T (American Telephone and Telegraph) deciding in the late 1970s to outsource its Shreveport, Louisiana, phone assembly operations to Singapore to save labor costs. By the late 1980s, AT&T discovered that phone assembly could be done even more cheaply in Thailand. Reich uses the example of AT&T to illustrate how outsourcing has eliminated many previously well-paying American manufacturing jobs. The example of AT&T effectively demonstrates the social problem of outsourcing, which increases the profits of companies—that is, their wealthy executives and investors—while laying off American workers and often forcing them into lower paying service jobs.

2   Almost all writing relies on exemplification to describe an issue or support a position. Such details are the stuff of writing, which is why exemplification is often combined with the other rhetorical modes of exposition, narration, description, and definition.

3   *Narration* also requires exemplification of detail to inform, entertain, instruct, and persuade. Barbara Ehrenreich's excerpt "Serving in Florida" from her 2001 book *Nickel and Dimed: On (Not) Getting By in America* exemplifies the challenges of the working poor to survive in this wealthy country. As a restaurant server, Ehrenreich remembers that one special irritation was the constant supervision that often required her to look busy when there was nothing to do. Once, she relates, a manager caught

her glancing at a newspaper during a lull in service, and—since she seemed to be idle—made her vacuum the entire restaurant with a cleaner that had a broken handle—thus she had to do it on her knees. This specific example, therefore, is powerful because it shows the reader an image of a worker humiliated—literally driven to her knees—by an unfeeling manager.

4   *Description*, of course, is another mode that relies on specific details and examples to show images of what the author wants us to see. In N. Scott Momaday's "The Way to Rainy Mountain," readers experience the images and feelings of the hard life on a Kiowa reservation in Oklahoma:

> The hardest weather in the world is there. Winter brings blizzards, hot tornadic winds arise in the spring, and in the summer the prairie is an anvil's edge. The grass turns brittle and brown, and it cracks beneath your feet. There are green belts along the rivers and creeks, linear groves of hickory and pecan, willow and witch hazel. At a distance in July or August the steaming foliage seems almost to writhe in fire. Great green and yellow grasshoppers are everywhere in the tall grass, popping up like corn to sting the flesh, and tortoises crawl about on the red earth...Loneliness is an aspect of the land. (215)

5   *Definition* as a rhetorical mode leaves the abstract world and enters the more accessible personal with interesting, informative examples. The famous anthropologist Margaret Mead, for example, in her essay "New Superstitions for Old," asks her readers, "But when you come to think about it, what is superstition?" Some superstitions, Mead explains, call up the "memory of...old folk belief" that has roots in "magic":

> Everyone...remembers a few of the observances of childhood—wishing on the first star; looking at the new moon over the right shoulder; avoiding the cracks in the sidewalk on the way to school while chanting, "Step on a crack, break your mother's back"; ...saying quickly, "Bread-and-butter" when a post or a tree separated you from the friend you were walking with.

6   Examples bring ideas alive. Specific and general exemplification explains a world of ideas.

- Exemplification
  - Uses examples to illustrate a general truth
  - May draw upon general or specific instances
  - May be used for support in many rhetorical modes

How to Mark a Book

Mortimer Adler

- **IE** Illustration and Exemplification
- **PA** Process Analysis
- **CD** Classification and Division
- **A** Analogy

1   You know you have to read "between the lines" to get the most out of anything. I want to persuade you to do something equally important in the course of your reading. I want to persuade you to "write between the lines." Unless you do, you are not likely to do the most efficient kind of reading.

2   I contend, quite bluntly, that marking up a book is not an act of mutilation but of love.

3   You shouldn't mark up a book which isn't yours. Librarians (or your friends) who lend you books expect you to keep them clean, and you should. If you decide that I am right about the usefulness of marking books, you will have to buy them. Most of the world's great books are available today, in reprint editions, at less than a dollar.

4   There are two ways in which one can own a book. The first is the property right you establish by paying for it, just as you pay for clothes and furniture. But this act of purchase is only the prelude to possession. Full ownership comes only when you have made it a part of yourself, and the best way to make yourself a part of it is by writing in it. An illustration may make the point clear. You buy a beefsteak and transfer it from the butcher's icebox to your own. But you do not own the beefsteak in the most important sense until you consume it and get it into your bloodstream. I am arguing that books, too, must be absorbed in your bloodstream to do you any good.

5   Confusion about what it means to *own* a book leads people to a false reverence for paper, binding, and type—a respect for the physical thing— the craft of the printer rather than the genius of the author. They forget that it is possible for a man to acquire the idea, to possess the beauty, which a great book contains, without staking his claim by pasting his bookplate inside the cover. Having a fine library doesn't prove that its owner has a mind enriched by books; it proves nothing more than that he, his father, or his wife, was rich enough to buy them.

6   There are three kinds of book owners. The first has all the standard sets and best-sellers—unread, untouched. (This deluded individual owns wood-pulp and ink, not books.) The second has a great many books—a few of them read through, most of them dipped into, but all of them as clean and shiny as the day they were bought. (This person would probably like to make books his own, but is restrained by a false respect for their physical appearance.) The third has a few books or many—every one of them dog-eared and dilapidated, shaken and loosened by continual use, marked and scribbled in from front to back. (This man owns books.)

7   Is it false respect, you may ask, to preserve intact and unblemished a beautifully printed book, an elegantly bound edition? Of course not. I'd no more scribble all over a first edition of *Paradise Lost* than I'd give my baby a set of crayons and an original Rembrandt! I wouldn't mark up a painting or a statue. Its soul, so to speak, is inseparable from its body. And the beauty of a rare edition or of a richly manufactured volume is like that of a painting or a statue.

8   But the soul of a book *can* be separated from its body. A book is more like the score of a piece of music than it is like a painting. No great musician confuses a symphony with the printed sheets of music. Arturo Toscanini reveres Brahms, but Toscanini's score of the C-minor Symphony is so thoroughly marked up that no one but the maestro himself can read it. The reason why a great conductor makes notations on his musical scores—marks them up again and again each time he returns to study them—is the reason why you should mark your books. If your respect for magnificent binding or typography gets in the way, buy yourself a cheap edition and pay your respects to the author.

9   Why is marking up a book indispensable to reading? First, it keeps you awake. (And I don't mean merely conscious; I mean wide awake.) In the second place, reading, if it is active, is thinking, and thinking tends to express itself in words, spoken or written. The marked book is usually the thought-through book. Finally, writing helps you remember the thoughts you had, or the thoughts the author expressed. Let me develop these three points.

10   If reading is to accomplish anything more than passing time, it must be active. You can't let your eyes glide across the lines of a book and come up with an understanding of what you have read. Now an ordinary piece of light fiction, like say, *Gone with the Wind*, doesn't require the most active kind of reading. The books you read for pleasure can be read in a state of relaxation, and nothing is lost. But a great book, rich in ideas and beauty,

a book that raises and tries to answer great fundamental questions, demands the most active reading of which you are capable. You don't absorb the ideas of John Dewey the way you absorb the crooning of Mr. Vallee. You have to reach for them. That you cannot do while you're asleep.

11   If, when you've finished reading a book, the pages are filled with your notes, you know that you read actively. The most famous active reader of great books I know is President Hutchins, of the University of Chicago. He also has the hardest schedule of business activities of any man I know. He invariably reads with a pencil, and sometimes, when he picks up a book and pencil in the evening, he finds himself, instead of making intelligent notes, drawing what he calls "caviar factories" on the margins. When that happens, he puts the book down. He knows he's too tired to read, and he's just wasting time.

12   But, you may ask, why is writing necessary? Well, the physical act of writing, with your own hand, brings words and sentences more sharply before your mind and preserves them better in your memory. To set down your reaction to important words and sentences you have read, and the questions they have raised in your mind, is to preserve those reactions and sharpen those questions.

13   Even if you wrote on a scratch pad, and threw the paper away when you had finished writing, your grasp of the book would be surer. But you don't have to throw the paper away. The margins (top and bottom, as well as side), the end-papers, the very space between the lines, are all available. They aren't sacred. And, best of all, your marks and notes become an integral part of the book and stay there forever. You can pick up the book the following week or year, and there are all your points of agreement, disagreement, doubt, and inquiry. It's like resuming an interrupted conversation with the advantage of being able to pick up where you left off.

14   And that is exactly what reading a book should be: a conversation between you and the author. Presumably he knows more about the subject than you do; naturally, you'll have the proper humility as you approach him. But don't let anybody tell you that a reader is supposed to be solely on the receiving end. Understanding is a two-way operation; learning doesn't consist in being an empty receptacle. The learner has to question himself and question the teacher. He even has to argue with the teacher, once he understands what the teacher is saying. And marking a book is literally an expression of your differences, or agreements of opinion, with the author.

READINGS

15   There are all kinds of devices for marking a book intelligently and fruitfully. Here's the way I do it:

1. *Underlining:* of major points, of important or forceful statements.

2. *Vertical lines at the margin:* to emphasize a statement already underlined.

3. *Star, asterisk, or other doo-dad at the margin:* to be used sparingly, to emphasize the ten or twenty most important statements in the book. (You may want to fold the bottom corner of each page on which you use such marks. It won't hurt the sturdy paper on which most modern books are printed, and you will be able to take the book off the shelf at any time and, by opening it at the folded-corner page, refresh your recollection of the book.)

4. *Numbers in the margin:* to indicate the sequence of points the author makes in developing a single argument.

5. *Numbers of other pages in the margin:* to indicate where else in the book the author made points relevant to the point marked; to tie up the ideas in a book, which, though they may be separated by many pages, belong together.

6. *Circling of key words or phrases.*

7. *Writing in the margin, or at the top or bottom of the page, for the sake of:* recording questions (and perhaps answers) which a passage raised in your mind; reducing a complicated discussion to a simple statement; recording the sequence of major points right through the book. I use the end-papers at the back of the book to make a personal index of the author's points in the order of their appearance.

16   The front end-papers are, to me, the most important. Some people reserve them for a fancy bookplate. I reserve them for fancy thinking. After I have finished reading the book and making my personal index on the back end-papers, I turn to the front and try to outline the book, not page by page, or point by point (I've already done that at the back), but as an integrated structure, with a basic unity and an order of parts. This outline is, to me, the measure of my understanding of the work.

17   If you're a die-hard anti-book-marker, you may object that the margins, the space between the lines, and the end-papers don't give you room enough. All right. How about using a scratch pad slightly smaller than the page-size of the book—so that the edges of the sheets won't protrude? Make your index, outlines, and even your notes on the pad, and then

insert these sheets permanently inside the front and back covers of the book.

18   Or, you may say that this business of marking books is going to slow up your reading. It probably will. That's one of the reasons for doing it. Most of us have been taken in by the notion that speed of reading is a measure of our intelligence. There is no such thing as the right speed for intelligent reading. Some things should be read quickly and effortlessly, and some should be read slowly and even laboriously. The sign of intelligence in reading is the ability to read different things according to their worth. In the case of good books, the point is not to see how many of them you can get through, but rather how many can get through you—how many you can make your own. A few friends are better than a thousand acquaintances. If this be your aim, as it should be, you will not be impatient if it takes more time and effort to read a great book than it does a newspaper.

19   You may have one final objection to marking books. You can't lend them to your friends because nobody else can read them without being distracted by your notes. Furthermore, you won't want to lend them because a marked copy is a kind of intellectual diary, and lending it is almost like giving your mind away.

20   If your friend wishes to read your "Plutarch's Lives," "Shakespeare," or "The Federalist Papers," tell him gently but firmly to buy a copy. You will lend him your car or your coat—but your books are as much a part of you as your head or your heart.

QUESTIONS TO CONSIDER

1. Describe what Adler means by "full ownership" of a book.

2. Define the three types of book owners Adler introduces. Which type are you? Why?

3. What are some benefits of marking in a book?

4. According to Adler, what is the most important part of the book? Why?

5. Adler addresses arguments against marking in books. Name at least three refutations he makes in this essay.

READINGS

READINGS

I Want to Be Miss America

Julia Alvarez

- **N** Narration
- **DES** Description
- **IE** Illustration and Exemplification
- **CC** Compare and Contrast
- **PA** Process Analysis
- **DEF** Definition

1 As young teenagers in our new country, my three sisters and I searched for clues on how to look as if we belonged here. We collected magazines, studied our classmates and our new TV, which was where we discovered the Miss America contest.

2 Watching the pageant became an annual event in our family. Once a year, we all plopped down in our parents' bedroom, with Mami and Papi presiding from their bed. In our nightgowns, we watched the fifty young women who had the American look we longed for.

3 The beginning was always the best part—all fifty contestants came on for one and only one appearance. In alphabetical order, they stepped forward and enthusiastically introduced themselves by name and state. "Hi! I'm! Susie! Martin! Miss! Alaska!" Their voices rang with false cheer. You could hear, not far off, years of high-school cheerleading, pom-poms, bleachers full of moon-eyed boys, and moms on phones, signing them up for all manner of lessons and making dentist appointments.

4 There they stood, fifty puzzle pieces forming the pretty face of America, so we thought, though most of the color had been left out, except for one, or possibly two, light-skinned black girls. If there was a "Hispanic," she usually looked all-American, and only the last name, López or Rodríguez, often mispronounced, showed a trace of a great-great-grandfather with a dark, curled mustache and a sombrero charging the Alamo. During the initial roll-call, what most amazed us was that some contestants were ever picked in the first place. There were homely girls with cross-eyed smiles or chipmunk cheeks. My mother would inevitably shake her head and say, "The truth is, these Americans believe in democracy—even in looks."

5 We were beginning to feel at home. Our acute homesickness had passed, and now we were like people recovered from a shipwreck, looking around at our new country, glad to be here. "I want to be in America," my mother hummed after we'd gone to see *West Side Story*, and her

four daughters chorused, "OK by me in America." We bought a house in Queens, New York, in a neighborhood that was mostly German and Irish, where we were the only "Hispanics." Actually, no one ever called us that. Our teachers and classmates at the local Catholic schools referred to us as "Porto Ricans" or "Spanish." No one knew where the Dominican Republic was on the map. "South of Florida," I explained, "in the same general vicinity as Bermuda and Jamaica." I could just as well have said west of Puerto Rico or east of Cuba or right next to Haiti, but I wanted us to sound like a vacation spot, not a Third World country, a place they would look down on.

6　　Although we wanted to look like we belonged here, the four sisters, our looks didn't seem to fit in. We complained about how short we were, about how our hair frizzed, how our figures didn't curve like those of the bathing beauties we'd seen on TV.

7　　"The grass always grows on the other side of the fence," my mother scolded. Her daughters looked fine just the way they were.

8　　But how could we trust her opinion about what looked good when she couldn't even get the sayings of our new country right? No, we knew better. We would have to translate our looks into English, iron and tweeze them out, straighten them, mold them into Made-in-the-U.S.A. beauty.

9　　So we painstakingly rolled our long, curly hair round and round, using our heads as giant rollers, ironing it until we had long, shining shanks, like our classmates and the contestants, only darker. Our skin was diagnosed by beauty consultants in department stores as sallow; we definitely needed a strong foundation to tone down that olive. We wore tights even in the summer to hide the legs Mami would not let us shave. We begged for permission, dreaming of the contestants' long, silky limbs. We were ten, fourteen, fifteen, and sixteen—merely children, Mami explained. We had long lives ahead of us in which to shave.

10　　We defied her. Giggly and red-faced, we all pitched in to buy a big tube of Nair at the local drugstore. We acted as if we were purchasing contraceptives. That night we crowded into the bathroom, and I, the most courageous along these lines, offered one of my legs as a guinea pig. When it didn't become gangrenous or fall off as Mami had predicted, we creamed the other seven legs. We beamed at each other; we were one step closer to that runway, those flashing cameras, those oohs and ahhs from the audience.

READINGS

11   Mami didn't even notice our Naired legs; she was too busy disapprov-
ing of the other changes. Our clothes, for one. "You're going to wear that
in public!" She'd gawk, as if to say, What will the Americans think of us?

12   "This is what the Americans wear," we would argue back.

13   But the dresses we had picked out made us look cheap, she said, like
bad, fast girls—gringas without vergüenza, without shame. She preferred
her choices: fuchsia skirts with matching vests, flowered dresses with
bows at the neck or gathers where you wanted to look slim, everything
bright and busy, like something someone might wear in a foreign country.

14   Our father didn't really notice our new look at all but, if called upon
to comment, would say absently that we looked beautiful. "Like Marilina
Monroe." Still, during the pageant, he would offer insights into what he
thought made a winner. "Personality, Mami," my father would say from
his post at the head of the bed, "Personality is the key," though his favorite contestants, whom he always championed in the name of personality, tended to be the fuller girls with big breasts who gushed shamelessly
at Bert Parks. "Ay, Papi," we would groan, rolling our eyes at each other.
Sometimes, as the girl sashayed back down the aisle, Papi would break
out in a little Dominican song that he sang whenever a girl had a lot of
swing in her walk:

> Yo no tumbo caña,
> Que la tumba el viento,
> Que la tumba Dora
> Con su movimiento!

> ("I don't have to cut the cane,
> The wind knocks it down,
> The wind of Dora's movement
> As she walks downtown.")

15   My father would stop on a New York City street when a young woman
swung by and sing this song out loud to the great embarrassment of his
daughters. We were sure that one day when we weren't around to make
him look like the respectable father of four girls, he would be arrested.

16   My mother never seemed to have a favorite contestant. She was an
ex-beauty herself, and no one seemed to measure up to her high standards. She liked the good girls who had common sense and talked about
their education and about how they owed everything to their mothers.
"Tell that to my daughters," my mother would address the screen, as if
none of us were there to hear her. If we challenged her—how exactly did

we not appreciate her?—she'd maintain a wounded silence for the rest of the evening. Until the very end of the show, that is, when all our disagreements were forgotten and we waited anxiously to see which of the two finalists holding hands on that near-empty stage would be the next reigning queen of beauty. How can they hold hands? I always wondered. Don't they secretly wish the other person would, well, die?

17   My sisters and I always had plenty of commentary on all the contestants. We were hardly strangers to this ritual of picking the beauty. In our own family, we had a running competition as to who was the prettiest of the four girls. We coveted one another's best feature: the oldest's dark, almond-shaped eyes, the youngest's great mane of hair, the third oldest's height and figure. I didn't have a preferred feature, but I was often voted the cutest, though my oldest sister liked to remind me that I had the kind of looks that wouldn't age well. Although she was only eleven months older than I was, she seemed years older, ages wiser. She bragged about the new kind of math she was learning in high school, called algebra, which she said I would never be able to figure out. I believed her. Dumb and excute, that's what I would grow up to be.

18   As for the prettiest Miss America, we sisters kept our choices secret until the very end. The range was limited—pretty white women who all really wanted to be wives and mothers. But even the small and inane set of options these girls represented seemed boundless compared with what we were used to. We were being groomed to go from being dutiful daughters to being dutiful wives with hymens intact. No stops along the way that might endanger the latter; no careers, no colleges, no shared apartments with girlfriends, no boyfriends, no social lives. But the young women on-screen, who were being held up as models in this new country, were in college, or at least headed there. They wanted to do this, they were going to do that with their lives. Everything in our native culture had instructed us otherwise: girls were to have no aspirations beyond being good wives and mothers.

19   Sometimes there would even be a contestant headed for law school or medical school. "I wouldn't mind having an office visit with her," my father would say, smirking. The women who caught my attention were the prodigies who bounded onstage and danced to tapes of themselves playing original compositions on the piano, always dressed in costumes they had sewn, with a backdrop of easels holding paintings they'd painted. "Overkill," my older sister insisted. But if one good thing came out of our watching this yearly parade of American beauties, it was that subtle

permission we all felt as a family: a girl could excel outside the home and still be a winner.

20   Every year, the queen came down the runway in her long gown with a sash like an old-world general's belt of ammunition. Down the walkway she paraded, smiling and waving while Bert sang his sappy song that made our eyes fill with tears. When she stopped at the very end of the stage and the camera zoomed in on her misty-eyed beauty and the credits began to appear on the screen, I always felt let down. I knew I would never be one of those girls, ever. It wasn't just the blond, blue-eyed looks or the beautiful, leggy figure. It was who she was—an American—and we were not. We were foreigners, dark-haired and dark-eyed with olive skin that could never, no matter the sun blocks or foundation makeup, be made into peaches and cream.

21   Had we been able to see into the future, beyond our noses, which we thought weren't the right shape; beyond our curly hair, which we wanted to be straight; and beyond the screen, which inspired us with a limited vision of what was considered beautiful in America, we would have been able to see the late sixties coming. Soon, ethnic looks would be in. Even Barbie, that quintessential white girl, would suddenly be available in different shades of skin color with bright, colorful outfits that looked like the ones Mami had picked out for us. Our classmates in college wore long braids like Native Americans and embroidered shawls and peasant blouses from South America, and long, diaphanous skirts and dangly earrings from India. They wanted to look exotic—they wanted to look like us.

22   We felt then a gratifying sense of inclusion, but it had unfortunately come too late. We had already acquired the habit of doubting ourselves as well as the place we came from. To this day, after three decades of living in America, I feel like a stranger in what I now consider my own country. I am still that young teenager sitting in front of the black-and-white TV in my parents' bedroom, knowing in my bones I will never be the beauty queen. There she is, Miss America, but even in my up-to-date, enlightened dreams, she never wears my face.

QUESTIONS TO CONSIDER

1.   The family in this essay gathers together each year to view the Miss America pageant. What annual family traditions do you remember for when you were younger? Provide a short paragraph about one of those traditions. See if you can do so in a form that parallels the items on which Alvarez focuses in her essay.

2. What are the details the author provides for an "American beauty"? How does the perspective on beauty change as she is growing up?

3. Did you compare yourself to some idealized image when you were a child? Explain. Did you achieve your idealized image, or did your desires evolve? Explain.

4. Why did the girls want to fit in? Explain.

READINGS

Is Google Making Us Stupid?

Nicholas Carr

- **AP** Argument and Persuasion
- **CE** Cause and Effect

1   "DAVE, STOP. STOP, WILL you? Stop, Dave. Will you stop, Dave?" So the supercomputer HAL pleads with the implacable astronaut Dave Bowman in a famous and weirdly poignant scene toward the end of Stanley Kubrick's *2001: A Space Odyssey.* Bowman, having nearly been sent to a deep-space death by the malfunctioning machine, is calmly, coldly disconnecting the memory circuits that control its artificial "brain." "Dave, my mind is going," HAL says, forlornly. "I can feel it. I can feel it."

2   I can feel it, too. Over the past few years I've had an uncomfortable sense that someone, or something, has been tinkering with my brain, remapping the neural circuitry, reprogramming the memory. My mind isn't going—so far as I can tell—but it's changing. I'm not thinking the way I used to think. I can feel it most strongly when I'm reading. Immersing myself in a book or a lengthy article used to be easy. My mind would get caught up in the narrative or the turns of the argument, and I'd spend hours strolling through long stretches of prose. That's rarely the case anymore. Now my concentration often starts to drift after two or three pages. I get fidgety, lose the thread, begin looking for something else to do. I feel as if I'm always dragging my wayward brain back to the text. The deep reading that used to come naturally has become a struggle.

3   I think I know what's going on. For more than a decade now, I've been spending a lot of time online, searching and surfing and sometimes adding to the great databases of the Internet. The Web has been a godsend to me as a writer. Research that once required days in the stacks or periodical rooms of libraries can now be done in minutes. A few Google searches, some quick clicks on hyperlinks, and I've got the telltale fact or pithy quote I was after. Even when I'm not working, I'm as likely as not to be foraging in the Web's info-thickets, reading and writing e-mails, scanning headlines and blog posts, watching videos and listening to podcasts, or just tripping from link to link to link. (Unlike footnotes, to which they're

sometimes likened, hyperlinks don't merely point to related works; they propel you toward them.)

4   For me, as for others, the Net is becoming a universal medium, the conduit for most of the information that flows through my eyes and ears and into my mind. The advantages of having immediate access to such an incredibly rich store of information are many, and they've been widely described and duly applauded. "The perfect recall of silicon memory," *Wired's* Clive Thompson has written, "can be an enormous boon to thinking." But that boon comes at a price. As the media theorist Marshall McLuhan pointed out in the 1960s, media are not just passive channels of information. They supply the stuff of thought, but they also shape the process of thought. And what the Net seems to be doing is chipping away my capacity for concentration and contemplation. My mind now expects to take in information the way the Net distributes it: in a swiftly moving stream of particles. Once I was a scuba diver in the sea of words. Now I zip along the surface like a guy on a Jet Ski.

5   I'm not the only one. When I mention my troubles with reading to friends and acquaintances—literary types, most of them—many say they're having similar experiences. The more they use the Web, the more they have to fight to stay focused on long pieces of writing. Some of the bloggers I follow have also begun mentioning the phenomenon. Scott Karp, who writes a blog about online media, recently confessed that he has stopped reading books altogether. "I was a lit major in college, and used to be [a] voracious book reader," he wrote. "What happened?" He speculates on the answer: "What if I do all my reading on the Web not so much because the way I read has changed, i.e., I'm just seeking convenience, but because the way I THINK has changed?"

6   Bruce Friedman, who blogs regularly about the use of computers in medicine, also has described how the Internet has altered his mental habits. "I now have almost totally lost the ability to read and absorb a longish article on the Web or in print," he wrote earlier this year. A pathologist who has long been on the faculty of the University of Michigan Medical School, Friedman elaborated on his comment in a telephone conversation with me. His thinking, he said, has taken on a "staccato" quality, reflecting the way he quickly scans short passages of text from many sources online. "I can't read *War and Peace* anymore," he admitted. "I've lost the ability to do that. Even a blog post of more than three or four paragraphs is too much to absorb. I skim it."

7   Anecdotes alone don't prove much. And we still await the long-term neurological and psychological experiments that will provide a definitive

READINGS

picture of how Internet use affects cognition. But a recently published study of online research habits, conducted by scholars from University College London, suggests that we may well be in the midst of a sea change in the way we read and think. As part of the five-year research program, the scholars examined computer logs documenting the behavior of visitors to two popular research sites, one operated by the British Library and one by a U.K. educational consortium, that provide access to journal articles, e-books, and other sources of written information. They found that people using the sites exhibited "a form of skimming activity," hopping from one source to another and rarely returning to any source they'd already visited. They typically read no more than one or two pages of an article or book before they would "bounce" out to another site. Sometimes they'd save a long article, but there's no evidence that they ever went back and actually read it. The authors of the study report:

> It is clear that users are not reading online in the traditional sense; indeed there are signs that new forms of "reading" are emerging as users "power browse" horizontally through titles, contents pages and abstracts going for quick wins. It almost seems that they go online to avoid reading in the traditional sense.

8   Thanks to the ubiquity of text on the Internet, not to mention the popularity of text messaging on cell phones, we may well be reading more today than we did in the 1970s or 1980s, when television was our medium of choice. But it's a different kind of reading, and behind it lies a different kind of thinking—perhaps even a new sense of the self. "We are not only *what* we read," says Maryanne Wolf, a developmental psychologist at Tufts University and the author of *Proust and the Squid: The Story and Science of the Reading Brain.* "We are *how* we read." Wolf worries that the style of reading promoted by the Net, a style that puts "efficiency" and "immediacy" above all else, may be weakening our capacity for the kind of deep reading that emerged when an earlier technology, the printing press, made long and complex works of prose commonplace. When we read online, she says, we tend to become "mere decoders of information." Our ability to interpret text, to make the rich mental connections that form when we read deeply and without distraction, remains largely disengaged.

9   Reading, explains Wolf, is not an instinctive skill for human beings. It's not etched into our genes the way speech is. We have to teach our minds how to translate the symbolic characters we see into the language we understand. And the media or other technologies we use in learning

and practicing the craft of reading play an important part in shaping the neural circuits inside our brains. Experiments demonstrate that readers of ideograms, such as the Chinese, develop a mental circuitry for reading that is very different from the circuitry found in those of us whose written language employs an alphabet. The variations extend across many regions of the brain, including those that govern such essential cognitive functions as memory and the interpretation of visual and auditory stimuli. We can expect as well that the circuits woven by our use of the Net will be different from those woven by our reading of books and other printed works.

10   Sometime in 1882, Friedrich Nietzsche bought a typewriter—a Malling Hansen Writing Ball, to be precise. His vision was failing, and keeping his eyes focused on a page had become exhausting and painful, often bringing on crushing headaches. He had been forced to curtail his writing, and he feared that he would soon have to give it up. The typewriter rescued him, at least for a time. Once he had mastered touch-typing, he was able to write with his eyes closed, using only the tips of his fingers. Words could once again flow from his mind to the page.

11   But the machine had a subtler effect on his work. One of Nietzsche's friends, a composer, noticed a change in the style of his writing. His already terse prose had become even tighter, more telegraphic. "Perhaps you will through this instrument even take to a new idiom," the friend wrote in a letter, noting that, in his own work, his "'thoughts' in music and language often depend on the quality of pen and paper."

12   "You are right," Nietzsche replied, "our writing equipment takes part in the forming of our thoughts." Under the sway of the machine, writes the German media scholar Friedrich A. Kittler, Nietzsche's prose "changed from arguments to aphorisms, from thoughts to puns, from rhetoric to telegram style."

13   The human brain is almost infinitely malleable. People used to think that our mental meshwork, the dense connections formed among the 100 billion or so neurons inside our skulls, was largely fixed by the time we reached adulthood. But brain researchers have discovered that that's not the case. James Olds, a professor of neuroscience who directs the Krasnow Institute for Advanced Study at George Mason University, says that even the adult mind "is very plastic." Nerve cells routinely break old connections and form new ones. "The brain," according to Olds, "has the ability to reprogram itself on the fly, altering the way it functions."

14   As we use what the sociologist Daniel Bell has called our "intellectual technologies"—the tools that extend our mental rather than our physical capacities—we inevitably begin to take on the qualities of those technologies. The mechanical clock, which came into common use in the 14th century, provides a compelling example. In *Technics and Civilization,* the historian and cultural critic Lewis Mumford described how the clock "disassociated time from human events and helped create the belief in an independent world of mathematically measurable sequences." The "abstract framework of divided time" became "the point of reference for both action and thought."

15   The clock's methodical ticking helped bring into being the scientific mind and the scientific man. But it also took something away. As the late MIT computer scientist Joseph Weizenbaum observed in his 1976 book, *Computer Power and Human Reason: From Judgment to Calculation,* the conception of the world that emerged from the widespread use of timekeeping instruments "remains an impoverished version of the older one, for it rests on a rejection of those direct experiences that formed the basis for, and indeed constituted, the old reality." In deciding when to eat, to work, to sleep, to rise, we stopped listening to our senses and started obeying the clock.

16   The process of adapting to new intellectual technologies is reflected in the changing metaphors we use to explain ourselves to ourselves. When the mechanical clock arrived, people began thinking of their brains as operating "like clockwork." Today, in the age of software, we have come to think of them as operating "like computers." But the changes, neuroscience tells us, go much deeper than metaphor. Thanks to our brain's plasticity, the adaptation occurs also at a biological level.

17   The Internet promises to have particularly far-reaching effects on cognition. In a paper published in 1936, the British mathematician Alan Turing proved that a digital computer, which at the time existed only as a theoretical machine, could be programmed to perform the function of any other information-processing device. And that's what we're seeing today. The Internet, an immeasurably powerful computing system, is subsuming most of our other intellectual technologies. It's becoming our map and our clock, our printing press and our typewriter, our calculator and our telephone, and our radio and TV.

18   When the Net absorbs a medium, that medium is re-created in the Net's image. It injects the medium's content with hyperlinks, blinking ads, and other digital gewgaws, and it surrounds the content with the content

of all the other media it has absorbed. A new e-mail message, for instance, may announce its arrival as we're glancing over the latest headlines at a newspaper's site. The result is to scatter our attention and diffuse our concentration.

19   The Net's influence doesn't end at the edges of a computer screen, either. As people's minds become attuned to the crazy quilt of Internet media, traditional media have to adapt to the audience's new expectations. Television programs add text crawls and pop-up ads, and magazines and newspapers shorten their articles, introduce capsule summaries, and crowd their pages with easy-to-browse info-snippets. When, in March of this year, *The New York Times* decided to devote the second and third pages of every edition to article abstracts, its design director, Tom Bodkin, explained that the "shortcuts" would give harried readers a quick "taste" of the day's news, sparing them the "less efficient" method of actually turning the pages and reading the articles. Old media have little choice but to play by the new-media rules.

20   Never has a communications system played so many roles in our lives—or exerted such broad influence over our thoughts—as the Internet does today. Yet, for all that's been written about the Net, there's been little consideration of how, exactly, it's reprogramming us. The Net's intellectual ethic remains obscure.

21   About the same time that Nietzsche started using his typewriter, an earnest young man named Frederick Winslow Taylor carried a stopwatch into the Midvale Steel plant in Philadelphia and began a historic series of experiments aimed at improving the efficiency of the plant's machinists. With the approval of Midvale's owners, he recruited a group of factory hands, set them to work on various metalworking machines, and recorded and timed their every movement as well as the operations of the machines. By breaking down every job into a sequence of small, discrete steps and then testing different ways of performing each one, Taylor created a set of precise instructions—an "algorithm," we might say today—for how each worker should work. Midvale's employees grumbled about the strict new regime, claiming that it turned them into little more than automatons, but the factory's productivity soared.

22   More than a hundred years after the invention of the steam engine, the Industrial Revolution had at last found its philosophy and its philosopher. Taylor's tight industrial choreography—his "system," as he liked to call it—was embraced by manufacturers throughout the country and, in time, around the world. Seeking maximum speed, maximum efficiency,

READINGS

and maximum output, factory owners used time-and-motion studies to organize their work and configure the jobs of their workers. The goal, as Taylor defined it in his celebrated 1911 treatise, *The Principles of Scientific Management*, was to identify and adopt, for every job, the "one best method" of work and thereby to effect "the gradual substitution of science for rule of thumb throughout the mechanic arts." Once his system was applied to all acts of manual labor, Taylor assured his followers, it would bring about a restructuring not only of industry but of society, creating a utopia of perfect efficiency. "In the past the man has been first," he declared; "in the future the system must be first."

23   Taylor's system is still very much with us; it remains the ethic of industrial manufacturing. And now, thanks to the growing power that computer engineers and software coders wield over our intellectual lives, Taylor's ethic is beginning to govern the realm of the mind as well. The Internet is a machine designed for the efficient and automated collection, transmission, and manipulation of information, and its legions of programmers are intent on finding the "one best method"—the perfect algorithm—to carry out every mental movement of what we've come to describe as "knowledge work."

24   Google's headquarters, in Mountain View, California—the Googleplex—is the Internet's high church, and the religion practiced inside its walls is Taylorism. Google, says its chief executive, Eric Schmidt, is "a company that's founded around the science of measurement," and it is striving to "systematize everything" it does. Drawing on the terabytes of behavioral data it collects through its search engine and other sites, it carries out thousands of experiments a day, according to the *Harvard Business Review,* and it uses the results to refine the algorithms that increasingly control how people find information and extract meaning from it. What Taylor did for the work of the hand, Google is doing for the work of the mind.

25   The company has declared that its mission is "to organize the world's information and make it universally accessible and useful." It seeks to develop "the perfect search engine," which it defines as something that "understands exactly what you mean and gives you back exactly what you want." In Google's view, information is a kind of commodity, a utilitarian resource that can be mined and processed with industrial efficiency. The more pieces of information we can "access" and the faster we can extract their gist, the more productive we become as thinkers.

26   Where does it end? Sergey Brin and Larry Page, the gifted young men who founded Google while pursuing doctoral degrees in computer science at Stanford, speak frequently of their desire to turn their search engine into an artificial intelligence, a HAL-like machine that might be connected directly to our brains. "The ultimate search engine is something as smart as people—or smarter," Page said in a speech a few years back. "For us, working on search is a way to work on artificial intelligence." In a 2004 interview with *Newsweek*, Brin said, "Certainly if you had all the world's information directly attached to your brain, or an artificial brain that was smarter than your brain, you'd be better off." Last year, Page told a convention of scientists that Google is "really trying to build artificial intelligence and to do it on a large scale."

27   Such an ambition is a natural one, even an admirable one, for a pair of math whizzes with vast quantities of cash at their disposal and a small army of computer scientists in their employ. A fundamentally scientific enterprise, Google is motivated by a desire to use technology, in Eric Schmidt's words, "to solve problems that have never been solved before," and artificial intelligence is the hardest problem out there. Why wouldn't Brin and Page want to be the ones to crack it?

28   Still, their easy assumption that we'd all "be better off" if our brains were supplemented, or even replaced, by an artificial intelligence is unsettling. It suggests a belief that intelligence is the output of a mechanical process, a series of discrete steps that can be isolated, measured, and optimized. In Google's world, the world we enter when we go online, there's little place for the fuzziness of contemplation. Ambiguity is not an opening for insight but a bug to be fixed. The human brain is just an outdated computer that needs a faster processor and a bigger hard drive.

29   The idea that our minds should operate as high-speed data-processing machines is not only built into the workings of the Internet, it is the network's reigning business model as well. The faster we surf across the Web—the more links we click and pages we view—the more opportunities Google and other companies gain to collect information about us and to feed us advertisements. Most of the proprietors of the commercial Internet have a financial stake in collecting the crumbs of data we leave behind as we flit from link to link—the more crumbs, the better. The last thing these companies want is to encourage leisurely reading or slow, concentrated thought. It's in their economic interest to drive us to distraction.

 READINGS

30   Maybe I'm just a worrywart. Just as there's a tendency to glorify technological progress, there's a countertendency to expect the worst of every new tool or machine. In Plato's *Phaedrus*, Socrates bemoaned the development of writing. He feared that, as people came to rely on the written word as a substitute for the knowledge they used to carry inside their heads, they would, in the words of one of the dialogue's characters, "cease to exercise their memory and become forgetful." And because they would be able to "receive a quantity of information without proper instruction," they would "be thought very knowledgeable when they are for the most part quite ignorant." They would be "filled with the conceit of wisdom instead of real wisdom." Socrates wasn't wrong—the new technology did often have the effects he feared—but he was shortsighted. He couldn't foresee the many ways that writing and reading would serve to spread information, spur fresh ideas, and expand human knowledge (if not wisdom).

31   The arrival of Gutenberg's printing press, in the 15th century, set off another round of teeth gnashing. The Italian humanist Hieronimo Squarciafico worried that the easy availability of books would lead to intellectual laziness, making men "less studious" and weakening their minds. Others argued that cheaply printed books and broadsheets would undermine religious authority, demean the work of scholars and scribes, and spread sedition and debauchery. As New York University professor Clay Shirky notes, "Most of the arguments made against the printing press were correct, even prescient." But, again, the doomsayers were unable to imagine the myriad blessings that the printed word would deliver.

32   So, yes, you should be skeptical of my skepticism. Perhaps those who dismiss critics of the Internet as Luddites or nostalgists will be proved correct, and from our hyperactive, data-stoked minds will spring a golden age of intellectual discovery and universal wisdom. Then again, the Net isn't the alphabet, and although it may replace the printing press, it produces something altogether different. The kind of deep reading that a sequence of printed pages promotes is valuable not just for the knowledge we acquire from the author's words but for the intellectual vibrations those words set off within our own minds. In the quiet spaces opened up by the sustained, undistracted reading of a book, or by any other act of contemplation, for that matter, we make our own associations, draw our own inferences and analogies, foster our own ideas. Deep reading, as Maryanne Wolf argues, is indistinguishable from deep thinking.

33   If we lose those quiet spaces, or fill them up with "content," we will sacrifice something important not only in our selves but in our culture. In a recent essay, the playwright Richard Foreman eloquently described what's at stake:

> I come from a tradition of Western culture, in which the ideal (my ideal) was the complex, dense and "cathedral-like" structure of the highly educated and articulate personality—a man or woman who carried inside themselves a personally constructed and unique version of the entire heritage of the West. [But now] I see within us all (myself included) the replacement of complex inner density with a new kind of self-evolving under the pressure of information overload and the technology of the "instantly available."

34   As we are drained of our "inner repertory of dense cultural inheritance," Foreman concluded, we risk turning into "'pancake people'— spread wide and thin as we connect with that vast network of information accessed by the mere touch of a button."

35   I'm haunted by that scene in *2001*. What makes it so poignant, and so weird, is the computer's emotional response to the disassembly of its mind: its despair as one circuit after another goes dark, its childlike pleading with the astronaut—"I can feel it. I can feel it. I'm afraid"—and its final reversion to what can only be called a state of innocence. HAL's outpouring of feeling contrasts with the emotionlessness that characterizes the human figures in the film, who go about their business with an almost robotic efficiency. Their thoughts and actions feel scripted, as if they're following the steps of an algorithm. In the world of *2001*, people have become so machinelike that the most human character turns out to be a machine. That's the essence of Kubrick's dark prophecy: as we come to rely on computers to mediate our understanding of the world, it is our own intelligence that flattens into artificial intelligence.

? QUESTIONS TO CONSIDER

1.   Nicholas Carr writes about the effect of technology generally and the Internet specifically on human thinking. How has the Internet become a part of your everyday life?

2.   The author uses the term "intelligence" in several different ways throughout the piece. What does he mean by this term?

3.   Carr is concerned that information is becoming a commodity. What does this mean and why is he concerned about it?

READINGS

4. What role do allusions and references play in this essay? Do you think they are effective?

5. Carr argues that Google is changing the way we think for the worse, but this is also an issue of access to technology. What factors are necessary for cheap and convenient access to the Internet?

You Left Out the Part About...

Ta-Nehisi Coates

- **N** Narration
- **DES** Description
- **IE** Illustration and Exemplification

- **CC** Compare and Contrast
- **AP** Argument and Persuasion

1   Last weekend, like seemingly half the country, I took my son to see "X-Men: First Class," the latest, and best, big-screen incarnation of the popular comic book franchise.

2   My son and I represent two generations of X-fans. I came of age in the '80s and '90s and can still recall when Xavier's students were lords of the Underground, and the phrase "comic book movie" conjured absurd images of David Hasselhoff donning an eye patch. The boy is of the present era, where the geeks and nerds throne and Hollywood is compelled to seriously contemplate the cinematic potential of B-listers Namor, Luke Cage and Ant-Man. Still, we were united across the ages in our love for the X-Men—patron-saints of the persecuted and the champions of freaks and pariahs across the globe.

3   In print, the X-Men are an elite team culled from a superpowered species of human. The mutants, as they are dubbed, are generally handled roughly by the rest of humanity and singled out for everything from enslavement to internment camps to genocide. As if to ram the allegory home, the X-Men, for much of their history, have hailed from across the spectrum of human existence. Over the decades, there have been gay X-Men, patrician X-Men, Jewish X-Men, Aboriginal X-Men, black X-Men with silver mohawks, X-Men hailing from Russia, Kentucky coal country, orphanages and a nightmarish future.

4   But as "First Class" roars to its final climactic scene, it appeals to an insidious suspension of disbelief; the heroic mutants of America, bravely opposing bigotry and fear, are revealed as not so much a spectrum of humankind, but as Eagle Scouts from Mayfield. Thus, "First Class" proves itself not merely an incredible film, but an incredible work of American historical fiction. Here is a period piece for our postracial times—in the era of Ella Baker and the Rev. Dr. Martin Luther King Jr., the most powerful adversaries of spectacular apartheid are a team of enlightened white dudes.

5   "First Class" is set in 1962. That was the year South Carolina marked the Civil War centennial by returning the Confederate Flag to the State Capitol; the year the University of Mississippi greeted its first black student, James Meredith, with a lethal race riot; the year George Wallace was elected governor of Alabama.

6   That was the year a small crowd of Americans gathered at the Lincoln Memorial and commemorated the 100th birthday of the Emancipation Proclamation. Only a single African-American was asked to speak (Thurgood Marshall, added under threat of boycott). In "First Class," 1962 finds our twin protagonists, Magneto and Professor X, also rallying before the Lincoln Memorial, not for protest or commemoration, but for a game of chess. "First Class" is not blind to societal evils, so much as it works to hold evil at an ocean's length. The film is rooted in its opposition to the comfortably foreign abomination of Nazism.

7   This is all about knowing your audience.

8   I am reminded of the House Republicans, opening the 112th Congress by reciting the Constitution, minus the slavery parts. I am reminded of the English professor last year who, responding to Huckleberry Finn's widespread banishment from public schools, was compelled to offer the Mark Twain classic, minus the nigger parts. I think of the Pentagon official, who this year justified the war in Afghanistan to soldiers by invoking the words of Dr. King, minus the "ultimate weakness of violence" parts. I am reminded of whole swaths of this country where historical fiction compels Americans to claim the Civil War was about states' rights, minus the "right to own people" part.

9   This is all about a convenient suspension of disbelief.

10   When we left the theater, my son and I knew we had experienced the most thrilling movie of the summer. "First Class" is narratively lean, beautifully acted and, at all the right moments, visually stunning. But I had experienced something else. My son is 10 and a romantic, as all 10-year-olds surely have the right to be. How then do I speak to him of this world's masterminds who render you a supporting actor in your own story? How do I speak of the Sentinels whose eyes melt history, until the world forgets that in 1962, the quintessential mutants of America were black?

11   Who do you think has the coolest power, Daddy?

12   His great caramel eyes were an amusement park.

13   You do, son.

❓ QUESTIONS TO CONSIDER

1. Coates is writing about a movie about a comic book set in 1962. What are some details the author provides about what was going in in the U.S. in 1962?

2. Is Coates suggesting there are parallels between the mutants and American blacks? Use passages from the essay to explain and support your response. (If your instructor wishes, use MLA form for the passages you quote.)

3. Where did Ta-Nehisi Coates grow up, and what is his son's name? (This is critical reading background information that you should have rounded up when this essay was assigned, right? Again, you may be asked to provide a correct MLA citation for where you found this information.)

4. Coates mentions the importance of avoiding historical fiction in the essay. Write about a time where you felt there was reframing of a historical time that was inaccurate. How did this reframing impact your view of that historical moment?

5. What is the significance of Coates' last statement to his son?

Learning to Read and Write

Frederick Douglass

- ■ **N** Narration
- ■ **PA** Process Analysis

1   I lived in Master Hugh's family about seven years. During this time, I succeeded in learning to read and write. In accomplishing this, I was compelled to resort to various stratagems. I had no regular teacher. My mistress, who had kindly commenced to instruct me, had, in compliance with the advice and direction of her husband, not only ceased to instruct, but had set her face against my being instructed by any one else. It is due, however, to my mistress to say of her, that she did not adopt this course of treatment immediately. She at first lacked the depravity indispensable to shutting me up in mental darkness. It was at least necessary for her to have some training in the exercise of irresponsible power, to make her equal to the task of treating me as though I were a brute.

2   My mistress was, as I have said, a kind and tender-hearted woman; and in the simplicity of her soul she commenced, when I first went to live with her, to treat me as she supposed one human being ought to treat another. In entering upon the duties of a slaveholder, she did not seem to perceive that I sustained to her the relation of a mere chattel, and that for her to treat me as a human being was not only wrong, but dangerously so. Slavery proved as injurious to her as it did to me. When I went there, she was a pious, warm, and tender-hearted woman. There was no sorrow or suffering for which she had not a tear. She had bread for the hungry, clothes for the naked, and comfort for every mourner that came within her reach. Slavery soon proved its ability to divest her of these heavenly qualities. Under its influence, the tender heart became stone, and the lamb-like disposition gave way to one of tiger-like fierceness. The first step in her downward course was in her ceasing to instruct me. She now commenced to practice her husband's precepts. She finally became even more violent in her opposition than her husband himself. She was not satisfied with simply doing as well as he had commanded; she seemed anxious to do better. Nothing seemed to make her more angry than to see me with a newspaper. She seemed to think that here lay the danger. I have had her rush at me with a face made all up of fury, and snatch from me a

newspaper, in a manner that fully revealed her apprehension. She was an apt woman; and a little experience soon demonstrated, to her satisfaction, that education and slavery were incompatible with each other.

3   From this time I was most narrowly watched. If I was in a separate room any considerable length of time, I was sure to be suspected of having a book, and was at once called to give an account of myself. All this, however, was too late. The first step had been taken. Mistress, in teaching me the alphabet, had given me the inch, and no precaution could prevent me from taking the *ell*.

4   The plan which I adopted, and the one by which I was most successful, was that of making friends of all the little white boys whom I met in the street. As many of these as I could, I converted into teachers. With their kindly aid, obtained at different times and in different places, I finally succeeded in learning to read. When I was sent on errands, I always took my book with me, and by doing one part of my errand quickly, I found time to get a lesson before my return. I used also to carry bread with me, enough of which was always in the house, and to which I was always welcome; for I was much better off in this regard than many of the poor white children in our neighborhood. This bread I used to bestow upon the hungry little urchins, who, in return, would give me that more valuable bread of knowledge. I am strongly tempted to give the names of two or three of those little boys, as a testimonial of the gratitude and affection I bear them; but prudence forbids;—not that it would injure me, but it might embarrass them; for it is almost an unpardonable offence to teach slaves to read in this Christian country. It is enough to say of the dear little fellows, that they lived on Philpot Street, very near Durgin and Bailey's ship-yard. I used to talk this matter of slavery over with them. I would sometimes say to them, I wished I could be as free as they would be when they got to be men. "You will be free as soon as you are twenty-one, *but I am a slave for life!* Have not I as good a right to be free as you have?" These words used to trouble them; they would express for me the liveliest sympathy, and console me with the hope that something would occur by which I might be free.

5   I was now about twelve years old, and the thought of being *a slave for life* began to bear heavily upon my heart. Just about this time, I got hold of a book entitled "The Columbian Orator." Every opportunity I got, I used to read this book. Among much of other interesting matter, I found in it a dialogue between a master and his slave. The slave was represented as having run away from his master three times. The dialogue represented

the conversation which took place between them, when the slave was retaken the third time. In this dialogue, the whole argument in behalf of slavery was brought forward by the master, all of which was disposed of by the slave. The slave was made to say some very smart as well as impressive things in reply to his master—things which had the desired though unexpected effect; for the conversation resulted in the voluntary emancipation of the slave on the part of the master.

6   In the same book, I met with one of Sheridan's mighty speeches on and in behalf of Catholic emancipation. These were choice documents to me. I read them over and over again with unabated interest. They gave tongue to interesting thoughts of my own soul, which had frequently flashed through my mind, and died away for want of utterance. The moral which I gained from the dialogue was the power of truth over the conscience of even a slaveholder. What I got from Sheridan was a bold denunciation of slavery, and a powerful vindication of human rights. The reading of these documents enabled me to utter my thoughts, and to meet the arguments brought forward to sustain slavery; but while they relieved me of one difficulty, they brought on another even more painful than the one of which I was relieved. The more I read, the more I was led to abhor and detest my enslavers. I could regard them in no other light than a band of successful robbers, who had left their homes, and gone to Africa, and stolen us from our homes, and in a strange land reduced us to slavery. I loathed them as being the meanest as well as the most wicked of men. As I read and contemplated the subject, behold! that very discontentment which Master Hugh had predicted would follow my learning to read had already come, to torment and sting my soul to unutterable anguish. As I writhed under it, I would at times feel that learning to read had been a curse rather than a blessing. It had given me a view of my wretched condition, without the remedy. It opened my eyes to the horrible pit, but to no ladder upon which to get out. In moments of agony, I envied my fellow-slaves for their stupidity. I have often wished myself a beast. I preferred the condition of the meanest reptile to my own. Any thing, no matter what, to get rid of thinking! It was this everlasting thinking of my condition that tormented me. There was no getting rid of it. It was pressed upon me by every object within sight or hearing, animate or inanimate. The silver trump of freedom had roused my soul to eternal wakefulness. Freedom now appeared, to disappear no more forever. It was heard in every sound, and seen in every thing. It was ever present to torment me with a sense of my wretched condition. I saw nothing without seeing it, I heard nothing without hearing it, and felt nothing without feeling it. It

looked from every star, it smiled in every calm, breathed in every wind, and moved in every storm.

7   I often found myself regretting my own existence, and wishing myself dead; and but for the hope of being free, I have no doubt but that I should have killed myself, or done something for which I should have been killed. While in this state of mind, I was eager to hear any one speak of slavery. I was a ready listener. Every little while, I could hear something about the abolitionists. It was some time before I found what the word meant. It was always used in such connections as to make it an interesting word to me. If a slave ran away and succeeded in getting clear, or if a slave killed his master, set fire to a barn, or did any thing very wrong in the mind of a slaveholder, it was spoken of as the fruit of *abolition*. Hearing the word in this connection very often, I set about learning what it meant. The dictionary afforded me little or no help. I found it was "the act of abolishing," but then I did not know what was to be abolished. Here I was perplexed. I did not dare to ask any one about its meaning, for I was satisfied that it was something they wanted me to know very little about. After a patient waiting, I got one of our city papers, containing an account of the number of petitions from the north, praying for the abolition of slavery in the District of Columbia, and of the slave trade between the States. From this time I understood the words *abolition* and *abolitionist*, and always drew near when that word was spoken, expecting to hear something of importance to myself and fellow-slaves. The light broke in upon me by degrees. I went one day down on the wharf of Mr. Waters; and seeing two Irishmen unloading a scow of stone, I went, unasked, and helped them. When we had finished, one of them came to me and asked me if I were a slave. I told him I was. He asked, "Are ye a slave for life?" I told him that I was. The good Irishman seemed to be deeply affected by the statement. He said to the other that it was a pity so fine a little fellow as myself should be a slave for life. He said it was a shame to hold me. They both advised me to run away to the north; that I should find friends there, and that I should be free, I pretended not to be interested in what they said, and treated them as if I did not understand them; for I feared they might be treacherous. White men have been known to encourage slaves to escape, and then, to get the reward, catch them and return them to their masters. I was afraid that these seemingly good men might use me so; but I nevertheless remembered their advice, and from that time I resolved to run away. I looked forward to a time at which it would be safe for me to escape. I was too young to think of doing so immediately; besides, I wished to learn how to write,

as I might have occasion to write my own pass. I consoled myself with the hope that I should one day find a good chance. Meanwhile, I would learn to write.

8   The idea as to how I might learn to write was suggested to me by being in Durgin and Bailey's ship-yard, and frequently seeing the ship carpenters, after hewing, and getting a piece of timber ready for use, write on the timber the name of that part of the ship for which it was intended. When a piece of timber was intended for the larboard side, it would be marked thus—"L." When a piece was for the starboard side, it would be marked thus—"S." A piece for the larboard side forward, would be marked thus—"L. F." When a piece was for starboard side forward, it would be marked thus—"S. F." For larboard aft, it would be marked thus—"L. A." For starboard aft, it would be marked thus—"S. A." I soon learned the names of these letters, and for what they were intended when placed upon a piece of timber in the ship yard. I immediately commenced copying them, and in a short time was able to make the four letters named. After that, when I met with any boy who I knew could write, I would tell him I could write as well as he. The next word would be, "I don't believe you. Let me see you try it." I would then make the letters which I had been so fortunate as to learn, and ask him to beat that. In this way I got a good many lessons in writing, which it is quite possible I should never have gotten in any other way. During this time, my copy-book was the board fence, brick wall, and pavement; my pen and ink was a lump of chalk. With these, I learned mainly how to write. I then commenced and continued copying the Italics in Webster's Spelling Book, until I could make them all without looking on the book. By this time, my little Master Thomas had gone to school, and learned how to write, and had written over a number of copy-books. These had been brought home, and shown to some of our near neighbors, and then laid aside. My mistress used to go to class meeting at the Wilk Street meetinghouse every Monday afternoon, and leave me to take care of the house. When left thus, I used to spend the time in writing in the spaces left in Master Thomas's copy-book, copying what he had written. I continued to do this until I could write a hand very similar to

that of Master Thomas. Thus, after a long, tedious effort for years, I finally succeeded in learning how to write.

QUESTIONS TO CONSIDER

1. Summarize Douglass's process of learning how to read and write. How does his journey towards literacy begin, and what tools does he find to assist him?

2. Why is learning to read so important to Douglass? To what extent does learning to read come to define him as a person? Find at least one specific quoted passage that illustrates Douglass's attitude towards literacy.

3. How does Douglass explain the conflict between literacy and slavery in his own experience? What explanation does he offer for why his master does not want him to learn how to read? What effect does the knowledge that literacy is prohibited have on Douglass?

Nickel and Dimed: On (Not) Getting By in America

Barbara Ehrenreich

- **N** Narration
- **DES** Description
- **IE** Illustration and Exemplification
- **CC** Compare and Contrast
- **PA** Process Analysis

1   At the beginning of June 1998 I leave behind everything that normally soothes the ego and sustains the body—home, career, companion, reputation, ATM card—for a plunge into the low-wage workforce. There, I become another, occupationally much diminished "Barbara Ehrenreich"—depicted on job-application forms as a divorced homemaker whose sole work experience consists of housekeeping in a few private homes. I am terrified, at the beginning, of being unmasked for what I am: a middle-class journalist setting out to explore the world that welfare mothers are entering, at the rate of approximately 50,000 a month, as welfare reform kicks in. Happily, though, my fears turn out to be entirely unwarranted: during a month of poverty and toil, my name goes unnoticed and for the most part unuttered. In this parallel universe where my father never got out of the mines and I never got through college, I am "baby," "honey," "blondie," and, most commonly, "girl."

2   My first task is to find a place to live. I figure that if I can earn $7 an hour—which, from the want ads, seems doable—I can afford to spend $500 on rent, or maybe, with severe economies, $600. In the Key West area, where I live, this pretty much confines me to flophouses and trailer homes—like the one, a pleasing fifteen-minute drive from town, that has no air-conditioning, no screens, no fans, no television, and, by way of diversion, only the challenge of evading the landlord's Doberman pinscher. The big problem with this place, though, is the rent, which at $675 a month is well beyond my reach. All right, Key West is expensive. But so is New York City, or the Bay Area, or Jackson Hole, or Telluride, or Boston, or any other place where tourists and the wealthy compete for living space with the people who clean their toilets and fry their hash browns. Still, it is a shock to realize that "trailer trash" has become, for me, a demographic category to aspire to.

3   So I decide to make the common trade-off between affordability and convenience, and go for a $500-a-month efficiency thirty miles up a two-lane highway from the employment opportunities of Key West,

meaning forty-five minutes if there's no road construction and I don't get caught behind some sun-dazed Canadian tourists. I hate the drive, along a roadside studded with white crosses commemorating the more effective head-on collisions, but it's a sweet little place—a cabin, more or less, set in the swampy back yard of the converted mobile home where my landlord, an affable TV repairman, lives with his bartender girlfriend. Anthropologically speaking, a bustling trailer park would be preferable, but here I have a gleaming white floor and a firm mattress, and the few resident bugs are easily vanquished.

4   Besides, I am not doing this for the anthropology. My aim is nothing so mistily subjective as to "experience poverty" or find out how it "really feels" to be a long-term low-wage worker. I've have enough unchosen encounters with poverty and the world of low-wage work to know it's not a place you want to visit for touristic purposes; it just smells too much like fear. And with all my real-life assets—bank account, IRA, health insurance, multiroom home—waiting indulgently in the background, I am, of course, thoroughly insulated from the terrors that afflict the genuinely poor.

5   No, this is a purely objective, scientific sort of mission. The humanitarian rationale for welfare reform—as opposed to the more punitive and stingy impulses that may actually have motivated it—is that work will lift poor women out of poverty while simultaneously inflating their self-esteem and hence their future value in the labor market. Thus, whatever the hassles involved in finding child care, transportation, etc., the transition from welfare to work will end happily, in greater prosperity for all. Now there are many problems with this comforting prediction, such as the fact that the economy will inevitably undergo a downturn, eliminating many jobs. Even without a downturn, the influx of a million former welfare recipients into the low-wage labor market could depress wages by as much as 11.9 percent, according to the Economic Policy Institute (EPI) in Washington, D.C.

6   But is it really possible to make a living on the kinds of jobs currently available to unskilled people? Mathematically, the answer is no, as can be shown by taking $6 to $7 an hour, perhaps subtracting a dollar or two an hour for child care, multiplying by 160 hours a month, and comparing the result to the prevailing rents. According to the National Coalition for the Homeless, for example, in 1998 it took, on average nation-wide, an hourly wage of $8.89 to afford a one-bedroom apartment, and the Preamble Center for Public Policy estimates that the odds against a typical welfare

recipient's landing a job at such a "living wage" are about 97 to 1. If these numbers are right, low-wage work is not a solution to poverty and possibly not even to homelessness.

7   It may seem excessive to put this proposition to an experimental test. As certain family members keep unhelpfully reminding me, the viability of low-wage work could be tested, after a fashion, without ever leaving my study. I could just pay myself $7 an hour for eight hours a day, charge myself for room and board, and total up the numbers after a month. Why leave the people and work that I love? But I am an experimental scientist by training. In that business, you don't just sit at a desk and theorize; you plunge into the everyday chaos of nature, where surprises lurk in the most mundane measurements. Maybe, when I got into it, I would discover some hidden economies in the world of the low-wage worker. After all, if 30 percent of the workforce toils for less than $8 an hour, according to the EPI, they may have found some tricks as yet unknown to me. Maybe—who knows?—I would even be able to detect in myself the bracing psychological effects of getting out of the house, as promised by the welfare wonks at places like the Heritage Foundation. Or, on the other hand, maybe there would be unexpected costs—physical, mental, or financial—to throw off all my calculations. Ideally, I should do this with two small children in tow, that being the welfare average, but mine are grown and no one is willing to lend me theirs for a month-long vacation in penury. So this is not the perfect experiment, just a test of the best possible case: an unencumbered woman, smart and even strong, attempting to live more or less off the land.

8   On the morning of my first full day of job searching, I take a red pen to the want ads, which are auspiciously numerous. Everyone in Key West's booming "hospitality industry" seems to be looking for someone like me—trainable, flexible, and with suitably humble expectations as to pay. I know I possess certain traits that might be advantageous—I'm white and, I like to think, well-spoken and poised—but I decide on two rules: One, I cannot use any skills derived from my education or usual work—not that there are a lot of want ads for satirical essayists anyway. Two, I have to take the best-paid job that is offered me and of course do my best to hold it, no Marxist rants or sneaking off to read novels in the ladies' room. In addition, I rule out various occupations for one reason or another: Hotel front-desk clerk, for example, which to my surprise is regarded as unskilled and pays around $7 an hour, gets eliminated because it involves standing in one spot for eight hours a day. Waitressing

is similarly something I'd like to avoid, because I remember it leaving me bone tired when I was eighteen, and I'm decades of varicosities and back pain beyond that now. Telemarketing, one of the first refuges of the suddenly indigent, can be dismissed on grounds of personality. This leaves certain supermarket jobs, such as deli clerk, or housekeeping in Key West's thousands of hotel and guest rooms. Housekeeping is especially appealing, for reasons both atavistic and practical: it's what my mother did before I came along, and it can't be too different from what I've been doing part-time, in my own home, all my life.

9   So I put on what I take to be a respectful-looking outfit of ironed Bermuda shorts and scooped-neck T-shirt and set out for a tour of the local hotels and supermarkets. Best Western, Econo Lodge, and Hojo's all let me fill out application forms, and these are, to my relief, interested in little more than whether I am a legal resident of the United States and have committed any felonies. My next stop is Winn-Dixie, the super-market, which turns out to have a particularly onerous application process, featuring a fifteen-minute "interview" by computer since, apparently, no human on the premises is deemed capable of representing the corporate point of view. I am conducted to a large room decorated with posters illustrating how to look "professional" (it helps to be white and, if female, permed) and warning of the slick promises that union organizers might try to tempt me with. The interview is multiple choice: Do I have anything, such as child-care problems, that might make it hard for me to get to work on time? Do I think safety on the job is the responsibility of management? Then, popping up cunningly out of the blue: How many dollars' worth of stolen goods have I purchased in the last year? Would I turn in a fellow employee if I caught him stealing? Finally, "Are you an honest person?"

10   Apparently, I ace the interview, because I am told that all I have to do is show up in some doctor's office tomorrow for a urine test. This seems to be a fairly general rule: if you want to stack Cheerio boxes or vacuum hotel rooms in chemically fascist America, you have to be willing to squat down and pee in front of some health worker (who has no doubt had to do the same thing herself). The wages Winn-Dixie is offering—$6 and a couple of dimes to start with—are not enough, I decide, to compensate for this indignity.

11   I lunch at Wendy's, where $4.99 gets you unlimited refills at the Mexican part of the Superbar, a comforting surfeit of refried beans and "cheese sauce." A teenage employee, seeing me studying the want ads, kindly offers me an application form, which I fill out, though here, too,

the pay is just $6 and change an hour. Then it's off for a round of the locally owned inns and guesthouses. At "The Palms," let's call it, a bouncy manager actually takes me around to see the rooms and meet the existing housekeepers, who, I note with satisfaction, look pretty much like me—faded ex-hippie types in shorts with long hair pulled back in braids. Mostly, though, no one speaks to me or even looks at me except to proffer an application form. At my last stop, a palatial B&B, I wait twenty minutes to meet "Max," only to be told that there are no jobs now but there should be one soon, since "nobody lasts more than a couple weeks." (Because none of the people I talked to knew I was a reporter, I have changed their names to protect their privacy and, in some cases perhaps, their jobs.)

12   Three days go like this, and, to my chagrin, no one out of the approximately twenty places I've applied calls me for an interview. I had been vain enough to worry about coming across as too educated for the jobs I sought, but no one even seems interested in finding out how overqualified I am. Only later will I realize that the want ads are not a reliable measure of the actual jobs available at any particular time. They are, as I should have guessed from Max's comment, the employers' insurance policy against the relentless turnover of the low-wage workforce. Most of the big hotels run ads almost continually, just to build a supply of applicants to replace the current workers as they drift away or are fired, so finding a job is just a matter of being at the right place at the right time and flexible enough to take whatever is being offered that day. This finally happens to me at one of the big discount hotel chains, where I go, as usual, for housekeeping and am sent, instead, to try out as a waitress at the attached "family restaurant," a dismal spot with a counter and about thirty tables that look out on a parking garage and features such tempting fare as "Pollish [sic] sausage and BBQ sauce" on 95-degree days. Phillip, the dapper young West Indian who introduces himself as the manager, interviews me with about as much enthusiasm as if he were a clerk processing me for Medicare, the principal questions being what shifts can I work and when can I start. I mutter something about being woefully out of practice as a waitress, but he's already on to the uniform: I'm to show up tomorrow wearing black slacks and black shoes; he'll provide the rust-colored polo shirt with HEARTHSIDE embroidered on it, though I might want to wear my own shirt to get to work, ha ha. At the word "tomorrow," something between fear and indignation rises in my chest. I want to say, "Thank you for your time, sir, but this is just an experiment, you know, not my actual life."

13   So begins my career at the Hearthside, I shall call it, one small profit center within a global discount hotel chain, where for two weeks I
work from 2:00 till 10:00 P.M. for $2.43 an hour plus tips. In some futile
bid for gentility, the management has barred employees from using the
front door, so my first day I enter through the kitchen, where a red-faced
man with shoulder-length blond hair is throwing frozen steaks against
the wall and yelling, "Fuck this shit!" "That's just Jack," explains Gail, the
wiry middle-aged waitress who is assigned to train me. "He's on the rag
again"—a condition occasioned, in this instance, by the fact that the cook
on the morning shift had forgotten to thaw out the steaks. For the next
eight hours, I run after the agile Gail, absorbing bits of instruction along
with fragments of personal tragedy. All food must be trayed, and the reason she's so tired today is that she woke up in a cold sweat thinking of her
boyfriend, who killed himself recently in an upstate prison. No refills on
lemonade. And the reason he was in prison is that a few DUIs caught up
with him, that's all, could have happened to anyone. Carry the creamers
to the table in a monkey bowl, never in your hand. And after he was gone
she spent several months living in her truck, peeing in a plastic pee bottle
and reading by candlelight at night, but you can't live in a truck in the
summer, since you need to have the windows down, which means anything can get in, from mosquitoes on up.

14   At least Gail puts to rest any fears I had of appearing overqualified.
From the first day on, I find that of all the things I have left behind, such
as home and identity, what I miss the most is competence. Not that I have
ever felt utterly competent in the writing business, in which one day's success augurs nothing at all for the next. But in my writing life, I at least have
some notion of procedure: do the research, make the outline, rough out a
draft, etc. As a server, though, I am beset by requests like bees: more iced
tea here, ketchup over there, a to-go box for table fourteen, and where are
the high chairs, anyway? Of the twenty-seven tables, up to six are usually
mine at any time, though on slow afternoons or if Gail is off, I sometimes
have the whole place to myself. There is the touch-screen computer-order-
ing system to master, which is, I suppose, meant to minimize server-cook
contact, but in practice requires constant verbal finetuning: "That's gravy on the mashed, okay? None on the meatloaf," and so forth—while the
cook scowls as if I were inventing these refinements just to torment him.
Plus, something I had forgotten in the years since I was eighteen: about a
third of a server's job is "side work" that's invisible to customers—sweep-
ing, scrubbing, slicing, refilling, and restocking. If it isn't all done, every

READINGS

little bit of it, you're going to face the 6:00 P.M. dinner rush defenseless and probably go down in flames. I screw up dozens of times at the beginning, sustained in my shame entirely by Gail's support—"It's okay, baby, every-one does that sometime"—because, to my total surprise and despite the scientific detachment I am doing my best to maintain, I care.

15   The whole thing would be a lot easier if I could just skate through it as Lily Tomlin in one of her waitress skits, but I was raised by the ab-surd Booker T. Washingtonian precept that says: If you're going to do something, do it well. In fact, "well" isn't good enough by half. Do it better than anyone has ever done it before. Or so said my father, who must have known what he was talking about because he managed to pull himself, and us with him, up from the mile-deep copper mines of Butte to the leafy suburbs of the Northeast, ascending from boilermakers to martinis be-fore booze beat out ambition. As in most endeavors I have encountered in my life, doing it "better than anyone" is not a reasonable goal. Still, when I wake up at 4:00 A.M. in my own cold sweat, I am not thinking about the writing deadlines I'm neglecting; I'm thinking about the table whose order I screwed up so that one of the boys didn't get his kiddie meal until the rest of the family had moved on to their Key Lime pies. That's the other powerful motivation I hadn't expected—the customers, or "patients," as I can't help thinking of them on account of the mysterious vulnerability that seems to have left them temporarily unable to feed themselves. After a few days at the Hearthside, I feel the service ethic kick in like a shot of oxytocin, the nurturance hormone. The plurality of my customers are hardworking locals—truck drivers, construction workers, even house-keepers from the attached hotel—and I want them to have the closest to a "fine dining" experience that the grubby circumstances will allow. No "you guys" for me; everyone over twelve is "sir" or "ma'am." I ply them with iced tea and coffee refills; I return, mid-meal, to inquire how everything is; I doll up their salads with chopped raw mushrooms, summer squash slic-es, or whatever bits of produce I can find that have survived their sojourn in the cold-storage room mold-free.

16   There is Benny, for example, a short, tight-muscled sewer repairman, who cannot even think of eating until he has absorbed a half hour of air-conditioning and ice water. We chat about hyperthermia and electro-lytes until he is ready to order some finicky combination like soup of the day, garden salad, and a side of grits. There are the German tourists who are so touched by my pidgin "Willkommen" and "Ist alles gut?" that they actually tip. (Europeans, spoiled by their trade-union-ridden, high-wage

welfare states, generally do not know that they are supposed to tip. Some restaurants, the Hearthside included, allow servers to "grat" their foreign customers, or add a tip to the bill. Since this amount is added before the customers have a chance to tip or not tip, the practice amounts to an automatic penalty for imperfect English.) There are the two dirt-smudged lesbians, just off their construction shift, who are impressed enough by my suave handling of the fly in the piña colada that they take the time to praise me to Stu, the assistant manager. There's Sam, the kindly retired cop, who has to plug up his tracheotomy hole with one finger in order to force the cigarette smoke into his lungs.

17   Sometimes I play with the fantasy that I am a princess who, in penance for some tiny transgression, has undertaken to feed each of her subjects by hand. But the non-princesses working with me are just as indulgent, even when this means flouting management rules—concerning, for example, the number of croutons that can go on a salad (six). "Put on all you want," Gail whispers, "as long as Stu isn't looking." She dips into her own tip money to buy biscuits and gravy for an out-of-work mechanic who's used up all his money on dental surgery, inspiring me to pick up the tab for his milk and pie. Maybe the same high levels of agape can be found throughout the "hospitality industry." I remember the poster decorating one of the apartments I looked at, which said, "If you seek happiness for yourself you will never find it. Only when you seek happiness for others will it come to you," or words to that effect—an odd sentiment, it seemed to me at the time, to find in the dank one-room basement apartment of a bellhop at the Best Western. At the Hearthside, we utilize whatever bits of autonomy we have to ply our customers with the illicit calories that signal our love. It is our job as servers to assemble the salads and desserts, pouring the dressings and squirting the whipped cream. We also control the number of butter patties our customers get and the amount of sour cream on their baked potatoes. So if you wonder why Americans are so obese, consider the fact that waitresses both express their humanity and earn their tips through the covert distribution of fats.

18   Ten days into it, this is beginning to look like a livable lifestyle. I like Gail, who is "looking at fifty" but moves so fast she can alight in one place and then another without apparently being anywhere between them. I clown around with Lionel, the teenage Haitian busboy, and catch a few fragments of conversation with Joan, the svelte fortyish hostess and militant feminist who is the only one of us who dares to tell Jack to shut the fuck up. I even warm up to Jack when, on a slow night and to make up

for a particularly unwarranted attack on my abilities, or so I imagine, he tells me about his glory days as a young man at "coronary school"—or do you say "culinary"?—in Brooklyn, where he dated a knock-out Puerto Rican chick and learned everything there is to know about food. I finish up at 10:00 or 10:30, depending on how much side work I've been able to get done during the shift, and cruise home to the tapes I snatched up at random when I left my real home—Marianne Faithfull, Tracy Chapman, Enigma, King Sunny Ade, the Violent Femmes—just drained enough for the music to set my cranium resonating but hardly dead. Midnight snack is Wheat Thins and Monterey Jack, accompanied by cheap white wine on ice and whatever AMC has to offer. To bed by 1:30 or 2:00, up at 9:00 or 10:00, read for an hour while my uniform whirls around in the landlord's washing machine, and then it's another eight hours spent following Mao's central instruction, as laid out in the Little Red Book, which was: Serve the people.

19   I could drift along like this, in some dreamy proletarian idyll, except for two things. One is management. If I have kept this subject on the margins thus far it is because I still flinch to think that I spent all those weeks under the surveillance of men (and later women) whose job it was to monitor my behavior for signs of sloth, theft, drug abuse, or worse. Not that managers and especially "assistant managers" in low-wage settings like this are exactly the class enemy. In the restaurant business, they are mostly former cooks or servers, still capable of pinch-hitting in the kitchen or on the floor, just as in hotels they are likely to be former clerks, and paid a salary of only about $400 a week. But everyone knows they have crossed over to the other side, which is, crudely put, corporate as opposed to human. Cooks want to prepare tasty meals; servers want to serve them graciously; but managers are there for only one reason—to make sure that money is made for some theoretical entity that exists far away in Chicago or New York, if a corporation can be said to have a physical existence at all. Reflecting on her career, Gail tells me ruefully that she had sworn, years ago, never to work for a corporation again. "They don't cut you no slack. You give and you give, and they take."

20   Managers can sit—for hours at a time if they want—but it's their job to see that no one else ever does, even when there's nothing to do, and this is why, for servers, slow times can be as exhausting as rushes. You start dragging out each little chore, because if the manager on duty catches you in an idle moment, he will give you something far nastier to do. So I wipe, I clean, I consolidate ketchup bottles and recheck the cheesecake supply, even tour the tables to make sure the customer evaluation forms are all

standing perkily in their places—wondering all the time how many calories I burn in these strictly theatrical exercises. When, on a particularly dead afternoon, Stu finds me glancing at a *USA Today* a customer has left behind, he assigns me to vacuum the entire floor with the broken vacuum cleaner that has a handle only two feet long, and the only way to do that without incurring orthopedic damage is to proceed from spot to spot on your knees.

21   On my first Friday at the Hearthside there is a "mandatory meeting for all restaurant employees," which I attend, eager for insight into our overall marketing strategy and the niche (your basic Ohio cuisine with a tropical twist?) we aim to inhabit. But there is no "we" at this meeting. Phillip, our top manager except for an occasional "consultant" sent out by corporate headquarters, opens it with a sneer: "The break room—it's disgusting. Butts in the ashtrays, newspapers lying around, crumbs." This windowless little room, which also houses the time clock for the entire hotel, is where we stash our bags and civilian clothes and take our half-hour meal breaks. But a break room is not a right, he tells us. It can be taken away. We should also know that the lockers in the break room and whatever is in them can be searched at any time. Then comes gossip; there has been gossip; gossip (which seems to mean employees talking among themselves) must stop. Off-duty employees are henceforth barred from eating at the restaurant, because "other servers gather around them and gossip." When Phillip has exhausted his agenda of rebukes, Joan complains about the condition of the ladies' room and I throw in my two bits about the vacuum cleaner. But I don't see any backup coming from my fellow servers, each of whom has subsided into her own personal funk; Gail, my role model, stares sorrowfully at a point six inches from her nose. The meeting ends when Andy, one of the cooks, gets up, muttering about breaking up his day off for this almighty bullshit.

22   Just four days later we are suddenly summoned into the kitchen at 3:30 P.M., even though there are live tables on the floor. We all—about ten of us—stand around Phillip, who announces grimly that there has been a report of some "drug activity" on the night shift and that, as a result, we are now to be a "drug-free" workplace, meaning that all new hires will be tested, as will possibly current employees on a random basis. I am glad that this part of the kitchen is so dark, because I find myself blushing as hard as if I had been caught toking up in the ladies' room myself: I haven't been treated this way—lined up in the corridor, threatened with locker searches, peppered with carelessly aimed accusations—since junior high

READINGS

school. Back on the floor, Joan cracks, "Next they'll be telling us we can't have sex on the job." When I ask Stu what happened to inspire the crackdown, he just mutters about "management decisions" and takes the opportunity to upbraid Gail and me for being too generous with the rolls. From now on there's to be only one per customer, and it goes out with the dinner, not with the salad. He's also been riding the cooks, prompting Andy to come out of the kitchen and observe—with the serenity of a man whose customary implement is a butcher knife—that "Stu has a death wish today."

23   Later in the evening, the gossip crystallizes around the theory that Stu is himself the drug culprit, that he uses the restaurant phone to order up marijuana and sends one of the late servers out to fetch it for him. The server was caught, and she may have ratted Stu out or at least said enough to cast some suspicion on him, thus accounting for his pissy behavior. Who knows? Lionel, the busboy, entertains us for the rest of the shift by standing just behind Stu's back and sucking deliriously on an imaginary joint.

24   The other problem, in addition to the less-than-nurturing management style, is that this job shows no sign of being financially viable. You might imagine, from a comfortable distance, that people who live, year in and year out, on $6 to $10 an hour have discovered some survival stratagems unknown to the middle class. But no. It's not hard to get my co-workers to talk about their living situations, because housing, in almost every case, is the principal source of disruption in their lives, the first thing they fill you in on when they arrive for their shifts. After a week, I have compiled the following survey:

- Gail is sharing a room in a well-known downtown flophouse for which she and a roommate pay about $250 a week. Her roommate, a male friend, has begun hitting on her, driving her nuts, but the rent would be impossible alone.

- Claude, the Haitian cook, is desperate to get out of the two-room apartment he shares with his girlfriend and two other, unrelated, people. As far as I can determine, the other Haitian men (most of whom only speak Creole) live in similarly crowded situations.

- Annette, a twenty-year-old server who is six months pregnant and has been abandoned by her boyfriend, lives with her mother, a postal clerk.

- Marianne and her boyfriend are paying $170 a week for a one-person trailer.

- Jack, who is, at $10 an hour, the wealthiest of us, lives in the trailer he owns, paying only the $400-a-month lot fee.

- The other white cook, Andy, lives on his dry-docked boat, which, as far as I can tell from his loving descriptions, can't be more than twenty feet long. He offers to take me out on it, once it's repaired, but the offer comes with inquiries as to my marital status, so I do not follow up on it.

- Tina and her husband are paying $60 a night for a double room in a Days Inn. This is because they have no car and the Days Inn is within walking distance of the Hearthside.

- When Marianne, one of the breakfast servers, is tossed out of her trailer for subletting (which is against the trailer-park rules), she leaves her boyfriend and moves in with Tina and her husband.

- Joan, who had fooled me with her numerous and tasteful outfits (hostesses wear their own clothes), lives in a van she parks behind a shopping center at night and showers in Tina's motel room. The clothes are from thrift shops.

25   It strikes me, in my middle-class solipsism, that there is gross improvidence in some of these arrangements. When Gail and I are wrapping silverware in napkins—the only task for which we are permitted to sit—she tells me she is thinking of escaping from her roommate by moving into the Days Inn herself. I am astounded: How can she even think of paying between $40 and $60 a day? But if I was afraid of sounding like a social worker, I come out just sounding like a fool. She squints at me in disbelief, "And where am I supposed to get a month's rent and a month's deposit for an apartment?" I'd been feeling pretty smug about my $500 efficiency, but of course it was made possible only by the $1,300 I had allotted myself for start-up costs when I began my low-wage life: $1,000 for the first month's rent and deposit, $100 for initial groceries and cash in my pocket, $200 stuffed away for emergencies. In poverty, as in certain propositions in physics, starting conditions are everything.

26   There are no secret economies that nourish the poor; on the contrary, there are a host of special costs. If you can't put up the two months' rent you need to secure an apartment, you end up paying through the nose for a room by the week. If you have only a room, with a hot plate at best, you can't save by cooking up huge lentil stews that can be frozen for the week ahead. You eat fast food, or the hot dogs and styrofoam cups of soup that can be microwaved in a convenience store. If you have no

money for health insurance—and the Hearthside's niggardly plan kicks in only after three months—you go without routine care or prescription drugs and end up paying the price. Gail, for example, was fine until she ran out of money for estrogen pills. She is supposed to be on the company plan by now, but they claim to have lost her application form and need to begin the paperwork all over again. So she spends $9 per migraine pill to control the headaches she wouldn't have, she insists, if her estrogen supplements were covered. Similarly, Marianne's boyfriend lost his job as a roofer because he missed so much time after getting a cut on his foot for which he couldn't afford the prescribed antibiotic.

27   My own situation, when I sit down to assess it after two weeks of work, would not be much better if this were my actual life. The seductive thing about waitressing is that you don't have to wait for payday to feel a few bills in your pocket, and my tips usually cover meals and gas, plus something left over to stuff into the kitchen drawer I use as a bank. But as the tourist business slows in the summer heat, I sometimes leave work with only $20 in tips (the gross is higher, but servers share about 15 percent of their tips with the busboys and bartenders). With wages included, this amounts to about the minimum wage of $5.15 an hour. Although the sum in the drawer is piling up, at the present rate of accumulation it will be more than a hundred dollars short of my rent when the end of the month comes around. Nor can I see any expenses to cut. True, I haven't gone the lentil-stew route yet, but that 's because I don't have a large cooking pot, pot holders, or a ladle to stir with (which cost about $30 at Kmart, less at thrift stores), not to mention onions, carrots, and the indispensable bay leaf. I do make my lunch almost every day—usually some slow-burning, high-protein combo like frozen chicken patties with melted cheese on top and canned pinto beans on the side. Dinner is at the Hearthside, which offers its employees a choice of BLT, fish sandwich, or hamburger for only $2. The burger lasts longest, especially if it's heaped with gut-puckering jalapeños, but by midnight my stomach is growling again.

28   So unless I want to start using my car as a residence, I have to find a second, or alternative, job. I call all the hotels where I filled out house-keeping applications weeks ago—the Hyatt, Holiday Inn, Econo Lodge, HoJo's, Best Western, plus a half dozen or so locally run guesthouses. Nothing. Then I start making the rounds again, wasting whole mornings waiting for some assistant manager to show up, even dipping into plac-es so creepy that the front-desk clerk greets you from behind bulletproof glass and sells pints of liquor over the counter. But either someone has

exposed my real-life housekeeping habits—which are, shall we say, mel-low—or I am at the wrong end of some infallible ethnic equation: most, but by no means all, of the working housekeepers I see on my job search-es are African Americans, Spanish-speaking, or immigrants from the Central European post-Communist world, whereas servers are almost invariably white and monolingually English-speaking. When I finally get a positive response, I have been identified once again as server material. Jerry's, which is part of a well-known national family restaurant chain and physically attached here to another budget hotel chain, is ready to use me at once. The prospect is both exciting and terrifying, because, with about the same number of tables and counter seats, Jerry's attracts three or four times the volume of customers as the gloomy old Hearthside.

29   Picture a fat person's hell, and I don't mean a place with no food. Instead there is everything you might eat if eating had no bodily conse-quences—cheese fries, chicken-fried steaks, fudge-laden desserts—only here every bite must be paid for, one way or another, in human discom-fort. The kitchen is a cavern, a stomach leading to the lower intestine that is the garbage and dishwashing area, from which issue bizarre smells combining the edible and the offal: creamy carrion, pizza barf, and that unique and enigmatic Jerry's scent—citrus fart. The floor is slick with spills, forcing us to walk through the kitchen with tiny steps, like Susan McDougal in leg irons. Sinks everywhere are clogged with scraps of let-tuce, decomposing lemon wedges, waterlogged toast crusts. Put your hand down on any counter and you risk being stuck to it by the film of ancient syrup spills, and this is unfortunate, because hands are utensils here, used for scooping up lettuce onto salad plates, lifting out pie slices, and even moving hash browns from one plate to another. The regulation poster in the single unisex restroom admonishes us to wash our hands thoroughly and even offers instructions for doing so, but there is always some vital substance missing—soap, paper towels, toilet paper—and I never find all three at once. You learn to stuff your pockets with napkins before going in there, and too bad about the customers, who must eat, though they don't realize this, almost literally out of our hands.

30   The break room typifies the whole situation: there is none, because there are no breaks at Jerry's. For six to eight hours in a row, you never sit except to pee. Actually, there are three folding chairs at a table immedi-ately adjacent to the bathroom, but hardly anyone ever sits here, in the very rectum of the gastro-architectural system. Rather, the function of the peritoilet area is to house the ashtrays in which servers and dishwashers

leave their cigarettes burning at all times, like votive candles, so that they don't have to waste time lighting up again when they dash back for a puff. Almost everyone smokes as if his or her pulmonary well-being depended on it—the multinational mélange of cooks, the Czech dishwashers, the servers, who are all American natives—creating an atmosphere in which oxygen is only an occasional pollutant. My first morning at Jerry's, when the hypoglycemic shakes set in, I complain to one of my fellow servers that I don't understand how she can go so long without food. "Well, I don't understand how you can go so long without a cigarette," she responds in a tone of reproach—because work is what you do for others; smoking is what you do for yourself. I don't know why the antismoking crusaders have never grasped the element of defiant self-nurturance that makes the habit so endearing to its victims—as if, in the American workplace, the only thing people have to call their own is the tumors they are nourishing and the spare moments they devote to feeding them.

31   Now, the Industrial Revolution is not an easy transition, especially when you have to zip through it in just a couple of days. I have gone from craft work straight into the factory, from the air-conditioned morgue of the Hearthside directly into the flames. Customers arrive in human waves, sometimes disgorged fifty at a time from their tour buses, peckish and whiny. Instead of two "girls" on the floor at once, there can be as many as six of us running around in our brilliant pink-and-orange Hawaiian shirts. Conversations, either with customers or fellow employees, seldom last more than twenty seconds at a time. On my first day, in fact, I am hurt by my sister servers' coldness. My mentor for the day is an emotionally un-inflected twenty-three-year-old, and the others, who gossip a little among themselves about the real reason someone is out sick today and the size of the bail bond someone else has had to pay, ignore me completely. On my second day, I find out why. "Well, it's good to see you again," one of them says in greeting. "Hardly anyone comes back after the first day." I feel powerfully vindicated—a survivor—but it would take a long time, probably months, before I could hope to be accepted into this sorority.

32   I start out with the beautiful, heroic idea of handling the two jobs at once, and for two days I almost do it: the breakfast/lunch shift at Jerry's, which goes till 2:00, arriving at the Hearthside at 2:10, and attempting to hold out until 10:00. In the ten minutes between jobs, I pick up a spicy chicken sandwich at the Wendy's drive-through window, gobble it down in the car, and change from khaki slacks to black, from Hawaiian to rust polo. There is a problem, though. When during the 3:00 to 4:00 P.M. dead

time I finally sit down to wrap silver, my flesh seems to bond to the seat. I try to refuel with a purloined cup of soup, as I've seen Gail and Joan do dozens of times, but a manager catches me and hisses "No eating!" though there's not a customer around to be offended by the sight of food making contact with a server's lips. So I tell Gail I'm going to quit, and she hugs me and says she might just follow me to Jerry's herself.

33   But the chances of this are minuscule. She has left the flophouse and her annoying roommate and is back to living in her beat-up old truck. But guess what? she reports to me excitedly later that evening: Phillip has given her permission to park overnight in the hotel parking lot, as long as she keeps out of sight, and the parking lot should be totally safe, since it's patrolled by a hotel security guard! With the Hearthside offering benefits like that, how could anyone think of leaving?

34   Gail would have triumphed at Jerry's, I'm sure, but for me it's a crash course in exhaustion management. Years ago, the kindly fry cook who trained me to waitress at a Los Angeles truck stop used to say: Never make an unnecessary trip; if you don't have to walk fast, walk slow; if you don't have to walk, stand. But at Jerry's the effort of distinguishing necessary from unnecessary and urgent from whenever would itself be too much of an energy drain. The only thing to do is to treat each shift as a one-time-only emergency: you've got fifty starving people out there, lying scattered on the battlefield, so get out there and feed them! Forget that you will have to do this again tomorrow, forget that you will have to be alert enough to dodge the drunks on the drive home tonight—just burn, burn, burn! Ideally, at some point you enter what servers call "a rhythm" and psychologists term a "flow state," in which signals pass from the sense organs directly to the muscles, bypassing the cerebral cortex, and a Zen-like emptiness sets in. A male server from the Hearthside's morning shift tells me about the time he "pulled a triple"—three shifts in a row, all the way around the clock—and then got off and had a drink and met this girl, and maybe he shouldn't tell me this, but they had sex right then and there, and it was like, beautiful.

35   But there's another capacity of the neuromuscular system, which is pain. I start tossing back drugstore-brand ibuprofen pills as if they were vitamin C, four before each shift, because an old mouse-related repetitive-stress injury in my upper back has come back to full-spasm strength, thanks to the tray carrying. In my ordinary life, this level of disability might justify a day of ice packs and stretching. Here I comfort myself with the Aleve commercial in which the cute blue-collar guy asks: If you quit after working four hours, what would your boss say? And the not-so-cute

blue-collar guy, who's lugging a metal beam on his back, answers: He'd fire me, that's what. But fortunately, the commercial tells us, we workers can exert the same kind of authority over our painkillers that our bosses exert over us. If Tylenol doesn't want to work for more than four hours, you just fire its ass and switch to Aleve.

36   True, I take occasional breaks from this life, going home now and then to catch up on e-mail and for conjugal visits (though I am careful to "pay" for anything I eat there), seeing *The Truman Show* with friends and letting them buy my ticket. And I still have those what-am-I-doing-here moments at work, when I get so homesick for the printed word that I obsessively reread the six-page menu. But as the days go by, my old life is beginning to look exceedingly strange. The e-mails and phone messages addressed to my former self come from a distant race of people with exotic concerns and far too much time on their hands. The neighborly market I used to cruise for produce now looks forbiddingly like a Manhattan yuppie emporium. And when I sit down one morning in my real home to pay bills from my past life, I am dazzled at the two- and three-figure sums owed to outfits like Club Body Tech and Amazon.com.

37   Management at Jerry's is generally calmer and more "professional" than at the Hearthside, with two exceptions. One is Joy, a plump, blowsy woman in her early thirties, who once kindly devoted several minutes to instructing me in the correct one-handed method of carrying trays but whose moods change disconcertingly from shift to shift and even within one. Then there's B.J., a.k.a. B.J. the Bitch, whose contribution is to stand by the kitchen counter and yell, "Nita, your order's up, move it!" or, "Barbara, didn't you see you've got another table out there? Come on, girl!" Among other things, she is hated for having replaced the whipped-cream squirt cans with big plastic whipped cream-filled baggies that have to be squeezed with both hands—because, reportedly, she saw or thought she saw employees trying to inhale the propellant gas from the squirt cans, in the hope that it might be nitrous oxide. On my third night, she pulls me aside abruptly and brings her face so close that it looks as if she's planning to butt me with her forehead. But instead of saying, "You're fired," she says, "You're doing fine." The only trouble is I'm spending time chatting with customers: "That's how they're getting you." Furthermore I am letting them "run me," which means harassment by sequential demands: you bring the ketchup and they decide they want extra Thousand Island; you bring that and they announce they now need a side of fries; and so on into distraction. Finally she tells me not to take her wrong. She

tries to say things in a nice way, but you get into a mode, you know, because everything has to move so fast.

38   I mumble thanks for the advice, feeling like I've just been stripped naked by the crazed enforcer of some ancient sumptuary law: No chatting for you, girl. No fancy service ethic allowed for the serfs. Chatting with customers is for the beautiful young college-educated servers in the downtown carpaccio joints, the kids who can make $70 to $100 a night. What had I been thinking? My job is to move orders from tables to kitchen and then trays from kitchen to tables. Customers are, in fact, the major obstacle to the smooth transformation of information into food and food into money—they are, in short, the enemy. And the painful thing is that I'm beginning to see it this way myself. There are the traditional asshole types—frat boys who down multiple Buds and then make a fuss because the steaks are so emaciated and the fries so sparse—as well as the variously impaired—due to age, diabetes, or literacy issues—who require patient nutritional counseling. The worst, for some reason, are the Visible Christians—like the ten-person table, all jolly and sanctified after Sunday-night service, who run me mercilessly and then leave me $1 on a $92 bill. Or the guy with the crucifixion T-shirt (SOMEONE TO LOOK UP TO) who complains that his baked potato is too hard and his iced tea too icy (I cheerfully fix both) and leaves no tip. As a general rule, people wearing crosses or WWJD? (What Would Jesus Do?) buttons look at us disapprovingly no matter what we do, as if they were confusing waitressing with Mary Magdalene's original profession.

39   I make friends, over time, with the other "girls" who work my shift: Nita, the tattooed twenty-something who taunts us by going around saying brightly, "Have we started making money yet?" Ellen, whose teenage son cooks on the graveyard shift and who once managed a restaurant in Massachusetts but won't try out for management here because she prefers being a "common worker" and not "ordering people around." Easygoing fiftyish Lucy, with the raucous laugh, who limps toward the end of the shift because of something that has gone wrong with her leg, the exact nature of which cannot be determined without health insurance. We talk about the usual girl things—men, children, and the sinister allure of Jerry's chocolate peanut-butter cream pie—though no one, I notice, ever brings up anything potentially expensive, like shopping or movies. As at the Hearthside, the only recreation ever referred to is partying, which requires little more than some beer, a joint, and a few close friends. Still, no one here is homeless, or cops to it anyway, thanks usually to a working

husband or boyfriend. All in all, we form a reliable mutual-support group: If one of us is feeling sick or overwhelmed, another one will "bev" a table or even carry trays for her. If one of us is off sneaking a cigarette or a pee, the others will do their best to conceal her absence from the enforcers of corporate rationality.

40   But my saving human connection—my oxytocin receptor, as it were—is George, the nineteen-year-old, fresh-off-the-boat Czech dishwasher. We get to talking when he asks me, tortuously, how much cigarettes cost at Jerry's. I do my best to explain that they cost over a dollar more here than at a regular store and suggest that he just take one from the half-filled packs that are always lying around on the break table. But that would be unthinkable. Except for the one tiny earring signaling his allegiance to some vaguely alternative point of view, George is a perfect straight arrow—crew-cut, hardworking, and hungry for eye contact. "Czech Republic," I ask, "or Slovakia?" and he seems delighted that I know the difference. "Václav Havel," I try. "Velvet Revolution, Frank Zappa?" "Yes, yes, 1989," he says, and I realize we are talking about history.

41   My project is to teach George English. "How are you today, George?" I say at the start of each shift. "I am good, and how are you today, Barbara?" I learn that he is not paid by Jerry's but by the "agent" who shipped him over—$5 an hour, with the agent getting the dollar or so difference between that and what Jerry's pays dishwashers. I learn also that he shares an apartment with a crowd of other Czech "dishers," as he calls them, and that he cannot sleep until one of them goes off for his shift, leaving a vacant bed. We are having one of our ESL sessions late one afternoon when B.J. catches us at it and orders "Joseph" to take up the rubber mats on the floor near the dishwashing sinks and mop underneath. "I thought your name was George," I say loud enough for B.J. to hear as she strides off back to the counter. Is she embarrassed? Maybe a little, because she greets me back at the counter with "George, Joseph—there are so many of them!" I say nothing, neither nodding nor smiling, and for this I am punished later when I think I am ready to go and she announces that I need to roll fifty more sets of silverware and isn't it time I mixed up a fresh four-gallon batch of bluecheese dressing? May you grow old in this place, B.J., is the curse I beam out at her when I am finally permitted to leave. May the syrup spills glue your feet to the floor.

42   I make the decision to move closer to Key West. First, because of the drive. Second and third, also because of the drive: gas is eating up $4 to $5 a day, and although Jerry's is as high-volume as you can get, the tips

average only 10 percent, and not just for a newbie like me. Between the base pay of $2.15 an hour and the obligation to share tips with the bus-boys and dishwashers, we're averaging only about $7.50 an hour. Then there is the $30 I had to spend on the regulation tan slacks worn by Jerry's servers—a setback it could take weeks to absorb. (I had combed the town's two downscale department stores hoping for something cheaper but decided in the end that these marked down Dockers, originally $49, were more likely to survive a daily washing.) Of my fellow servers, every-one who lacks a working husband or boyfriend seems to have a second job: Nita does something at a computer eight hours a day; another welds. Without the forty-five-minute commute, I can picture myself working two jobs and having the time to shower between them.

43   So I take the $500 deposit I have coming from my landlord, the $400 I have earned toward the next month's rent, plus the $200 reserved for emergencies, and use the $1,100 to pay the rent and deposit on trailer number 46 in the Overseas Trailer Park, a mile from the cluster of budget hotels that constitute Key West's version of an industrial park. Number 46 is about eight feet in width and shaped like a barbell inside, with a narrow region—because of the sink and the stove—separating the bedroom from what might optimistically be called the "living" area, with its two-per-son table and half-sized couch. The bathroom is so small my knees rub against the shower stall when I sit on the toilet, and you can't just leap out of the bed, you have to climb down to the foot of it in order to find a patch of floor space to stand on. Outside, I am within a few yards of a liquor store, a bar that advertises "free beer tomorrow," a convenience store, and a Burger King—but no supermarket or, alas, laundromat. By reputation, the Overseas park is a nest of crime and crack, and I am hoping at least for some vibrant, multicultural street life. But desolation rules night and day, except for a thin stream of pedestrian traffic heading for their jobs at the Sheraton or 7-Eleven. There are not exactly people here but what amounts to canned labor, being preserved from the heat between shifts.

44   In line with my reduced living conditions, a new form of ugliness aris-es at Jerry's. First we are confronted—via an announcement on the com-puters through which we input orders—with the new rule that the hotel bar is henceforth off-limits to restaurant employees. The culprit, I learn through the grapevine, is the ultra-efficient gal who trained me—another trailer-home dweller and a mother of three. Something had set her off one morning, so she slipped out for a nip and returned to the floor impaired. This mostly hurts Ellen, whose habit it is to free her hair from its rubber

band and drop by the bar for a couple of Zins before heading home at the end of the shift, but all of us feel the chill. Then the next day, when I go for straws, for the first time I find the dry-storage room locked. Ted, the portly assistant manager who opens it for me, explains that he caught one of the dishwashers attempting to steal something, and, unfortunately, the miscreant will be with us until a replacement can be found—hence the locked door. I neglect to ask what he had been trying to steal, but Ted tells me who he is—the kid with the buzz cut and the earring. You know, he's back there right now.

45   I wish I could say I rushed back and confronted George to get his side of the story. I wish I could say I stood up to Ted and insisted that George be given a translator and allowed to defend himself, or announced that I'd find a lawyer who'd handle the case pro bono. The mystery to me is that there's not much worth stealing in the dry-storage room, at least not in any fenceable quantity: "Is Gyorgi here, and am having 200—maybe 250—ketchup packets. What do you say?" My guess is that he had taken—if he had taken anything at all—some Saltines or a can of cherry-pie mix, and that the motive for taking it was hunger.

46   So why didn't I intervene? Certainly not because I was held back by the kind of moral paralysis that can pass as journalistic objectivity. On the contrary, something new—something loathsome and servile—had infected me, along with the kitchen odors that I could still sniff on my bra when I finally undressed at night. In real life I am moderately brave, but plenty of brave people shed their courage in concentration camps, and maybe something similar goes on in the infinitely more congenial milieu of the low-wage American workplace. Maybe, in a month or two more at Jerry's, I might have regained my crusading spirit. Then again, in a month or two I might have turned into a different person altogether—say, the kind of person who would have turned George in.

47   But this is not something I am slated to find out. When my month-long plunge into poverty is almost over, I finally land my dream job—housekeeping. I do this by walking into the personnel office of the only place I figure I might have some credibility, the hotel attached to Jerry's, and confiding urgently that I have to have a second job if I am to pay my rent and, no, it couldn't be front desk clerk. "All right," the personnel lady fairly spits, "So it's housekeeping," and she marches me back to meet Maria, the housekeeping manager, a tiny, frenetic Hispanic woman who greets me as "babe" and hands me a pamphlet emphasizing the need for a positive attitude. The hours are nine in the morning till whenever, the pay

is $6.10 an hour, and there's one week of vacation a year. I don't have to ask about health insurance once I meet Carlotta, the middle-aged African-American woman who will be training me. Carla, as she tells me to call her, is missing all of her top front teeth.

48   On that first day of housekeeping and last day of my entire project—although I don't yet know it's the last—Carla is in a foul mood. We have been given nineteen rooms to clean, most of them "checkouts," as opposed to "stay-overs," that require the whole enchilada of bed-stripping, vacuuming, and bathroom-scrubbing. When one of the rooms that had been listed as a stay-over turns out to be a checkout, Carla calls Maria to complain, but of course to no avail. "So make up the motherfucker," Carla orders me, and I do the beds while she sloshes around the bathroom. For four hours without a break I strip and remake beds, taking about four and a half minutes per queen-sized bed, which I could get down to three if there were any reason to. We try to avoid vacuuming by picking up the larger specks by hand, but often there is nothing to do but drag the monstrous vacuum cleaner—it weighs about thirty pounds—off our cart and try to wrestle it around the floor. Sometimes Carla hands me the squirt bottle of "BAM" (an acronym for something that begins, ominously, with "butyric"; the rest has been worn off the label) and lets me do the bathrooms. No service ethic challenges me here to new heights of performance. I just concentrate on removing the pubic hairs from the bathtubs, or at least the dark ones that I can see.

49   I had looked forward to the breaking-and-entering aspect of cleaning the stay overs, the chance to examine the secret, physical existence of strangers. But the contents of the rooms are always banal and surprisingly neat—zipped up shaving kits, shoes lined up against the wall (there are no closets), flyers for snorkeling trips, maybe an empty wine bottle or two. It is the TV that keeps us going, from *Jerry* to *Sally* to *Hawaii Five-O* and then on to the soaps. If there's something especially arresting, like "Won't Take No for an Answer" on *Jerry,* we sit down on the edge of a bed and giggle for a moment as if this were a pajama party instead of a terminally dead-end job. The soaps are the best, and Carla turns the volume up full blast so that she won't miss anything from the bathroom or while the vacuum is on. In room 503, Marcia confronts Jeff about Lauren. In 505, Lauren taunts poor cuckolded Marcia. In 511, Helen offers Amanda $10,000 to stop seeing Eric, prompting Carla to emerge from the bathroom to study Amanda's troubled face. "You take it, girl," she advises. "I would for sure."

50   The tourists' rooms that we clean and, beyond them, the far more expensively appointed interiors in the soaps, begin after a while to merge. We have entered a better world—a world of comfort where every day is a day off, waiting to be filled up with sexual intrigue. We, however, are only gatecrashers in this fantasy, forced to pay for our presence with backaches and perpetual thirst. The mirrors, and there are far too many of them in hotel rooms, contain the kind of person you would normally find pushing a shopping cart down a city street—bedraggled, dressed in a damp hotel polo shirt two sizes too large, and with sweat dribbling down her chin like drool. I am enormously relieved when Carla announces a half-hour meal break, but my appetite fades when I see that the bag of hot-dog rolls she has been carrying around on our cart is not trash salvaged from a check-out but what she has brought for her lunch.

51   When I request permission to leave at about 3:30, another house-keeper warns me that no one has so far succeeded in combining house-keeping at the hotel with serving at Jerry's: "Some kid did it once for five days, and you're no kid." With that helpful information in mind, I rush back to number 46, down four Advils (the name brand this time), shower, stooping to fit into the stall, and attempt to compose myself for the on-coming shift. So much for what Marx termed the "reproduction of labor power," meaning the things a worker has to do just so she'll be ready to work again. The only unforeseen obstacle to the smooth transition from job to job is that my tan Jerry's slacks, which had looked reasonably clean by 40-watt bulb last night when I handwashed my Hawaiian shirt, prove by daylight to be mottled with ketchup and ranch dressing stains. I spend most of my hour-long break between jobs attempting to remove the edi-ble portions with a sponge and then drying the slacks over the hood of my car in the sun.

52   I can do this two-job thing, is my theory, if I can drink enough caf-feine and avoid getting distracted by George's ever more obvious suffer-ing. The first few days after being caught he seemed not to understand the trouble he was in, and our chirpy little conversations had continued. But the last couple of shifts he's been listless and unshaven, and tonight he looks like the ghost we all know him to be, with dark half-moons hanging from his eyes. At one point, when I am briefly immobilized by the task of filling little paper cups with sour cream for baked potatoes, he comes over and looks as if he'd like to explore the limits of our shared vocabulary, but I am called to the floor for a table. I resolve to give him all my tips that night and to hell with the experiment in low-wage money management.

At eight, Ellen and I grab a snack together standing at the mephitic end of the kitchen counter, but I can only manage two or three mozzarella sticks and lunch had been a mere handful of McNuggets. I am not tired at all, I assure myself, though it may be that there is simply no more "I" left to do the tiredness monitoring. What I would see, if I were more alert to the situation, is that the forces of destruction are already massing against me. There is only one cook on duty, a young man named Jesus ("Hay-Sue," that is) and he is new to the job. And there is Joy, who shows up to take over in the middle of the shift, wearing high heels and a long, clingy white dress and fuming as if she'd just been stood up in some cocktail bar.

53   Then it comes, the perfect storm. Four of my tables fill up at once. Four tables is nothing for me now, but only so long as they are obligingly staggered. As I bev table 27, tables 25, 28, and 24 are watching enviously. As I bev 25, 24 glowers because their bevs haven't even been ordered. Twenty-eight is four yuppyish types, meaning everything on the side and agonizing instructions as to the chicken Caesars. Twenty-five is a middle-aged black couple, who complain, with some justice, that the iced tea isn't fresh and the tabletop is sticky. But table 24 is the meteorological event of the century: ten British tourists who seem to have made the decision to absorb the American experience entirely by mouth. Here everyone has at least two drinks—iced tea and milk shake, Michelob and water (with lemon slice, please)—and a huge promiscuous orgy of breakfast specials, mozz sticks, chicken strips, quesadillas, burgers with cheese and without, sides of hash browns with cheddar, with onions, with gravy, seasoned fries, plain fries, banana splits. Poor Jesus! Poor me! Because when I arrive with their first tray of food—after three prior trips just to refill bevs—Princess Di refuses to eat her chicken strips with her pancake-and-sausage special, since, as she now reveals, the strips were meant to be an appetizer. Maybe the others would have accepted their meals, but Di, who is deep into her third Michelob, insists that everything else go back while they work on their "starters." Meanwhile, the yuppies are waving me down for more decaf and the black couple looks ready to summon the NAACP.

54   Much of what happened next is lost in the fog of war. Jesus starts going under. The little printer on the counter in front of him is spewing out orders faster than he can rip them off, much less produce the meals. Even the invincible Ellen is ashen from stress. I bring table 24 their reheated main courses, which they immediately reject as either too cold or fossilized by the microwave. When I return to the kitchen with their trays

(three trays in three trips), Joy confronts me with arms akimbo: "What is this?" She means the food—the plates of rejected pancakes, hash browns in assorted flavors, toasts, burgers, sausages, eggs. "Uh, scrambled with cheddar," I try, "and that's..." "NO," she screams in my face. "Is it a traditional, a super-scramble, an eye-opener?" I pretend to study my check for a clue, but entropy has been up to its tricks, not only on the plates but in my head, and I have to admit that the original order is beyond reconstruction. "You don't know an eye-opener from a traditional?" she demands in outrage. All I know, in fact, is that my legs have lost interest in the current venture and have announced their intention to fold. I am saved by a yuppie (mercifully not one of mine) who chooses this moment to charge into the kitchen to bellow that his food is twenty-five minutes late. Joy screams at him to get the hell out of her kitchen, please, and then turns on Jesus in a fury, hurling an empty tray across the room for emphasis.

55   I leave. I don't walk out, I just leave. I don't finish my side work or pick up my credit-card tips, if any, at the cash register or, of course, ask Joy's permission to go. And the surprising thing is that you can walk out without permission, that the door opens, that the thick tropical night air parts to let me pass, that my car is still parked where I left it. There is no vindication in this exit, no fuck-you surge of relief, just an overwhelming, dank sense of failure pressing down on me and the entire parking lot. I had gone into this venture in the spirit of science, to test a mathematical proposition, but somewhere along the line, in the tunnel vision imposed by long shifts and relentless concentration, it became a test of myself, and clearly I have failed. Not only had I flamed out as a housekeeper/server, I had even forgotten to give George my tips, and, for reasons perhaps best known to hardworking, generous people like Gail and Ellen, this hurts. I don't cry, but I am in a position to realize, for the first time in many years, that the tear ducts are still there, and still capable of doing their job.

56   When I moved out of the trailer park, I gave the key to number 46 to Gail and arranged for my deposit to be transferred to her. She told me that Joan is still living in her van and that Stu had been fired from the Hearthside. I never found out what happened to George.

57   In one month, I had earned approximately $1,040 and spent $517 on food, gas, toiletries, laundry, phone, and utilities. If I had remained in my $500 efficiency, I would have been able to pay the rent and have $22 left over (which is $78 less than the cash I had in my pocket at the start of the month). During this time I bought no clothing except for the required slacks and no prescription drugs or medical care (I did finally buy some

vitamin B to compensate for the lack of vegetables in my diet). Perhaps I could have saved a little on food if I had gotten to a supermarket more often, instead of convenience stores, but it should be noted that I lost almost four pounds in four weeks, on a diet weighted heavily toward burgers and fries.

58   How former welfare recipients and single mothers will (and do) survive in the low-wage workforce, I cannot imagine. Maybe they will figure out how to condense their lives—including child-raising, laundry, romance, and meals—into the couple of hours between full-time jobs. Maybe they will take up residence in their vehicles, if they have one. All I know is that I couldn't hold two jobs and I couldn't make enough money to live on with one. And I had advantages unthinkable to many of the long term poor—health, stamina, a working car, and no children to care for and support. Certainly nothing in my experience contradicts the conclusion of Kathryn Edin and Laura Lein, in their recent book *Making Ends Meet: How Single Mothers Survive Welfare and Low-Wage Work,* that low-wage work actually involves more hardship and deprivation than life at the mercy of the welfare state. In the coming months and years, economic conditions for the working poor are bound to worsen, even without the almost inevitable recession. As mentioned earlier, the influx of former welfare recipients into the low-skilled workforce will have a depressing effect on both wages and the number of jobs available. A general economic downturn will only enhance these effects, and the working poor will of course be facing it without the slight, but nonetheless often saving, protection of welfare as a backup.

59   The thinking behind welfare reform was that even the humblest jobs are morally uplifting and psychologically buoying. In reality they are likely to be fraught with insult and stress. But I did discover one redeeming feature of the most abject low-wage work—the camaraderie of people who are, in almost all cases, far too smart and funny and caring for the work they do and the wages they're paid. The hope, of course, is that someday these people will come to know what they're worth, and take appropriate action.

—1999

QUESTIONS TO CONSIDER

1. What stories stand out from Barbara Ehrenreich's experiences? What stories does she tell about her own struggles, and what stories does she share about her coworkers' hardships? Which seem to be most effective?

2. Beyond the financial struggles of working a job that pays minimum wage, Ehrenreich identifies a number of other, related problems that she and her coworkers encounter. What are these problems? Does Ehrenreich seem to offer any solutions?

3. What audience does Ehrenreich seem to be targeting with this piece of undercover journalism? What do you think is her purpose in writing about her work, and how can you tell?

4. What is her tone? What specific words, phrases, and passages reveal her attitude towards her subject?

5. This selection from her book, *Nickel and Dimed*, focuses on low wage labor in the United States. Have you ever worked a difficult job, a job that did not pay well, or a job in which you felt particularly unappreciated? How did your experience compare with the experiences Ehrenreich describes?

Freewriting

Peter Elbow

- **IE** Illustration and Exemplification
- **PA** Process Analysis

1   The most effective way I know to improve your writing is to do free-writing exercises regularly. At least three times a week. They are some-times called "automatic writing," "babbling," or "jabbering" exercises. The idea is simply to write for ten minutes (later on, perhaps fifteen or twenty). Don't stop for anything. Go quickly without rushing. Never stop to look back, to cross something out, to wonder how to spell something, to wonder what word or thought to use, or to think about what you are doing. If you can't think of a word or a spelling, just use a squiggle or else write "I can't think what to say, I can't think what to say" as many times as you want; or repeat the last word you wrote over and over again; or anything else. The only requirement is that you *never* stop.

2   What happens to a freewriting exercise is important. It must be a piece of writing which, even if someone else reads it, doesn't send any ripples back to you. It is like writing something and putting it in a bottle in the sea. Freewritings help you by providing no feedback at all. When I assign one, I invite the writer to let me read it, but also tell him to keep it if he prefers.

3   Here is an example of a fairly coherent exercise (sometimes they are very incoherent, which is fine):

I think I'll write what's on my mind, but the only thing on my mind right now is what to write for ten minutes. I've never done this before and I'm not prepared in any way—the sky is cloudy today, how's that? now I'm afraid I won't be able to think of what to write when I get to the end of the sentence—well, here I am at the end of the sentence— here I am again, again, again, again, at least I'm still writing—Now I ask is there some reason to be happy that I'm still writing—ah yes! Here comes the question again—What am I getting out of this? What point is there in it? It's almost obscene to always ask it but I seem to question everything that way and I was gonna say something else pertaining to that but I got so busy writing down the first part that I forgot what I was leading into. This is kind of fun oh don't stop writing—cars and trucks speeding by somewhere out the window, pens clittering across peoples' papers. The sky is still cloudy—is it symbolic that I should be mentioning it? Huh? I dunno. Maybe I should try colors, blue, red, dirty words—wait a minute—no can't do that, orange, yellow, arm tired, green pink violet magenta lavender red brown black green—now I can't think of any more colors—just about done—relief? maybe.

4   Freewriting may seem crazy but actually it makes simple sense. Think of the difference between speaking and writing. Writing has the advantage of permitting more editing. But that's its downfall too. Almost everyone interposes a massive and complicated series of editings between the time the words start to be born into consciousness and when they finally come off the end of the pencil or typewriter onto the page. This is partly because schooling makes us obsessed with the "mistakes" we make in writing. Many people constantly think about spelling and grammar as they try to write. I am always thinking about the awkwardness, wordiness, and general mushiness of my natural verbal product as I try to write down words.

5   But it's not just "mistakes" or "bad writing" we edit as we write. We also edit unacceptable thoughts and feelings, as we do in speaking. In writing there is more time to do it so the editing is heavier: when speaking, there's someone right there waiting for a reply and he'll get bored or think we're crazy if we don't come out with *something*. Most of the time in speaking, we settle for the catch-as-catch-can way in which the words tumble out. In writing, however, there's a chance to try to get them right. But the opportunity to get them right is a terrible burden: you can work for two hours trying to get a paragraph "right" and discover it's not right at all. And then give up.

6   Editing, *in itself,* is not the problem. Editing is usually necessary if we want to end up with something satisfactory. The problem is that editing goes on *at the same time* as producing. The editor is, as it were, constantly looking over the shoulder of the producer and constantly fiddling with what he's doing while he's in the middle of trying to do it. No wonder the producer gets nervous, jumpy, inhibited, and finally can't be coherent. It's an unnecessary burden to try to think of words and also worry at the same time whether they're the right words.

7   The main thing about freewriting is that it is *nonediting*. It is an exercise in bringing together the process of producing words and putting

them down on the page. Practiced regularly, it undoes the ingrained habit of editing at the same time you are trying to produce. It will make writing less blocked because words will come more easily. You will use up more paper, but chew up fewer pencils.

8   Next time you write, notice how often you stop yourself from writing down something you were going to write down. Or else cross it out after it's been written. "Naturally," you say, "it wasn't any good." But think for a moment about the occasions when you spoke well. Seldom was it because you first got the beginning right. Usually it was a matter of a halting or even a garbled beginning, but you kept going and your speech finally became coherent and even powerful. There is a lesson here for writing: trying to get the beginning just right is a formula for failure—and probably a secret tactic to make yourself give up writing. Make some words, whatever they are, and then grab hold of that line and reel in as hard as you can. Afterwards you can throw away lousy beginnings and make new ones. This is the quickest way to get into good writing.

9   The habit of compulsive, premature editing doesn't just make writing hard. It also makes writing dead. Your voice is damped out by all the interruptions, changes, and hesitations between the consciousness and the page. In your natural way of producing words there is a sound, a texture, a rhythm—a voice—which is the main source of power in your writing. I don't know how it works, but this voice is the force that will make a reader listen to you. Maybe you don't like your voice; maybe people have made fun of it. But it's the only voice you've got. It's your only source of power. You better get back into it, no matter what you think of it. If you keep writing in it, it may change into something you like better. But if you abandon it, you'll likely never have a voice and never be heard.

10   Freewritings are vacuums. Gradually you will begin to carry over into your regular writing some of the voice, force, and connectedness that creep into those vacuums.

READINGS

? QUESTIONS TO CONSIDER

1. What are some uses of writing that you can think of? Try brainstorming several verb phrases (like "recording information"). What do you need to be able to do in order to do any of these actions successfully?

2. Peter Elbow has quipped, "The precondition for writing well is being able to write badly and to write when you are not in the mood." What do you think he means by this?

3. What's the primary problem Elbow focuses on in this piece? In your experiences, what gets in the way of you improving your writing or writing well?

4. What does Elbow see as the biggest strength in anyone's writing?

5. What does Elbow see as the relationship between "the producer" and "the editor"?

6. How does your writing process differ from the freewriting process that Elbow describes? What seems most challenging about freewriting? What seems most useful?

7. All writing has an audience and purpose. What are the audience and purpose of this piece of writing?

Supersaturation, or, The Media Torrent and Disposable Feeling

Todd Gitlin

- ■ **DES** Description
- ■ **CC** Compare and Contrast
- ■ **DEF** Definition
- ■ **CE** Cause and Effect

1   On my bedroom wall hangs a print of Vermeer's *The Concert*, painted around 1660. A young woman is playing a spinet. A second woman, probably her maid, holds a letter. A cavalier stands between them, his back to us. A landscape is painted on the raised lid of the spinet, and on the wall hang two paintings, a landscape and *The Procuress*, a work by Baburen, another Dutch artist, depicting a man and two women in a brothel. As in many seventeenth-century Dutch paintings, the domestic space is decorated by paintings. In wealthy Holland, many homes, and not only bourgeois ones, featured such renderings of the outer world. These pictures were pleasing, but more: they were proofs of taste and prosperity, amusements and news at once.

2   Vermeer froze instants, but instants that spoke of the relative constancy of the world in which his subjects lived. If he had painted the same room in the same house an hour, a day, or a month later, the letter in the maid's hand would have been different, and the woman might have been playing a different selection, but the paintings on the far wall would likely have been the same. There might have been other paintings, etchings, and prints elsewhere in the house, but they would not have changed much from month to month, year to year.

3   In what was then the richest country in the world, "everyone strives to embellish his house with precious pieces, especially the room toward the street," as one English visitor to Amsterdam wrote in 1640, noting that he had observed paintings in bakeries, butchers' shops, and the workshops of blacksmiths and cobblers. Of course, the number of paintings, etchings, and prints in homes varied considerably. One tailor owned five paintings, for example, while at the high end, a 1665 inventory of a lavish patrician's house in Amsterdam held two maps and thirteen paintings in one grand room, twelve paintings in his widow's bedroom, and seven in the maid's room. Still, compared with today's domestic imagery, the grandest Dutch inventories of that prosperous era were tiny. Even in the

better-off households depicted by Vermeer, the visual field inhabited by his figures was relatively scanty and fixed.

4   Today, Vermeer's equivalent, if he were painting domestic scenes, or shooting a spread for *Vanity Fair,* or directing commercials or movies, would also display his figures against a background of images; and if his work appeared on-screen, there is a good chance that he would mix in a soundtrack as well. Most of the images would be portraits of individuals who have never walked in the door—not in the flesh—and yet are recognized and welcomed, though not like actual persons. They would rapidly segue into others—either because they had been edited into a video montage, or because they appear on pages meant to be leafed through. Today's Vermeer would discover that the private space of the home offers up vastly more impressions of the larger world than was possible in 1660. In seventeenth-century Delft, painters did not knock on the door day and night offering fresh images for sale. Today, though living space has been set apart from working space, as would have been the case only for the wealthier burghers of Vermeer's time, the outside world has entered the home with a vengeance—in the profusion of media.

5   The flow of images and sounds through the households of the rich world, and the richer parts of the poor world, seems unremarkable today. Only a visitor from an earlier century or an impoverished country could be startled by the fact that life is now played out against a shimmering multitude of images and sounds, emanating from television, videotapes, videodiscs, video games, VCRs, computer screens, digital displays of all sorts, always in flux, chosen partly at will, partly by whim, supplemented by words, numbers, symbols, phrases, fragments, all passing through screens that in a single minute can display more pictures than a prosperous seventeenth-century Dutch household contained over several lifetimes, portraying in one day more individuals than the Dutch burgher would have beheld in the course of years, and in one week more bits of what we have come to call "information" than all the books in all the households in Vermeer's Delft. And this is not yet to speak of our sonic surroundings: the music, voices, and sound effects from radios, CD players, and turntables. Nor is it to speak of newspapers, magazines, newsletters, and books. Most of the faces we shall ever behold, we shall behold in the form of images.

6   Because they arrive with sound, at home, in the car, the elevator, or the waiting room, today's images are capable of attracting our attention during much of the day. We may ignore most of them most of the time,

take issue with them or shrug them off (or think we are shrugging them off), but we must do the work of dispelling them—and even then, we know we can usher them into our presence whenever we like. Iconic plenitude is the contemporary condition, and it is taken for granted. To grow up in this culture is to grow into an expectation that images and sounds will be there for us on command, and that the stories they compose will be succeeded by still other stories, all bidding for our attention, all striving to make sense, all, in some sense, *ours*. Raymond Williams, the first analyst to pay attention to the fact that television is not just pictures but flow, and not just flow but drama upon drama, pointed out more than a quarter century ago, long before hundred-channel cable TV and VCRs, that

> we have never as a society acted so much or watched so many others acting...[W]hat is really new...is that drama...is built into the rhythms of everyday life. In earlier periods drama was important at a festival, in a season, or as a conscious journey to a theater; from honouring Dionysus or Christ to taking in a show. What we have now is drama as habitual experience: more in a week, in many cases, than most human beings would previously have seen in a lifetime.

7   Around the time Vermeer painted *The Concert*, Blaise Pascal, who worried about the seductive power of distraction among the French royalty, wrote that "near the persons of kings there never fail to be a great number of people who see to it that amusement follows business, and who watch all the time of their leisure to supply them with delights and games, so that there is no blank in it." In this one respect, today almost everyone—even the poor—in the rich countries resembles a king, attended by the courtiers of the media offering a divine right of choice.

Measures of Magnitude

8   Statistics begin—but barely—to convey the sheer magnitude of this in-touchness, access, exposure, plenitude, glut, however we want to think of it.

9   In 1999, a television set was on in the average American household more than seven hours a day, a figure that has remained fairly steady since 1983. According to the measurements of the A. C. Nielsen Company, the standard used by advertisers and the television business itself, the average individual watched television about four hours a day, not counting the time when the set was on but the individual in question was not watching. When Americans were asked to keep diaries of how they spend their time, the time spent actually watching dropped to a still striking three

READINGS

hours a day—probably an undercount. In 1995, of those who watched, the percentage who watched "whatever's on," as opposed to any specific program, was 43 percent, up from 29 percent in 1979. Though cross-national comparisons are elusive because of differences in measurement systems, the numbers in other industrialized nations seem to be comparable—France, for example, averaging three and a half hours per person. One survey of forty-three nations showed the United States ranking third in viewing hours, after Japan and Mexico. None of this counts time spent discussing programs, reading about their stars, or thinking about either.

10   Overall, wrote one major researcher in 1990, "watching TV is the dominant leisure activity of Americans, consuming 40 percent of the average person's free time as a primary activity [when people give television their undivided attention]. Television takes up more than half of our free time if you count...watching TV while doing something else like eating or reading...[or] when you have the set on but you aren't paying attention to it." Sex, race, income, age, and marital status make surprisingly little difference in time spent. Neither, at this writing, has the Internet diminished total media use, even if you don't count the Web as part of the media. While Internet users do watch 28 percent less television, they spend more time than nonusers playing video games and listening to the radio and recorded music—obviously a younger crowd. Long-term users (four or more years) say they go on-line for more than two hours a day, and boys and girls alike spend the bulk of their Internet time entertaining themselves with games, hobbies, and the like. In other words, the Internet redistributes the flow of unlimited media but does not dry it up. When one considers the overlapping and additional hours of exposure to radio, magazines, newspapers, compact discs, movies (available via a range of technologies as well as in theaters), and comic books, as well as the accompanying articles, books, and chats about what's on or was on or is coming up via all these means, it is clear that the media flow into the home—not to mention outside—has swelled into a torrent of immense force and constancy, an accompaniment *to* life that has become a central experience *of* life.

11   The place of media in the lives of children is worth special attention—not simply because children are uniquely impressionable but because their experience shapes everyone's future; if we today take a media-soaked environment for granted, surely one reason is that we grew up in it and can no longer see how remarkable it is. Here are some findings from a national survey of media conditions among American children

aged two through eighteen. The average American child lives in a household with 2.9 televisions, 1.8 VCRs, 3.1 radios, 2.6 tape players, 2.1 CD players, 1.4 video game players, and 1 computer. Ninety-nine percent of these children live in homes with one or more TVs, 97 percent with a VCR, 97 percent with a radio, 94 percent with a tape player, 90 percent with a CD player, 70 percent with a video game player, 69 percent with a computer. Eighty-eight percent live in homes with two or more TVs, 60 percent in homes with three or more. Of the 99 percent with a TV, 74 percent have cable or satellite service. And so on, and on, and on.

12   The uniformity of this picture is no less astounding. A great deal about the lives of children depends on their race, sex, and social class, but access to major media does not. For TV, VCR, and radio ownership, rates do not vary significantly among white, black, and Hispanic children, or between girls and boys. For television and radio, rates do not vary significantly according to the income of the community.

13   How accessible, then, is the media cavalcade at home? Of children eight to eighteen, 65 percent have a TV in their bedrooms, 86 percent a radio, 81 percent a tape player, 75 percent a CD player. Boys and girls are not significantly different in possessing this bounty, though the relative usages do vary by medium. Researchers also asked children whether the television was "on in their homes even if no one is watching 'most of the time,' 'some of the time,' 'a little of the time,' or 'never.'" Homes in which television is on "most of the time" are termed *constant television households*. By this measure, 42 percent of all American households with children are constant television households.

14   Blacks are more likely than whites or Hispanics to experience TV in their lives: 56 percent of black children live in constant television households (and 69 percent have a TV in their bedrooms, compared to 48 percent of whites). The lower the family education and the median income of the community, the greater the chance that a household is a constant television household.

15   As for time, the average child spent six hours and thirty-two minutes per day exposed to media of all kinds, of which the time spent reading books and magazines—not counting schoolwork—averaged about forty-five minutes. For ages two to seven, the average for total media was four hours and seventeen minutes; for ages eight to thirteen, eight hours and eight minutes, falling to seven hours and thirty-five minutes for ages fourteen to eighteen. Here, race and social class do count. Black children are most exposed, followed by Hispanics, than whites. At all age levels, the

READINGS

amount of exposure to all media varies inversely with class, from six hours and fifty-nine minutes a day for children in households where the median income for the zip code is under $25,000 to six hours and two minutes for children whose zip code median income is over $40,000. The discrepancy for TV exposure is especially pronounced, ranging from three hours and six minutes a day for children whose zip code incomes are under $25,000 to two hours and twenty-nine minutes for children whose zip code incomes are over $40,000. Still, these differences are not vast. Given everything that divides the rich from the poor, the professional from the working class—differences in physical and mental health, infant mortality, longevity, safety, vulnerability to crime, prospects for stable employment, and so on—the class differences in media access and use are surprisingly slender. So are the differences between American and western European children, the latter averaging six hours a day total, though in Europe only two and a quarter of those hours are spent with TV.

16   All such statistics are crude, of course. Most of them register the time that people *say* they spend. They are—thankfully—not checked by total surveillance. Moreover, the meaning of *exposure* is hard to assess, since the concept encompasses rapt attention, vague awareness, oblivious coexistence, and all possible shadings in between. As the images glide by and the voices come and go, how can we assess what goes on in people's heads? Still, the figures do convey some sense of the media saturation with which we live—and so far we have counted only what can be counted at home. These numbers don't take into account the billboards, the TVs at bars and on planes, the Muzak in restaurants and shops, the magazines in the doctor's waiting room, the digital displays at the gas pump and over the urinal, the ads, insignias, and logos whizzing by on the sides of buses and taxis, climbing the walls of buildings, making announcements from caps, bags, T-shirts, and sneakers. To vary our experience, we can pay to watch stories about individuals unfold across larger-than-lifesize movie screens, or visit theme parks and troop from image to image, display to display. Whenever we like, on foot or in vehicles, we can convert ourselves into movable nodes of communication, thanks to car radios, tape, CD, and game players, cell phones, beepers, Walkmen, and the latest in "personal communication systems"—and even if we ourselves refrain, we find ourselves drawn willy-nilly into the soundscape that others broadcast around us.

17   Crucially, who we are is how we live our time—or *spend* it, to use the term that registers its intrinsic scarcity. What we believe, or say we believe, is less important. We vote for a way of life with our time. And increasingly, when we are not at work or asleep, we are in the media torrent. (Sometimes at work, we are also there, listening to the radio or checking out sports scores, pin-ups, or headlines on the Internet.) Steadily more inhabitants of the wealthy part of the world have the means, incentives, and opportunities to seek private electronic companionship. The more money we have to spend, the more personal space each household member gets. With personal space comes solitude, but this solitude is instantly crowded with images and soundtracks. To a degree that was unthinkable in the seventeenth century, life experience has become an experience in the presence of media.

? QUESTIONS TO CONSIDER

1. Why were wealthy Dutch "domestic spaces" decorated with numerous paintings in the 17th century? According to Gitlin, what is the modern equivalent of this? Why is this important?

2. How is our modern relationship with drama different now from how it was in the past?

3. In what ways do we live in a "media-soaked environment"?

4. What is a "constant television household?" How many televisions do you have in your house? Do you ever leave the television on when you are not paying attention? Why?

5. What is the relationship between household income and how much television children watch?

Salvation

Langston Hughes

- **N** Naration
- **DES** Description
- **DEF** Definition

1   I was saved from sin when I was going on thirteen. But not really saved. It happened like this. There was a big revival at my Auntie Reed's church. Every night for weeks there had been much preaching, singing, praying, and shouting, and some very hardened sinners had been brought to Christ, and the membership of the church had grown by leaps and bounds. Then just before the revival ended, they held a special meeting for children, "to bring the young lambs to the fold." My aunt spoke of it for days ahead. That night I was escorted to the front row and placed on the mourners' bench with all the other young sinners, who had not yet been brought to Jesus.

2   My aunt told me that when you were saved you saw a light, and something happened to you inside! and Jesus came into your life! and God was with you from then on! She said you could see and hear and feel Jesus in your soul. I believed her. I had heard a great many old people say the same thing and it seemed to me they ought to know. So I sat there calmly in the hot, crowded church, waiting for Jesus to come to me.

3   The preacher preached a wonderful rhythmical sermon, all moans and shouts and lonely cries and dire pictures of hell, and then he sang a song about the ninety and nine safe in the fold, but one little lamb was left out in the cold. Then he said: "Won't you come? Won't you come to Jesus? Young lambs, won't you come?" and he held out his arms to all us young sinners there on the mourners' bench. And the little girls cried. And some of them jumped up and went to Jesus right away. But most of us just sat there.

4   A great many old people came and knelt around us and prayed, old women with jet-black faces and braided hair, old men with work-gnarled hands. And the church sang a song about the lower lights are burning, some poor sinners to be saved. And the whole building rocked with prayer and song.

5   Still I kept waiting to *see* Jesus.

6   Finally all the young people had gone to the altar and were saved, but one boy and me. He was a rounder's son named Westley. Westley and I were surrounded by sisters and deacons praying. It was very hot in the church, and getting late now. Finally Westley said to me in a whisper: "God damn! I'm tired o' sitting here. Let's get up and be saved." So he got up and was saved.

7   Then I was left all alone on the mourners' bench. My aunt came and knelt at my knees and cried, while prayers and songs swirled all around me in the little church. The whole congregation prayed for me alone, in a mighty wail of moans and voices. And I kept waiting serenely for Jesus, waiting, waiting—but he didn't come. I wanted to see him, but nothing happened to me. Nothing! I wanted something to happen to me, but nothing happened.

8   I heard the songs and the minister saying: "Why don't you come? My dear child, why don't you come to Jesus? Jesus is waiting for you. He wants you. Why don't you come? Sister Reed, what is this child's name?"

9   "Langston," my aunt sobbed.

10   "Langston, why don't you come? Why don't you come and be saved? Oh, lamb of God! Why don't you come?"

11   Now it was really getting late. I began to be ashamed of myself, holding everything up so long. I began to wonder what God thought about Westley, who certainly hadn't seen Jesus either, but who was now sitting proudly on the platform, swinging his knickerbockered legs and grinning down at me, surrounded by deacons and old women on their knees praying. God had not struck Westley dead for taking his name in vain or for lying in the temple. So I decided that maybe to save further trouble, I'd better lie, too, and say that Jesus had come, and get up and be saved.

12   So I got up.

13   Suddenly the whole room broke into a sea of shouting, as they saw me rise. Waves of rejoicing swept the place. Women leaped in the air. My aunt threw her arms around me. The minister took me by the hand and led me to the platform.

14   When things quieted down, in a hushed silence, punctuated by a few ecstatic "amens," all the new young lambs were blessed in the name of God. Then joyous singing filled the room.

15   That night, for the last time in my life but one—for I was a big boy twelve years old—I cried. I cried, in bed alone, and couldn't stop. I buried my head under the quilts, but my aunt heard me. She woke up and told my uncle I was crying because the Holy Ghost had come into my life, and

READINGS

because I had seen Jesus. But I was really crying because I couldn't bear to tell her that I had lied, that I had deceived everybody in the church, and I hadn't seen Jesus, and that now l didn't believe there was a Jesus any more, since he didn't come to help me.

QUESTIONS TO CONSIDER

1. What does the reader learn about young Langston? What kind of person is he? What makes him act as he does? How does Hughes develop this "character"?

2. For a short essay, Hughes includes a fair amount of dialogue. Whom is Hughes quoting, and what is the effect of these lines? Special consideration needs to be given to Westley.

3. The essay is densely packed with vivid description. What or whom is Hughes describing, and what effect does this description have on the reader?

4. Consider the forces at work here on young Langston and his experience. What are they, and how do they contribute to the devastation he describes at the end of the essay?

5. Consider some of the writing techniques Hughes employs. Why is the essay entitled "Salvation"? What is the effect of the first two sentences? What impact on the essay do the two one-sentence paragraphs (5 and 12) have? What is the purpose of the many exclamation points in paragraph 2?

When Bright Girls Decide that Math Is "a Waste of Time"

Susan Jacoby

- **AP** Argument and Persuasion
- **CE** Cause and Effect

1   Susannah, a 16-year-old who has always been an A student in every subject from algebra to English, recently informed her parents that she intended to drop physics and calculus in her senior year of high school and replace them with a drama seminar and a work-study program. She expects a major in art or history in college, she explained, and "any more science or math will just be a waste of my time."

2   Her parents were neither concerned by nor opposed to her decision. "Fine, dear," they said. Their daughter is, after all, an outstanding student. What does it matter if, at age 16, she has taken a step that may limit her understanding of both machines and the natural world for the rest of her life?

3   This kind of decision, in which girls turn away from studies that would give them a sure footing in the world of science and technology, is a self-inflicted female disability that is, regrettably, almost as common today as it was when I was in high school. If Susannah had announced that she had decided to stop taking English in her senior year, her mother and father would have been horrified. I also think they would have been a good deal less sanguine about her decision if she were a boy.

4   In saying that scientific and mathematical ignorance is a self-inflicted female wound, I do not, obviously, mean that cultural expectations play no role in the process. But the world does not conspire to deprive modern women of access to science as it did in the 1930s, when Rosalyn S. Yalow, the Nobel Prize winning physicist, graduated from Hunter College and was advised to go work as a secretary because no graduate school would admit her to its physics department. The current generation of adolescent girls—and their parents, bred on old expectations about women's interests—are active conspirators in limiting their own intellectual development.

5   It is true that the proportion of young women in science-related graduate and professional schools, most notably medical schools, has

increased significantly in the past decade. It is also true that so few women were studying advanced science and mathematics before the early 1970s that the percentage increase in female enrollment does not yet translate into large numbers of women actually working in science.

6   The real problem is that so many girls eliminate themselves from any serious possibility of studying science as a result of decisions made during the vulnerable period of midadolescence, when they are most likely to be influenced—on both conscious and subconscious levels—by the traditional belief that math and science are "masculine" subjects.

7   During the teen-age years the well-documented phenomenon of "math anxiety" strikes girls who never had any problem handling numbers during earlier schooling. Some men, too, experience this syndrome—a form of panic, akin to a phobia, at any task involving numbers—but women contribute the overwhelming majority of sufferers. The onset of acute math anxiety during the teen-age years is, as Stalin was fond of saying, "not by accident."

8   In adolescence girls begin to fear that they will be unattractive to boys if they are typed as "brains." Science and math epitomize unfeminine braininess in a way that, say, foreign languages do not. High-school girls who pursue an advanced interest in science and math (unless they are students at special institutions like the Bronx High School of Science where everyone is a brain) usually find that they are greatly outnumbered by boys in their classes. They are, therefore, intruding on male turf at a time when their sexual confidence, as well as that of the boys, is most fragile.

9   A 1981 assessment of female achievement in mathematics, based on research conducted under a National Institute for Education grant, found significant differences in the mathematical achievements of 9th and 12th graders. At age 13 girls were equal to or slightly better than boys in tests involving algebra, problem solving and spatial ability; four years later the boys had outstripped the girls.

10   It is not mysterious that some very bright high-school girls suddenly decide that math is "too hard" and "a waste of time." In my experience, self-sabotage of mathematical and scientific ability is often a conscious process. I remember deliberately pretending to be puzzled by geometry problems in my sophomore year in high school. A male teacher called me in after class and said, in a baffled tone, "I don't see how you can be having so much trouble when you got straight A's last year in my algebra class."

11   The decision to avoid advanced biology, chemistry, physics and calculus in high school automatically restricts academic and professional choices that ought to be wide open to anyone beginning college. At all coeducational universities women are overwhelmingly concentrated in the fine arts, social sciences and traditionally female departments like education. Courses leading to degrees in science- and technology-related fields are filled mainly by men.

12   In my generation, the practical consequences of mathematical and scientific illiteracy are visible in the large number of special programs to help professional women overcome the anxiety they feel when they are promoted into jobs that require them to handle statistics.

13   The consequences of this syndrome should not, however, be viewed in narrowly professional terms. Competence in science and math does not mean one is going to become a scientist or mathematician any more than competence in writing English means one is going to become a professional writer. Scientific and mathematical illiteracy—which has been cited in several recent critiques by panels studying American education from kindergarten through college—produces an incalculably impoverished vision of human experience.

14   Scientific illiteracy is not, of course, the exclusive province of women. In certain intellectual circles it has become fashionable to proclaim a willed, aggressive ignorance about science and technology. Some female writers specialize in ominous, uninformed diatribes against genetic research as a plot to remove control of childbearing from women, while some well-known men of letters proudly announce that they understand absolutely nothing about computers, or, for that matter, about electricity. This lack of understanding is nothing in which women or men ought to take pride.

15   Failure to comprehend either computers or chromosomes leads to a terrible sense of helplessness, because the profound impact of science on everyday life is evident even to those who insist they don't, won't, can't understand why the changes are taking place. At this stage of history women are more prone to such feelings of helplessness than men because the culture judges their ignorance less harshly and because women themselves acquiesce in that indulgence.

16   Since there is ample evidence of such feelings in adolescence, it is up to parents to see that their daughters do not accede to the old stereotypes about "masculine" and "feminine" knowledge. Unless we want our

daughters to share our intellectual handicaps, we had better tell them no, they can't stop taking mathematics and science at the ripe old age of 16.

? QUESTIONS TO CONSIDER

1. What is the purpose of an education according to Jacoby? Why does she believe that girls and boys alike need a strong math and science education?

2. Select one sentence that could serve as Jacoby's thesis. (Remember that Jacoby isn't writing a college essay, so you may choose a sentence from any section of the essay, not just the first paragraph, to use as the thesis.) Explain why you selected this sentence as the umbrella statement to represent the entire essay.

3. Do your own internet research on the participation of women and girls in STEM (science, technology, engineering, and math) fields. How has women's involvement in these fields changed, if at all, from the time when Jacoby published this piece?

4. In your experience, have you been encouraged (or discouraged) in certain fields of study or hobbies because of your gender? Following Jacoby's model, compose your own short essay in which you explain the gender stereotypes you have encountered related to your own pursuits or observed in your classes, your family, or your workplace.

READINGS

My Creature from the Black Lagoon

Stephen King

- **N** Narration
- **CC** Compare and Contrast

1 The first movie I can remember seeing as a kid was *Creature from the Black Lagoon.* It was at the drive-in, and unless it was a second-run job I must have been about seven, because the film, which starred Richard Carlson and Richard Denning, was released in 1954. It was also originally released in 3-D, but I cannot remember wearing the glasses, so perhaps I did see a rerelease.

2 I remember only one scene clearly from the movie, but it left a lasting impression. The hero (Carlson) and the heroine (Julia Adams, who looked absolutely spectacular in a one-piece white bathing suit) are on an expedition somewhere in the Amazon basin. They make their way up a swampy, narrow waterway and into a wide pond that seems an idyllic South American version of the Garden of Eden.

3 But the creature is lurking—naturally. It's a scaly, batrachian monster that is remarkably like Lovecraft's half-breed, degenerate aberrations—the crazed and blasphemous results of liaisons between gods and human women (I told you it's difficult to get away from Lovecraft). This monster is slowly and patiently barricading the mouth of the stream with sticks and branches, irrevocably sealing the party of anthropologists in.

4 I was barely old enough to read at that time, the discovery of my father's box of weird fiction still years away. I have a vague memory of boyfriends in my mom's life during that period—from 1952 until 1958 or so; enough of a memory to be sure she had a social life, not enough to even guess if she had a sex life. There was Norville, who smoked Luckies and kept three fans going in his two-room apartment during the summer; and there was Milt, who drove a Buick and wore gigantic blue shorts in the summertime; and another fellow, very small, who was, I believe, a cook in a French restaurant. So far as I know, my mother came close to marrying none of them. She'd gone that route once. Also, that was a time when a woman, once married, became a shadow figure in the process of decision-making and bread-winning. I think my mom, who could be stubborn, intractable, grimly persevering and nearly impossible to discourage, had

gotten a taste for captaining her own life. And so she went out with guys, but none of them became permanent fixtures.

5   It was Milt we were out with that night, he of the Buick and the large blue shorts. He seemed to genuinely like my brother and me, and to genuinely not mind having us along in the back seat from time to time (it may be that when you have reached the calmer waters of your early forties, the idea of necking at the drive-in no longer appeals so strongly...even if you have a Buick as large as a cabin cruiser to do it in). By the time the Creature made his appearance, my brother had slithered down onto the floor of the back and had fallen asleep. My mother and Milt were talking, perhaps passing a Kool back and forth. They don't matter, at least not in this context; nothing matters except the big black-and-white images up on the screen, where the unspeakable Thing is walling the handsome hero and the sexy heroine into...into...the Black Lagoon!

6   I knew, watching, that the Creature had become *my* Creature; I had bought it. Even to a seven-year-old, it was not a terribly convincing Creature. I did not know then it was good old Ricou Browning, the famed underwater stuntman, in a molded latex suit, but I surely knew it was some guy in some kind of a monster suit...just as I knew that, later on that night, he would visit me in the black lagoon of my dreams, looking much more realistic. He might be waiting in the closet when we got back; he might be standing slumped in the blackness of the bathroom at the end of the hall, stinking of algae and swamp rot, all ready for a post-midnight snack of small boy. Seven isn't old, but it is old enough to know that you get what you pay for. You own it, you bought it, it's yours. It is old enough to feel the dowser suddenly come alive, grow heavy, and roll over in your hands, pointing at hidden water.

7   My reaction to the Creature on that night was perhaps the perfect reaction, the one every writer of horror fiction or director who has worked in the field hopes for when he or she uncaps a pen or a lens: total emotional involvement, pretty much undiluted by any real thinking process—and you understand, don't you, that when it comes to horror movies, the only thought process really necessary to break the mood is for a friend to lean over and whisper, "See the zipper running down his back?"

8   I think that only people who have worked in the field for some time truly understand how fragile this stuff really is, and what an amazing commitment it imposes on the reader or viewer of intellect and maturity. When Coleridge spoke of "the suspension of disbelief" in his essay on imaginative poetry, I believe he knew that disbelief is not like a balloon,

which may be suspended in air with a minimum of effort; it is like a lead weight, which has to be hoisted with a clean and a jerk and held up by main force. Disbelief isn't light; it's heavy. The difference in sales between Arthur Hailey and H. P. Lovecraft may exist because everyone believes in cars and banks, but it takes a sophisticated and muscular intellectual act to believe, even for a little while, in Nyarlathotep, the Blind Faceless One, the Howler in the Night. And whenever I run into someone who expresses a feeling along the lines of, "I don't read fantasy or go to any of those movies; none of it's real," I feel a kind of sympathy. They simply can't lift the weight of fantasy. The muscles of the imagination have grown too weak.

9   In this sense, kids are the perfect audience for horror. The paradox is this: children, who are physically quite weak, lift the weight of unbelief with ease. They are the jugglers of the invisible world—a perfectly understandable phenomenon when you consider the perspective they must view things from. Children deftly manipulate the logistics of Santa Claus's entry on Christmas Eve (he can get down small chimneys by making himself small, and if there's no chimney there's the letter slot, and if there's no letter slot there's always the crack under the door), the Easter Bunny, God (big guy, sorta old, white beard, throne), Jesus ("How do you think he turned the water into wine?" I asked my son Joe when he—Joe, not Jesus—was five; Joe's idea was that he had something "kinda like magic Kool-Aid, you get what I mean?"), the devil (big guy, red skin, horse feet, tail with an arrow on the end of it, Snidely Whiplash moustache), Ronald McDonald, the Burger King, the Keebler Elves, Dorothy and Toto, the Lone Ranger and Tonto, a thousand more. Most parents think they understand this openness better than, in many cases, they actually do, and try to keep their children away from anything that smacks too much of horror and terror—. "Rated PG (or G in the case of *The Andromeda Strain*), but may be too intense for younger children," the ads for *Jaws* read—believing, I suppose, that to allow their kids to go to a real horror movie would be tantamount to rolling a live hand grenade into a nursery school.

10   But one of the odd Doppler effects that seems to occur during the selective forgetting that is so much a part of "growing up" is the fact that almost *everything* has a scare potential for the child under eight. Children are literally afraid of their own shadows at the right time and place. There is the story of the four-year-old who refused to go to bed at night without a light on in his closet. His parents at last discovered he was frightened of a creature he had heard his father speak of often; this creature, which had

grown large and dreadful in the child's imagination, was the "twi-night double-header."

11   Seen in this light, even Disney movies are minefields of terror, and the animated cartoons, which will apparently be released and rereleased even unto the end of the world, are usually the worst offenders. There are adults today, who, when questioned, will tell you that the most frightening thing they saw at the movies as children was Bambi's father shot by the hunter, or Bambi and his mother running before the forest fire. Other Disney memories which are right up there with the batrachian horror inhabiting the Black Lagoon include the marching brooms that have gone totally out of control in *Fantasia* (and for the small child, the real horror inherent in the situation is probably buried in the implied father-son relationship between Mickey Mouse and the old sorcerer; those brooms are making a terrible mess, and when the sorcerer/father gets home, there may be PUNISHMENT....This sequence might well send the child of strict parents into an ecstasy of terror); the night on Bald Mountain from the same film; the witches in *Snow White* and *Sleeping Beauty,* one with her enticingly red poisoned apple (and what small child is not taught early to fear the idea of POISON?), the other with her deadly spinning wheel; this holds all the way up to the relatively innocuous *One Hundred and One Dalmatians,* which features the logical granddaughter of those Disney witches from the thirties and forties—the evil Cruella DeVille, with her scrawny, nasty face, her loud voice (grownups sometimes forget how terrified young children are of loud voices, which come from the giants of their world, the adults), and her plan to kill all the dalmatian puppies (read "children," if you're a little person) and turn them into dogskin coats.

12   Yet it is the parents, of course, who continue to underwrite the Disney procedure of release and rerelease, often discovering goosebumps on their own arms as they rediscover what terrified them as children... because what the good horror film (or horror sequence in what may be billed a "comedy" or an "animated cartoon") does above all else is to knock the adult props out from under us and tumble us back down the slide into childhood. And there our own shadow may once again become that of a mean dog, a gaping mouth, or a beckoning dark figure.

13   Perhaps the supreme realization of this return to childhood comes in David Cronenberg's marvelous horror film *The Brood,* where a disturbed woman is literally producing "children of rage" who go out and murder the members of her family, one by one. About halfway through the film, her father sits dispiritedly on the bed in an upstairs room, drinking and

mourning his wife, who has been the first to feel the wrath of the brood. We cut to the bed itself...and clawed hands suddenly reach out from beneath it and dig into the carpeting near the doomed father's shoes. And so Cronenberg pushes us down the slide; we are four again, and all of our worst surmises about what might be lurking under the bed have turned out to be true.

14   The irony of all this is that children are better able to deal with fantasy and terror *on its own terms* than their elders are. You'll note I've italicized the phrase "on its own terms." An adult is able to deal with the cataclysmic terror of something like *The Texas Chainsaw Massacre* because he or she understands that it is all make-believe, and that when the take is done the dead people will simply get up and wash off the stage blood. The child is not so able to make this distinction, and *Chainsaw Massacre* is quite rightly rated R. Little kids do not need this scene, any more than they need the one at the end of *The Fury* where John Cassavetes quite literally blows apart. But the point is, if you put a little kid of six in the front row at a screening of *The Texas Chainsaw Massacre* along with an adult who was temporarily unable to distinguish between make-believe and "real things" (as Danny Torrance, the little boy in *The Shining* puts it)—if, for instance, you had given the adult a hit of Yellow Sunshine LSD about two hours before the movie started—my guess is that the kid would have maybe a week's worth of bad dreams. The adult might spend a year or so in a rubber room, writing home with Crayolas.

15   A certain amount of fantasy and horror in a child's life seems to me a perfectly okay, useful sort of thing. Because of the size of their imaginative capacity, children are able to handle it, and because of their unique position in life, they are able to put such feelings to work. They understand their position very well, too. Even in such a relatively ordered society as our own, they understand that their survival is a matter almost totally out of their hands. Children are "dependents" up until the age of eight or so in every sense of the word; dependent on mother and father (or some reasonable facsimile thereof) not only for food, clothing, and shelter, but dependent on them not to crash the car into a bridge abutment, to meet the school bus on time, to walk them home from Cub Scouts or Brownies, to buy medicines with childproof caps, dependent on them to make sure they don't electrocute themselves while screwing around with the toaster or while trying to play with Barbie's Beauty Salon in the bathtub.

16   Running directly counter to this necessary dependence is the survival directive built into all of us. The child realizes his or her essential lack

of control, and I suspect it is this very realization which makes the child uneasy. It is the same sort of free-floating anxiety that many air travelers feel. They are not afraid because they believe air travel to be unsafe; they are afraid because they have surrendered control, and if something goes wrong all they can do is sit there clutching air-sick bags or the in-flight magazine. To surrender control runs counter to the survival directive. Conversely, while a thinking, informed person may understand intellectually that travel by car is much more dangerous than flying, he or she is still apt to feel much more comfortable behind the wheel, because she/he has control...or at least an illusion of it.

17   This hidden hostility and anxiety toward the airline pilots of their lives may be one explanation why, like the Disney pictures which are released during school vacations in perpetuity, the old fairy tales also seem to go on forever. A parent who would raise his or her hands in horror at the thought of taking his/her child to see *Dracula* or *The Changeling* (with its pervasive imagery of the drowning child) would be unlikely to object to the baby sitter reading "Hansel and Gretel" to the child before bedtime. But consider: the tale of Hansel and Gretel begins with deliberate abandonment (oh yes, the stepmother masterminds that one, but she is the symbolic mother all the same, and the father is a spaghetti-brained nurd who goes along with everything she suggests even though he knows it's wrong—thus we can see her as amoral, him as actively evil in the Biblical and Miltonian sense), it progresses to kidnapping (the witch in the candy house), enslavement, illegal detention, and finally justifiable homicide and cremation. Most mothers and fathers would never take their children to see *Survive*, that quickie Mexican exploitation flick about the rugby players who survived the aftermath of a plane crash in the Andes by eating their dead teammates, but these same parents find little to object to in "Hansel and Gretel," where the witch is fattening the children up so she can eat them. We give this stuff to the kids almost instinctively, understanding on a deeper level, perhaps, that such fairy stories are the perfect points of crystallization for those fears and hostilities.

18   Even anxiety-ridden air travelers have their own fairy tales—all those *Airport* movies, which, like "Hansel and Gretel" and all those Disney cartoons, show every sign of going on forever...but which should only be viewed on Thanksgivings, since all of them feature a large cast of turkeys.

19   My gut reaction to *Creature from the Black Lagoon* on that long-ago night was a kind of terrible, waking swoon. The nightmare was happening right in front of me; every hideous possibility that human flesh is heir to was being played out on that drive-in screen.

20   Approximately twenty-two years later, I had a chance to see *Creature from the Black Lagoon* again—not on TV, with any kind of dramatic build and mood broken up by adverts for used cars, K-Tel disco anthologies, and Underalls pantyhose, thank God, but intact, uncut...and even in 3-D. Guys like me who wear glasses have a hell of a time with 3-D, you know; ask anyone who wears specs how they like those nifty little cardboard glasses they give you when you walk in the door. If 3-D ever comes back in a big way, I'm going to take myself down to the local Pearle Vision Center and invest seventy bucks in a special pair of prescription lenses: one red, one blue. Annoying glasses aside, I should add that I took my son Joe with me—he was then five, about the age I had been myself, that night at the drive-in (and imagine my surprise—my *rueful* surprise—to discover that the movie which had so terrified me on that long-ago night had been rated G by the MPAA...just like the Disney pictures).

21   As a result, I had a chance to experience that weird doubling back in time that I believe most parents only experience at the Disney films with their children, or when reading them the Pooh books or perhaps taking them to the Shrine or the Barnum & Bailey circus. A popular record is apt to create a particular "set" in a listener's mind, precisely because of its brief life of six weeks to three months, and "golden oldies" continue to be played because they are the emotional equivalent of freeze-dried coffee. When the Beach Boys come on the radio singing "Help Me, Rhonda," there is always that wonderful second or two when I can re-experience the wonderful, guilty joy of copping my first feel (and if you do the mental subtraction from my present age of thirty-three, you'll see that I was a little backward in that respect). Movies and books do the same thing, although I would argue that the mental set, its depth and texture, tends to be a little richer, a little more complex, when re-experiencing films, and a lot more complex when dealing with books.

22   With Joe that day I experienced *Creature from the Black Lagoon* from the other end of the telescope, but this particular theory of set identification still applied; in fact, it prevailed. Time and age and experience have all left their marks on me, just as they have on you; time is not a river, as Einstein theorized—it's a big fucking buffalo herd that runs us down and eventually mashes us into the ground, dead and bleeding, with a hearing-aid plugged into one ear and a colostomy bag instead of a .44 clapped on one leg. Twenty-two years later I knew that the Creature was really good old Ricou Browning, the famed underwater stuntman, in a molded latex suit, and the suspension of disbelief, that mental clean-and-jerk, had

become a lot harder to accomplish. But I did it, which may mean nothing, or which may mean (I hope!) that the buffalo haven't got me yet. But when that weight of disbelief was finally up there, the old feelings came flooding in, as they flooded in some five years ago when I took Joe and my daughter Naomi to their first movie, a reissue of *Snow White and the Seven Dwarves*. There is a scene in that film where, after Snow White has taken a bite from the poisoned apple, the dwarves take her into the forest, weeping copiously. Half the audience of little kids was also in tears; the lower lips of the other half were trembling. The set identification in that case was strong enough so that I was also surprised into tears. I hated myself for being so blatantly manipulated, but manipulated I was, and there I sat, blubbering into my beard over a bunch of cartoon characters. But it wasn't Disney that manipulated me; I did it myself. It was the kid inside who wept, surprised out of dormancy and into schmaltzy tears...but at least awake for awhile.

23   During the final two reels of *Creature from the Black Lagoon*, the weight of disbelief is nicely balanced somewhere above my head, and once again director Jack Arnold places the symbols in front of me and produces the old equation of the fairy tales, each symbol as big and as easy to handle as a child's alphabet block. Watching, the child awakes again and knows that this is what dying is like. Dying is when the Creature from the Black Lagoon dams up the exit. Dying is when the monster gets you.

24   In the end, of course, the hero and heroine, very much alive, not only survive but triumph—as Hansel and Gretel do. As the drive-in floodlights over the screen came on and the projector flashed its GOOD NIGHT, DRIVE SAFELY slide on that big white space (along with the virtuous suggestion that you ATTEND THE CHURCH OF YOUR CHOICE), there was a brief feeling of relief, almost of resurrection. But the feeling that stuck longest was the swooning sensation that good old Richard Carlson and good old Julia Adams were surely going down for the third time, and the image that remains forever after is of the creature slowly and patiently walling its victims into the Black Lagoon; even now I can see it peering over that growing wall of mud and sticks.

25   Its eyes. Its ancient eyes.

? QUESTIONS TO CONSIDER

1. Why does King begin and end his article with a tale from his childhood?

2. What is "suspension of disbelief"? Why does King claim that writing a horror story can be more difficult than writing a "realistic" story?

3. How is disbelief like a "lead weight"? Why are children better able to manage this weight than adults?

4. What are the similarities between horror movies and fairy tales? How is this comparison important to King's article?

5. Do you believe that Disney movies are "minefields of terror"? Was there a time when you were afraid of a particular scene in a Disney movie? If so, what was it?

Letter from Birmingham Jail

Martin Luther King Jr.

- **IE** Illustration and Exemplification
- **CC** Compare and Contrast
- **DEF** Definition
- **AP** Argument and Persuasion

1   My Dear Fellow Clergymen: While confined here in the Birmingham city jail, I came across your recent statement calling my present activities "unwise and untimely." Seldom do I pause to answer criticism of my work and ideas. If I sought to answer all the criticisms that cross my desk, my secretaries would have little time for anything other than such correspondence in the course of the day, and I would have no time for constructive work. But since I feel that you are men of genuine good will and that your criticisms are sincerely set forth, I want to try to answer your statement in what I hope will be patient and reasonable terms.

2   I think I should indicate why I am here in Birmingham, since you have been influenced by the view which argues against "outsiders coming in." I have the honor of serving as president of the Southern Christian Leadership Conference, an organization operating in every southern state, with headquarters in Atlanta, Georgia. We have some eighty-five affiliated organizations across the South, and one of them is the Alabama Christian Movement for Human Rights. Frequently we share staff, educational, and financial resources with our affiliates. Several months ago the affiliate here in Birmingham asked us to be on call to engage in a nonviolent direct-action program if such were deemed necessary. We readily consented, and when the hour came we lived up to our promise. So I, along with several members of my staff, am here because I was invited here. I am here because I have organizational ties here.

3   But more basically, I am in Birmingham because injustice is here. Just as the prophets of the eighth century B.C. left their villages and carried their "thus saith the Lord" far beyond the boundaries of their home towns, and just as the Apostle Paul left his village of Tarsus and carried the gospel of Jesus Christ to the far corners of the Greco-Roman world, so am I compelled to carry the gospel of freedom beyond my own home town. Like Paul, I must constantly respond to the Macedonian call for aid.

4   Moreover, I am cognizant of the interrelatedness of all communities and states. I cannot sit idly by in Atlanta and not be concerned about what happens in Birmingham. Injustice anywhere is a threat to justice everywhere. We are caught in an inescapable network of mutuality, tied in a single garment of destiny. Whatever affects one directly, affects all indirectly. Never again can we afford to live with the narrow, provincial "outside agitator" idea. Anyone who lives inside the United States can never be considered an outsider anywhere within its bounds.

5   You deplore the demonstration taking place in Birmingham. But your statement, I am sorry to say, fails to express a similar concern for the conditions that brought about the demonstrations. I am sure that none of you would want to rest content with the superficial kind of social analysis that deals merely with effects and does not grapple with underlying causes. It is unfortunate that demonstrations are taking place in Birmingham, but it is even more unfortunate that the city's white power structure left the Negro community with no alternative.

6   In any nonviolent campaign there are four basic steps: collection of the facts to determine whether injustices exist; negotiation; self-purification; and direct action. We have gone through all these steps in Birmingham. There can be no gainsaying the fact that racial injustice engulfs this community. Birmingham is probably the most thoroughly segregated city in the United States. Its ugly record of brutality is widely known. Negroes have experienced grossly unjust treatment in the courts. There have been more unsolved bombings of Negro homes and churches in Birmingham than in any other city in the nation. These are the hard, brutal facts of the case. On the basis of these conditions, Negro leaders sought to negotiate with the city fathers. But the latter consistently refused to engage in good-faith negotiation.

7   Then, last September, came the opportunity to talk with leaders of Birmingham's economic community. In the course of the negotiations, certain promises were made by the merchants—for example, to remove the stores' humiliating racial signs. On the basis of these promises, the Reverend Fred Shuttlesworth and the leaders of the Alabama Christian Movement for Human Rights agreed to a moratorium on all demonstrations. As the weeks and months went by, we realized that we were the victims of a broken promise. A few signs, briefly removed, returned; the others remained.

8   As in so many past experiences, our hopes had been blasted, and the shadow of deep disappointment settled upon us. We had no alternative

except to prepare for direct action, whereby we would present our very bodies as a means of laying our case before the conscience of the local and the national community. Mindful of the difficulties involved, we decided to undertake a process of self-purification. We began a series of workshops on nonviolence, and we repeatedly asked ourselves: "Are you able to accept blows without retaliating?" "Are you able to endure the ordeal of jail?" We decided to schedule our direct-action program for the Easter season, realizing that except for Christmas, this is the main shopping period of the year. Knowing that a strong economic-withdrawal program would be the byproduct of direct action, we felt that this would be the best time to bring pressure to bear on the merchants for the needed change.

9 Then it occurred to us that Birmingham's mayoralty election was coming up in March, and we speedily decided to postpone action until after election day. When we discovered that the Commissioner of Public Safety, Eugene "Bull" Connor, had piled up enough votes to be in the run-off, we decided again to postpone action until the day after the run-off so that the demonstrations could not be used to cloud the issues. Like many others, we waited to see Mr. Connor defeated, and to this end we endured postponement after postponement. Having aided in this community need, we felt that our direct-action program could be delayed no longer.

10 You may well ask: "Why direct action? Why sit-ins, marches, and so forth? Isn't negotiation a better path?" You are quite right in calling for negotiation. Indeed, this is the very purpose of direct action. Nonviolent direct action seeks to create such a crisis and foster such a tension that a community which has constantly refused to negotiate is forced to confront the issue. It seeks so to dramatize the issue that it can no longer be ignored. My citing the creation of tension as part of the work of the nonviolent-resister may sound rather shocking. But I must confess that I am not afraid of the word "tension." I have earnestly opposed violent tension, but there is a type of constructive, nonviolent tension which is necessary for growth. Just as Socrates felt that it was necessary to create a tension in the mind so that individuals could rise from the bondage of myths and half-truths to the unfettered realm of creative analysis and objective appraisal, so must we see the need for nonviolent gadflies to create the kind of tension in society that will help men rise from the dark depths of prejudice and racism to the majestic heights of understanding and brotherhood.

11   The purpose of our direct-action program is to create a situation so crisis-packed that it will inevitably open the door to negotiation. I therefore concur with you in your call for negotiation. Too long has our beloved Southland been bogged down in a tragic effort to live in monologue rather than dialogue.

12   One of the basic points in your statement is that the action that I and my associates have taken in Birmingham is untimely. Some have asked: "Why didn't you give the new city administration time to act?" The only answer that I can give to this query is that the new Birmingham administration must be prodded about as much as the outgoing one, before it will act. We are sadly mistaken if we feel that the election of Albert Boutwell as mayor will bring the millennium to Birmingham. While Mr. Boutwell is a much more gentle person than Mr. Connor, they are both segregationists, dedicated to maintenance of the status quo. I have hope that Mr. Boutwell will be reasonable enough to see the futility of massive resistance to desegregation. But he will not see this without pressure from devotees of civil rights. My friends, I must say to you that we have not made a single gain in civil rights without determined legal and nonviolent pressure. Lamentably, it is an historical fact that privileged groups seldom give up their privileges voluntarily. Individuals may see the moral light and voluntarily give up their unjust posture; but as Reinhold Niebuhr has reminded us, groups tend to be more immoral than individuals.

13   We know through painful experience that freedom is never voluntarily given by the oppressor; it must be demanded by the oppressed. Frankly, I have yet to engage in a direct-action campaign that was "well timed" in the view of those who have not suffered unduly from the disease of segregation. For years now I have heard the word "Wait!" It rings in the ear of every Negro with piercing familiarity. This "Wait" has almost always meant "Never." We must come to see, with one of our distinguished jurists, that "justice too long delayed is justice denied."

14   We have waited for more than 340 years for our constitutional and God-given rights. The nations of Asia and Africa are moving with jetlike speed toward gaining political independence, but we still creep at horse-and-buggy pace toward gaining a cup of coffee at a lunch counter. Perhaps it is easy for those who have never felt the stinging darts of segregation to say, "Wait." But when you have seen vicious mobs lynch your mothers and fathers at will and drown your sisters and brothers at whim; when you have seen hate-filled policemen curse, kick, and even kill your black brothers and sisters; when you see the vast majority of your twenty million

Negro brothers smothering in an airtight cage of poverty in the midst of an affluent society; when you suddenly find your tongue twisted and your speech stammering as you seek to explain to your six-year-old daughter why she can't go to the public amusement park that has just been advertised on television, and see tears welling up in her eyes when she is told that Funtown is closed to colored children, and see ominous clouds of inferiority beginning to form in her little mental sky, and see her beginning to distort her personality by developing an unconscious bitterness toward white people; when you have to concoct an answer for a five-year-old son who is asking: "Daddy, why do white people treat colored people so mean?"; when you take a cross-country drive and find it necessary to sleep night after night in the uncomfortable corners of your automobile because no motel will accept you; when you are humiliated day in and day out by nagging signs reading "white" and "colored"; when your first name becomes "nigger," your middle name becomes "boy" (however old you are) and your last name becomes "John," and your wife and mother are never given the respected title "Mrs."; when you are harried by day and haunted by night by the fact that you are a Negro, living constantly at tiptoe stance, never quite knowing what to expect next, and are plagued with inner fears and outer resentments; when you are forever fighting a degenerating sense of "nobodiness"—then you will understand why we find it difficult to wait. There comes a time when the cup of endurance runs over, and men are no longer willing to be plunged into the abyss of despair. I hope, sirs, you can understand our legitimate and unavoidable impatience.

15   You express a great deal of anxiety over our willingness to break laws. This is certainly a legitimate concern. Since we so diligently urge people to obey the Supreme Court's decision of 1954 outlawing segregation in the public schools, at first glance it may seem rather paradoxical for us consciously to break laws. One may well ask: "How can you advocate breaking some laws and obeying others?" The answer lies in the fact that there are two types of laws: just and unjust. I would be the first to advocate obeying just laws. One has not only a legal but a moral responsibility to obey just laws. Conversely, one has a moral responsibility to disobey unjust laws. I would agree with St. Augustine that "an unjust law is no law at all."

16   Now, what is the difference between the two? How does one determine whether a law is just or unjust? A just law is a man-made code that squares with the moral law or the law of God. An unjust law is a code that is out of harmony with the moral law. To put it in the terms of St. Thomas

Aquinas: An unjust law is a human law that is not rooted in eternal law and natural law. Any law that uplifts human personality is just. Any law that degrades human personality is unjust. All segregation statutes are unjust because segregation distorts the soul and damages the personality. It gives the segregator a false sense of superiority and the segregated a false sense of inferiority. Segregation, to use the terminology of the Jewish philosopher Martin Buber, substitutes an "I-it" relationship for an "I-thou" relationship and ends up relegating persons to the status of things. Hence segregation is not only politically, economically, and sociologically unsound, it is morally wrong and sinful. Paul Tillich has said that sin is separation. Is not segregation an existential expression of man's tragic separation, his awful estrangement, his terrible sinfulness? Thus it is that I can urge men to obey the 1954 decision of the Supreme Court, for it is morally right; and I can urge them to disobey segregation ordinances, for they are morally wrong.

17   Let us consider a more concrete example of just and unjust laws. An unjust law is a code that a numerical or power majority group compels a minority group to obey but does not make binding on itself. This is *difference* made legal. By the same token, a just law is a code that a majority compels a minority to follow and that it is willing to follow itself. This is *sameness* made legal.

18   Let me give another explanation. A law is unjust if it is inflicted on a minority that, as a result of being denied the right to vote, had no part in enacting or devising the law. Who can say that the legislature of Alabama which set up that state's segregation laws was democratically elected? Throughout Alabama all sorts of devious methods are used to prevent Negroes from becoming registered voters, and there are some counties in which, even though Negroes constitute a majority of the population, not a single Negro is registered. Can any law enacted under such circumstances be considered democratically structured?

19   Sometimes a law is just on its face and unjust in its application. For instance, I have been arrested on a charge of parading without a permit. Now, there is nothing wrong in having an ordinance which requires a permit for a parade. But such an ordinance becomes unjust when it is used to maintain segregation and to deny citizens the First Amendment privilege of peaceful assembly and protest.

20   I hope you are able to see the distinction I am trying to point out. In no sense do I advocate evading or defying the law, as would the rabid segregationist. That would lead to anarchy. One who breaks an unjust law

READINGS

must do so openly, lovingly, and with a willingness to accept the penalty. I submit that an individual who breaks a law that conscience tells him is unjust, and who willingly accepts the penalty of imprisonment in order to arouse the conscience of the community over its injustice, is in reality expressing the highest respect for law.

21   Of course, there is nothing new about this kind of civil disobedience. It was evidenced sublimely in the refusal of Shadrach, Meshach, and Abednego to obey the laws of Nebuchadnezzar, on the ground that a higher moral law was at stake. It was practiced superbly by the early Christians, who were willing to face hungry lions and the excruciating pain of chopping blocks rather than submit to certain unjust laws of the Roman Empire. To a degree, academic freedom is a reality today because Socrates practiced civil disobedience. In our own nation, the Boston Tea Party represented a massive act of civil disobedience.

22   We should never forget that everything Adolf Hitler did in Germany was "legal" and everything the Hungarian freedom fighters did in Hungary was "illegal." It was "illegal" to aid and comfort a Jew in Hitler's Germany. Even so, I am sure that, had I lived in Germany at the time, I would have aided and comforted my Jewish brothers. If today I lived in a Communist country where certain principles dear to the Christian faith are suppressed, I would openly advocate disobeying that country's anti-religious laws.

23   I must make two honest confessions to you, my Christian and Jewish brothers. First, I must confess that over the past few years I have been gravely disappointed with the white moderate. I have almost reached the regrettable conclusion that the Negro's great stumbling block in his stride toward freedom is not the White Citizen's Counciler or the Ku Klux Klanner, but the white moderate, who is more devoted to "order" than to justice; who prefers a negative peace which is the absence of tension to a positive peace which is the presence of justice; who constantly says: "I agree with you in the goal you seek, but I cannot agree with your methods of direct action"; who paternalistically believes he can set the timetable for another man's freedom; who lives by a mythical concept of time and who constantly advises the Negro to wait for a "more convenient season." Shallow understanding from people of good will is more frustrating than absolute misunderstanding from people of ill will. Lukewarm acceptance is much more bewildering than outright rejection.

24   I had hoped that the white moderate would understand that law and order exist for the purpose of establishing justice and that when they fail

in this purpose they become the dangerously structured dams that block the flow of social progress. I had hoped that the white moderate would understand that the present tension in the South is a necessary phase of the transition from an obnoxious negative peace, in which the Negro passively accepted his unjust plight, to a substantive and positive peace, in which all men will respect the dignity and worth of human personality. Actually, we who engage in nonviolent direct action are not the creators of tension. We merely bring to the surface the hidden tension that is already alive. We bring it out in the open, where it can be seen and dealt with. Like a boil that can never be cured so long as it is covered up but must be opened with all its ugliness to the natural medicines of air and light, injustice must be exposed, with all the tension its exposure creates, to the light of human conscience and the air of national opinion before it can be cured.

25   In your statement you assert that our actions, even though peaceful, must be condemned because they precipitate violence. But is this a logical assertion? Isn't this like condemning a robbed man because his possession of money precipitated the evil act of robbery? Isn't this like condemning Socrates because his unswerving commitment to truth and his philosophical inquiries precipitated the act by the misguided populace in which they made him drink hemlock? Isn't this like condemning Jesus because his unique God-consciousness and never-ceasing devotion to God's will precipitated the evil act of crucifixion? We must come to see that, as the federal courts have consistently affirmed, it is wrong to urge an individual to cease his efforts to gain his basic constitutional rights because the quest may precipitate violence. Society must protect the robbed and punish the robber.

26   I had also hoped that the white moderate would reject the myth concerning time in relation to the struggle for freedom. I have just received a letter from a white brother in Texas. He writes: "All Christians know that the colored people will receive equal rights eventually, but it is possible that you are in too great a religious hurry. It has taken Christianity almost two thousand years to accomplish what it has. The teachings of Christ take time to come to earth." Such an attitude stems from a tragic misconception of time, from the strangely irrational notion that there is something in the very flow of time that will inevitably cure all ills. Actually, time itself is neutral; it can be used either destructively or constructively. More and more I feel that the people of ill will have used time much more effectively than have the people of good will. We will have to repent in this

generation not merely for the hateful words and actions of the bad people but for the appalling silence of the good people. Human progress never rolls in on wheels of inevitability; it comes through the tireless efforts of men willing to be co-workers with God, and without this hard work, time itself becomes an ally of the forces of social stagnation. We must use time creatively, in the knowledge that the time is always ripe to do right. Now is the time to make real the promise of democracy and transform our pending national elegy into a creative psalm of brotherhood. Now is the time to lift our national policy from the quicksand of racial injustice to the solid rock of human dignity.

27   You speak of our activity in Birmingham as extreme. At first I was rather disappointed that fellow clergymen would see my nonviolent efforts as those of an extremist. I began thinking about the fact that I stand in the middle of two opposing forces in the Negro community. One is a force of complacency, made up in part of Negroes who, as a result of long years of oppression, are so drained of self-respect and a sense of "somebodiness" that they have adjusted to segregation; and in part of a few middle-class Negroes who, because of a degree of academic and economic security and because in some ways they profit by segregation, have become insensitive to the problems of the masses. The other force is one of bitterness and hatred, and it comes perilously close to advocating violence. It is expressed in the various black nationalist groups that are springing up across the nation, the largest and best-known being Elijah Muhammad's Muslim movement. Nourished by the Negro's frustration over the continued existence of racial discrimination, this movement is made up of people who have lost faith in America, who have absolutely repudiated Christianity, and who have concluded that the white man is an incorrigible "devil."

28   I have tried to stand between these two forces, saying that we need emulate neither the "do-nothingism" of the complacent nor the hatred and despair of the black nationalist. For there is the more excellent way of love and nonviolent protest. I am grateful to God that, through the influence of the Negro church, the way of nonviolence became an integral part of our struggle.

29   If this philosophy had not emerged, by now many streets of the South would, I am convinced, be flowing with blood. And I am further convinced that if our white brothers dismiss as "rabble-rousers" and "outside agitators" those of us who employ nonviolent direct action, and if they refuse to support our nonviolent efforts, millions of Negroes will, out of

frustration and despair, seek solace and security in black-nationalist ide-
ologies—a development that would inevitably lead to a frightening racial
nightmare.

30   Oppressed people cannot remain oppressed forever. The yearning for
freedom eventually manifests itself, and that is what has happened to the
American Negro. Something within has reminded him of his birthright of
freedom, and something without has reminded him that it can be gained.
Consciously or unconsciously, he has been caught up by the *Zeitgeist*,
and with his black brothers of Africa and his brown and yellow brothers
of Asia, South America, and the Caribbean, the United States Negro is
moving with a sense of great urgency toward the promised land of racial justice. If one recognizes this vital urge that has engulfed the Negro
community, one should readily understand why public demonstrations
are taking place. The Negro has many pent-up resentments and latent
frustrations, and he must release them. So let him march; let him make
prayer pilgrimages to the city hall; let him go on freedom rides—and try to
understand why he must do so. If his repressed emotions are not released
in nonviolent ways, they will seek expression through violence; this is not
a threat but a fact of history. So I have not said to my people: "Get rid of
your discontent." Rather, I have tried to say that this normal and healthy
discontent can be channeled into the creative outlet of nonviolent direct
action. And now this approach is being termed extremist.

31   But though I was initially disappointed at being categorized as an
extremist, as I continued to think about the matter I gradually gained
a measure of satisfaction from the label. Was not Jesus an extremist for
love: "Love your enemies, bless them that curse you, do good to them that
hate you, and pray for them which despitefully use you, and persecute
you." Was not Amos an extremist for justice: "Let justice roll down like
waters and righteousness like an ever-flowing stream." Was not Paul an
extremist for the Christian gospel: "I bear in my body the marks of the
Lord Jesus." Was not Martin Luther an extremist: "Here I stand; I cannot
do otherwise, so help me God." And John Bunyan: "I will stay in jail to the
end of my days before I make a butchery of my conscience." And Abraham
Lincoln: "This nation cannot survive half slave and half free." And Thomas
Jefferson: "We hold these truths to be self-evident, that all men are created equal...." So the question is not whether we will be extremists, but
what kind of extremists we will be. Will we be extremists for hate or for
love? Will we be extremists for the preservation of injustice or for the extension of justice? In that dramatic scene on Calvary's hill three men were

crucified. We must never forget that all three were crucified for the same crime—the crime of extremism. Two were extremists for immorality, and thus fell below their environment. The other, Jesus Christ, was an extremist for love, truth, and goodness, and thereby rose above his environment. Perhaps the South, the nation, and the world are in dire need of creative extremists.

32   I had hoped that the white moderate would see this need. Perhaps I was too optimistic; perhaps I expected too much. I suppose I should have realized that few members of the oppressor race can understand the deep groans and passionate yearnings of the oppressed race, and still fewer have the vision to see that injustice must be rooted out by strong, persistent, and determined action. I am thankful, however, that some of our white brothers in the South have grasped the meaning of this social revolution and committed themselves to it. They are still all too few in quantity, but they are big in quality. Some—such as Ralph McGill, Lillian Smith, Harry Golden, James McBride Dabbs, Ann Braden, and Sarah Patton Boyle—have written about our struggle in eloquent and prophetic terms. Others have marched with us down nameless streets of the South. They have languished in filthy, roach-infested jails, suffering the abuse and brutality of policemen who view them as "dirty nigger-lovers." Unlike so many of their moderate brothers and sisters, they have recognized the urgency of the moment and sensed the need for powerful "action" antidotes to combat the disease of segregation.

33   Let me take note of my other major disappointment. I have been so greatly disappointed with the white church and its leadership. Of course, there are some notable exceptions. I am not unmindful of the fact that each of you has taken some significant stands on this issue. I commend you, Reverend Stallings, for your Christian stand on this past Sunday, in welcoming Negroes to your worship service on a nonsegregated basis. I commend the Catholic leaders of this state for integrating Spring Hill College several years ago.

34   But despite these notable exceptions, I must honestly reiterate that I have been disappointed with the church. I do not say this as one of those negative critics who can always find something wrong with the church. I say this as a minister of the gospel, who loves the church; who was nurtured in its bosom; who has been sustained by its spiritual blessings and who will remain true to it as long as the cord of life shall lengthen.

35   When I was suddenly catapulted into the leadership of the bus protest in Montgomery, Alabama, a few years ago, I felt we would be supported

by the white church. I felt that the white ministers, priests, and rabbis of the South would be among our strongest allies. Instead, some have been outright opponents, refusing to understand the freedom movement and misrepresenting its leaders; all too many others have been more cautious than courageous and have remained silent behind the anesthetizing security of stained-glass windows.

36   In spite of my shattered dreams, I came to Birmingham with the hope that the white religious leadership of this community would see the justice of our cause and, with deep moral concern, would serve as the channel through which our just grievances could reach the power structure. I had hoped that each of you would understand. But again I have been disappointed.

37   I have heard numerous southern religious leaders admonish their worshipers to comply with a desegregation decision because it is the law, but I have longed to hear white ministers declare: "Follow this decree because integration is morally right and because the Negro is your brother." In the midst of blatant injustices inflicted upon the Negro, I have watched white churchmen stand on the sideline and mouth pious irrelevancies and sanctimonious trivialities. In the midst of a mighty struggle to rid our nation of racial and economic injustice, I have heard many ministers say: "Those are social issues, with which the gospel has no real concern." And I have watched many churches commit themselves to a completely otherworldly religion which makes a strange, unbiblical distinction between body and soul, between the sacred and the secular.

38   I have traveled the length and breadth of Alabama, Mississippi, and all the other southern states. On sweltering summer days and crisp autumn mornings I have looked at the South's beautiful churches with their lofty spires pointing heavenward. I have beheld the impressive outlines of her massive religious education buildings. Over and over I have found myself asking: "What kind of people worship here? Who is their God? Where were their voices when the lips of Governor Barnett dripped with words of interposition and nullification? Where were they when Governor Wallace gave a clarion call for defiance and hatred? Where were their voices of support when bruised and weary Negro men and women decided to rise from the dark dungeons of complacency to the bright hills of creative protest?"

39   Yes, these questions are still in my mind. In deep disappointment I have wept over the laxity of the church. But be assured that my tears have been tears of love. There can be no deep disappointment where

READINGS

there is not deep love. Yes, I love the church. How could I do otherwise? I am in the rather unique position of being the son, the grandson, and the great-grandson of preachers. Yes, I see the church as the body of Christ. But, Oh! How we have blemished and scarred that body through social neglect and through fear of being nonconformists.

40   There was a time when the church was very powerful—in the time when the early Christians rejoiced at being deemed worthy to suffer for what they believed. In those days the church was not merely a thermometer that recorded the ideas and principles of popular opinion; it was a thermostat that transformed the mores of society. Whenever the early Christians entered a town, the people in power became disturbed and immediately sought to convict the Christians for being "disturbers of the peace" and "outside agitators." But the Christians pressed on, in the conviction that they were "a colony of heaven," called to obey God rather than man. Small in number, they were big in commitment. They were too God-intoxicated to be "astronomically intimidated." By their effort and example they brought an end to such ancient evils as infanticide and gladiatorial contests.

41   Things are different now. So often the contemporary church is a weak, ineffectual voice with an uncertain sound. So often it is an archdefender of the status quo. Far from being disturbed by the presence of the church, the power structure of the average community is consoled by the church's silent—and often even vocal—sanction of things as they are.

42   But the judgment of God is upon the church as never before. If today's church does not recapture the sacrificial spirit of the early church, it will lose its authenticity, forfeit the loyalty of millions, and be dismissed as an irrelevant social club with no meaning for the twentieth century. Every day I meet young people whose disappointment with the church has turned into outright disgust.

43   Perhaps I have once again been too optimistic. Is organized religion too inextricably bound to the status quo to save our nation and the world? Perhaps I must turn my faith to the inner spiritual church, the church within the church, as the true *ekklesia* and the hope of the world. But again I am thankful to God that some noble souls from the ranks of organized religion have broken loose from the paralyzing chains of conformity and joined us as active partners in the struggle for freedom. They have left their secure congregations and walked the streets of Albany, Georgia, with us. They have gone down the highways of the South on tortuous rides for freedom. Yes, they have gone to jail with us. Some have been dismissed

from their churches, have lost the support of their bishops and fellow ministers. But they have acted in the faith that right defeated is stronger than evil triumphant. Their witness has been the spiritual salt that has preserved the true meaning of the gospel in these troubled times. They have carved a tunnel of hope through the dark mountain of disappointment.

44   I hope the church as a whole will meet the challenge of this decisive hour. But even if the church does not come to the aid of justice, I have no despair about the future. I have no fear about the outcome of our struggle in Birmingham, even if our motives are at present misunderstood. We will reach the goal of freedom in Birmingham and all over the nation, because the goal of America is freedom. Abused and scorned though we may be, our destiny is tied up with America's destiny. Before the pilgrims landed at Plymouth, we were here. Before the pen of Jefferson etched the majestic words of the Declaration of Independence across the pages of history, we were here. For more than two centuries our forebears labored in this country without wages; they made cotton king; they built the homes of their masters while suffering gross injustice and shameful humiliation—and yet out of a bottomless vitality they continued to thrive and develop. If the inexpressible cruelties of slavery could not stop us, the opposition we now face will surely fail. We will win our freedom because the sacred heritage of our nation and the eternal will of God are embodied in our echoing demands.

45   Before closing I feel impelled to mention one other point in your statement that has troubled me profoundly. You warmly commended the Birmingham police force for keeping "order" and "preventing violence." I doubt that you would have so warmly commended the police force if you had seen its dogs sinking their teeth into unarmed, nonviolent Negroes. I doubt that you would so quickly commend the policemen if you were to observe their ugly and inhumane treatment of Negroes here in the city jail; if you were to watch them push and curse old Negro women and young Negro girls; if you were to see them slap and kick old Negro men and young boys; if you were to observe them, as they did on two occasions, refuse to give us food because we wanted to sing our grace together. I cannot join you in your praise of the Birmingham police department.

46   It is true that the police have exercised a degree of discipline in handling the demonstrators. In this sense they have conducted themselves rather "nonviolently" in public. But for what purpose? To preserve the evil system of segregation. Over the past few years I have consistently preached that nonviolence demands that the means we use must be as pure as the ends we seek. I have tried to make clear that it is wrong to

use immoral means to attain moral ends. But now I must affirm that it is just as wrong, or perhaps even more so, to use moral means to preserve immoral ends. Perhaps Mr. Connor and his policemen have been rather nonviolent in public, as was Chief Pritchett in Albany, Georgia, but they used the moral means of nonviolence to maintain the immoral end of racial injustice. As T. S. Eliot has said: "The last temptation is the greatest treason: To do the right deed for the wrong reason."

47   I wish you had commended the Negro sit-inners and demonstrators of Birmingham for their sublime courage, their willingness to suffer, and their amazing discipline in the midst of great provocation. One day the South will recognize its real heroes. They will be the James Merediths, with the noble sense of purpose that enables them to face jeering and hostile mobs, and with the agonizing loneliness that characterizes the life of the pioneer. They will be old, oppressed, battered Negro women, symbolized in a seventy-two-year-old woman in Montgomery, Alabama, who rose up with a sense of dignity and with her people decided not to ride segregated buses, and who responded with ungrammatical profundity to one who inquired about her weariness: "My feets is tired, but my soul is at rest." They will be the young high school and college students, the young ministers of the gospel and a host of their elders, courageously and nonviolently sitting in at lunch counters and willingly going to jail for conscience's sake. One day the South will know that when these disinherited children of God sat down at lunch counters, they were in reality standing up for what is best in the American dream and for the most sacred values in our Judaeo-Christian heritage, thereby bringing our nation back to those great wells of democracy which were dug deep by the founding fathers in their formulation of the Constitution and the Declaration of Independence.

48   Never before have I written so long a letter. I'm afraid it is much too long to take your precious time. I can assure you that it would have been much shorter if I had been writing from a comfortable desk, but what else can one do when he is alone in a narrow jail cell, other than write long letters, think long thoughts, and pray long prayers?

49   If I have said anything in this letter that overstates the truth and indicates an unreasonable impatience, I beg you to forgive me. If I have said anything that understates the truth and indicates my having a patience that allows me to settle for anything less than brotherhood, I beg God to forgive me.

50   I hope this letter finds you strong in the faith. I also hope that circumstances will soon make it possible for me to meet each of you, not as an integrationist or a civil-rights leader but as a fellow clergyman and a Christian brother. Let us all hope that the dark clouds of racial prejudice will soon pass away and the deep fog of misunderstanding will be lifted from our fear-drenched communities, and in some not too distant tomorrow the radiant stars of love and brotherhood will shine over our great nation with all their scintillating beauty.

—Yours for the Cause of Peace and Brotherhood, Martin Luther King, Jr.

QUESTIONS TO CONSIDER

1. According to King's letter, name the four basic steps for a non-violent campaign.

2. Identify at least five rhetorical strategies in "Letter from Birmingham Jail." What is the effect of each approach on King's audience?

3. Who is King writing the letter to and why?

4. Explain the two different types of laws King discusses: just and unjust.

5. What is your favorite quote or segment of "Letter from Birmingham Jail"? How does this concept relate to the present?

Stone Soup

Barbara Kingsolver

- **AP** Argument and Persuasion
- **CC** Compare and Contrast

1   In the catalog of family values, where do we rank an occasion like this? A curly-haired boy who wanted to run before he walked, age seven now, a soccer player scoring a winning goal. He turns to the bleachers with his fists in the air and a smile wide as a gap-toothed galaxy. His own cheering section of grown-ups and kids all leap to their feet and hug each other, delirious with love for this boy. He's Andy, my best friend's son. The cheering section includes his mother and her friends, his brother, his father and stepmother, a stepbrother and stepsister, and a grandparent. Lucky is the child with this many relatives on hand to hail a proud accomplishment. I'm there too, witnessing a family fortune. But in spite of myself, defensive words take shape in my head. I am thinking: I dare *anybody* to call this a broken home.

2   Families change, and remain the same. Why are our names for home so slow to catch up to the truth of where we live?

3   When I was a child, I had two parents who loved me without cease. One of them attended every excuse for attention I ever contrived, and the other made it to the ones with higher production values, like piano recitals and appendicitis. So I was a lucky child too. I played with a set of paper dolls called "The Family of Dolls," four in number, who came with the factory-assigned names of Dad, Mom, Sis, and Junior. I think you know what they looked like, at least before I loved them to death and their heads fell off.

4   Now I've replaced the dolls with a life. I knit my days around my daughter's survival and happiness, and am proud to say her head is still on. But we aren't the Family of Dolls. Maybe you're not, either. And if not, even though you are statistically no oddity, it's probably been suggested to you in a hundred ways that yours isn't exactly a real family, but an impostor family, a harbinger of cultural ruin, a slapdash substitute—something like counterfeit money. Here at the tail end of our century, most of us are up to our ears in the noisy business of trying to support and love a thing called family. But there's a current in the air with ferocious moral force

that finds its way even into political campaigns, claiming there is only one right way to do it, the Way It Has Always Been.

5   In the face of a thriving, particolored world, this narrow view is so pickled and absurd I'm astonished that it gets airplay. And I'm astonished that it still stings.

6   Every parent has endured the arrogance of a child-unfriendly grump sitting in judgment, explaining what those kids of ours really need (for example, "a good licking"). If we're polite, we move our crew to another bench in the park. If we're forthright (as I am in my mind, only, for the rest of the day), we fix them with a sweet imperious stare and say, "Come back and let's talk about it after you've changed a thousand diapers."

7   But it's harder somehow to shrug off the Family-of-Dolls Family Values crew when they judge (from their safe distance) that divorced people, blended families, gay families, and single parents are failures. That our children are at risk, and the whole arrangement is messy and embarrassing. A marriage that ends is not called "finished," it's called *failed*. The children of this family may have been born to a happy union, but now they are called *the children of divorce*.

8   I had no idea how thoroughly these assumptions overlaid my culture until I went through divorce myself. I wrote to a friend: "This might be worse than being widowed. Overnight I've suffered the same losses—companionship, financial and practical support, my identity as a wife and partner, the future I'd taken for granted. I am lonely, grieving, and hard-pressed to take care of my household alone. But instead of bringing casseroles, people are acting like I had a fit and broke up the family china."

9   Once upon a time I held these beliefs about divorce: that everyone who does it could have chosen not to do it. That it's a lazy way out of marital problems. That it selfishly puts personal happiness ahead of family integrity. Now I tremble for my ignorance. It's easy, in fortunate times, to forget about the ambush that could leave your head reeling: serious mental or physical illness, death in the family, abandonment, financial calamity, humiliation, violence, despair.

10   I started out like any child, intent on being the Family of Dolls. I set upon young womanhood believing in most of the doctrines of my generation: I wore my skirts four inches above the knee. I had the Barbie with her zebra-striped swimsuit and a figure unlike anything found in nature. And I understood the Prince Charming Theory of Marriage, a quest for Mr. Right that ends smack dab where you find him. I did not completely understand that another whole story *begins* there, and no fairy tale prepared

me for the combination of bad luck and persistent hope that would interrupt my dream and lead me to other arrangements. Like a cancer diagnosis, a dying marriage is a thing to fight, to deny, and finally, when there's no choice left, to dig in and survive. Casseroles would help. Likewise, I imagine it must be a painful reckoning in adolescence (or later on) to realize one's own true love will never look like the soft-focus fragrance ads because Prince Charming (surprise!) is a princess. Or vice versa. Or has skin the color your parents didn't want you messing with, except in the Crayola box.

11   It's awfully easy to hold in contempt the straw broken home, and that mythical category of persons who toss away nuclear family for the sheer fun of it. Even the legal terms we use have a suggestion of caprice. I resent the phrase "irreconcilable differences," which suggests a stubborn refusal to accept a spouse's little quirks. This is specious. Every happily married couple I know has loads of irreconcilable differences. Negotiating where to set the thermostat is not the point. A nonfunctioning marriage is a slow asphyxiation. It is waking up despised each morning, listening to the pulse of your own loneliness before the radio begins to blare its raucous gospel that you're nothing if you aren't loved. It is sharing your airless house with the threat of suicide or other kinds of violence, while the ghost that whispers, "Leave here and destroy your children," has passed over every door and nailed it shut. Disassembling a marriage in these circumstances is as much *fun* as amputating your own gangrenous leg. You do it, if you can, to save a life—or two, or more.

12   I know of no one who really went looking to hoe the harder row, especially the daunting one of single parenthood. Yet it seems to be the most American of customs to blame the burdened for their destiny. We'd like so desperately to believe in freedom and justice for all, we can hardly name that rogue bad luck, even when he's a close enough snake to bite us. In the wake of my divorce, some friends (even a few close ones) chose to vanish, rather than linger within striking distance of misfortune.

13   But most stuck around, bless their hearts, and if I'm any the wiser for my trials, it's from having learned the worth of steadfast friendship. And also, what not to say. The least helpful question is: "Did you want the divorce, or didn't you?" Did I want to keep that gangrenous leg, or not? How to explain, in a culture that venerates choice: two terrifying options are much worse than none at all. Give me any day the quick hand of cruel fate that will leave me scarred but blameless. As it was, I kept thinking of that wicked third-grade joke in which some boy comes up behind you and

grabs your ear, starts in with a prolonged tug, and asks, "Do you want this ear any longer?"

14   Still, the friend who holds your hand and says the wrong thing is made of dearer stuff than the one who stays away. And generally, through all of it, you live. My favorite fictional character, Kate Vaiden (in the novel by Reynolds Price), advises: "Strength just comes in one brand—you stand up at sunrise and meet what they send you and keep your hair combed."

15   Once you've weathered the straits, you get to cross the tricky juncture from casualty to survivor. If you're on your feet at the end of a year or two, and have begun putting together a happy new existence, those friends who were kind enough to feel sorry for you when you needed it must now accept you back to the ranks of the living. If you're truly blessed, they will dance at your second wedding. Everybody else, for heaven's sake, should stop throwing stones.

16   Arguing about whether nontraditional families deserve pity or tolerance is a little like the medieval debate about left-handedness as a mark of the devil. Divorce, remarriage, single parenthood, gay parents, and blended families simply are. They're facts of our time. Some of the reasons listed by sociologists for these family reconstructions are: the idea of marriage as a romantic partnership rather than a pragmatic one; a shift in women's expectations, from servility to self-respect and independence; and longevity (prior to antibiotics no marriage was expected to last many decades—in Colonial days the average couple lived to be married less than twelve years). Add to all this, our growing sense of entitlement to happiness and safety from abuse. Most would agree these are all good things. Yet their result—a culture in which serial monogamy and the consequent reshaping of families are the norm—gets diagnosed as "failing."

17   For many of us, once we have put ourselves Humpty-Dumpty-wise back together again, the main problem with our reorganized family is that other people think we have a problem. My daughter tells me the only time she's uncomfortable about being the child of divorced parents is when her friends say they feel sorry for her. It's a bizarre sympathy, given that half the kids in her school and nation are in the same boat, pursuing childish happiness with the same energy as their married-parent peers. When anyone asks how *she* feels about it, she spontaneously lists the benefits: our house is in the country and we have a dog, but she can go to her dad's neighborhood for the urban thrills of a pool and sidewalks for roller-skating. What's more, she has three sets of grandparents!

READINGS

18   Why is it surprising that a child would revel in a widened family and the right to feel at home in more than one house? Isn't it the opposite that should worry us—a child with no home at all, or too few resources to feel safe? The child at risk is the one whose parents are too immature themselves to guide wisely; too diminished by poverty to nurture; too far from opportunity to offer hope. The number of children in the U.S. living in poverty at this moment is almost unfathomably large: twenty percent. There are families among us that need help all right, and by no means are they new on the landscape. The rate at which teenage girls had babies in 1957 (ninety-six per thousand) was twice what it is now. That remarkable statistic is ignored by the religious right—probably because the teen birth rate was cut in half mainly by legalized abortion. In fact, the policy gatekeepers who coined the phrase "family values" have steadfastly ignored the desperation of too-small families, and since 1979 have steadily reduced the amount of financial support available to a single parent. But, this camp's most outspoken attacks seem aimed at the notion of families getting too complex, with add-ons and extras such as a gay parent's partner, or a remarried mother's new husband and his children.

19   To judge a family's value by its tidy symmetry is to purchase a book for its cover. There's no moral authority there. The famous family comprised of Dad, Mom, Sis, and Junior living as an isolated economic unit is not built on historical bedrock. In *The Way We Never Were,* Stephanie Coontz writes, "Whenever people propose that we go back to the traditional family, I always suggest that they pick a ballpark date for the family they have in mind." Colonial families were tidily disciplined, but their members (meaning everyone but infants) labored incessantly and died young. Then the Victorian family adopted a new division of labor, in which women's role was domestic and children were allowed time for study and play, but this was an upper-class construct supported by myriad slaves. Coontz writes, "For every nineteenth-century middle-class family that protected its wife and child within the family circle, there was an Irish or German girl scrubbing floors...a Welsh boy mining coal to keep the home-baked goodies warm, a black girl doing the family laundry, a black mother and child picking cotton to be made into clothes for the family, and a Jewish or an Italian daughter in a sweatshop making 'ladies' dresses or artificial flowers for the family to purchase."

20   The abolition of slavery brought slightly more democratic arrangements, in which extended families were harnessed together in cottage industries; at the turn of the century came a steep rise in child labor in

mines and sweatshops. Twenty percent of American children lived in orphanages at the time; their parents were not necessarily dead, but couldn't afford to keep them.

21   During the Depression and up to the end of World War II, many millions of U.S. households were more multigenerational than nuclear. Women my grandmother's age were likely to live with a fluid assortment of elderly relatives, in-laws, siblings, and children. In many cases they spent virtually every waking hour working in the company of other women—a companionable scenario in which it would be easier, I imagine, to tolerate an estranged or difficult spouse. I'm reluctant to idealize a life of so much hard work and so little spousal intimacy, but its advantage may have been resilience. A family so large and varied would not easily be brought down by a single blow: it could absorb a death, long illness, an abandonment here or there, and any number of irreconcilable differences.

22   The Family of Dolls came along midcentury as a great American experiment. A booming economy required a mobile labor force and de-manded that women surrender jobs to returning soldiers. Families came to be defined by a single breadwinner. They struck out for single-family homes at an earlier age than ever before, and in unprecedented num-bers they raised children in suburban isolation. The nuclear family was launched to sink or swim.

23   More than a few sank. Social historians corroborate that the subur-ban family of the postwar economic boom, which we have recently select-ed as our definition of "traditional," was no panacea. Twenty-five percent of Americans were poor in the mid-1950s, and as yet there were no food stamps. Sixty percent of the elderly lived on less than $1,000 a year, and most had no medical insurance. In the sequestered suburbs, alcoholism and sexual abuse of children were far more widespread than anyone imagined.

24   Expectations soared, and the economy sagged. It's hard to depend on one other adult for everything, come what may. In the last three decades, that amorphous, adaptable structure we call "family" has been reshaped once more by economic tides. Compared with fifties families, mothers are far more likely now to be employed. We are statistically more likely to di-vorce, and to live in blended families or other extranuclear arrangements. We are also more likely to plan and space our children, and to rate our marriages as " happy." We are less likely to suffer abuse without recourse, or to stare out at our lives through a glaze of prescription tranquilizers. Our aged parents are less likely to be destitute, and we're half as likely to have a teenage daughter turn up a mother herself. All in all, I would say

that if "intact" in modern family-values jargon means living quietly desperate in the bell jar, then hip-hip-hooray for "broken." A neat family model constructed to service the Baby Boom economy seems to be returning gradually to a grand, lumpy shape that human families apparently have tended toward since they first took root in the Olduvai Gorge. We're social animals, deeply fond of companionship, and children love best to run in packs. If there is a *normal* for humans, at all, I expect it looks like two or three Families of Dolls, connected variously by kinship and passion, shuffled like cards and strewn over several shoeboxes.

25   The sooner we can let go of the fairy tale of families functioning perfectly in isolation, the better we might embrace the relief of community. Even the admirable parents who've stayed married through thick and thin are very likely, at present, to incorporate other adults into their families— household help and baby-sitters if they can afford them, or neighbors and grandparents if they can't. For single parents, this support is the rock-bottom definition of family. And most parents who have split apart, however painfully, still manage to maintain family continuity for their children, creating in many cases a boisterous phenomenon that Constance Ahrons in her book *The Good Divorce* calls the "binuclear family." Call it what you will—when ex-spouses beat swords into plowshares and jump up and down at a soccer game together, it makes for happy kids.

26   Cinderella, look, who needs her? All those evil stepsisters? That story always seemed like too much cotton-picking fuss over clothes. A childhood tale that fascinated me more was the one called "Stone Soup," and the gist of it is this: Once upon a time, a pair of beleaguered soldiers straggled home to a village empty-handed, in a land ruined by war. They were famished, but the villagers had so little they shouted evil words and slammed their doors. So the soldiers dragged out a big kettle, filled it with water, and put it on a fire to boil. They rolled a clean round stone into the pot, while the villagers peered through their curtains in amazement.

27   "What kind of soup is that?" they hooted.

28   "Stone soup," the soldiers replied. "Everybody can have some when it's done."

29   "Well, thanks," one matron grumbled, coming out with a shriveled carrot. "But it'd be better if you threw this in."

30   And so on, of course, a vegetable at a time, until the whole suspicious village managed to feed itself grandly.

31   Any family is a big empty pot, save for what gets thrown in. Each stew turns out different. Generosity, a resolve to turn bad luck into good, and respect for variety—these things will nourish a nation of children. Name-calling and suspicion will not. My soup contains a rock or two of hard times, and maybe yours does too. I expect it's a heck of a bouillabaisse.

QUESTIONS TO CONSIDER

1. How does Barbara Kingsolver characterize her family? Compare and contrast her family with the "family of dolls" she describes.

2. What is the message of Kingsolver's essay?

3. Why does Kingsolver italicize certain words in "Stone Soup"? What effect do these italics have on your reading of her essay?

4. Who do you think is the intended audience for Kingsolver's essay? What clues make you think this is the audience?

5. How does Kingsolver establish her own credibility in the eyes of her audience?

READINGS

The Death of Horatio Alger

Paul Krugman

- **N** Narration
- **PA** Process Analysis

1   The other day I found myself reading a leftist rag that made outrageous claims about America. It said that we are becoming a society in which the poor tend to stay poor, no matter how hard they work; in which sons are much more likely to inherit the socioeconomic status of their father than they were a generation ago.

2   The name of the leftist rag? *Business Week*, which published an article titled "Waking Up From the American Dream." The article summarizes recent research showing that social mobility in the United States (which was never as high as legend had it) has declined considerably over the past few decades. If you put that research together with other research that shows a drastic increase in income and wealth inequality, you reach an uncomfortable conclusion: America looks more and more like a class-ridden society.

3   And guess what? Our political leaders are doing everything they can to fortify class inequality, while denouncing anyone who complains—or even points out what is happening—as a practitioner of "class warfare."

4   Let's talk first about the facts on income distribution. Thirty years ago we were a relatively middle-class nation. It had not always been thus: Gilded Age America was a highly unequal society, and it stayed that way through the 1920s. During the 1930s and '40s, however, America experienced what the economic historians Claudia Goldin and Robert Margo have dubbed the Great Compression: a drastic narrowing of income gaps, probably as a result of New Deal policies. And the new economic order persisted for more than a generation: Strong unions; taxes on inherited wealth, corporate profits and high incomes; close public scrutiny of corporate management—all helped to keep income gaps relatively small. The economy was hardly egalitarian, but a generation ago the gross inequalities of the 1920s seemed very distant.

5   Now they're back. According to estimates by the economists Thomas Piketty and Emmanuel Saez—confirmed by data from the Congressional

Budget Office—between 1973 and 2000 the average real income of the bottom 90 percent of American taxpayers actually fell by 7 percent. Meanwhile, the income of the top 1 percent rose by 148 percent, the income of the top 0.1 percent rose by 343 percent, and the income of the top 0.01 percent rose 599 percent. (Those numbers exclude capital gains, so they're not an artifact of the stock market bubble.) The distribution of income in the United States has gone right back to Gilded Age levels of inequality.

6   Never mind, say the apologists, who churn out papers with titles like that of a 2001 Heritage Foundation piece, "Income Mobility and the Fallacy of Class-Warfare Arguments." America, they say, isn't a caste society—people with high incomes this year may have low incomes next year and vice versa, and the route to wealth is open to all. That's where those commies at *Business Week* come in: As they point out (and as economists and sociologists have been pointing out for some time), America actually is more of a caste society than we like to think. And the caste lines have lately become a lot more rigid.

7   The myth of income mobility has always exceeded the reality. As a general rule, once they've reached their 30s, people don't move up and down the income ladder very much. Conservatives often cite studies like a 1992 report by Glenn Hubbard, a Treasury official under the elder Bush who later became chief economic adviser to the younger Bush, that purport to show large numbers of Americans moving from low-wage to high-wage jobs during their working lives. But what these studies measure, as the economist Kevin Murphy put it, is mainly "the guy who works in the college bookstore and has a real job by his early 30s." Serious studies that exclude this sort of pseudo-mobility show that inequality in average incomes over long periods isn't much smaller than inequality in annual incomes.

8   It is true, however, that America was once a place of substantial intergenerational mobility: Sons often did much better than their fathers. A classic 1978 survey found that among adult men whose fathers were in the bottom 25 percent of the population as ranked by social and economic status, 23 percent had made it into the top 25 percent. In other words, during the first thirty years or so after World War II, the American dream of upward mobility was a real experience for many people.

9   Now for the shocker. The *Business Week* piece cites a new survey of today's adult men, which finds that this number has dropped to only 10 percent. That is, over the past generation upward mobility has fallen

READINGS

drastically. Very few children of the lower class are making their way to even moderate affluence. This goes along with other studies indicating that rags-to-riches stories have become vanishingly rare, and that the correlation between fathers' and sons' incomes has risen in recent decades. In modern America, it seems, you're quite likely to stay in the social and economic class into which you were born.

10   *Business Week* attributes this to the "Wal-Martization" of the economy, the proliferation of dead-end, low-wage jobs and the disappearance of jobs that provide entry to the middle class. That's surely part of the explanation. But public policy plays a role—and will, if present trends continue, play an even bigger role in the future.

11   Put it this way: Suppose that you actually liked a caste society, and you were seeking ways to use your control of the government to further entrench the advantages of the haves against the have-nots. What would you do?

12   One thing you would definitely do is get rid of the estate tax, so that large fortunes can be passed on to the next generation. More broadly, you would seek to reduce tax rates both on corporate profits and on unearned income such as dividends and capital gains, so that those with large accumulated or inherited wealth could more easily accumulate even more. You'd also try to create tax shelters mainly useful for the rich. And more broadly still, you'd try to reduce tax rates on people with high incomes, shifting the burden to the payroll tax and other revenue sources that bear most heavily on people with lower incomes.

13   Meanwhile, on the spending side, you'd cut back on healthcare for the poor, on the quality of public education, and on state aid for higher education. This would make it more difficult for people with low incomes to climb out of their difficulties and acquire the education essential to upward mobility in the modern economy.

14   And just to close off as many routes to upward mobility as possible, you'd do everything possible to break the power of unions, and you'd privatize government functions so that well-paid civil servants could be replaced with poorly paid private employees.

15   It all sounds sort of familiar, doesn't it?

16   Where is this taking us? Thomas Piketty, whose work with Saez has transformed our understanding of income distribution, warns that current policies will eventually create "a class of rentiers in the U.S., whereby a small group of wealthy but untalented children controls vast segments of the U.S. economy and penniless, talented children simply can't compete."

If he's right—and I fear that he is—we will end up suffering not only from injustice, but from a vast waste of human potential.

17   Goodbye, Horatio Alger. And goodbye, American Dream.

QUESTIONS TO CONSIDER

1. What type of tone is set at the beginning of the article? What kind of vocabulary does Krugman use to achieve this? What do you think he is trying to accomplish?

2. What is a "caste society," and in what ways is America similar to one?

3. What is the American dream of "upward mobility"? Is it a reality now, or was it something of the past? How has this changed over time in America?

4. According to Krugman, what are the ways to effectively establish a caste society? Is this similar to current American policies?

5. What is Krugman's main argument in this article? Do you agree? Why?

The College Dropout Boom

David Leonhardt

- **CE** Cause and Effect
- **PA** Process Analysis

1   One of the biggest decisions Andy Blevins has ever made, and one of the few he now regrets, never seemed like much of a decision at all. It just felt like the natural thing to do.

2   In the summer of 1995, he was moving boxes of soup cans, paper towels and dog food across the floor of a supermarket warehouse, one of the biggest buildings here in southwest Virginia. The heat was brutal. The job had sounded impossible when he arrived fresh off his first year of college, looking to make some summer money, still a skinny teenager with sandy blond hair and a narrow, freckled face.

3   But hard work done well was something he understood, even if he was the first college boy in his family. Soon he was making bonuses on top of his $6.75 an hour, more money than either of his parents made. His girlfriend was around, and so were his hometown buddies. Andy acted more outgoing with them, more relaxed. People in Chilhowie noticed that.

4   It was just about the perfect summer. So the thought crossed his mind: maybe it did not have to end. Maybe he would take a break from college and keep working. He had been getting C's and D's, and college never felt like home, anyway.

5   "I enjoyed working hard, getting the job done, getting a paycheck," Mr. Blevins recalled. "I just knew I didn't want to quit."

6   So he quit college instead, and with that, Andy Blevins joined one of the largest and fastest-growing groups of young adults in America. He became a college dropout, though nongraduate may be the more precise term.

7   Many people like him plan to return to get their degrees, even if few actually do. Almost one in three Americans in their mid-20's now fall into this group, up from one in five in the late 1960's, when the Census Bureau began keeping such data. Most come from poor and working-class families.

8   The phenomenon has been largely overlooked in the glare of posi-tive news about the country's gains in education. Going to college has become the norm throughout most of the United States, even in many places where college was once considered an exotic destination—places like Chilhowie (pronounced chill-HOW-ee), an Appalachian hamlet with a simple brick downtown. At elite universities, classrooms are filled with women, blacks, Jews and Latinos, groups largely excluded two genera-tions ago. The American system of higher learning seems to have become a great equalizer.

9   In fact, though, colleges have come to reinforce many of the advan-tages of birth. On campuses that enroll poorer students, graduation rates are often low. And at institutions where nearly everyone graduates— small colleges like Colgate, major state institutions like the University of Colorado and elite private universities like Stanford—more students today come from the top of the nation's income ladder than they did two decades ago.

10   Only 41 percent of low-income students entering a four-year college managed to graduate within five years, the Department of Education found in a study last year, but 66 percent of high-income students did. That gap had grown over recent years. "We need to recognize that the most serious domestic problem in the United States today is the widen-ing gap between the children of the rich and the children of the poor," Lawrence H. Summers, the president of Harvard, said last year when an-nouncing that Harvard would give full scholarships to all its lowest-in-come students. "And education is the most powerful weapon we have to address that problem."

11   There is certainly much to celebrate about higher education today. Many more students from all classes are getting four-year degrees and reaping their benefits. But those broad gains mask the fact that poor and working-class students have nevertheless been falling behind; for them, not having a degree remains the norm.

12   That loss of ground is all the more significant because a college edu-cation matters much more now than it once did. A bachelor's degree, not a year or two of courses, tends to determine a person's place in today's globalized, computerized economy. College graduates have received steady pay increases over the past two decades, while the pay of everyone else has risen little more than the rate of inflation.

13   As a result, despite one of the great education explosions in modern history, economic mobility—moving from one income group to another

READINGS

over the course of a lifetime—has stopped rising, researchers say. Some recent studies suggest that it has declined over the last generation.

14   Put another way, children seem to be following the paths of their parents more than they once did. Grades and test scores, rather than privilege, determine success today, but that success is largely being passed down from one generation to the next. A nation that believes that everyone should have a fair shake finds itself with a kind of inherited meritocracy.

15   In this system, the students at the best colleges may be diverse—male and female and of various colors, religions and hometowns—but they tend to share an upper-middle-class upbringing. An old joke that Harvard's idea of diversity is putting a rich kid from California in the same room as a rich kid from New York is truer today than ever; Harvard has more students from California than it did in years past and just as big a share of upper-income students.

16   Students like these remain in college because they can hardly imagine doing otherwise. Their parents, understanding the importance of a bachelor's degree, spent hours reading to them, researching school districts and making it clear to them that they simply must graduate from college.

17   Andy Blevins says that he too knows the importance of a degree, but that he did not while growing up, and not even in his year at Radford University, 66 miles up the Interstate from Chilhowie. Ten years after trading college for the warehouse, Mr. Blevins, 29, spends his days at the same supermarket company. He has worked his way up to produce buyer, earning $35,000 a year with health benefits and a 401(k) plan. He is on a path typical for someone who attended college without getting a four-year degree. Men in their early 40's in this category made an average of $42,000 in 2000. Those with a four-year degree made $65,000.

18   Still boyish-looking but no longer rail thin, Mr. Blevins says he has many reasons to be happy. He lives with his wife, Karla, and their year-old son, Lucas, in a small blue-and-yellow house at the end of a cul-de-sac in the middle of a stunningly picturesque Appalachian valley. He plays golf with some of the same friends who made him want to stay around Chilhowie.

19   But he does think about what might have been, about what he could be doing if he had the degree. As it is, he always feels as if he is on thin ice. Were he to lose his job, he says, everything could slip away with it. What kind of job could a guy without a college degree get? One night, while talking to his wife about his life, he used the word "trapped."

20   "Looking back, I wish I had gotten that degree," Mr. Blevins said in his soft-spoken lilt. "Four years seemed like a thousand years then. But I wish I would have just put in my four years."

The Barriers

21   Why so many low-income students fall from the college ranks is a question without a simple answer. Many high schools do a poor job of preparing teenagers for college. Many of the colleges where lower-income students tend to enroll have limited resources and offer a narrow range of majors, leaving some students disenchanted and unwilling to continue.

22   Then there is the cost. Tuition bills scare some students from even applying and leave others with years of debt. To Mr. Blevins, like many other students of limited means, every week of going to classes seemed like another week of losing money—money that might have been made at a job.

23   "The system makes a false promise to students," said John T. Casteen III, the president of the University of Virginia, himself the son of a Virginia shipyard worker.

24   Colleges, Mr. Casteen said, present themselves as meritocracies in which academic ability and hard work are always rewarded. In fact, he said, many working-class students face obstacles they cannot overcome on their own.

25   For much of his 15 years as Virginia's president, Mr. Casteen has focused on raising money and expanding the university, the most prestigious in the state. In the meantime, students with backgrounds like his have become ever scarcer on campus. The university's genteel nickname, the Cavaliers, and its aristocratic sword-crossed coat of arms seem appropriate today. No flagship state university has a smaller proportion of low-income students than Virginia. Just 8 percent of undergraduates last year came from families in the bottom half of the income distribution, down from 11 percent a decade ago.

26   That change sneaked up on him, Mr. Casteen said, and he has spent a good part of the last year trying to prevent it from becoming part of his legacy.Starting with next fall's freshman class, the university will charge no tuition and require no loans for students whose parents make less than twice the poverty level, or about $37,700 a year for a family of four. The university has also increased financial aid to middle-income students.

27   To Mr. Casteen, these are steps to remove what he describes as "artificial barriers" to a college education placed in the way of otherwise

READINGS

deserving students. Doing so "is a fundamental obligation of a free culture," he said.

28   But the deterrents to a degree can also be homegrown. Many low-income teenagers know few people who have made it through college. A majority of the nongraduates are young men, and some come from towns where the factory work ethic, to get working as soon as possible, remains strong, even if the factories themselves are vanishing. Whatever the reasons, college just does not feel normal.

29   "You get there and you start to struggle," said Leanna Blevins, Andy's older sister, who did get a bachelor's degree and then went on to earn a Ph.D. at Virginia studying the college experiences of poor students. "And at home your parents are trying to be supportive and say, 'Well, if you're not happy, if it's not right for you, come back home. It's O.K.' And they think they're doing the right thing. But they don't know that maybe what the student needs is to hear them say, 'Stick it out just one semester. You can do it. Just stay there. Come home on the weekend, but stick it out.'"

30   Today, Ms. Blevins, petite and high-energy, is helping to start a new college a few hours' drive from Chilhowie for low-income students. Her brother said he had daydreamed about attending it and had talked to her about how he might return to college.

31   For her part, Ms. Blevins says, she has daydreamed about having a life that would seem as natural as her brother's, a life in which she would not feel like an outsider in her hometown. Once, when a high-school teacher asked students to list their goals for the next decade, Ms. Blevins wrote, "having a college degree" and "not being married."

32   "I think my family probably thinks I'm liberal," Ms. Blevins, who is now married, said with a laugh, "that I've just been educated too much and I'm gettin' above my raisin'."

33   Her brother said that he just wanted more control over his life, not a new one. At a time when many people complain of scattered lives, Mr. Blevins can stand in one spot—his church parking lot, next to a graveyard—and take in much of his world. "That's my parents' house," he said one day, pointing to a sliver of roof visible over a hill. "That's my uncle's trailer. My grandfather is buried here. I'll probably be buried here."

Taking Class into Account

34   Opening up colleges to new kinds of students has generally meant one thing over the last generation: affirmative action. Intended to right the wrongs of years of exclusion, the programs have swelled the number

of women, blacks and Latinos on campuses. But affirmative action was never supposed to address broad economic inequities, just the ones that stem from specific kinds of discrimination.

35   That is now beginning to change. Like Virginia, a handful of other colleges are not only increasing financial aid but also promising to give weight to economic class in granting admissions. They say they want to make an effort to admit more low-income students, just as they now do for minorities and children of alumni.

36   "The great colleges and universities were designed to provide for mobility, to seek out talent," said Anthony W. Marx, president of Amherst College. "If we are blind to the educational disadvantages associated with need, we will simply replicate these disadvantages while appearing to make decisions based on merit."

37   With several populous states having already banned race-based preferences and the United States Supreme Court suggesting that it may outlaw such programs in a couple of decades, the future of affirmative action may well revolve around economics. Polls consistently show that programs based on class backgrounds have wider support than those based on race.

38   The explosion in the number of nongraduates has also begun to get the attention of policy makers. This year, New York became one of a small group of states to tie college financing more closely to graduation rates, rewarding colleges more for moving students along than for simply admitting them. Nowhere is the stratification of education more vivid than here in Virginia, where Thomas Jefferson once tried, and failed, to set up the nation's first public high schools. At a modest high school in the Tidewater city of Portsmouth, not far from Mr. Casteen's boyhood home, a guidance office wall filled with college pennants does not include one from rarefied Virginia. The colleges whose pennants are up—Old Dominion University and others that seem in the realm of the possible— have far lower graduation rates.

39   Across the country, the upper middle class so dominates elite universities that high-income students, on average, actually get slightly more financial aid from colleges than low-income students do. These elite colleges are so expensive that even many high-income students receive large grants. In the early 1990's, by contrast, poorer students got 50 percent more aid on average than the wealthier ones, according to the College Board, the organization that runs the SAT entrance exams.

40   At the other end of the spectrum are community colleges, the two-year institutions that are intended to be feeders for four-year colleges. In

READINGS

nearly every one are tales of academic success against tremendous odds: a battered wife or a combat veteran or a laid-off worker on the way to a better life. But overall, community colleges tend to be places where dreams are put on hold.

41   Most people who enroll say they plan to get a four-year degree eventually; few actually do. Full-time jobs, commutes and children or parents who need care often get in the way. One recent national survey found that about 75 percent of students enrolling in community colleges said they hoped to transfer to a four-year institution. But only 17 percent of those who had entered in the mid-1990's made the switch within five years, according to a separate study. The rest were out working or still studying toward the two-year degree.

42   "We here in Virginia do a good job of getting them in," said Glenn Dubois, chancellor of the Virginia Community College System and himself a community college graduate. "We have to get better in getting them out."

'I wear a tie every day'

43   College degree or not, Mr. Blevins has the kind of life that many Americans say they aspire to. He fills it with family, friends, church and a five-handicap golf game. He does not sit in traffic commuting to an office park. He does not talk wistfully of a relocated brother or best friend he sees only twice a year. He does not worry about who will care for his son while he works and his wife attends community college to become a physical therapist. His grandparents down the street watch Lucas, just as they took care of Andy and his two sisters when they were children. When Mr. Blevins comes home from work, it is his turn to play with Lucas, tossing him into the air and rolling around on the floor with him and a stuffed elephant.

44   Mr. Blevins also sings in a quartet called the Gospel Gentlemen. One member is his brother-in-law; another lives on Mr. Blevins's street. In the long white van the group owns, they wend their way along mountain roads on their way to singing dates at local church functions, sometimes harmonizing, sometimes ribbing one another or talking about where to buy golf equipment.

45   Inside the churches, the other singers often talk to the audience between songs, about God or a grandmother or what a song means to them. Mr. Blevins rarely does, but his shyness fades once he is back in the van with his friends.

46   At the warehouse, he is usually the first to arrive, around 6:30 in the morning. The grandson of a coal miner, he takes pride, he says, in having moved up to become a supermarket buyer. He decides which bananas, grapes, onions and potatoes the company will sell and makes sure that there are always enough. Most people with his job have graduated from college.

47   "I'm pretty fortunate to not have a degree but have a job where I wear a tie every day," he said.

48   He worries about how long it will last, though, mindful of what happened to his father, Dwight, a decade ago. A high school graduate, Dwight Blevins was laid off from his own warehouse job and ended up with another one that paid less and offered a smaller pension.

49   "A lot of places, they're not looking that you're trained in something," Andy Blevins said one evening, sitting on his back porch. "They just want you to have a degree."

50   Figuring out how to get one is the core quandary facing the nation's college nongraduates. Many seem to want one. In a *New York Times* poll, 43 percent of them called it essential to success, while 42 percent of college graduates and 32 percent of high-school dropouts did. This in itself is a change from the days when "college boy" was an insult in many working-class neighborhoods. But once students take a break—the phrase that many use instead of drop out—the ideal can quickly give way to reality. Family and work can make a return to school seem even harder than finishing it in the first place.

51   After dropping out of Radford, Andy Blevins enrolled part-time in a community college, trying to juggle work and studies. He lasted a year. From time to time in the decade since, he has thought about giving it another try. But then he has wondered if that would be crazy. He works every third Saturday, and his phone rings on Sundays when there is a problem with the supply of potatoes or apples. "It never ends," he said. "There's never a lull."

52   To spend more time with Lucas, Mr. Blevins has already cut back on his singing. If he took night classes, he said, when would he ever see his little boy? Anyway, he said, it would take years to get a degree part-time. To him, it is a tug of war between living in the present and sacrificing for the future.

READINGS

Few Breaks for the Needy

53   The college admissions system often seems ruthlessly meritocratic. Yes, children of alumni still have an advantage. But many other pillars of the old system—the polite rejections of women or blacks, the spots reserved for graduates of Choate and Exeter—have crumbled.

54   This was the meritocracy Mr. Casteen described when he greeted the parents of freshmen in a University of Virginia lecture hall late last summer. Hailing from all 50 states and 52 foreign countries, the students were more intelligent and better prepared than he and his classmates had been, he told the parents in his quiet, deep voice. The class included 17 students with a perfect SAT score.

55   If anything, children of privilege think that the system has moved so far from its old-boy history that they are now at a disadvantage when they apply, because colleges are trying to diversify their student rolls. To get into a good college, the sons and daughters of the upper middle class often talk of needing a higher SAT score than, say, an applicant who grew up on a farm, in a ghetto or in a factory town. Some state legislators from Northern Virginia's affluent suburbs have argued that this is a form of geographic discrimination and have quixotically proposed bills to outlaw it.

56   But the conventional wisdom is not quite right. The elite colleges have not been giving much of a break to the low-income students who apply. When William G. Bowen, a former president of Princeton, looked at admissions records recently, he found that if test scores were equal a low-income student had no better chance than a high-income one of getting into a group of 19 colleges, including Harvard, Yale, Princeton, Williams and Virginia. Athletes, legacy applicants and minority students all got in with lower scores on average. Poorer students did not.

57   The findings befuddled many administrators, who insist that admissions officers have tried to give poorer applicants a leg up. To emphasize the point, Virginia announced this spring that it was changing its admissions policy from "need blind"—a term long used to assure applicants that they would not be punished for seeking financial aid—to "need conscious." Administrators at Amherst and Harvard have also recently said that they would redouble their efforts to take into account the obstacles students have overcome.

58   "The same score reflects more ability when you come from a less fortunate background," Mr. Summers, the president of Harvard, said. "You haven't had a chance to take the test-prep course. You went to a school

that didn't do as good a job coaching you for the test. You came from a home without the same opportunities for learning."

59   But it is probably not a coincidence that elite colleges have not yet turned this sentiment into action. Admitting large numbers of low-income students could bring clear complications. Too many in a freshman class would probably lower the college's average SAT score, thereby damaging its ranking by *U.S. News & World Report,* a leading arbiter of academic prestige. Some colleges, like Emory University in Atlanta, have climbed fast in the rankings over precisely the same period in which their percentage of low-income students has tumbled. The math is simple: when a college goes looking for applicants with high SAT scores, it is far more likely to find them among well-off teenagers.

60   More spots for low-income applicants might also mean fewer for the children of alumni, who make up the fund-raising base for universities. More generous financial aid policies will probably lead to higher tuition for those students who can afford the list price. Higher tuition, lower ranking, tougher admission requirements: they do not make for an easy marketing pitch to alumni clubs around the country. But Mr. Casteen and his colleagues are going ahead, saying the pendulum has swung too far in one direction.

61   That was the mission of John Blackburn, Virginia's easy-going admissions dean, when he rented a car and took to the road recently. Mr. Blackburn thought of the trip as a reprise of the drives Mr. Casteen took 25 years earlier, when he was the admissions dean, traveling to churches and community centers to persuade black parents that the university was finally interested in their children.

62   One Monday night, Mr. Blackburn came to Big Stone Gap, in a mostly poor corner of the state not far from Andy Blevins's town. A community college there was holding a college fair, and Mr. Blackburn set up a table in a hallway, draping it with the University of Virginia's blue and orange flag.

63   As students came by, Mr. Blackburn would explain Virginia's new admissions and financial aid policies. But he soon realized that the Virginia name might have been scaring off the very people his pitch was intended for. Most of the students who did approach the table showed little interest in the financial aid and expressed little need for it. One man walked up to Mr. Blackburn and introduced his son as an aspiring doctor. The father was an ophthalmologist. Other doctors came by, too. So did some lawyers.

64   "You can't just raise the UVa flag," Mr. Blackburn said, packing up his materials at the end of the night, "and expect a lot of low-income kids to come out."

65   When the applications started arriving in his office this spring, there seemed to be no increase in those from low-income students. So Mr. Blackburn extended the deadline two weeks for everybody, and his colleagues also helped some applicants with the maze of financial aid forms. Of 3,100 incoming freshmen, it now seems that about 180 will qualify for the new financial aid program, up from 130 who would have done so last year. It is not a huge number, but Virginia administrators call it a start.

A Big Decision

66   On a still-dark February morning, with the winter's heaviest snowfall on the ground, Andy Blevins scraped off his Jeep and began his daily drive to the supermarket warehouse. As he passed the home of Mike Nash, his neighbor and fellow gospel singer, he noticed that the car was still in the driveway. For Mr. Nash, a school counselor and the only college graduate in the singing group, this was a snow day.

67   Mr. Blevins later sat down with his calendar and counted to 280: the number of days he had worked last year. Two hundred and eighty days— six days a week most of the time—without ever really knowing what the future would hold.

68   "I just realized I'm going to have to do something about this," he said, "because it's never going to end."

69   In the weeks afterward, his daydreaming about college and his conversations about it with his sister Leanna turned into serious research. He requested his transcripts from Radford and from Virginia Highlands Community College and figured out that he had about a year's worth of credits. He also talked to Leanna about how he could become an elementary school teacher. He always felt that he could relate to children, he said. The job would take up 180 days, not 280. Teachers do not usually get laid off or lose their pensions or have to take a big pay cut to find new work.

70   So the decision was made. On May 31, Andy Blevins says, he will return to Virginia Highlands, taking classes at night; the Gospel Gentlemen are no longer booking performances. After a year, he plans to take classes by video and on the Web that are offered at the community college but run by Old Dominion, a Norfolk, Va., university with a big group of working-class students.

71   "I don't like classes, but I've gotten so motivated to go back to school,"
Mr. Blevins said. "I don't want to, but, then again, I do."

72   He thinks he can get his bachelor's degree in three years. If he gets it
at all, he will have defied the odds.

? QUESTIONS TO CONSIDER

1. What does Leonhardt mean by "meritocracy"?

2. Why does Andy Blevins regret his decision?

3. Why do students from different economic backgrounds have different experiences in college?

4. What are some of the reasons lower-income students have a higher chance of becoming nongraduates?

5. Do you think colleges should give weight to economic class in granting admissions and admit more low-income students? Why or why not?

READINGS

Being Country

Bobbie Ann Mason

- **N** Narration
- **IE** Illustration and Exemplification
- **CC** Compare and Contrast
- **DEF** Definition

1   One day Mama and Granny were shelling beans and talking about the proper method of drying apples. I was nearly eleven and still entirely absorbed with the March girls in *Little Women*. Drying apples was not in my dreams. Beth's death was weighing darkly on me at that moment, and I threw a little tantrum—what Mama called a hissy fit.

2   "Can't y'all talk about anything but food?" I screamed.

3   There was a shocked silence. "Well, what else is there?" Granny asked.

4   Granny didn't question a woman's duties, but I did. I didn't want to be hulling beans in a hot kitchen when I was fifty years old. I wanted to *be* somebody, maybe an airline stewardess. Also, I had been listening to the radio. I had notions.

5   Our lives were haunted by the fear of crop failure. We ate as if we didn't know where our next meal might come from. All my life I have had a recurrent food dream: I face a buffet or cafeteria line, laden with beautiful foods. I spend the entire dream choosing the foods I want. My anticipation is deliciously agonizing. I always wake up just as I've made my selections but before I get to eat.

6   Working with food was fraught with anxiety and desperation. In truth, no one in memory had missed a meal—except Peyton Washam on the banks of Panther Creek wistfully regarding his seed corn. But the rumble of poor Peyton's belly must have survived to trouble our dreams. We were at the mercy of nature, and it wasn't to be trusted. My mother watched the skies at evening for a portent of the morrow. A cloud that went over and then turned around and came back was an especially bad sign. Our livelihood—even our lives—depended on forces outside our control.

7   I think this dependence on nature was at the core of my rebellion. I hated the constant sense of helplessness before vast forces, the continuous threat of failure. Farmers didn't take initiative, I began to see; they reacted to whatever presented itself. I especially hated women 's part in the dependence.

8   My mother allowed me to get spoiled. She never even tried to teach me to cook.

9   "You didn't want to learn," she says now. "You were a lady of leisure, and you didn't want to help. You had your nose in a book."

10   I believed progress meant freedom from the field and the range. That meant moving to town, I thought.

11   Because we lived on the edge of Mayfield, I was acutely conscious of being country. I felt inferior to people in town because we grew our food and made our clothes, while they bought whatever they needed. Although we were self- sufficient and resourceful and held clear title to our land, we lived in a state of psychological poverty. As I grew older, this acute sense of separation from town affected me more deeply. I began to sense that the fine life in town—celebrated in magazines, on radio, in movies—was denied us. Of course we weren't poor at all. Poor people had too many kids, and they weren't landowners; they rented decrepit little houses with plank floors and trash in the yard. "Poor people are wormy and eat wild onions," Mama said. We weren't poor, but we were country.

12   We had three wardrobes—everyday clothes, school clothes, and Sunday clothes. We didn't wear our school clothes at home, but we could wear them to town. When we got home from church, we had to change back into everyday clothes before we ate Mama's big Sunday dinner.

13   "Don't eat in your good clothes!" Mama always cried. "You'll spill something on them."

14   Mama always preferred outdoor life, but she was a natural cook. At harvest time, after she'd come in from the garden and put out a wash, she would whip out a noontime dinner for the men in the field—my father and grandfather and maybe some neighbors and a couple of hired hands: fried chicken with milk gravy, ham, mashed potatoes, lima beans, field peas, corn, slaw, sliced tomatoes, fried apples, biscuits, and peach pie. This was not considered a banquet, only plain hearty food, fuel for work. All the ingredients except the flour, sugar, and salt came from our farm— the chickens, the hogs, the milk and butter, the Irish potatoes, the beans, peas, corn, cabbage, apples, peaches. Nothing was processed, except by Mama. She was always butchering and plucking and planting and hoeing and shredding and slicing and creaming (scraping cobs for the creamed corn) and pressure-cooking and canning and freezing and thawing and mixing and shaping and baking and frying.

15   We would eat our pie right on the same plate as our turnip greens so as not to mess up another dish. The peach cobbler oozed all over the

turnip-green juice and the pork grease. "It all goes to the same place," Mama said. It was boarding-house reach, no "Pass the peas, please." Conversation detracted from the sensuous pleasure of filling yourself. A meal required meat and vegetables and dessert. The beverages were milk and iced tea ("ice-tea"). We never used napkins or ate tossed salad. Our salads were Jell-O and slaw. We ate "poke salet" and wilted lettuce. Mama picked tender, young pokeweed in the woods in the spring, before it turned poison, and cooked it a good long time to get the bitterness out. We liked it with vinegar and minced boiled eggs. Wilted lettuce was tender new lettuce, shredded, with sliced radishes and green onions, and blasted with hot bacon grease to blanch the rawness. "Too many fresh vegetables in summer gives people the scours," Daddy said.

16   Food was better in town, we thought. It wasn't plain and everyday. The centers of pleasure were there—the hamburger and barbecue places, the movie shows, all the places to buy things. Woolworth's, with the pneumatic tubes overhead rushing money along a metallic mole tunnel up to a balcony; Lochridge & Ridgway, with an engraved sign on the third-story cornice: stoves, appliances, plows. On the mezzanine at that store, I bought my first phonograph records, brittle 78s of big-band music—Woody Herman and Glenn Miller, and Glen Gray and his Casa Loma Orchestra playing "No Name Jive." A circuit of the courthouse square took you past the grand furniture stores, the two dime stores, the shoe stores, the men's stores, the ladies' stores, the banks, the drugstores. You'd walk past the poolroom and an exhaust fan would blow the intoxicating smell of hamburgers in your face. Before she bought a freezer, Mama stored meat in a rented food locker in town, near the ice company. She stored the butchered calf there, and she fetched hunks of him each week to fry. But hamburgers in town were better. They were greasier, and they came in waxed-paper packages.

17   At the corner drugstore, on the square, Mama and Janice and I sat at filigreed wrought-iron tables on a black-and-white mosaic tile floor, eating peppermint ice cream. It was very cold in there, under the ceiling fans. The ice cream was served elegantly, in paper cones sunk into black plastic holders. We were uptown.

18   The A&P grocery, a block away, reeked of the rich aroma of ground coffee. Daddy couldn't stand the smell of coffee, but Mama loved it. Daddy retched and scoffed in his exaggerated fashion. "I can't stand that smell!" Granny perked coffee, and Granddaddy told me it would turn a child black. I hated coffee. I wouldn't touch it till I was thirty. We savored

store-bought food—coconuts, pineapples, and Vienna sausages and potted meat in little cans that opened with keys. We rarely went to the uptown A&P. We usually traded at a small mom-and-pop grocery, where the proprietors slapped the hands of black children who touched the candy case. I wondered if they were black from coffee.

QUESTIONS TO CONSIDER

1. What do you think Mason means when she says, "I wanted to *be* somebody" in paragraph 4?

2. Throughout "Being Country," Mason compares and contrasts her experience of rural farm life with the appeal of glamorous town life. What is the major take away from this? Do you have a better understanding of Mason and her experiences because of it?

3. Mason writes that "food was better in town…it wasn't plain and everyday." Do you think there's a sense of irony about this statement? A sense of longing?

4. How does Mason's writing style and tone affect your understanding and opinion of the essay? How does Mason use imagery and anecdotes to get across her point? Do you think this is effective?

5. It is obvious that Mason longs for not only different surroundings, but a different lifestyle. Have you ever longed for a different lifestyle? If you have experienced a major lifestyle change, did it meet your expectations or were you left longing for the lifestyle you left behind?

READINGS

Designer Genes

Bill McKibben

- **IE** Illustration and Exemplification
- **AP** Argument and Persuasion
- **CE** Cause and Effect

1   I grew up in a household where we were very suspicious of dented cans. Dented cans were, according to my mother, a well-established gateway to botulism, and botulism was a bad thing, worse than swimming immediately after lunch. It was one of those bad things measured in extinctions, as in "three tablespoons of botulism toxin could theoretically kill every human on Earth." Or something like that.

2   So I refused to believe the early reports, a few years back, that socialites had begun injecting dilute strains of the toxin into their brows in an effort to temporarily remove the vertical furrow that appears between one's eyes as one ages. It sounded like a Monty Python routine, some clinic where they daubed your soles with plague germs to combat athlete's foot. But I was wrong to doubt. As the world now knows, Botox has become, in a few short years, a staple weapon in the cosmetic arsenal—so prevalent that, in the words of one writer, "it is now rare in certain social enclaves to see a woman over the age of thirty-five with the ability to look angry." With their facial muscles essentially paralyzed, actresses are having trouble acting; since the treatment requires periodic booster shots, doctors warn that "you could marry a woman (or a man) with a flawlessly even face and wind up with someone who four months later looks like a Shar-Pei." But never mind—now you can get Botoxed in strip mall storefronts and at cocktail parties.

3   People, in other words, will do fairly far-out things for less-than-pressing causes. And more so all the time: public approval of "aesthetic surgery" has grown fifty percent in the United States in the last decade. But why stop there? Once you accept the idea that our bodies are essentially plastic, and that it's okay to manipulate that plastic, there's no reason to think that consumers would balk because "genes" were involved instead of, say, "toxins." Especially since genetic engineering would not promote your own vanity, but instead be sold as a boon to your child.

4   The vision of genetic engineers is to do to humans what we have already done to salmon and wheat, pine trees and tomatoes. That is, to make them better in some way; to delete, modify, or add genes in developing embryos so that the cells of the resulting person will produce proteins that make them taller and more muscular, or smarter and less aggressive, maybe handsome and possibly straight. Even happy. As early as 1993, a March of Dimes poll found that forty-three percent of Americans would engage in genetic engineering "simply to enhance their children's looks or intelligence."

5   Ethical guidelines promulgated by the scientific oversight boards so far prohibit actual attempts at human genetic engineering, but researchers have walked right to the line, maybe even stuck their toes a trifle over. In the spring of 2001, for instance, a fertility clinic in New Jersey impregnated fifteen women with embryos fashioned from their own eggs, their partner's sperm, and a small portion of an egg donated by a second woman. The procedure was designed to work around defects in the would-be mother's egg—but in at least two of the cases, tests showed the resulting babies carried genetic material from all three "parents."

6   And so the genetic modification of humans is not only possible, it's coming fast; a mix of technical progress and shifting mood means it could easily happen in the next few years. Consider what happened with plants. A decade ago, university research farms were growing small plots of genetically modified grain and vegetables. Sometimes activists who didn't like what they were doing would come and rip the plants up, one by one. Then, all of a sudden in the mid-1990s, before anyone had paid any real attention, farmers had planted half the corn and soybean fields in America with transgenic seed.

7   Every time you turn your back this technology creeps a little closer. Gallops, actually, growing and spreading as fast as the internet. One moment you've sort of heard of it; the next moment it's everywhere. But we haven't done it yet. For the moment we remain, if barely, a fully human species. And so we have time yet to consider, to decide, to act. This is arguably the biggest decision humans will ever make.

8   Right up until this decade, the genes that humans carried in their bodies were exclusively the result of chance—of how the genes of the sperm and the egg, the father and the mother, combined. The only way you could intervene in the process was by choosing who you would mate with—and that was as much wishful thinking as anything else, as generation upon generation of surprised parents have discovered.

 READINGS

9   But that is changing. We now know two different methods to change human genes. The first, and less controversial, is called somatic gene therapy. Somatic gene therapy begins with an existing individual—someone with, say, cystic fibrosis. Researchers try to deliver new, modified genes to some of her cells, usually by putting the genes aboard viruses they inject into the patient, hoping that the viruses will infect the cells and thereby transmit the genes. Somatic gene therapy is, in other words, much like medicine. You take an existing patient with an existing condition, and you in essence try and convince her cells to manufacture the medicine she needs.

10   Germline genetic engineering on the other hand is something very novel indeed. "Germ" here refers not to microbes, but to the egg and sperm cells, the germ cells of the human being. Scientists intent on genetic engineering would probably start with a fertilized embryo a week or so old. They would tease apart the cells of that embryo, and then, selecting one, they would add to, delete, or modify some of its genes. They could also insert artificial chromosomes containing predesigned genes. They would then take the cell, place it inside an egg whose nucleus had been removed, and implant the resulting new embryo inside a woman. The embryo would, if all went according to plan, grow into a genetically engineered child. His genes would be pushing out proteins to meet the particular choices made by his parents, and by the companies and clinicians they were buying the genes from. Instead of coming solely from the combination of his parents, and thus the combination of their parents, and so on back through time, those genes could come from any other person, or any other plant or animal, or out of the thin blue sky. And once implanted they will pass to his children, and on into time.

11   But all this work will require one large change in our current way of doing business. Instead of making babies by making love, we will have to move conception to the laboratory. You need to have the embryo out there where you can work on it—to make the necessary copies, try to add or delete genes, and then implant the one that seems likely to turn out best. Gregory Stock, a researcher at the University of California and an apostle of the new genetic technologies, says that "the union of egg and sperm from two individuals... would be too unpredictable with intercourse." And once you've got the embryo out on the lab bench, gravity disappears altogether. "Ultimately," says Michael West, CEO of Advanced Cell Technology, the firm furthest out on the cutting edge of these technologies, "the dream of biologists is to have the sequence of DNA, the programming code of life, and to be able to edit it the way you can a document on a word processor."

12   Does it sound far-fetched? We began doing it with animals (mice) in 1978, and we've managed the trick with most of the obvious mammals, except one. Some of the first germline interventions might be semi-medical. You might, say some advocates, start by improving "visual and auditory acuity," first to eliminate nearsightedness or prevent deafness, then to "improve artistic potential." But why stop there? "If something has evolved elsewhere, then it is possible for us to determine its genetic basis and transfer it into the human genome," says Princeton geneticist Lee Silver—just as we have stuck flounder genes into strawberries to keep them from freezing, and jellyfish genes into rabbits and monkeys to make them glow in the dark.

13   But would we actually do this? Is there any real need to raise these questions as more than curiosities, or will the schemes simply fade away on their own, ignored by the parents who are their necessary consumers?

14   Anyone who has entered a baby supply store in the last few years knows that even the soberest parents can be counted on to spend virtually unlimited sums in pursuit of successful offspring. What if the "Baby Einstein" video series, which immerses "learning enabled" babies in English, Spanish, Japanese, Hebrew, German, Russian, and French, could be bolstered with a little gene- tweaking to improve memory? What if the Wombsongs prenatal music system, piping in Brahms to your waiting fetus, could be supplemented with an auditory upgrade? One sociologist told *The New York Times* we'd crossed the line from parenting to "product development," and even if that remark is truer in Manhattan than elsewhere, it's not hard to imagine what such attitudes will mean across the affluent world.

15   Here's one small example. In the 1980s, two drug companies were awarded patents to market human growth hormone to the few thousand American children suffering from dwarfism. The FDA thought the market would be very small, so HGH was given "orphan drug status," a series of special market advantages designed to reward the manufacturers for taking on such an unattractive business. But within a few years, HGH had become one of the largest-selling drugs in the country, with half a billion dollars in sales. This was not because there'd been a sharp increase in the number of dwarves, but because there'd been a sharp increase in the number of parents who wanted to make their slightly short children taller. Before long the drug companies were arguing that the children in the bottom five percent of their normal height range were in fact in need of three to five shots a week of HGH. Take elevenyear-old Marco Oriti. At

READINGS

four foot one, he was about four inches shorter than average, and project-ed to eventually top out at five foot four. This was enough to convince his parents to start on a six-day-a-week HGH regimen, which will cost them $150,000 over the next four years. "You want to give your child the edge no matter what," said his mother.

16   A few of the would-be parents out on the current cutting edge of the reproduction revolution—those who need to obtain sperm or eggs for in vitro fertilization—exhibit similar zeal. Ads started appearing in Ivy League college newspapers a few years ago: couples were willing to pay $50,000 for an egg, provided the donor was at least five feet, ten inches tall, white, and had scored 1400 on her SATs. There is, in other words, a market just waiting for the first clinic with a catalogue of ger-mline modifications, a market that two California artists proved when they opened a small boutique, Gene Genies Worldwide, in a trendy part of Pasadena. Tran Kim-Trang and Karl Mihail wanted to get people thinking more deeply about these emerging technologies, so they outfitted their store with petri dishes and models of the double helix, and printed up brochures highlighting traits with genetic links: creativity, extroversion, thrill-seeking criminality. When they opened the doors, they found peo-ple ready to shell out for designer families (one man insisted he wanted the survival ability of a cockroach). The "store" was meant to be ironic, but the irony was lost on a culture so deeply consumer that this kind of manipulation seems like the obvious next step. "Generally, people refused to believe this store was an art project," says Tran. And why not? The next store in the mall could easily have been a Botox salon.

17   But say you're not ready. Say you're perfectly happy with the prospect of a child who shares the unmodified genes of you and your partner. Say you think that manipulating the DNA of your child might be dangerous, or presumptuous, or icky? How long will you be able to hold that line if the procedure begins to spread among your neighbors? Maybe not so long as you think: if germline manipulation actually does begin, it seems likely to set off a kind of biological arms race. "Suppose parents could add thirty points to their child's IQ," asks MIT economist Lester Thurow. "Wouldn't you want to do it? And if you don't, your child will be the stupidest in the neighborhood."

18   That's precisely what it might feel like to be the parent facing the choice. Individual competition more or less defines the society we've built, and in that context love can almost be defined as giving your kids what they need to make their way in the world. Deciding not to soup them up...well, it could come to seem like child abuse.

19   Of course, the problem about arms races is that you never really get anywhere. If everyone's adding thirty IQ points, then having an IQ of one hundred fifty won't get you any closer to Stanford than you were at the outset. The very first athlete engineered to use twice as much oxygen as the next guy will be unbeatable in the Tour de France—but in no time he'll merely be the new standard. You'll have to do what he did to be in the race, but your upgrades won't put you ahead, merely back on a level playing field. You might be able to argue that society as a whole was helped, because there was more total brainpower at work, but your kid won't be any closer to the top of the pack. All you'll be able to do is guarantee she won't be left hopelessly far behind.

20   In fact, the arms-race problem has an extra ironic twist when it comes to genetic manipulation. The United States and the Soviet Union could, and did, keep adding new weapons to their arsenals over the decades. But with germline manipulation, you get only one shot; the extra chromosome you stick in your kid when he's born is the one he carries throughout his life. So let's say baby Sophie has a state-of-the-art gene job: her parents paid for the proteins discovered by, say, 2005 that, on average, yielded ten extra IQ points. By the time Sophie is five, though, scientists will doubtless have discovered ten more genes linked to intelligence. Now anyone with a platinum card can get twenty IQ points, not to mention a memory boost and a permanent wrinkle-free brow. So by the time Sophie is twenty-five and in the job market, she's already more or less obsolete— the kids coming out of college just plain have better hardware.

21   "For all his billions, Bill Gates could not have purchased a single genetic enhancement for his son Rory John," writes Gregory Stock, at the University of California. "And you can bet that any enhancements a billion dollars can buy Rory's child in 2030 will seem crude alongside those available for modest sums in 2060." It's not, he adds, "so different from upgraded software. You'll want the new release."

22   The vision of one's child as a nearly useless copy of Windows 95 should make parents fight like hell to make sure we never get started down this path. But the vision gets lost easily in the gushing excitement about "improving" the opportunities for our kids.

23   Beginning the hour my daughter came home from the hospital, I spent part of every day with her in the woods out back, showing her trees and ferns and chipmunks and frogs. One of her very first words was "birch," and you couldn't have asked for a prouder papa. She got her middle name from the mountain we see out the window; for her fifth birthday

she got her own child-sized canoe; her school wardrobe may not be re-lentlessly up-to-date but she's never lacked for hiking boots. As I write these words, she's spending her first summer at sleep-away camp, one we chose because the kids sleep in tents and spend days in the mountains. All of which is to say that I have done everything in my power to try and mold her into a lover of the natural world. That is where my deepest sat-isfactions lie, and I want the same for her. It seems benign enough, but it has its drawbacks; it means less time and money and energy for trips to the city and music lessons and so forth. As time goes on and she develops stronger opinions of her own, I yield more and more, but I keep trying to stack the deck, to nudge her in the direction that's meant something to me. On a Saturday morning, when the question comes up of what to do, the very first words out of my mouth always involve yet another hike. I can't help myself.

24   In other words, we already "engineer" our offspring in some sense of the word: we do our best, and often our worst, to steer them in particular directions. And our worst can be pretty bad. We all know people whose lives were blighted trying to meet the expectations of their parents. We've all seen the crazed devotion to getting kids into the right schools, the right professions, the right income brackets. Parents try and pass down their prejudices, their politics, their attitude toward the world ("we've got to toughen that kid up—he's going to get walked all over"). There are fa-thers who start teaching the curveball at the age of four, and sons made to feel worthless if they don't make the Little League traveling team. People move house so that their kids can grow up with the right kind of school-mates. They threaten to disown them for marrying African Americans, or for not marrying African Americans. No dictator anywhere has ever tried to rule his subjects with as much attention to detail as the average modern parent.

25   Why not take this just one small step further? Why not engineer chil-dren to up the odds that all that nudging will stick? In the words of Lee Silver, the Princeton geneticist, "Why not seize this power? Why not con-trol what has been left to chance in the past? Indeed, we control all other aspects of our children's lives and identities through powerful social and environmental influences...On what basis can we reject positive genetic influences on a person's essence when we accept the rights of parents to benefit their children in every other way?" If you can buy your kid three years at Deerfield, four at Harvard, and three more at Harvard Law, why shouldn't you be able to turbocharge his IQ a bit?

26   But most likely the answer has already occurred to you as well. Because you know plenty of people who managed to rebel successfully against whatever agenda their parents laid out for them, or who took that agenda and bent it to fit their own particular personality. In our society that's often what growing up is all about—the sometimes excruciatingly difficult, frequently liberating break with the expectations of your parents. The decision to join the Peace Corps (or, the decision to leave the commune where you grew up and go to business school). The discovery that you were happiest davening in an Orthodox shul three hours a day, much to the consternation of your good suburban parents who almost always made it to Yom Kippur services; the decision that, much as you respected the Southern Baptist piety of your parents, the Bible won't be your watchword.

27   Without the grounding offered by tradition, the search for the "authentic you" can be hard; our generations contain the first people who routinely shop religions, for instance. But the sometimes poignant difficulty of finding yourself merely underscores how essential it is. Silver says the costs of germline engineering and a college education might be roughly comparable; in both cases, he goes on, the point is to "increase the chances the child will become wiser in some way, and better able to achieve success and happiness." But that's half the story, at best. College is where you go to be exposed to a thousand new influences, ideas that should be able to take you in almost any direction. It's where you go to get out from under your parents' thumb, to find out that you actually don't have to go to law school if you don't want to. As often as not, the harder parents try and wrench their kids in one direction, the harder those kids eventually fight to determine their own destiny. I am as prepared as I can be for the possibility—the probability—that Sophie will decide she wants to live her life in the concrete heart of Manhattan. It's her life (and perhaps her kids will have a secret desire to come wander in the woods with me).

28   We try and shape the lives of our kids—to "improve" their lives, as we would measure improvement—but our gravity is usually weak enough that kids can break out of it if and when they need to. (When it isn't, when parents manage to bend their children to the point of breaking, we think of them as monstrous.) "Many of the most creative and valuable human lives are the result of particularly difficult struggles" against expectation and influence, writes the legal scholar Martha Nussbaum.

29   That's not how a genetic engineer thinks of his product. He works to ensure absolute success. Last spring an Israeli researcher announced that he had managed to produce a featherless chicken. This constituted an

READINGS

improvement, to his mind, because "it will be cheaper to produce since its lack of feathers means there is no need to pluck it before it hits the shelves." Also, poultry farmers would no longer have to ventilate their vast barns to keep their birds from overheating. "Feathers are a waste," the scientist explained. "The chickens are using feed to produce something that has to be dumped, and the farmers have to waste electricity to overcome that fact." Now, that engineer was not trying to influence his chickens to shed their feathers because they'd be happier and the farmer would be happier and everyone would be happier. He was inserting a gene that created a protein that made good and certain they would not be producing feathers. Just substitute, say, an even temperament for feathers, and you'll know what the human engineers envision.

30   "With reprogenetics," writes Lee Silver, "parents can gain complete control [emphasis mine] over their destiny, with the ability to guide and enhance the characteristics of their children, and their children's children as well." Such parents would not be calling their children on the phone at annoyingly frequent intervals to suggest that it's time to get a real job; instead, just like the chicken guy, they would be inserting genes that produced proteins that would make their child behave in certain ways throughout his life. You cannot rebel against the production of that protein. Perhaps you can still do everything in your power to defeat the wishes of your parents, but that protein will nonetheless be pumped out relentlessly into your system, defining who you are. You won't grow feathers, no matter how much you want them. And maybe they can engineer your mood enough that your lack of plumage won't even cross your mind.

31   Such children will, in effect, be assigned a goal by their programmers: "intelligence," "even temper," "athleticism." (As with chickens, the market will doubtless lean in the direction of efficiency. It may be hard to find genes for, say, dreaminess.) Now two possibilities arise. Perhaps the programming doesn't work very well, and your kid spells poorly, or turns moody, or can't hit the inside fastball. In the present world, you just tell yourself that that's who he is. But in the coming world, he'll be, in essence, a defective product. Do you still accept him unconditionally? Why? If your new Jetta got thirty miles to the gallon instead of the forty it was designed to get, you'd take it back. You'd call it a lemon. If necessary, you'd sue.

32   Or what if the engineering worked pretty well, but you decided, too late, that you'd picked the wrong package, hadn't gotten the best features? Would you feel buyer's remorse if the kid next door had a better ear, a stronger arm?

33   Say the gene work went a little awry and left you with a kid who had some serious problems; what kind of guilt would that leave you with? Remember, this is not a child created by the random interaction of your genes with those of your partner, this is a child created with specific intent. Does *Consumer Reports* start rating the various biotech offerings?

34   What if you had a second child five years after the first, and by that time the upgrades were undeniably improved: how would you feel about the first kid? How would he feel about his new brother, the latest model?

35   The other outcome—that the genetic engineering works just as you had hoped—seems at least as bad. Now your child is a product. You can take precisely as much pride in her achievements as you take in the achievements of your dishwashing detergent. It was designed to produce streak-free glassware, and she was designed to be sweet-tempered, social, and smart. And what can she take pride in? Her good grades? She may have worked hard, but she'll always know that she was spec'ed for good grades. Her kindness to others? Well, yes, it's good to be kind— but perhaps it's not much of an accomplishment once the various genes with some link to sociability have been catalogued and manipulated. I have no doubt that these qualms would be one of the powerful psychological afflictions of the future—at least until someone figures out a fix that keeps the next generations from having such bad thoughts.

36   Britain's chief rabbi, Jonathan Sacks, was asked, a few years ago, about the announcement that Italian doctors were trying to clone humans. "If there is a mystery at the heart of human condition, it is otherness: the otherness of man and woman, parent and child. It is the space we make for otherness that makes love something other than narcissism." I remember so well the feeling of walking into the maternity ward with Sue, and walking out with Sue and Sophie: where there had been two there were now, somehow, three, each of us our own person, but now commanded to make a family, a place where we all could thrive. She was so mysterious, that Sophie, and in many ways she still is. There are times when, like every parent, I see myself reflected in her, and times when I wonder if she's even related. She's ours to nurture and protect, but she is who she is. That's the mystery and the glory of any child.

37   Mystery, however, is not one of the words that thrills engineers. They try and deliver solid bridges, unyielding dams, reliable cars. We wouldn't want it any other way. The only question is if their product line should be expanded to include children.

38   Right now both the genes, and the limits that they set on us, connect us with every human that came before. Human beings can look at rock

art carved into African cliffs and French caves thirty thousand years ago and feel an electric, immediate kinship. We've gone from digging sticks to combines, and from drum circles to symphony orchestras (and back again to drum circles), but we still hear in the same range and see in the same spectrum, still produce adrenaline and dopamine in the same ways, still think in many of the same patterns. We are, by and large, the same people, more closely genetically related to one another than we may be to our engineered grandchildren.

39   These new technologies show us that human meaning dangles by a far thinner thread than we had thought. If germline genetic engineering ever starts, it will accelerate endlessly and unstoppably into the future, as individuals make the calculation that they have no choice but to equip their kids for the world that's being made. The first child whose genes come in part from some corporate lab, the first child who has been "enhanced" from what came before—that's the first child who will glance back over his shoulder and see a gap between himself and human history.

40   These would be mere consumer decisions—but that also means that they would benefit the rich far more than the poor. They would take the gap in power, wealth, and education that currently divides both our society and the world at large, and write that division into our very biology. A sixth of the American population lacks health insurance of any kind— they can't afford to go to the doctor for a checkup. And much of the rest of the world is far worse off. If we can't afford the fifty cents a person it would take to buy bed nets to protect most of Africa from malaria, it is unlikely we will extend to anyone but the top tax bracket these latest forms of genetic technology. The injustice is so obvious that even the strongest proponents of genetic engineering make little attempt to deny it. "Anyone who accepts the right of affluent parents to provide their children with an expensive private school education cannot use 'unfairness' as a reason for rejecting the use of reprogenetic technologies," says Lee Silver.

41   These new technologies, however, are not yet inevitable. Unlike global warming, this genie is not yet out of the bottle. But if germline genetic engineering is going to be stopped, it will have to happen now, before it's quite begun. It will have to be a political choice, that is—one we make not as parents but as citizens, not as individuals but as a whole, thinking not only about our own offspring but about everyone.

42   So far the discussion has been confined to a few scientists, a few philosophers, a few ideologues. It needs to spread widely, and quickly, and loudly. The stakes are absurdly high, nothing less than the meaning of being human. And given the seductions that we've seen—the intuitively

and culturally delicious prospect of a better child—the arguments against must be not only powerful but also deep. They'll need to resonate on the same intuitive and cultural level. We'll need to feel in our gut the reasons why, this time, we should tell Prometheus thanks, but no thanks.

QUESTIONS TO CONSIDER

1. What is McKibben's thesis statement? Does McKibben explicitly state his thesis or is it broadly insinuated throughout the article? Do you agree or disagree with him?

2. What are the biggest drawbacks that McKibben presents against germline genetic engineering? Do you agree with McKibben's comment that these drawbacks would have negative social consequences for both underprivileged people and society as a whole?

3. Why does McKibben compare germline genetic engineering to upgrading computer software? Do you think this analogy is effective? Why or why not?

4. Do you agree with McKibben that genetic engineering could lead to a "biological arms race"?

5. As McKibben states in his article, there are already people who are receptive to the idea of genetic engineering. Likewise, there are people who are against the idea of it as well. What is your stance on the issue? What pros and cons do you think could come from genetic engineering?

READINGS

The Way to Rainy Mountain

N. Scott Momaday

- **N** Narration
- **DES** Description
- **DEF** Definition

1   A single knoll rises out of the plain in Oklahoma, north and west of the Wichita Range. For my people, the Kiowas, it is an old landmark and they gave it the name Rainy Mountain. The hardest weather in the world is there. Winter brings blizzards, hot tornadic winds arise in the spring, and in the summer the prairie is an anvil's edge. The grass turns brittle and brown, and it cracks beneath your feet. There are green belts along the rivers and creeks, linear groves of hickory and pecan, willow and witch hazel. At a distance in July and August the steaming foliage seems almost to writhe in fire. Great green and yellow grasshoppers are everywhere in the tall grass, popping up like corn to sting the flesh, and tortoises crawl about on the earth going nowhere in plenty of time. Loneliness is an aspect of the land. All things in the plain are isolate; there is no confusion of objects in the eye, but *one* hill or *one* tree or *one* man. To look upon that landscape in the early morning, with the sun at your back, is to lose the sense of proportion. Your imagination comes to life, and this, you think, is where Creation was begun.

2   I returned to Rainy Mountain in July. My grandmother had died in the spring, and I wanted to be at her grave. She had lived to be very old and at last infirm. Her only living daughter was with her when she died, and I was told that in death her face was that of a child.

3   I like to think of her as a child. When she was born, the Kiowas were living the last great moment of their history. For more than a hundred years they had controlled the open range from the Smoky Hill River to the Red, from the head-waters of the Canadian to the fork of the Arkansas and Cimarron. In alliance with the Comanches, they had ruled the whole of the southern Plains. War was their sacred business, and they were among the finest horsemen the world has ever known. But warfare for the Kiowas was preeminently a matter of disposition rather than of survival, and they never understood the grim, unrelenting advance of the U.S. Cavalry. When at last, divided and ill-provisioned, they were driven

onto the Staked Plains in the cold rains of autumn, they fell into panic. In Palo Duro Canyon they abandoned their crucial stores to pillage and had nothing then but their lives. In order to save themselves, they surrendered to the soldiers at Fort Sill and were imprisoned in the old stone corral that now stands as a military museum. My grandmother was spared the humiliation of those high gray walls by eight or ten years, but she must have known from birth the affliction of defeat, the dark brooding of old warriors.

4   Her name was Aho, and she belonged to the last culture to evolve in North America. Her forebears came down from the high country in western Montana nearly three centuries ago. They were a mountain people, a mysterious tribe of hunters whose language has never been positively classified in any major group. In the late seventeenth century they began a long migration to the south and east. It was a journey toward the dawn, and it led to a golden age. Along the way the Kiowas were befriended by the Crows, who gave them the culture and religion of the Plains. They acquired horses, and their ancient nomadic spirit was suddenly free of the ground. They acquired Tai-me, the sacred Sun Dance doll, from that moment the object and symbol of their worship, and so shared in the divinity of the sun. Not least, they acquired the sense of destiny, therefore courage and pride. When they entered upon the southern Plains they had been transformed. No longer were they slaves to the simple necessity of survival; they were a lordly and dangerous society of fighters and thieves, hunters and priests of the sun. According to their origin myth, they entered the world through a hollow log. From one point of view, their migration was the fruit of old prophecy, for indeed they emerged from a sunless world.

5   Although my grandmother lived her long life in the shadow of Rainy Mountain, the immense landscape of the continental interior lay like memory in her blood. She could tell of the Crows, whom she had never seen, and of the Black Hills, where she had never been. I wanted to see in reality what she had seen more perfectly in the mind's eye, and traveled fifteen hundred miles to begin my pilgrimage.

6   Yellowstone, it seemed to me, was the top of the world, a region of deep lakes and dark timber, canyons and waterfalls. But, beautiful as it is, one might have the sense of confinement there. The skyline in all directions is close at hand, the high wall of the woods and deep cleavages of shade. There is a perfect freedom in the mountains, but it belongs to the eagle and the elk, the badger and the bear. The Kiowas reckoned their stature by the distance they could see, and they were bent and blind in the wilderness.

7   Descending eastward, the highland meadows are a stairway to the plain. In July the inland slope of the Rockies is luxuriant with flax and the buckwheat, stonecrop and larkspur. The earth unfolds and the limit of the land recedes. Clusters of trees, and animals grazing far in the distance, cause the vision to reach away and wonder to build upon the mind. The sun follows a longer course in the day, and the sky is immense beyond all comparison. The great billowing clouds that sail upon it are shadows that move upon the grain like water, dividing light. Farther down, in the land of the Crows and Blackfeet, the plain is yellow. Sweet clover takes hold of the hills and bends upon itself to cover and seal the soil. There the Kiowas paused on their way; they had come to the place where they must change their lives. The sun is at home on the plains. Precisely there does it have the certain character of a god. When the Kiowas came to the land of the Crows, they could see the dark lees of the hills at dawn across the Bighorn River, the profusion of light on the grain shelves, the oldest deity ranging after the solstices. Not yet would they veer southward to the caldron of the land that lay below; they must wean their blood from the northern winter and hold the mountains a while longer in their view. They bore Tai-me in procession to the east.

8   A dark mist lay over the Black Hills, and the land was like iron. At the top of a ridge I caught sight of Devil's Tower upthrust against the gray sky as if in the birth of time the core of the earth had broken through its crust and the motion of the world was begun. There are things in nature that engender an awful quiet in the heart of man; Devil's Tower is one of them. Two centuries ago, because they could not do otherwise, the Kiowas made a legend at the base of the rock. My grandmother said:

Eight children were there at play, seven sisters and their brother. Suddenly the boy was struck dumb; he trembled and began to run upon his hands and feet. His fingers became claws, and his body was covered with fur. Directly there was a bear where the boy had been. The sisters were terrified; they ran, and the bear after them. They came to the stump of a great tree, and the tree spoke to them. It bade them climb upon it, and as they did so it began to rise into the air. The bear came to kill them, but they were just beyond its reach. It reared against the tree and scored the bark all around with its claws. The seven sisters were borne into the sky, and they became the stars of the Big Dipper.

9   From that moment, and so long as the legend lives, the Kiowas have kinsmen in the night sky. Whatever they were in the mountains, they could be no more. However tenuous their well-being, however much they had suffered and would suffer again, they had found a way out of the wilderness.

10   My grandmother had a reverence for the sun, a holy regard that now is all but gone out of mankind. There was a wariness in her, and an ancient awe. She was a Christian in her later years, but she had come a long way about, and she never forgot her birthright. As a child she had been to the Sun Dances; she had taken part in those annual rites, and by them she had learned the restoration of her people in the presence of Tai-me. She was about seven when the last Kiowa Sun Dance was held in 1887 on the Washita River above Rainy Mountain Creek. The buffalo were gone. In order to consummate the ancient sacrifice—to impale the head of a buffalo bull upon the medicine tree—a delegation of old men journeyed into Texas, there to beg and barter for an animal from the Goodnight herd. She was ten when the Kiowas came together for the last time as a living Sun Dance culture. They could find no buffalo; they had to hang an old hide from the sacred tree. Before the dance could begin, a company of soldiers rode out from Fort Sill under orders to disperse the tribe. Forbidden without cause the essential act of their faith, having seen the wild herds slaughtered and left to rot upon the ground, the Kiowas backed away forever from the medicine tree. That was July 20, 1890, at the great bend of the Washita. My grandmother was there. Without bitterness, and for as long as she lived, she bore a vision of deicide.

11   Now that I can have her only in memory, I see my grandmother in the several postures that were peculiar to her: standing at the wood stove on a winter morning and turning meat in a great iron skillet; sitting at the south window, bent above her beadwork, and afterwards, when her vision failed, looking down for a long time into the fold of her hands; going out upon a cane, very slowly as she did when the weight of age came upon her; praying. I remember her most often at prayer. She made long, rambling prayers out of suffering and hope, having seen many things. I was never sure that I had the right to hear, so exclusive were they of all mere custom and company. The last time I saw her she prayed standing by the side of her bed at night, naked to the waist, the light of a kerosene lamp moving upon her dark skin. Her long, black hair, always drawn and braided in the day, lay upon her shoulders and against her breasts like a shawl. I do not speak Kiowa, and I never understood her prayers, but

there was something inherently sad in the sound, some merest hesitation upon the syllables of sorrow. She began in a high and descending pitch, exhausting her breath to silence; then again and again—and always the same intensity of effort, of something that is, and is not, like urgency in the human voice. Transported so in the dancing light among the shadows of her room, she seemed beyond the reach of time. But that was illusion; I think I knew then that I should not see her again.

12   Houses are like sentinels in the plain, old keepers of the weather watch. There, in a very little while, wood takes on the appearance of great age. All colors wear soon away in the wind and rain, and then the wood is burned gray and the grain appears and the nails turn red with rust. The windowpanes are black and opaque; you imagine there is nothing within, and indeed there are many ghosts, bones given up to the land. They stand here and there against the sky, and you approach them for a longer time than you expect. They belong in the distance; it is their domain.

13   Once there was a lot of sound in my grandmother's house, a lot of coming and going, feasting and talk. The summers there were full of excitement and reunion. The Kiowas are a summer people; they abide the cold and keep to themselves, but when the season turns and the land becomes warm and vital they cannot hold still; an old love of going returns upon them. The aged visitors who came to my grandmother's house when I was a child were made of lean and leather, and they bore themselves upright. They wore great black hats and bright ample shirts that shook in the wind. They rubbed fat upon their hair and wound their braids with strips of colored cloth. Some of them painted their faces and carried the scars of old and cherished enmities. They were an old council of warlords, come to remind and be reminded of who they were. Their wives and daughters served them well. The women might indulge themselves; gossip was at once the mark and compensation of their servitude. They made loud and elaborate talk among themselves, full of jest and gesture, fright and false alarm. They went abroad in fringed and flowered shawls, bright beadwork and German silver. They were at home in the kitchen, and they prepared meals that were banquets.

14   There were frequent prayer meetings, and great nocturnal feasts. When I was a child I played with my cousins outside, where the lamplight fell upon the ground and the singing of the old people rose up around us and carried away into the darkness. There were a lot of good things to eat, a lot of laughter and surprise. And afterwards, when the quiet returned, I lay

down with my grandmother and could hear the frogs away by the river and feel the motion of the air.

15   Now there is a funeral silence in the rooms, the endless wake of some final word. The walls have closed in upon my grandmother's house. When I returned to it in mourning, I saw for the first time in my life how small it was. It was late at night, and there was a white moon, nearly full. I sat for a long time on the stone steps by the kitchen door. From there I could see out across the land; I could see the long row of trees by the creek, the low light upon the rolling plains, and the stars of the Big Dipper. Once I looked at the moon and caught sight of a strange thing. A cricket had perched upon the handrail, only a few inches away from me. My line of vision was such that the creature filled the moon like a fossil. It had gone there, I thought, to live and die, for there, of all places, was its small definition made whole and eternal. A warm wind rose up and purled like the longing within me.

16   The next morning I awoke at dawn and went out on the dirt road to Rainy Mountain. It was already hot, and the grasshoppers began to fill the air. Still, it was early in the morning, and the birds sang out of the shadows. The long yellow grass on the mountain shone in the bright light, and a scissortail hied above the land. There, where it ought to be, at the end of a long and legendary way, was my grandmother's grave. Here and there on the dark stones were ancestral names. Looking back once, I saw the mountain and came away.

? QUESTIONS TO CONSIDER

1. How does the landscape of Rainy Mountain represent Momaday's identity?

2. What connects Momaday to his Native American heritage?

3. Explain the significance of the Big Dipper.

4. In addition to losing his grandmother, what else has Momaday lost?

5. Contrast Momaday's experience at Rainy Mountain to his grandmother's experiences.

The Maker's Eye: Revising Your Own Manuscripts

Donald M. Murray

- **IE** Illustration and Exemplification
- **CD** Classification and Division
- **PA** Process Analysis
- **A** Analogy

1   When students complete a first draft, they consider the job of writing done—and their teachers too often agree. When professional writers complete a first draft, they usually feel that they are at the start of the writing process. When a draft is completed, the job of writing can begin.

2   That difference in attitude is the difference between amateur and professional, inexperience and experience, journeyman and craftsman. Peter F. Drucker, the prolific business writer, calls his first draft "the zero draft"—after that he can start counting. Most writers share the feeling that the first draft, and all of those which follow, are opportunities to discover what they have to say and how best they can say it.

3   To produce a progression of drafts, each of which says more and says it more clearly, the writer has to develop a special kind of reading skill. In school we are taught to decode what appears on the page as finished writing. Writers, however, face a different category of possibility and responsibility when they read their own drafts. To them the words on the page are never finished. Each can be changed and rearranged, can set off a chain reaction of confusion or clarified meaning. This is a different kind of reading, which is possibly more difficult and certainly more exciting.

4   Writers must learn to be their own best enemy. They must accept the criticism of others and be suspicious of it; they must accept the praise of others and be even more suspicious of it. Writers cannot depend on others. They must detach themselves from their own pages so that they can apply both their caring and their craft to their own work.

5   Such detachment is not easy. Science-fiction writer Ray Bradbury supposedly puts each manuscript away for a year to the day and then rereads it as a stranger. Not many writers have the discipline or the time to do this. We must read when our judgment may be at its worst, when we are close to the euphoric moment of creation.

6   Then the writer, counsels novelist Nancy Hale, "should be critical of everything that seems to him most delightful in his style. He should excise

what he most admires, because he wouldn't thus admire it if he weren't... in a sense protecting it from criticism." John Ciardi, the poet, adds, "The last act of the writing must be to become one's own reader. It is, I suppose, a schizophrenic process, to begin passionately and to end critically, to begin hot and to end cold; and, more important, to be passion-hot and critic-cold at the same time."

7 Most people think that the principal problem is that writers are too proud of what they have written. Actually, a greater problem for most professional writers is one shared by the majority of students. They are overly critical, think everything is dreadful, tear up page after page, never complete a draft, see the task as hopeless.

8 The writer must learn to read critically but constructively, to cut what is bad, to reveal what is good. Eleanor Estes, the children's book author, explains: "The writer must survey his work critically, coolly, as though he were a stranger to it. He must be willing to prune, expertly and hard-heartedly. At the end of each revision, a manuscript may look... worked over, torn apart, pinned together, added to, deleted from, words changed and words changed back. Yet the book must maintain its original freshness and spontaneity."

9 Most readers underestimate the amount of rewriting it usually takes to produce spontaneous reading. This is a great disadvantage to the student writer, who sees only a finished product and never watches the craftsman who takes the necessary step back, studies the work carefully, returns to the task, steps back, returns, steps back, again and again. Anthony Burgess, one of the most prolific writers in the English-speaking world, admits, "I might revise a page twenty times." Roald Dahl, the popular children's writer, states, "By the time I'm nearing the end of a story, the first part will have been reread and altered and corrected at least 150 times...Good writing is essentially rewriting. I am positive of this."

10 Rewriting isn't virtuous. It isn't something that ought to be done. It is simply something that most writers find they have to do to discover what they have to say and how to say it. It is a condition of the writer's life.

11 There are, however, a few writers who do little formal rewriting, primarily because they have the capacity and experience to create and review a large number of invisible drafts in their minds before they approach the page. And some writers slowly produce finished pages, performing all the tasks of revision simultaneously, page by page, rather than draft by draft. But it is still possible to see the sequence followed by most writers most of the time in rereading their own work.

12   Most writers scan their drafts first, reading as quickly as possible to catch the larger problems of subject and form, and then move in closer and closer as they read and write, reread and rewrite.

13   The first thing writers look for in their drafts is *information*. They know that a good piece of writing is built from specific, accurate, and interesting information. The writer must have an abundance of information from which to construct a readable piece of writing.

14   Next writers look for *meaning* in the information. The specifics must build to a pattern of significance. Each piece of specific information must carry the reader toward meaning.

15   Writers reading their own drafts are aware of *audience*. They put themselves in the reader's situation and make sure that they deliver information which a reader wants to know or needs to know in a manner which is easily digested. Writers try to be sure that they anticipate and answer the questions a critical reader will ask when reading the piece of writing.

16   Writers make sure that the *form* is appropriate to the subject and the audience. Form, or genre, is the vehicle which carries meaning to the reader, but form cannot be selected until the writer has adequate information to discover its significance and an audience which needs or wants that meaning.

17   Once writers are sure the form is appropriate, they must then look at the *structure*, the order of what they have written. Good writing is built on a solid framework of logic, argument, narrative, or motivation which runs through the entire piece of writing and holds it together. This is the time when many writers find it most effective to outline as a way of visualizing the hidden spine by which the piece of writing is supported.

18   The element on which writers spend a majority of their time is *development*. Each section of a piece of writing must be adequately developed. It must give readers enough information so that they are satisfied. How much information is enough? That's as difficult as asking how much garlic belongs in a salad. It must be done to taste, but most beginning writers underdevelop, underestimating the reader's hunger for more information.

19   As writers solve development problems, they often have to consider questions of *dimension*. There must be a pleasing and effective proportion among all the parts of the piece of writing. There is a continual process of subtracting and adding to keep the piece of writing in balance.

20   Finally, writers have to listen to their own voices. *Voice* is the force which drives a piece of writing forward. It is an expression of the writer's

authority and concern. It is what is between the words on the page, what glues the piece of writing together. A good piece of writing is always marked by a consistent, individual voice.

21   As writers read and reread, write and rewrite, they move closer and closer to the page until they are doing line-by-line editing. Writers read their own pages with infinite care. Each sentence, each line, each clause, each phrase, each word, each mark of punctuation, each section of white space between the type has to contribute to the clarification of meaning.

22   Slowly the writer moves from word to word, looking through language to see the subject. As a word is changed, cut or added, as a construction is rearranged, all the words used before that moment and all those that follow that moment must be considered and reconsidered.

23   Writers often read aloud at this stage of the editing process, muttering or whispering to themselves, calling on the ear's experience with language. Does this sound right—or that? Writers edit, shifting back and forth from eye to page to ear to page. I find I must do this careful editing in short runs, no more than fifteen or twenty minutes at a stretch, or I become too kind with myself. I begin to see what I hope is on the page, not what actually is on the page.

24   This sounds tedious if you haven't done it, but actually it is fun. Making something right is immensely satisfying, for writers begin to learn what they are writing about by writing. Language leads them to meaning, and there is the joy of discovery, of understanding, of making meaning clear as the writer employs the technical skills of language.

25   Words have double meanings, even triple and quadruple meanings. Each word has its own potential of connotation and denotation. And when writers rub one word against the other, they are often rewarded with a sudden insight, an unexpected clarification.

26   The maker's eye moves back and forth from word to phrase to sentence to paragraph to sentence to phrase to word. The maker's eye sees the need for variety and balance, for a firmer structure, for a more appropriate form. It peers into the interior of the paragraph, looking for coherence, unity, and emphasis, which make meaning clear.

27   I learned something about this process when my first bifocals were prescribed. I had ordered a larger section of the reading portion of the glass because of my work, but even so, I could not contain my eyes within this new limit of vision. And I still find myself taking off my glasses and bending my nose toward the page, for my eyes unconsciously flick back and forth across the page, back to another page, forward to still another, as I try to see each evolving line in relation to every other line.

28   When does this process end? Most writers agree with the great Russian writer Tolstoy, who said, "I scarcely ever reread my published writings, if by chance I come across a page, it always strikes me: all this must be rewritten; this is how I should have written it."

29   The maker's eye is never satisfied, for each word has the potential to ignite new meaning. This article has been twice written all the way through the writing process, and it was published four years ago. Now it is to be republished in a book. The editors made a few small suggestions, and then I read it with my maker's eye. Now it has been re-edited, re-re-vised, re-read, and re-re-edited, for each piece of writing to the writer is full of potential and alternatives.

30   A piece of writing is never finished. It is delivered to a deadline, torn out of the typewriter on demand, sent off with a sense of accomplishment and shame and pride and frustration. If only there were a couple more days, time for just another run at it, perhaps then...

QUESTIONS TO CONSIDER

Comprehension

1. In paragraph 2, what does the writer Peter Drucker mean by "the zero draft" and why is it important for the student writer to understand?

2. In paragraphs 4 and 5, describe the significance of "detachment" to the serious writer. What does Murray mean when he asserts that "writers must learn to be their own best enemy"?

3. Which one of Murray's italicized features of writing—*information, meaning, audience, form, structure, development, dimension,* and *voice*—is most important to student writers looking to improve their work?

Rhetoric

1. What is the effect of Murray's providing so many author examples? Is it persuasive or random and confusing?

2. What does Murray mean by his expression "the maker's eye"? What does his title say about the relationship of writing to making and reading?

3. How does Murray's "bifocal" analogy work in paragraph 27? Do you think it is an effective example?

Writing

1. What would you say was some of the best advice that college students might take from Murray's essay?

2. Have your own attitudes towards revising changed over the years? What changed them, or why haven't they changed? Compare your own writing and revising process to Murray's comments and process.

Shooting an Elephant

George Orwell

- **N** Narration
- **DES** Description

- **IE** Illustration and Exemplification
- **AP** Argument and Persuasion

1   In Moulmein, in lower Burma, I was hated by large numbers of people—the only time in my life that I have been important enough for this to happen to me. I was sub-divisional police officer of the town, and in an aimless, petty kind of way anti-European feeling was very bitter. No one had the guts to raise a riot, but if a European woman went through the bazaars alone somebody would probably spit betel juice over her dress. As a police officer I was an obvious target and was baited whenever it seemed safe to do so. When a nimble Burman tripped me up on the football field and the referee (another Burman) looked the other way, the crowd yelled with hideous laughter. This happened more than once. In the end the sneering yellow faces of young men that met me everywhere, the insults hooted after me when I was at a safe distance, got badly on my nerves. The young Buddhist priests were the worst of all. There were several thousands of them in the town and none of them seemed to have anything to do except stand on street corners and jeer at Europeans.

2   All this was perplexing and upsetting. For at that time I had already made up my mind that imperialism was an evil thing and the sooner I chucked up my job and got out of it the better. Theoretically—and secretly, of course—I was all for the Burmese and all against their oppressors, the British. As for the job I was doing, I hated it more bitterly than I can perhaps make clear. In a job like that you see the dirty work of Empire at close quarters. The wretched prisoners huddling in the stinking cages of the lock-ups, the grey, cowed faces of the long-term convicts, the scarred buttocks of the men who had been Bogged with bamboos—all these oppressed me with an intolerable sense of guilt. But I could get nothing into perspective. I was young and ill-educated and I had had to think out my problems in the utter silence that is imposed on every Englishman in the East. I did not even know that the British Empire is dying, still less did I know that it is a great deal better than the younger empires that are going to supplant it. All I knew was that I was stuck between my hatred of

the empire I served and my rage against the evil-spirited little beasts who tried to make my job impossible. With one part of my mind I thought of the British Raj as an unbreakable tyranny, as something clamped down, *in saecula saeculorum*, upon the will of prostrate peoples; with another part I thought that the greatest joy in the world would be to drive a bayonet into a Buddhist priest's guts. Feelings like these are the normal by-products of imperialism; ask any Anglo-Indian official, if you can catch him off duty.

3   One day something happened which in a roundabout way was enlightening. It was a tiny incident in itself, but it gave me a better glimpse than I had had before of the real nature of imperialism—the real motives for which despotic governments act. Early one morning the sub-inspector at a police station the other end of the town rang me up on the phone and said that an elephant was ravaging the bazaar. Would I please come and do something about it? I did not know what I could do, but I wanted to see what was happening and I got on to a pony and started out. I took my rifle, an old .44 Winchester and much too small to kill an elephant, but I thought the noise might be useful *in terrorem*. Various Burmans stopped me on the way and told me about the elephant's doings. It was not, of course, a wild elephant, but a tame one which had gone "must." It had been chained up, as tame elephants always are when their attack of "must" is due, but on the previous night it had broken its chain and escaped. Its mahout, the only person who could manage it when it was in that state, had set out in pursuit, but he had taken the wrong direction and was now twelve hours' journey away, and in the morning the elephant had suddenly reappeared in the town. The Burmese population had no weapons and were quite helpless against it. It had already destroyed somebody's bamboo hut, killed a cow, and raided some fruit-stalls and devoured the stock; also it had met the municipal rubbish van, and, when the driver jumped out and took to his heels, had turned the van over and inflicted violences upon it.

4   The Burmese sub-inspector and some Indian constables were waiting for me in the quarter where the elephant had been seen. It was a very poor quarter, a labyrinth of squalid bamboo huts, thatched with palm-leaf, winding all over a steep hillside. I remember that it was a cloudy, stuffy morning at the beginning of the rains. We began questioning the people as to where the elephant had gone, and, as usual, failed to get any definite information. That is invariably the case in the East; a story always sounds clear enough at a distance, but the nearer you get to the scene of

READINGS

events the vaguer it becomes. Some of the people said that the elephant had gone in one direction, some said that he had gone in another, some professed not even to have heard of any elephant. I had almost made up my mind that the whole story was a pack of lies, when we heard yells a little distance away. There was a loud, scandalized cry of "Go away, child! Go away this instant!" and an old woman with a switch in her hand came round the corner of a hut, violently shooing away a crowd of naked children. Some more women followed, clicking their tongues and exclaiming; evidently there was something there that the children ought not to have seen. I rounded the hut and saw a man's dead body sprawling in the mud. He was an Indian, a black Dravidian coolie, almost naked, and he could not have been dead many minutes. The people said that the elephant had come suddenly upon him round the corner of the hut, caught him with its trunk, put its foot on his back, and ground him into the earth. This was the rainy season and the ground was soft, and his face had scored a trench a foot deep and a couple of yards long. He was lying on his belly with arms crucified and head sharply twisted to one side. His face was coated with mud, the eyes wide open, the teeth bared and grinning with an expression of unendurable agony. (Never tell me, by the way, that the dead look peaceful. Most of the corpses I have seen looked devilish.) The friction of the great beast's foot had stripped the skin from his back as neatly as one skins a rabbit. As soon as I saw the dead man I sent an orderly to a friend's house nearby to borrow an elephant rifle. I had already sent back the pony, not wanting it to go mad with fright and throw me if it smelled the elephant.

5   The orderly came back in a few minutes with a rifle and five cartridges, and meanwhile some Burmans had arrived and told us that the elephant was in the paddy fields below, only a few hundred yards away. As I started forward practically the whole population of the quarter flocked out of their houses and followed me. They had seen the rifle and were all shouting excitedly that I was going to shoot the elephant. They had not shown much interest in the elephant when he was merely ravaging their homes, but it was different now that he was going to be shot. It was a bit of fun to them, as it would be to an English crowd; besides, they wanted the meat. It made me vaguely uneasy. I had no intention of shooting the elephant—I had merely sent for the rifle to defend myself if necessary— and it is always unnerving to have a crowd following you. I marched down the hill, looking and feeling a fool, with the rifle over my shoulder and an ever-growing army of people jostling at my heels. At the bottom, when

you got away from the huts, there was a metalled road and beyond that a miry waste of paddy fields a thousand yards across, not yet ploughed but soggy from the first rains and dotted with coarse grass. The elephant was standing eighty yards from the road, his left side towards us. He took not the slightest notice of the crowd's approach. He was tearing up bunches of grass, beating them against his knees to clean them and stuffing them into his mouth.

6   I had halted on the road. As soon as I saw the elephant I knew with perfect certainty that I ought not to shoot him. It is a serious matter to shoot a working elephant—it is comparable to destroying a huge and costly piece of machinery—and obviously one ought not to do it if it can possibly be avoided. And at that distance, peacefully eating, the elephant looked no more dangerous than a cow. I thought then and I think now that his attack of "must" was already passing off; in which case he would merely wander harmlessly about until the mahout came back and caught him. Moreover, I did not in the least want to shoot him. I decided that I would watch him for a little while to make sure that he did not turn savage again, and then go home.

7   But at that moment I glanced round at the crowd that had followed me. It was an immense crowd, two thousand at the least and growing every minute. It blocked the road for a long distance on either side. I looked at the sea of yellow faces above the garish clothes—faces all happy and excited over this bit of fun, all certain that the elephant was going to be shot. They were watching me as they would watch a conjurer about to perform a trick. They did not like me, but with the magical rifle in my hands I was momentarily worth watching. And suddenly I realised that I should have to shoot the elephant after all. The people expected it of me and I had got to do it; I could feel their two thousand wills pressing me forward, irresistibly. And it was at this moment, as I stood there with the rifle in my hands, that I first grasped the hollowness, the futility of the white man's dominion in the East. Here was I, the white man with his gun, standing in front of the unarmed native crowd—seemingly the leading actor of the piece; but in reality I was only an absurd puppet pushed to and fro by the will of those yellow faces behind. I perceived in this moment that when the white man turns tyrant it is his own freedom that he destroys. He becomes a sort of hollow, posing dummy, the conventionalised figure of a sahib. For it is the condition of his rule that he shall spend his life in trying to impress the "natives," and so in every crisis he has got to do what the "natives" expect of him. He wears a mask, and his face grows to fit it.

I had got to shoot the elephant. I had committed myself to doing it when I sent for the rifle. A sahib has got to act like a sahib; he has got to appear resolute, to know his own mind and do definite things. To come all that way, rifle in hand, with two thousand people marching at my heels, and then to trail feebly away, having done nothing—no, that was impossible. The crowd would laugh at me. And my whole life, every white man's life in the East, was one long struggle not to be laughed at.

8   But I did not want to shoot the elephant. I watched him beating his bunch of grass against his knees, with that preoccupied grandmotherly air that elephants have. It seemed to me that it would be murder to shoot him. At that age I was not squeamish about killing animals, but I had never shot an elephant and never wanted to. (Somehow it always seems worse to kill a *large* animal.) Besides, there was the beast's owner to be considered. Alive, the elephant was worth at least a hundred pounds; dead, he would only be worth the value of his tusks—five pounds, possibly. But I had got to act quickly. I turned to some experienced-looking Burmans who had been there when we arrived, and asked them how the elephant had been behaving. They all said the same thing: he took no notice of you if you left him alone, but he might charge if you went too close to him.

9   It was perfectly clear to me what I ought to do. I ought to walk up to within, say, twenty-five yards of the elephant and test his behaviour. If he charged I could shoot, if he took no notice of me it would be safe to leave him until the mahout came back. But also I knew that I was going to do no such thing. I was a poor shot with a rifle and the ground was soft mud into which one would sink at every step. If the elephant charged and I missed him, I should have about as much chance as a toad under a steamroller. But even then I was not thinking particularly of my own skin, only the watchful yellow faces behind. For at that moment, with the crowd watching me, I was not afraid in the ordinary sense, as I would have been if I had been alone. A white man mustn't be frightened in front of "natives"; and so, in general, he isn't frightened. The sole thought in my mind was that if anything went wrong those two thousand Burmans would see me pursued, caught, trampled on, and reduced to a grinning corpse like that Indian up the hill. And if that happened it was quite probable that some of them would laugh. That would never do. There was only one alternative. I shoved the cartridges into the magazine and lay down on the road to get a better aim.

10   The crowd grew very still, and a deep, low, happy sigh, as of people who see the theatre curtain go up at last, breathed from innumerable

throats. They were going to have their bit of fun after all. The rifle was a beautiful German thing with cross-hair sights. I did not then know that in shooting an elephant one should shoot to cut an imaginary bar running from ear-hole to ear-hole. I ought, therefore, as the elephant was sideways on, to have aimed straight at his ear-hole; actually I aimed several inches in front of this, thinking the brain would be further forward.

11 When I pulled the trigger I did not hear the bang or feel the kick— one never does when a shot goes home—but heard the devilish roar of glee that went up from the crowd. In that instant, in too short a time, one would have thought, even for the bullet to get there, a mysterious, terrible change had come over the elephant. He neither stirred nor fell, but every line of his body had altered. He looked suddenly stricken, shrunken, immensely old, as though the frightful impact of the bullet had paralysed him without knocking him down. At last, after what seemed a long time—it might have been five seconds, I dare say—he sagged flabbily to his knees. His mouth slobbered. An enormous senility seemed to have settled upon him. One could have imagined him thousands of years old. I fired again into the same spot. At the second shot he did not collapse but climbed with desperate slowness to his feet and stood weakly upright, with legs sagging and head drooping. I fired a third time. That was the shot that did for him. You could see the agony of it jolt his whole body and knock the last remnant of strength from his legs. But in falling he seemed for a moment to rise, for as his hind legs collapsed beneath him he seemed to tower upwards like a huge rock toppling, his trunk reaching skyward like a tree. He trumpeted, for the first and only time. And then down he came, his belly towards me, with a crash that seemed to shake the ground even where I lay.

12 I got up. The Burmans were already racing past me across the mud. It was obvious that the elephant would never rise again, but he was not dead. He was breathing very rhythmically with long rattling gasps, his great mound of a side painfully rising and falling. His mouth was wide open—I could see far down into caverns of pale pink throat. I waited a long time for him to die, but his breathing did not weaken. Finally I fired my two remaining shots into the spot where I thought his heart must be. The thick blood welled out of him like red velvet, but still he did not die. His body did not even jerk when the shots hit him, the tortured breathing continued without a pause. He was dying, very slowly and in great agony, but in some world remote from me where not even a bullet could damage him further. I felt that I had got to put an end to that dreadful noise. It

seemed dreadful to see the great beast lying there, powerless to move and yet powerless to die, and not even to be able to finish him. I sent back for my small rifle and poured shot after shot into his heart and down his throat. They seemed to make no impression. The tortured gasps continued as steadily as the ticking of a clock.

13   In the end I could not stand it any longer and went away. I heard later that it took him half an hour to die. Burmans were bringing dahs and baskets even before I left, and I was told they had stripped his body almost to the bones by the afternoon.

14   Afterwards, of course, there were endless discussions about the shooting of the elephant. The owner was furious, but he was only an Indian and could do nothing. Besides, legally I had done the right thing, for a mad elephant has to be killed, like a mad dog, if its owner fails to control it. Among the Europeans opinion was divided. The older men said I was right, the younger men said it was a damn shame to shoot an elephant for killing a coolie, because an elephant was worth more than any damn Coringhee coolie. And afterwards I was very glad that the coolie had been killed; it put me legally in the right and it gave me a sufficient pretext for shooting the elephant. I often wondered whether any of the others grasped that I had done it solely to avoid looking a fool.

QUESTIONS TO CONSIDER

1. Does Orwell have the freedom to choose whether or not to shoot the elephant? Why or why not?

2. At what point in the story is Orwell committed to shooting the elephant?

3. What is the significance of describing the elephant's death in such detail?

4. Why do the people want the elephant shot?

5. Explain Orwell's rapport with the Burmans.

A Note to Young Immigrants

Mitali Perkins

- **AP** Argument and Persuasion
- **DES** Description
- **IE** Illustration and Exemplification

- **CE** Cause and Effect
- **DEF** Definition

1   Be ready: You lose a lot once you're tossed into the mainstream. You lose a place that feels like home, a community where the basics are understood, where conversations can begin at a deeper level. No easy havens await you, no places to slip into with a sigh of relief, saying, "At last, a place where everybody is like me." In the neighborhood, you're like a pinch of chili tossed into a creamy pot. You lose the sharpness of your ethnic flavor quickly but find that you can never fully dissolve.

2   You lose the ability to forget about race. You're aware of it everywhere in town, like a woman aware of her gender in a roomful of men. You dodge stereotypes at school by underperforming or overachieving. You wonder if you're invisible to the opposite sex because you're foreign or because you're unattractive.

3   You lose a language. You still speak your parents' language, but it will soon begin to feel foreign to lips, pen and mind. Your heart won't forget as quickly; it will reserve a space for this mother tongue, your instructor of emotion, whispered in love and hurled in anger. Your heart language will speak words that tremble through tears; it will join you with others in the camaraderie of uncontrollable laughter. In your new language, English, you enjoy the lyrical cadence of poetry and glimpse the depth of ancient epics, but your heart will remain insatiable.

4   You lose the advantage of parents who can interpret the secrets of society. Your friends learn the art of conversation, the habits of mealtimes, the nuances of relationships, even the basics of bathroom behavior, from their parents. Your own parents' social etiquette sometimes leads to confusion or embarrassment in the outside world. You begin to take on the responsibility of buffering your parents from a culture that is even more foreign to them. You translate this new world's secrets for them.

5   You lose the stabilizing power of traditions. The year is not punctuated by rituals your grandmother and great-grandmother celebrated. Holidays in this new place lack the power to evoke nostalgia and renew

childlike wonder. Your parents' feasts of celebration fall on days when you have to go to school.

6   You lose the chance to disappear into the majority anywhere in your new world. In the new neighborhood, you draw reactions common to minorities—outright racism, patronizing tokenism, enthusiasm from curious culture-seekers. If you travel across the seas to neighborhoods where your parents grew up, you're greeted with curious, appraising stares. You're too tall or too short; you move your arms and hips differently when you walk; you smile too often or not often enough; you employ the confusing nonverbal gestures from another world.

7   But don't get discouraged. In fact, you should feel quite the opposite. There is good news about life in the melting pot. There are gains to offset the losses, if you manage not to melt away altogether. You're boiled down, refined to your own distinctiveness. You realize early that virtues are not the property of one heritage; you discover a self powerful enough to balance the best of many worlds.

8   A part of you rises above the steamy confusion of diversity to glimpse the common and universal. You recognize the ache that makes us all feel like strangers, even in the middle of comfortable homogeneity. You understand the soul's craving for a real home because yours is never sated with a counterfeit version.

9   So take time to mourn your losses, but remember to revel in the gains. Learn to embrace a litany of genuine labels—words like *stranger, pilgrim, sojourner, wayfarer*. Stride past the lure of false destinations, intent on traveling to a place where, at last, everyone can feel at home.

[2005]

? QUESTIONS TO CONSIDER

1. Perkins discusses several items that get lost when immigrants assimilate into a new land. List 3–5 characteristics that are lost. How might losing these characteristics impact the person?

2. Perkins writes about what is lost when immigrants assimilate to mainstream culture. Write about a time when you had to sacrifice a part of your identity to fit into mainstream culture. What was sacrificed? Did you regret the decision? Explain.

3. What is one family tradition or ritual you would prefer not to lose? Explain.

4. To balance the losses about which he writes, what gains does the author suggest might also be available to young immigrants?

5. Perkins suggests in paragraphs 3 and 6 that race is a consideration for immigrants. How aware of race or ethnicity are you in your day-to-day life? Explain.

6. Do you believe assimilating into mainstream culture for immigrants is overemphasized in the general public? Explain.

7. Perkins cites several descriptions throughout the essay. Which descriptions are the most effective? Explain.

8. The bulk of the essay is told in second person "you" voice. Do you believe this was effective? Why or why not? Would the essay be more or less effective if written in first person (I) or third person (she or they) point of view?

The Allegory of the Cave

Plato

- **AP** Argument and Persuasion
- **IE** Illustration and Exemplification
- **CC** Compare and Contrast
- **A** Analogy
- **CE** Cause and Effect

The Allegory of the Cave is found in Book IV of Plato's The Republic, *his dialogues on justice, society, and rulers (especially the philosopher kings who rule Plato's Utopian city of Kallipolis).*

The following selection is taken from the Benjamin Jowett translation (Vintage, 1991), pp. 253–261.

1 [Socrates] And now, I said, let me show in a figure how far our nature is enlightened or unenlightened:—Behold! human beings living in a underground cave, which has a mouth open towards the light and reaching all along the cave; here they have been from their childhood, and have their legs and necks chained so that they cannot move, and can only see before them, being prevented by the chains from turning round their heads. Above and behind them a fire is blazing at a distance, and between the fire and the prisoners there is a raised way; and you will see, if you look, a low wall built along the way, like the screen which marionette players have in front of them, over which they show the puppets.

2 [Glaucon] I see.

3 [Socrates] And do you see, I said, men passing along the wall carrying all sorts of vessels, and statues and figures of animals made of wood and stone and various materials, which appear over the wall? Some of them are talking, others silent.

4 [Glaucon] You have shown me a strange image, and they are strange prisoners.

5 [Socrates] Like ourselves, I replied; and they see only their own shadows, or the shadows of one another, which the fire throws on the opposite wall of the cave?

6 [Glaucon] True, he said; how could they see anything but the shadows if they were never allowed to move their heads?

7 [Socrates] And of the objects which are being carried in like manner they would only see the shadows?

8 [Glaucon] Yes, he said.

9   [Socrates] And if they were able to converse with one another, would they not suppose that they were naming what was actually before them?

10   [Glaucon] Very true.

11   [Socrates] And suppose further that the prison had an echo which came from the other side, would they not be sure to fancy when one of the passers-by spoke that the voice which they heard came from the passing shadow?

12   [Glaucon] No question, he replied.

13   [Socrates] To them, I said, the truth would be literally nothing but the shadows of the images.

14   [Glaucon] That is certain.

15   [Socrates] And now look again, and see what will naturally follow if the prisoners are released and disabused of their error. At first, when any of them is liberated and compelled suddenly to stand up and turn his neck round and walk and look towards the light, he will suffer sharp pains; the glare will distress him, and he will be unable to see the realities of which in his former state he had seen the shadows; and then conceive some one saying to him, that what he saw before was an illusion, but that now, when he is approaching nearer to being and his eye is turned towards more real existence, he has a clearer vision,—what will be his reply? And you may further imagine that his instructor is pointing to the objects as they pass and requiring him to name them,—will he not be perplexed? Will he not fancy that the shadows which he formerly saw are truer than the objects which are now shown to him?

16   [Glaucon] Far truer.

17   [Socrates] And if he is compelled to look straight at the light, will he not have a pain in his eyes which will make him turn away to take refuge in the objects of vision which he can see, and which he will conceive to be in reality clearer than the things which are now being shown to him?

18   [Glaucon] True, he said.

19   [Socrates] And suppose once more, that he is reluctantly dragged up a steep and rugged ascent, and held fast until he's forced into the presence of the sun himself, is he not likely to be pained and irritated? When he approaches the light his eyes will be dazzled, and he will not be able to see anything at all of what are now called realities.

20   [Glaucon] Not all in a moment, he said.

21   [Socrates] He will require to grow accustomed to the sight of the upper world. And first he will see the shadows best, next the reflections of men and other objects in the water, and then the objects themselves; then

he will gaze upon the light of the moon and the stars and the spangled heaven; and he will see the sky and the stars by night better than the sun or the light of the sun by day?

22   [Glaucon] Certainly.

23   [Socrates] Last of all he will be able to see the sun, and not mere reflections of him in the water, but he will see him in his own proper place, and not in another; and he will contemplate him as he is.

24   [Glaucon] Certainly.

25   [Socrates] He will then proceed to argue that this is he who gives the season and the years, and is the guardian of all that is in the visible world, and in a certain way the cause of all things which he and his fellows have been accustomed to behold?

26   [Glaucon] Clearly, he said, he would first see the sun and then reason about him.

27   [Socrates] And when he remembered his old habitation, and the wisdom of the cave and his fellow-prisoners, do you not suppose that he would felicitate himself on the change, and pity them?

28   [Glaucon] Certainly, he would.

29   [Socrates] And if they were in the habit of conferring honors among themselves on those who were quickest to observe the passing shadows and to remark which of them went before, and which followed after, and which were together; and who were therefore best able to draw conclusions as to the future, do you think that he would care for such honors and glories, or envy the possessors of them? Would he not say with Homer, *"Better to be the poor servant of a poor master, and to endure anything, rather than think as they do and live after their manner?"*

30   [Glaucon] Yes, he said, I think that he would rather suffer anything than entertain these false notions and live in this miserable manner.

31   [Socrates] Imagine once more, I said, such a one coming suddenly out of the sun to be replaced in his old situation; would he not be certain to have his eyes full of darkness?

32   [Glaucon] To be sure, he said.

33   [Socrates] And if there were a contest, and he had to compete in measuring the shadows with the prisoners who had never moved out of the cave, while his sight was still weak, and before his eyes had become steady (and the time which would be needed to acquire this new habit of sight might be very considerable) would he not be ridiculous? Men would say of him that up he went and down he came without his eyes; and that it was better not even to think of ascending; and if any one tried to loose

another and lead him up to the light, let them only catch the offender, and they would put him to death.

34   [Glaucon] No question, he said.

35   [Socrates] This entire allegory, I said, you may now append, dear Glaucon, to the previous argument; the prison-house is the world of sight, the light of the fire is the sun, and you will not misapprehend me if you interpret the journey upwards to be the ascent of the soul into the intellectual world according to my poor belief, which, at your desire, I have expressed—whether rightly or wrongly God knows. But, whether true or false, my opinion is that in the world of knowledge the idea of good appears last of all, and is seen only with an effort; and, when seen, is also inferred to be the universal author of all things beautiful and right, parent of light and of the lord of light in this visible world, and the immediate source of reason and truth in the intellectual; and that this is the power upon which he who would act rationally, either in public or private life must have his eye fixed.

36   [Glaucon] I agree, he said, as far as I am able to understand you.

37   [Socrates] Moreover, I said, you must not wonder that those who attain to this beatific vision are unwilling to descend to human affairs; for their souls are ever hastening into the upper world where they desire to dwell; which desire of theirs is very natural, if our allegory may be trusted.

38   [Glaucon] Yes, very natural.

39   [Socrates] And is there anything surprising in one who passes from divine contemplations to the evil state of man, misbehaving himself in a ridiculous manner; if, while his eyes are blinking and before he has become accustomed to the surrounding darkness, he is compelled to fight in courts of law, or in other places, about the images or the shadows of images of justice, and is endeavoring to meet the conceptions of those who have never yet seen absolute justice?

40   [Glaucon] Anything but surprising, he replied.

41   [Socrates] Any one who has common sense will remember that the bewilderments of the eyes are of two kinds, and arise from two causes, either from coming out of the light or from going into the light, which is true of the mind's eye, quite as much as of the bodily eye; and he who remembers this when he sees any one whose vision is perplexed and weak, will not be too ready to laugh; he will first ask whether that soul of man has come out of the brighter light, and is unable to see because unaccustomed to the dark, or having turned from darkness to the day is dazzled by excess of light. And he will count the one happy in his condition and

 READINGS

state of being, and he will pity the other; or, if he have a mind to laugh at the soul which comes from below into the light, there will be more reason in this than in the laugh which greets him who returns from above out of the light into the cave.

42   [Glaucon] That, he said, is a very just distinction.

43   [Socrates] But then, if I am right, certain professors of education must be wrong when they say that they can put a knowledge into the soul which was not there before, like sight into blind eyes.

44   [Glaucon] They undoubtedly say this, he replied.

45   [Socrates] Whereas, our argument shows that the power and capacity of learning exists in the soul already; and that just as the eye was unable to turn from darkness to light without the whole body, so too the instrument of knowledge can only by the movement of the whole soul be turned from the world of becoming into that of being, and learn by degrees to endure the sight of being, and of the brightest and best of being, or in other words, of the good.

46   [Glaucon] Very true.

47   [Socrates] And must there not be some art which will effect conversion in the easiest and quickest manner; not implanting the faculty of sight, for that exists already, but has been turned in the wrong direction, and is looking away from the truth?

48   [Glaucon] Yes, he said, such an art may be presumed.

49   [Socrates] And whereas the other so-called virtues of the soul seem to be akin to bodily qualities, for even when they are not originally innate they can be implanted later by habit and exercise, the virtue of wisdom more than anything else contains a divine element which always remains, and by this conversion is rendered useful and profitable; or, on the other hand, hurtful and useless. Did you never observe the narrow intelligence flashing from the keen eye of a clever rogue—how eager he is, how clearly his paltry soul sees the way to his end; he is the reverse of blind, but his keen eyesight is forced into the service of evil, and he is mischievous in proportion to his cleverness.

50   [Glaucon] Very true, he said.

51   [Socrates] But what if there had been a circumcision of such natures in the days of their youth; and they had been severed from those sensual pleasures, such as eating and drinking, which, like leaden weights, were attached to them at their birth, and which drag them down and turn the vision of their souls upon the things that are below—if, I say, they had been released from these impediments and turned in the opposite direction,

the very same faculty in them would have seen the truth as keenly as they see what their eyes are turned to now.

52   [Glaucon] Very likely.

53   [Socrates] Yes, I said; and there is another thing which is likely, or rather a necessary inference from what has preceded, that neither the uneducated and uninformed of the truth, nor yet those who never make an end of their education, will be able ministers of State; not the former, because they have no single aim of duty which is the rule of all their ac- tions, private as well as public; nor the latter, because they will not act at all except upon compulsion, fancying that they are already dwelling apart in the islands of the blest.

54   [Glaucon] Very true, he replied.

55   [Socrates] Then, I said, the business of us who are the founders of the State will be to compel the best minds to attain that knowledge which we have already shown to be the greatest of all—they must continue to ascend until they arrive at the good; but when they have ascended and seen enough we must not allow them to do as they do now.

56   [Glaucon] What do you mean?

57 [Socrates] I mean that they remain in the upper world: but this must not be allowed; they must be made to descend again among the prisoners in the cave, and partake of their labors and honors, whether they are worth having or not.

58   [Glaucon] But is not this unjust? he said; ought we to give them a worse life, when they might have a better?

59   [Socrates] You have again forgotten, my friend, I said, the intention of the legislator, who did not aim at making any one class in the State happy above the rest; the happiness was to be in the whole State, and he held the citizens together by persuasion and necessity, making them benefactors of the State, and therefore benefactors of one another; to this end he cre- ated them, not to please themselves, but to be his instruments in binding up the State.

60   [Glaucon] True, he said, I had forgotten.

61   [Socrates] Observe, Glaucon, that there will be no injustice in com- pelling our philosophers to have a care and providence of others; we shall explain to them that in other States, men of their class are not obliged to share in the toils of politics: and this is reasonable, for they grow up at their own sweet will, and the government would rather not have them. Being self-taught, they cannot be expected to show any gratitude for a culture which they have never received. But we have brought you into

the world to be rulers of the hive, kings of yourselves and of the other citizens, and have educated you far better and more perfectly than they have been educated, and you are better able to share in the double duty. Wherefore each of you, when his turn comes, must go down to the general underground abode, and get the habit of seeing in the dark. When you have acquired the habit, you will see ten thousand times better than the inhabitants of the cave, and you will know what the several images are, and what they represent, because you have seen the beautiful and just and good in their truth. And thus our State which is also yours will be a reality, and not a dream only, and will be administered in a spirit unlike that of other States, in which men fight with one another about shadows only and are distracted in the struggle for power, which in their eyes is a great good. Whereas the truth is that the State in which the rulers are most reluctant to govern is always the best and most quietly governed, and the State in which they are most eager, the worst.

62   [Glaucon] Quite true, he replied.

63   [Socrates] And will our pupils, when they hear this, refuse to take their turn at the toils of State, when they are allowed to spend the greater part of their time with one another in the heavenly light?

64   [Glaucon] Impossible, he answered; for they are just men, and the commands which we impose upon them are just; there can be no doubt that every one of them will take office as a stern necessity, and not after the fashion of our present rulers of State.

65   [Socrates] Yes, my friend, I said; and there lies the point. You must contrive for your future rulers another and a better life than that of a ruler, and then you may have a well-ordered State; for only in the State which offers this, will they rule who are truly rich, not in silver and gold, but in virtue and wisdom, which are the true blessings of life. Whereas if they go to the administration of public affairs, poor and hungering after their own private advantage, thinking that hence they are to snatch the chief good, order there can never be; for they will be fighting about office, and the civil and domestic broils which thus arise will be the ruin of the rulers themselves and of the whole State.

66   [Glaucon] Most true, he replied.

67   [Socrates] And the only life which looks down upon the life of political ambition is that of true philosophy. Do you know of any other?

68   [Glaucon] Indeed, I do not, he said.

69   [Socrates] And those who govern ought not to be lovers of the task? For, if they are, there will be rival lovers, and they will fight.

70   [Glaucon] No question.

71   [Socrates] Who then are those whom we shall compel to be guardians? Surely they will be the men who are wisest about affairs of State, and by whom the State is best administered, and who at the same time have other honors and another and a better life than that of politics?

72   [Glaucon] They are the men, and I will choose them, he replied.

73   [Socrates] And now shall we consider in what way such guardians will be produced, and how they are to be brought from darkness to light,—as some are said to have ascended from the world below to the gods?

74   [Glaucon] By all means, he replied.

75   [Socrates] The process, I said, is not the turning over of an oyster-shell, but the turning round of a soul passing from a day which is little better than night to the true day of being, that is, the ascent from below, which we affirm to be true philosophy?

76   [Glaucon] Quite so.

QUESTIONS TO CONSIDER

1. What is the meaning behind Plato's allegory?

2. Why do the prisoners believe that the shadows are real? Are they wrong?

3. How do the other prisoners react to what the escaped prisoner tells them about the outside world? Why?

4. How does Plato's allegory relate to today's media?

5. Have you ever changed your opinion about a particular topic? Was it easy to change your thinking? What brought about this change?

Sex Ed

Anna Quindlen

- **IE** Illustration and Exemplification
- **DEF** Definition
- **AP** Argument and Persuasion
- **CE** Cause and Effect

1   Several years ago I spent the day at a family planning clinic in one of New York City's poorest neighborhoods. I sat around a Formica table with a half dozen sixteen-year-old girls and listened with some amazement as they showed off their knowledge of human sexuality.

2   They knew how long sperm lived inside the body, how many women out of a hundred using a diaphragm were statistically likely to get pregnant and the medical term for the mouth of the cervix. One girl pointed out all the parts of the female reproductive system on a placard; another recited the stages of the ovulation cycle from day one to twenty-eight. There was just one problem with this performance: Although the results of their laboratory tests would not be available for fifteen more minutes, every last one of them was pregnant.

3   I always think of that day when someone suggests that sex education at school is a big part of the answer to the problem of teenage pregnancy. I happen to be a proponent of such programs; I think human sexuality is a subject for dispassionate study, like civics and ethics and dozens of other topics that have a moral component. I'd like my sons to know as much as possible about how someone gets pregnant, how pregnancy can be avoided, and what it means when avoidance techniques have failed.

4   I remember adolescence about as vividly as I remember anything, however, and I am not in the least convinced that that information alone will significantly alter the rate of teenage pregnancy. It seemed to me that day in the clinic, and on days I spent at schools and on street corners, that teenage pregnancy has a lot more to do with what it means to be a teenager than with how someone gets pregnant. When I was in high school, at the tail end of the sixties, there was a straightforward line on sex among my friends. Boys could have it; girls couldn't. A girl who was not a virgin pretended she was. A girl who was sleeping with her boyfriend, no matter how long-playing the relationship, pretended she was not.

5   It is the nature of adolescence that there is no past and no future, only the present, burning as fierce, bright, and merciless as a bare light bulb. Girls had sex with boys because nothing seemed to matter except right now, not pregnancy, not parental disapprobation, nothing but those minutes, this dance, that face, those words. Most of them knew that pregnancy could result, but they assured themselves that they would be the lucky ones who would not get caught. Naturally, some of them were wrong, and in my experience they did one of three things: They went to Puerto Rico for a mysterious weekend trip; visited an aunt in some faraway state for three months and came back with empty eyes and a vague reputation; or got married, quickly, in Empire-waist dresses.

6   What seems to have changed most since then is that there is little philosophical counterpoint, hypocritical or not, to the raging hormones of adolescence, and that so many of the once-hidden pregnancies are hidden no more.

7   Not long after the day at the family planning clinic, I went to a public high school in the suburbs. In the girl's room was this graffito: Jennifer Is a Virgin. I asked the kids about it and they said it was shorthand for geek, nerd, weirdo, somebody who was so incredibly out of it that they were in high school and still hadn't had sex. If you were a virgin, they told me, you just lied about it so that no one would think you were that immature. The girls in the family planning clinic told me much the same thing— that everyone did it, that the boys wanted it, that not doing it made them seem out of it. The only difference, really, was that the girls in the clinic were poor and would have their babies, and the girls in the high school were well-to-do and would have abortions. Pleasure didn't seem to have very much to do with sex for either group. After she learned she was pregnant, one of the girls at the clinic said, without a trace of irony, that she hoped childbirth didn't hurt as much as sex had. Birth control was easily disposed of in both cases. The pill, the youngsters said, could give you a stroke; the IUD could make you sterile. A diaphragm was disgusting.

8   One girl told me the funniest thing her boyfriend—a real original thinker—had told her: They couldn't use condoms because it was like taking a shower with a raincoat on. She was a smart girl and pretty, and I wanted to tell her that it sounded as if she was sleeping with a jerk who didn't deserve her. But that is the kind of basic fact of life that must be taught not in the classroom, not by a stranger, but at home by the family. It is this that, finally, I will try to teach my sons about sex, after I've explained fertile periods and birth control and all the other mechanics

that are important to understand but never really go to the heart of the matter: I believe I will say that when you sleep with someone you take off a lot more than your clothes.

QUESTIONS TO CONSIDER

1. What are Quindlen's thoughts about sex education? Does she approve or disapprove? Do you agree or disagree with her?

2. The last line of the article says that "when you sleep with someone you take off a lot more than your clothes." What do you think this means? How does it relate to the rest of the article?

3. In the last paragraph, Quindlen states that certain areas of sex education should be taught by family members instead of in a classroom. What are your thoughts on this statement?

4. Do you think the examples Quindlen gives throughout the essay are effective? How do they help underscore the thesis of the essay?

5. Quindlen states that she believes sex education is important to discuss in the classroom as it relates to teenage pregnancy and sexuality. What do you think are the advantages and disadvantages of sex education courses? Do you think sex education can help reduce the problem of teen pregnancy?

Why the Rich Are Getting Richer, and the Poor, Poorer

Robert B. Reich

- **IE** Illustration and Exemplification
- **CC** Compare and Contrast
- **CD** Classification and Division
- **AP** Argument and Persuasion
- **PA** Process Analysis

1   Regardless of how your job is officially classified (manufacturing, service, managerial, technical, secretarial, and so on), or the industry in which you work (automotive, steel, computer, advertising, finance, food processing), your real competitive position in the world economy is coming to depend on the function you perform in it. Herein lies the basic reason why incomes are diverging. The fortunes of routine producers are declining. In-person servers are also becoming poorer, although their fates are less clear-cut. But symbolic analysts—who solve, identify, and broker new problems—are, by and large, succeeding in the world economy.

2   All Americans used to be in roughly the same economic boat. Most rose or fell together as the corporations in which they were employed, the industries comprising such corporations, and the national economy as a whole became more productive—or languished. But national borders no longer define our economic fates. We are now in different boats, one sinking rapidly, one sinking more slowly, and the third rising steadily.

3   The boat containing routine producers is sinking rapidly. Recall that by midcentury routine production workers in the United States were paid relatively well. The giant pyramid-like organizations at the core of each major industry coordinated their prices and investments—avoiding the harsh winds of competition and thus maintaining healthy earnings. Some of these earnings, in turn, were reinvested in new plants and equipment (yielding ever-larger-scale economies); another portion went to top managers and investors. But a large and increasing portion went to middle managers and production workers. Work stoppages posed such a threat to high-volume production that organized labor was able to exact an ever-larger premium for its cooperation. And the pattern of wages established within the core corporations influenced the pattern throughout the national economy. Thus the growth of a relatively affluent middle class, able to purchase all the wondrous things produced in high volume by the core corporations.

4   But, as has been observed, the core is rapidly breaking down into global webs which earn their largest profits from clever problem-solving, -identifying, and brokering. As the costs of transporting standard things and of communicating information about them continue to drop, profit margins on high-volume, standardized production are thinning, because there are few barriers to entry. Modern factories and state-of-the-art machinery can be installed almost anywhere on the globe. Routine producers in the United States, then, are in direct competition with millions of routine producers in other nations. Twelve thousand people are added to the world's population every hour, most of whom, eventually, will happily work for a small fraction of the wages of routine producers in America.

5   The consequence is clearest in older, heavy industries, where high-volume, standardized production continues its ineluctable move to where labor is cheapest and most accessible around the world. Thus, for example, the Maquiladora factories cluttered along the Mexican side of the U.S. border in the sprawling shanty towns of Tijuana, Mexicali, Nogales, Agua Prieta, and Ciudad Juarez—factories owned mostly by Americans, but increasingly by Japanese—in which more than a half million routine producers assemble parts into finished goods to be shipped into the United States.

6   The same story is unfolding worldwide. Until the late 1970s, AT&T had depended on routine producers in Shreveport, Louisiana, to assemble standard telephones. It then discovered that routine producers in Singapore would perform the same tasks at a far lower cost. Facing intense competition from other global webs, AT&T's strategic brokers felt compelled to switch. So in the early 1980s they stopped hiring routine producers in Shreveport and began hiring cheaper routine producers in Singapore. But under this kind of pressure for ever-lower high-volume production costs, today's Singaporean can easily end up as yesterday's Louisianan. By the late 1980s, AT&T's strategic brokers found that routine producers in Thailand were eager to assemble telephones for a small fraction of the wages of routine producers in Singapore. Thus, in 1989, AT&T stopped hiring Singaporeans to make telephones and began hiring even cheaper routine producers in Thailand.

7   The search for ever lower wages has not been confined to heavy industry. Routine data processing is equally footloose. Keypunch operators located anywhere around the world can enter data into computers, linked by satellite or transoceanic fiber-optic cable, and take it out again. As the rates charged by satellite networks continue to drop, and as more

satellites and fiber-optic cables become available (reducing communication costs still further), routine data processors in the United States
find themselves in ever more direct competition with their counterparts
abroad, who are often eager to work for far less.

8   By 1990, keypunch operators in the United States were earning, at
most, $6.50 per hour. But keypunch operators throughout the rest of
the world were willing to work for a fraction of this. Thus, many potential American data-processing jobs were disappearing, and the wages
and benefits of the remaining ones were in decline. Typical was Saztec
International, a $20-million-a-year data-processing firm headquartered
in Kansas City, whose American strategic brokers contracted with routine
data processors in Manila and with American-owned firms that needed
such data-processing services. Compared with the average Philippine
income of $1,700 per year, data-entry operators working for Saztec earn
the princely sum of $2,650. The remainder of Saztec's employees were
American problem-solvers and -identifiers, searching for ways to improve
the worldwide system and find new uses to which it could be put.

9   By 1990, American Airlines was employing over 1,000 data processors in Barbados and the Dominican Republic to enter names and flight
numbers from used airline tickets (flown daily to Barbados from airports
around the United States) into a giant computer bank located in Dallas.
Chicago publisher R. R. Donnelley was sending entire manuscripts
to Barbados for entry into computers in preparation for printing. The
New York Life Insurance Company was dispatching insurance claims to
Castleisland, Ireland, where routine producers, guided by simple directions, entered the claims and determined the amounts due, then instantly
transmitted the computations back to the United States. (When the firm
advertised in Ireland for twenty-five data-processing jobs, it received six
hundred applications.) And McGraw-Hill was processing subscription
renewal and marketing information for its magazines in nearby Galway.
Indeed, literally millions of routine workers around the world were receiving information, converting it into computer-readable form, and then
sending it back—at the speed of electronic impulses—whence it came.

10   The simple coding of computer software has also entered into world
commerce. India, with a large English-speaking population of technicians
happy to do routine programming cheaply, is proving to be particularly attractive to global webs in need of this service. By 1990, Texas Instruments
maintained a software development facility in Bangalore, linking fifty
Indian programmers by satellite to TI's Dallas headquarters. Spurred by

READINGS

this and similar ventures, the Indian government was building a teleport in Poona, intended to make it easier and less expensive for many other firms to send their routine software design specifications for coding.

11   This shift of routine production jobs from advanced to developing nations is a great boon to many workers in such nations who otherwise would be jobless or working for much lower wages. These workers, in turn, now have more money with which to purchase symbolic-analytic services from advanced nations (often embedded within all sorts of complex products). The trend is also beneficial to everyone around the world who can now obtain high-volume, standardized products (including information and software) more cheaply than before.

12   But these benefits do not come without certain costs. In particular the burden is borne by those who no longer have good-paying routine production jobs within advanced economies like the United States. Many of these people used to belong to unions or at least benefited from prevailing wage rates established in collective bargaining agreements. But as the old corporate bureaucracies have flattened into global webs, bargaining leverage has been lost. Indeed, the tacit national bargain is no more.

13   Despite the growth in the number of new jobs in the United States, union membership has withered. In 1960, 35 percent of all nonagricultural workers in America belonged to a union. But by 1980 that portion had fallen to just under a quarter, and by 1989 to about 17 percent. Excluding government employees, union membership was down to 13.4 percent. This was a smaller proportion even than in the early 1930s, before the National Labor Relations Act created a legally protected right to labor representation. The drop in membership has been accompanied by a growing number of collective bargaining agreements to freeze wages at current levels, reduce wage levels of entering workers, or reduce wages overall. This is an important reason why the long economic recovery that began in 1982 produced a smaller rise in unit labor costs than any of the eight recoveries since World War l—the low rate of unemployment during its course notwithstanding.

14   Routine production jobs have vanished fastest in traditional unionized industries (autos, steel, and rubber, for example), where average wages have kept up with inflation. This is because the jobs of older workers in such industries are protected by seniority; the youngest workers are the first to be laid off. Faced with a choice of cutting wages or cutting the number of jobs, a majority of union members (secure in the knowledge that there are many who are junior to them who will be laid off first) often have voted for the latter.

15   Thus the decline in union membership has been most striking among young men entering the work force without a college education. In the early 1950s, more than 40 percent of this group joined unions; by the late 1980s, less than 20 percent (if public employees are excluded, less than 10 percent). In steelmaking, for example, although many older workers remained employed, almost half of all routine steelmaking jobs in America vanished between 1974 and 1988 (from 480,000 to 260,000). Similarly with automobiles: During the 1980s, the United Auto Workers lost 500,000 members—one-third of their total at the start of the decade. General Motors alone cut 150,000 American production jobs during the 1980s (even as it added employment abroad). Another consequence of the same phenomenon: The gap between the average wages of unionized and nonunionized workers widened dramatically—from 14.6 percent in 1973 to 20.4 percent by end of the 1980s. The lesson is clear. If you drop out of high school or have no more than a high school diploma, do not expect a good routine production job to be awaiting you.

16   Also vanishing are lower- and middle-level management jobs involving routine production. Between 1981 and 1986, more than 780,000 foremen, supervisors, and section chiefs lost their jobs through plant closings and layoffs. Large numbers of assistant division heads, assistant directors, assistant managers, and vice presidents also found themselves jobless. GM shed more than 40,000 white-collar employees and planned to eliminate another 25,000 by the mid-1990s. As America's core pyramids metamorphosed into global webs, many middle-level routine producers were as obsolete as routine workers on the line.

17   As has been noted, foreign-owned webs are hiring some Americans to do routine production in the United States. Philips, Sony, and Toyota factories are popping up all over—to the self-congratulatory applause of the nation's governors and mayors, who have lured them with promises of tax abatements and new sewers, among other amenities. But as these ebullient politicians will soon discover, the foreign-owned factories are highly automated and will become far more so in years to come. Routine production jobs account for a small fraction of the cost of producing most items in the United States and other advanced nations, and this fraction will continue to decline sharply as computer-integrated robots take over. In 1977, it took routine producers thirty-five hours to assemble an automobile in the United States; it is estimated that by the mid-1990s, Japanese-owned factories in America will be producing finished automobiles using only eight hours of a routine producer's time.

READINGS

18   The productivity and resulting wages of American workers who run
such robotic machinery may be relatively high, but there may not be
many such jobs to go around. A case in point: In the late 1980s, Nippon
Steel joined with America's ailing Inland Steel to build a new $400 million
cold-rolling mill fifty miles west of Gary, Indiana. The mill was celebrated
for its state-of-the-art technology, which cut the time to produce a coil of
steel from twelve days to about one hour. In fact, the entire plant could
be run by a small team of technicians, which became clear when Inland
subsequently closed two of its old cold-rolling mills, laying off hundreds
of routine workers. Governors and mayors take note: Your much-bally-
hooed foreign factories may end up employing distressingly few of your
constituents.

19   Overall, the decline in routine jobs has hurt men more than women.
This is because the routine production jobs held by men in high-volume
metal-bending manufacturing industries had paid higher wages than the
routine production jobs held by women in textiles and data processing.
As both sets of jobs have been lost, American women in routine production have gained more equal footing with American men—equally poor
footing, that is. This is a major reason why the gender gap between male
and female wages began to close during the 1980s.

20   The second of the three boats, carrying in-person servers, is sinking
as well, but somewhat more slowly and unevenly. Most in-person servers
are paid at or just slightly above the minimum wage and many work only
part-time, with the result that their take-home pay is modest, to say the
least. Nor do they typically receive all the benefits (health care, life insurance, disability, and so forth) garnered by routine producers in large manufacturing corporations or by symbolic analysts affiliated with the more
affluent threads of global webs. In-person servers are sheltered from the
direct effects of global competition and, like everyone else, benefit from
access to lower-cost products from around the world. But they are not
immune to its indirect effects.

21   For one thing, in-person servers increasingly compete with former
routine production workers, who, no longer able to find well-paying routine production jobs, have few alternatives but to seek in-person service
jobs. The Bureau of Labor Statistics estimates that of the 2.8 million manufacturing workers who lost their jobs during the early 1980s, fully one-
third were rehired in service jobs paying at least 20 percent less. In-person
servers must also compete with high school graduates and dropouts who
years before had moved easily into routine production jobs but no longer
can. And if demographic predictions about the American work force in

the first decades of the twenty-first century are correct (and they are likely to be, since most of the people who will comprise the work force are already identifiable), most new entrants into the job market will be black or Hispanic men, or women—groups that in years past have possessed relatively weak technical skills. This will result in an even larger number of people crowding into in-person services. Finally, in-person servers will be competing with growing numbers of immigrants, both legal and illegal, for whom in-person services will comprise the most accessible jobs. (It is estimated that between the mid-1980s and the end of the century, about a quarter of all workers entering the American labor force will be immigrants.)

22   Perhaps the fiercest competition that in-person servers face comes from labor-saving machinery (much of it invented, designed, fabricated, or assembled in other nations, of course). Automated tellers, computerized cashiers, automatic car washes, robotized vending machines, self-service gasoline pumps, and all similar gadgets substitute for the human beings that customers once encountered. Even telephone operators are fast disappearing, as electronic sensors and voice simulators become capable of carrying on conversations that are reasonably intelligent and always polite. Retail sales workers—among the largest groups of in-person servers—are similarly imperiled. Through personal computers linked to television screens, tomorrow's consumers will be able to buy furniture, appliances, and all sorts of electronic toys from their living rooms—examining the merchandise from all angles, selecting whatever color, size, special features, and price seem most appealing, and then transmitting the order instantly to warehouses from which the selections will be shipped directly to their homes. So, too, with financial transactions, airline and hotel reservations, rental car agreements, and similar contracts, which will be executed between consumers in their homes and computer banks somewhere else on the globe.

23   Advanced economies like the United States will continue to generate sizable numbers of new in-person service jobs, of course, the automation of older ones notwithstanding. For every bank teller who loses her job to an automated teller, three new jobs open for aerobics instructors. Human beings, it seems, have an almost insatiable desire for personal attention. But the intense competition nevertheless ensures that the wages of in-person servers will remain relatively low. In-person servers—working on their own, or else dispersed widely amid many small establishments, filling all sorts of personal-care niches—cannot readily organize themselves into labor unions or create powerful lobbies to limit the impact of such competition.

24   In two respects, demographics will work in favor of in-person servers, buoying their collective boat slightly. First, as has been noted, the rate of growth of the American work force is slowing. In particular, the number of young workers is shrinking. Between 1985 and 1995, the number of the eighteen- to twenty-four-year-olds will have declined by 17.5 percent. Thus, employers will have more incentive to hire and train in-person servers whom they might previously have avoided. But this demographic relief from the competitive pressures will be only temporary. The cumulative procreative energies of the postwar baby-boomers (born between 1946 and 1964) will result in a new surge of workers by 2010 or thereabouts. And immigration—both legal and illegal—shows every sign of increasing in years to come.

25   Next, by the second decade of the twenty-first century, the number of Americans aged sixty-five and over will be rising precipitously, as the baby-boomers reach retirement age and live longer. Their life expectancies will lengthen not just because fewer of them will have smoked their way to their graves and more will have eaten better than their parents, but also because they will receive all sorts of expensive drugs and therapies designed to keep them alive—barely. By 2035, twice as many Americans will be elderly as in 1988, and the number of octogenarians is expected to triple. As these decaying baby-boomers ingest all the chemicals and receive all the treatments, they will need a great deal of personal attention. Millions of deteriorating bodies will require nurses, nursing-home operators, hospital administrators, orderlies, home-care providers, hospice aides, and technicians to operate and maintain all the expensive machinery that will monitor and temporarily stave off final disintegration. There might even be a booming market for euthanasia specialists. In-person servers catering to the old and ailing will be in strong demand.

26   One small problem: the decaying baby-boomers will not have enough money to pay for these services. They will have used up their personal savings years before. Their Social Security payments will, of course, have been used by the government to pay for the previous generation's retirement and to finance much of the budget deficits of the 1980s. Moreover, with relatively fewer young Americans in the population, the supply of housing will likely exceed the demand, with the result that the boomers' major investments—their homes—will be worth less (in inflation-adjusted dollars) when they retire than they planned for. In consequence, the huge cost of caring for the graying boomers will fall on many of the same people who will be paid to care for them. It will be like a great sump pump:

In-person servers of the twenty-first century will have an abundance of health-care jobs, but a large portion of their earnings will be devoted to Social Security payments and income taxes, which will in turn be used to pay their salaries. The net result: No real improvement in their standard of living.

27   The standard of living of in-person servers also depends, indirectly, on the standard of living of the Americans they serve who are engaged in world commerce. To the extent that *these* Americans are richly reward-ed by the rest of the world for what they contribute, they will have more money to lavish upon in-person services. Here we find the only form of "trickle-down" economics that has a basis in reality. A waitress in a town whose major factory has just been closed is unlikely to earn a high wage or enjoy much job security; in a swank resort populated by film producers and banking moguls, she is apt to do reasonably well. So, too, with na-tions. In-person servers in Bangladesh may spend their days performing roughly the same tasks as in-person servers in the United States, but have a far lower standard of living for their efforts. The difference comes in the value that their customers add to the world economy.

28   Unlike the boats of routine producers and in-person servers, howev-er, the vessel containing America's symbolic analysts is rising. Worldwide demand for their insights is growing as the ease and speed of commu-nicating them steadily increases. Not every symbolic analyst is rising as quickly or as dramatically as every other, of course; symbolic analysts at the low end are barely holding their own in the world economy. But sym-bolic analysts at the top are in such great demand worldwide that they have difficulty keeping track of all their earnings. Never before in history has opulence on such a scale been gained by people who have earned it, and done so legally.

29   Among symbolic analysts in the middle range are American sci-entists and researchers who are busily selling their discoveries to glob-al enterprise webs. They are not limited to American customers. If the strategic brokers in General Motors' headquarters refuse to pay a high price for a new means of making high-strength ceramic engines dreamed up by a team of engineers affiliated with Carnegie Mellon University in Pittsburgh, the strategic brokers of Honda or Mercedes-Benz are likely to be more than willing.

30   So, too, with the insights of America's ubiquitous management consultants, which are being sold for large sums to eager entrepreneurs in Europe and Latin America. Also, the insights of America's energy

consultants, sold for even larger sums to Arab sheikhs. American design engineers are providing insights to Olivetti, Mazda, Siemens, and other global webs; American marketers, techniques for learning what world-wide consumers will buy; American advertisers, ploys for ensuring that they actually do. American architects are issuing designs and blueprints for opera houses, art galleries, museums, luxury hotels, and residential complexes in the world's major cities; American commercial proper-ty developers, marketing these properties to worldwide investors and purchasers.

31   Americans who specialize in the gentle art of public relations are in demand by corporations, governments, and politicians in virtually ev-ery nation. So, too, are American political consultants, some of whom, at this writing, are advising the Hungarian Socialist Party, the remnant of Hungary's ruling Communists, on how to salvage a few parliamenta-ry seats in the nation's first free election in more than forty years. Also at this writing, a team of American agricultural consultants is advising the managers of a Soviet farm collective employing 1,700 Russians eighty miles outside Moscow. As noted, American investment bankers and law-yers specializing in financial circumnavigations are selling their insights to Asians and Europeans who are eager to discover how to make large amounts of money by moving large amounts of money.

32   Developing nations, meanwhile, are hiring American civil engineers to advise on building roads and dams. The present thaw in the Cold War will no doubt expand these opportunities. American engineers from Bechtel (a global firm notable for having employed both Caspar Weinberger and George Shultz for much larger sums than either earned in the Reagan administration) have begun helping the Soviets design and install a new generation of nuclear reactors. Nations also are hir-ing American bankers and lawyers to help them renegotiate the terms of their loans with global banks, and Washington lobbyists to help them with Congress, the Treasury, the World Bank, the IMF, and other politi-cally sensitive institutions. In fits of obvious desperation, several nations emerging from communism have even hired American economists to teach them about capitalism.

33   Almost everyone around the world is buying the skills and insights of Americans who manipulate oral and visual symbols—musicians, sound engineers, film producers, makeup artists, directors, cinematographers, actors and actresses, boxers, scriptwriters, songwriters, and set design-ers. Among the wealthiest of symbolic analysts are Steven Spielberg, Bill

Cosby, Charles Schulz, Eddie Murphy, Sylvester Stallone, Madonna, and other star directors and performers—who are almost as well known on the streets of Dresden and Tokyo as in the Back Bay of Boston. Less well rewarded but no less renowned are the unctuous anchors on Turner Broadcasting's Cable News, who appear daily, via satellite, in places ranging from Vietnam to Nigeria. Vanna White is the world's most-watched game-show hostess. Behind each of these familiar faces is a collection of American problem-solvers, -identifiers, and brokers who train, coach, advise, promote, amplify, direct, groom, represent, and otherwise add value to their talents.

34   There are also the insights of senior American executives who occupy the world headquarters of global "American" corporations and the national or regional headquarters of global "foreign" corporations. Their insights are duly exported to the rest of the world through the webs of global enterprise. IBM does not export many machines from the United States, for example. Big Blue makes machines all over the globe and services them on the spot. Its prime American exports are symbolic and analytic. From IBM's world headquarters in Armonk, New York, emanate strategic brokerage and related management services bound for the rest of the world. In return, IBM's top executives are generously rewarded.

35   The most important reason for this expanding world market and increasing global demand for the symbolic and analytic insights of Americans has been the dramatic improvement in worldwide communication and transportation technologies. Designs, instructions, advice, and visual and audio symbols can be communicated more and more rapidly around the globe, with ever-greater precision and at ever-lower cost. Madonna's voice can be transported to billions of listeners, with perfect clarity, on digital compact discs. A new invention emanating from engineers in Battelle's laboratory in Columbus, Ohio, can be sent almost anywhere via modem, in a form that will allow others to examine it in three dimensions through enhanced computer graphics. When face-to-face meetings are still required—and videoconferencing will not suffice—it is relatively easy for designers, consultants, advisers, artists, and executives to board supersonic jets and, in a matter of hours, meet directly with their worldwide clients, customers, audiences, and employees.

36   With rising demand comes rising compensation. Whether in the form of licensing fees, fees for service, salaries, or shares in final profits, the economic result is much the same. There are also nonpecuniary rewards. One of the best-kept secrets among symbolic analysts is that so

many of them enjoy their work. In fact, much of it does not count as work at all, in the traditional sense. The work of routine producers and in-person servers is typically monotonous; it causes muscles to tire or weaken and involves little independence or discretion. The "work" of symbolic analysts, by contrast, often involves puzzles, experiments, games, a significant amount of chatter, and substantial discretion over what to do next. Few routine producers or in-person servers would "work" if they did not need to earn the money. Many symbolic analysts would "work" even if money were no object.

37   At midcentury, when America was a national market dominated by core pyramid-shaped corporations, there were constraints on the earnings of people at the highest rungs. First and most obviously, the market for their services was largely limited to the borders of the nation. In addition, whatever conceptual value they might contribute was small relative to the value gleaned from large scale—and it was dependent on large scale for whatever income it was to summon. Most of the problems to be identified and solved had to do with enhancing the efficiency of production and improving the flow of materials, parts, assembly, and distribution. Inventors searched for the rare breakthrough revealing an entirely new product to be made in high volume; management consultants, executives, and engineers thereafter tried to speed and synchronize its manufacture, to better achieve scale efficiencies; advertisers and marketers sought then to whet the public's appetite for the standard item that emerged. Since white-collar earnings increased with larger scale, there was considerable incentive to expand the firm; indeed, many of America's core corporations grew far larger than scale economies would appear to have justified.

38   By the 1990s, in contrast, the earnings of symbolic analysts were limited neither by the size of the national market nor by the volume of production of the firms with which they were affiliated. The marketplace was worldwide, and conceptual value was high relative to value added from scale efficiencies.

39   There had been another constraint on high earnings, which also gave way by the 1990s. At midcentury, the compensation awarded to top executives and advisors of the largest of America's core corporations could not be grossly out of proportion to that of low-level production workers. It would be unseemly for executives who engaged in highly visible rounds of bargaining with labor unions, and who routinely responded to government requests to moderate prices, to take home wages and benefits wildly

in excess of what other Americans earned. Unless white-collar executives restrained themselves, moreover, blue-collar production workers could not be expected to restrain their own demands for higher wages. Unless both groups exercised restraint, the government could not be expected to forbear from imposing direct controls and regulations.

40   At the same time, the wages of production workers could not be allowed to sink too low, lest there be insufficient purchasing power in the economy. After all, who would buy all the goods flowing out of American factories if not American workers? This, too, was part of the tacit bargain struck between American managers and their workers.

41   Recall the oft-repeated corporate platitude of the era about the chief executive's responsibility to carefully weigh and balance the interests of the corporation's disparate stakeholders. Under the stewardship of the corporate statesman, no set of stakeholders—least of all white-collar executives—was to gain a disproportionately large share of the benefits of corporate activity; nor was any stakeholder—especially the average worker—to be left with a share that was disproportionately small. Banal though it was, this idea helped to maintain the legitimacy of the core American corporation in the eyes of most Americans, and to ensure continued economic growth.

42   But by the 1990s, these informal norms were evaporating, just as (and largely because) the core American corporation was vanishing. The links between top executives and the American production worker were fading: An ever-increasing number of subordinates and contractees were foreign, and a steadily growing number of American routine producers were working for foreign-owned firms. An entire cohort of middle-level managers, who had once been deemed "white collar," had disappeared; and, increasingly, American executives were exporting their insights to global enterprise webs.

43   As the American corporation itself became a global web almost indistinguishable from any other, its stakeholders were turning into a large and diffuse group, spread over the world. Such global stakeholders were less visible, and far less noisy, than national stakeholders. And as the American corporation sold its goods and services all over the world, the purchasing power of American workers became far less relevant to its economic survival.

44   Thus have the inhibitions been removed. The salaries and benefits of America's top executives, and many of their advisers and consultants, have soared to what years before would have been unimaginable heights, even as those of other Americans have declined.

? QUESTIONS TO CONSIDER

1. What does Reich mean when he says that Americans used to be in "roughly the same economic boat"? What impact does this have on economic inequality?

2. What impact has globalization had on "routine producers"? What are the advantages and disadvantages of the shift in routine production jobs from advanced to developing nations?

3. What is the reason for the decline in union membership? What is the result of this decline?

4. According to Reich, who are "in-person servers," and what impact will aging baby boomers have on them? Who are "symbolic analysts" and why are they thriving in the current economy?

5. How does visibility influence the salaries and benefits of America's top executives? Why?

Family Values

Richard Rodriguez

- **N** Narration
- **DEF** Definition
- **CD** Classification and Division

- **AP** Argument and Persuasion
- **CE** Cause and Effect

1   I am sitting alone in my car, in front of my parents' house—a middle-aged man with a boy's secret to tell. What words will I use to tell them? I hate the word *gay*, find its little affirming sparkle more pathetic than assertive. I am happier with the less polite *queer*. But to my parents I would say *homosexual*, avoiding the Mexican slang *joto* (I had always heard it said in our house with hints of condescension), though *joto* is less mocking than the sissy-boy *maricon*.

2   The buzz on everyone's lips now: Family values. The other night on TV, the vice president of the United States, his arm around his wife, smiled into the camera and described homosexuality as "mostly a choice." But how would he know? Homosexuality never felt like a choice to me.

3   A few minutes ago Rush Limbaugh, the radio guy with a voice that reminds me, for some reason, of a butcher's arms, was banging his console and booming a near-reasonable polemic about family values. Limbaugh was not very clear about which values exactly he considers to be family values. A divorced man who lives alone in New York?

4   My parents live on a gray, treeless street in San Francisco not far from the ocean. Probably more than half of the neighborhood is immigrant. India lives next door to Greece, who lives next door to Russia. I wonder what the Chinese lady next door to my parents makes of the politicians' phrase *family values.*

5   What immigrants know, what my parents certainly know, is that when you come to this country, you risk losing your children. The assurance of family—continuity, inevitability—is precisely what America encourages its children to overturn. *Become your own man.* We who are native to this country know this too, of course, though we are likely to deny it. Only a society so guilty about its betrayal of family would tolerate the pieties of politicians regarding family values.

6   On the same summer day that Republicans were swarming in Houston (buzzing about family values), a friend of mine who escaped family values awhile back and who now wears earrings resembling intra-uterine devices, was complaining to me over coffee about the Chinese. The Chinese will never take over San Francisco, my friend said, because the Chinese do not want to take over San Francisco. The Chinese do not even *see* San Francisco! All they care about is their damn families. All they care about is double-parking smack in front of the restaurant on Clement Street and pulling granny out of the car—and damn anyone who happens to be in the car behind them or the next or the next.

7   Politicians would be horrified by such an American opinion, of course. But then, what do politicians, Republicans or Democrats, really know of our family life? Or what are they willing to admit? Even in that area where they could reasonably be expected to have something to say— regarding the relationship of family life to our economic system—the politicians say nothing. Republicans celebrate American economic free-dom, but Republicans don't seem to connect that economic freedom to the social breakdown they find appalling. Democrats, on the other hand, if more tolerant of the drift from familial tradition, are suspicious of the very capitalism that creates social freedom.

8   How you become free in America: Consider the immigrant. He gets a job. Soon he is earning more money than his father ever made (his father's authority is thereby subtly undermined). The immigrant begins living a life his father never knew. The immigrant moves from one job to another, changes houses. His economic choices determine his home address—not the other way around. The immigrant is on his way to becoming his own man.

9   When I was broke a few years ago and trying to finish a book, I lived with my parents. What a thing to do! A major theme of America is leaving home. We trust the child who forsakes family connections to make it on his own. We call that the making of a man.

10   Let's talk about this man stuff for a minute. America's ethos is anti-domestic. We may be intrigued by blood that runs through wealth—the Kennedys or the Rockefellers—but they seem European to us. Which is to say, they are movies. They are Corleones. Our real pledge of allegiance: We say in America that nothing about your family—your class, your race, your pedigree—should be as important as what you yourself achieve. We end up in 1992 introducing ourselves by first names.

11   What authority can Papa have in a country that formed its identity in an act of Oedipal rebellion against a mad British king? Papa is a joke in

America, a stock sitcom figure—Archie Bunker or Homer Simpson. But my Mexican father went to work every morning, and he stood in a white smock, making false teeth, oblivious of the shelves of grinning false teeth mocking his devotion.

12   The nuns in grammar school—my wonderful Irish nuns—used to push Mark Twain on me. I distrusted Huck Finn, he seemed like a gringo kid I would steer clear of in the schoolyard. (He was too confident.) I realize now, of course, that Huck is the closest we have to a national hero. We trust the story of a boy who has no home and is restless for the river. (Huck's Pap is drunk.) Americans are more forgiving of Huck's wildness than of the sweetness of the Chinese boy who walks to school with his mama or grandma. (There is no worse thing in America than to be a mama's boy, nothing better than to be a real boy—all boy—like Huck, who eludes Aunt Sally, and is eager for the world of men.)

13   There's a bent old woman coming up the street. She glances nervously as she passes my car. What would you tell us, old lady, of family values in America?

14   America is an immigrant country, we say. Motherhood—parenthood—is less our point than adoption. If I had to assign gender to America, I would note the consensus of the rest of the world. When America is burned in effigy, a male is burned. Americans themselves speak of Uncle Sam.

15   Like the Goddess of Liberty, Uncle Sam has no children of his own. He steals children to make men of them, mocks all reticence, all modesty, all memory. Uncle Sam is a hectoring Yankee, a skinflint uncle, gaunt, uncouth, unloved. He is the American Savonarola—hater of moonshine, destroyer of stills, burner of cocaine. Sam has no patience with mamas' boys.

16   You betray Uncle Sam by favoring private over public life, by seeking to exempt yourself, by cheating on your income taxes, by avoiding jury duty, by trying to keep your boy on the farm.

17   Mothers are traditionally the guardians of the family—against America—though even Mom may side with America against queers and deserters, at least when the Old Man is around. Premature gray hair. Arthritis in her shoulders. Bowlegged with time, red hands. In their fiercely flowered housedresses, mothers are always smarter than fathers in America. But in reality they are betrayed by their children who leave. In a thousand ways. They end up alone.

18   We kind of like the daughter who was a tomboy. Remember her? It was always easier to be a tomboy in America than a sissy. Americans

admired Annie Oakley more than they admired Liberace (who, nevertheless, always remembered his mother). But today we do not admire Annie
Oakley when we see Mom becoming Annie Oakley.

19   The American household now needs two incomes, everyone says.
Meaning: Mom is *forced* to leave home out of economic necessity. But lots
of us know lots of moms who are sick and tired of being mom, or only
mom. It's like the nuns getting fed up, teaching kids for all those years and
having those kids grow up telling stories of how awful Catholic school
was! Not every woman in America wants her life's work to be forgiveness.
Today there are moms who don't want their husbands' names. And the
most disturbing possibility: What happens when Mom doesn't want to be
Mom at all? Refuses pregnancy?

20   Mom is only becoming an American like the rest of us. Certainly, people all over the world are going to describe the influence of feminism on
women (all over the world) as their "Americanization." And rightly so.

21   Nothing of this, of course, will the politician's wife tell you. The politician's
wife is careful to follow her husband's sentimental reassurances that
nothing has changed about America except perhaps for the sinister influence of deviants. Like myself.

22   I contain within myself an anomaly at least as interesting as the
Republican Party's version of family values. I am a homosexual Catholic, a
communicant in a tradition that rejects even as it upholds me.

23   I do not count myself among those Christians who proclaim themselves protectors of family values. They regard me as no less an enemy of
the family than the "radical feminists." But the joke about families that all
homosexuals know is that we are the ones who stick around and make
families possible. Call on us. I can think of 20 or 30 examples. A gay son
or daughter is the only one who is "free" (married brothers and sisters
are too busy). And, indeed, because we have admitted the inadmissible
about ourselves (that we are queer)—we are adepts at imagination—we
can even imagine those who refuse to imagine us. We can imagine Mom's
loneliness, for example. If Mom needs to be taken to church or to the
doctor or ferried between Christmas dinners, depend on the gay son or
lesbian daughter.

24   I won't deny that the so-called gay liberation movement, along with
feminism, undermined the heterosexual household, if that's what politicians mean when they say family values. Against churchly reminders that
sex was for procreation, the gay bar as much as the birth-control pill taught
Americans not to fear sexual pleasure. In the past two decades—and, not

coincidentally, parallel to the feminist movement—the gay liberation movement moved a generation of Americans toward the idea of a childless adulthood. If the women's movement was ultimately more concerned about getting out of the house and into the workplace, the gay movement was in its way more subversive to Puritan America because it stressed the importance of play.

25   Several months ago, the society editor of the morning paper in San Francisco suggested (on a list of "must haves") that every society dame must have at least one gay male friend. A ballet companion. A lunch date. The remark was glib and incorrect enough to beg complaints from homosexual readers, but there was a truth about it as well. Homosexual men have provided women with an alternate model of masculinity. And the truth: The Old Man, God bless him, is a bore. Thus are we seen as preserving marriages? Even Republican marriages?

26   For myself, homosexuality is a deep brotherhood but does not involve domestic life. Which is why, my married sisters will tell you, I can afford the time to be a writer. And why are so many homosexuals such wonderful teachers and priests and favorite aunts, if not because we are freed from the house? On the other hand, I know lots of homosexual couples (male and female) who model their lives on the traditional heterosexual version of domesticity and marriage. Republican politicians mock the notion of a homosexual marriage, but ironically such marriages honor the heterosexual marriage by imitating it.

27   "The only loving couples I know," a friend of mine recently remarked, "are all gay couples."

28   This woman was not saying that she does not love her children or that she is planning a divorce. But she was saying something about the sadness of American domestic life: the fact that there is so little joy in family intimacy. Which is perhaps why gossip (public intrusion into the private) has become a national industry. All day long, in forlorn houses, the television lights up a freakish parade of husbands and mothers-in-law and children upon the stage of Sally or Oprah or Phil. They tell on each other. The audience ooohhhs. Then a psychiatrist-shaman appears at the end to dispense prescriptions—the importance of family members granting one another more "space."

29   The question I desperately need to ask you is whether we Americans have ever truly valued the family. We are famous, or our immigrant ancestors were famous, for the willingness to leave home. And it is ironic that a crusade under the banner of family values has been taken up by those who would otherwise pass themselves off as patriots. For they seem not

READINGS

to understand America, nor do I think they love the freedoms America grants. Do they understand why, in a country that prizes individuality and is suspicious of authority, children are disinclined to submit to their parents? You cannot celebrate American values in the public realm without expecting them to touch our private lives. As Barbara Bush remarked recently, family values are also neighborhood values. It may be harmless enough for Barbara Bush to recall a sweeter America— Midland, Texas, in the 1950s. But the question left begging is why we chose to leave Midland, Texas. Americans like to say that we can't go home again. The truth is that we don't want to go home again, don't want to be known, recognized. Don't want to respond in the same old ways. (And you know you will if you go back there.)

30   Little 10-year-old girls know that there are reasons for getting away from the family. They learn to keep their secrets—under lock and key—addressed to Dear Diary. Growing up queer, you learn to keep secrets as well. In no place are those secrets more firmly held than within the family house. You learn to live in closets. I know a Chinese man who arrived in America about 10 years ago. He got a job and made some money. And during that time he came to confront his homosexuality. And then his family arrived. I do not yet know the end of this story.

31   The genius of America is that it permits children to leave home, it permits us to become different from our parents. But the sadness, the loneliness of America, is clear too.

32   Listen to the way Americans talk about immigrants. If, on the one hand, there is impatience when today's immigrants do not seem to give up their family, there is also a fascination with this reluctance. In Los Angeles, Hispanics are considered people of family. Hispanic women are hired to be at the center of the American family—to babysit and diaper, to cook and to clean and to ease the dying. Hispanic attachment to family is seen by many Americans, I think, as the reason why Hispanics don't get ahead. But if Asians privately annoy us for being so family oriented, they are also stereotypically celebrated as the new "whiz kids" in school. Don't Asians go to college, after all, to honor their parents?

33   More important still is the technological and economic ascendancy of Asia, particularly Japan, on the American imagination. Americans are starting to wonder whether perhaps the family values of Asia put the United States at a disadvantage. The old platitude had it that ours is a vibrant, robust society for being a society of individuals. Now we look to Asia and see team effort paying off.

34   In this time of national homesickness, of nostalgia, for how we imagine America used to be, there are obvious dangers. We are going to start blaming each other for the loss. Since we are inclined, as Americans, to think of ourselves individually, we are disinclined to think of ourselves as creating one another or influencing one another.

35   But it is not the politician or any political debate about family values that has brought me here on a gray morning to my parents' house. It is some payment I owe to my youth and to my parents' youth. I imagine us sitting in the living room, amid my mother's sentimental doilies and the family photographs, trying to take the measure of the people we have turned out to be in America.

36   A San Francisco poet, when he was in the hospital and dying, called a priest to his bedside. The old poet wanted to make his peace with Mother Church. He wanted baptism. The priest asked why. "Because the Catholic Church has to accept me," said the poet. "Because I am a sinner."

37   Isn't willy-nilly inclusiveness the point, the only possible point to be derived from the concept of family? Curiously, both President Bush and Vice President Quayle got in trouble with their constituents recently for expressing a real family value. Both men said that they would try to dissuade a daughter or granddaughter from having an abortion. But, finally, they said they would support her decision, continue to love her, never abandon her.

38   There are families that do not accept. There are children who are forced to leave home because of abortions or homosexuality. There are family secrets that Papa never hears. Which is to say there are families that never learn the point of families.

39   But there she is at the window. My mother has seen me and she waves me in. Her face asks: Why am I sitting outside? (Have they, after all, known my secret for years and kept it, out of embarrassment, not knowing what to say?) Families accept, often by silence. My father opens the door to welcome me in.

? QUESTIONS TO CONSIDER

1.   Rodriguez begins and ends this article with a specific event. What is it? Why do you think he chose to structure it this way?

2.   What does Rodriguez mean by "family values"?

3.   How do "family values" differ between Americans and families that have immigrated to the United States?

4. What are some reasons behind the breakdown of "family values" in America?

5. What does Rodriguez mean by "Americanization"? How is the term important to the ideas in this article?

The Lonely, Good Company of Books

Richard Rodriguez

- **N** Narration
- **IE** Illustration and Exemplification

1   From an early age I knew that my mother and father could read and write both Spanish and English. I had observed my father making his way through what, I now suppose, must have been income tax forms. On other occasions I waited apprehensively while my mother read onion-paper letters airmailed from Mexico with news of a relative's illness or death. For both my parents, however, reading was something done out of necessity and as quickly as possible. Never did I see either of them read an entire book. Nor did I see them read for pleasure. Their reading consisted of work manuals, prayer books, newspapers, recipes....

2   In our house each school year would begin with my mother's careful instruction: "Don't write in your books so we can sell them at the end of the year." The remark was echoed in public by my teachers, but only in part: "Boys and girls, don't write in your books. You must learn to treat them with great care and respect."

3   OPEN THE DOORS OF YOUR MIND WITH BOOKS, read the red and white poster over the nun's desk in early September. It soon was apparent to me that reading was the classroom's central activity. Each course had its own book. And the information gathered from a book was unquestioned. READ TO LEARN, the sign on the wall advised in December. I privately wondered: What was the connection between reading and learning? Did one learn something only by reading it? Was an idea only an idea if it could be written down? In June, CONSIDER BOOKS YOUR BEST FRIENDS. Friends? Reading was, at best, only a chore. I needed to look up whole paragraphs of words in a dictionary. Lines of type were dizzying, the eye having to move slowly across the page, then down, and across.... The sentences of the first books I read were coolly impersonal. Toned hard. What most bothered me, however, was the isolation reading required. To console myself for the loneliness I'd feel when I read, I tried reading in a very soft voice. Until: "Who is doing all that talking to his neighbor?" Shortly after, remedial reading classes were arranged for me with a very old nun.

4   At the end of each school day, for nearly six months, I would meet with her in the tiny room that served as the school's library but was actually only a storeroom for used textbooks and a vast collection of *National Geographics.* Everything about our sessions pleased me: the smallness of the room; the noise of the janitor's broom hitting the edge of the long hallway outside the door; the green of the sun, lighting the wall; and the old woman's face blurred white with a beard. Most of the time we took turns. I began with my elementary text. Sentences of astonishing simplicity seemed to me lifeless and drab: "The boys ran from the rain...She wanted to sing...The kite rose in the blue." Then the old nun would read from her favorite books, usually biographies of early American presidents. Playfully she ran through complex sentences, calling the words alive with her voice, making it seem that the author somehow was speaking directly to me. I smiled just to listen to her. I sat there and sensed for the very first time some possibility of fellowship between reader and writer, a communication, never *intimate* like that I heard spoken words at home convey, but one nonetheless *personal.*

5   One day the nun concluded a session by asking me why I was so reluctant to read by myself. I tried to explain; said something about the way written words made me feel alone—almost, I wanted to add but didn't, as when I spoke to myself in a room just emptied of furniture. She studied my face as I spoke; she seemed to be watching more than listening. In an uneventful voice she replied that I had nothing to fear. Didn't I realize that reading would open up whole new worlds? A book could open doors for me. It could introduce me to people and show me places I never imagined existed. She gestured toward the bookshelves. (Bare-breasted African women danced, and the shiny hubcaps of automobiles on the back covers of the *Geographic* gleamed in my mind.) I listened with respect. But her words were not very influential. I was thinking then of another consequence of literacy, one I was too shy to admit but nonetheless trusted. Books were going to make me "educated." *That* confidence enabled me, several months later, to overcome my fear of the silence.

6   In fourth grade I embarked upon a grandiose reading program. "Give me the names of important books," I would say to startled teachers. They soon found out that I had in mind "adult books." I ignored their suggestions of anything I suspected was written for children. (Not until I was in college, as a result, did I read *Huckleberry Finn* or *Alice's Adventures in Wonderland.*) Instead, I read *The Scarlet Letter* and Franklin's *Autobiography.* And whatever I read I read for extra credit. Each time I finished a book, I reported

the achievement to a teacher and basked in the praise my effort earned. Despite my best efforts, however, there seemed to be more and more books I needed to read. At the library I would literally tremble as I came upon whole shelves of books I hadn't read. So I read and I read and I read: *Great Expectations*; all the short stories of Kipling; *The Babe Ruth Story;* the entire first volume of the *Encyclopedia Britannica* (A-Anstey); *The Iliad; Moby Dick; Gone with the Wind; The Good Earth; Ramona; Forever Amber; The Lives of the Saints; Crime and Punishment; The Pearl....* Librarians who initially frowned when I checked out the maximum ten books at a time started saving books they thought I might like. Teachers would say to the rest of the class, "I only wish the rest of you took reading as seriously as Richard obviously does."

7   But at home I would hear my mother wondering, "What do you see in your books?" (Was reading a hobby like her knitting? Was so much reading even healthy for a boy? Was it a sign of "brains"? Or was it just a convenient excuse for not helping around the house on Saturday mornings?) Always, "What do you see...?"

8   What *did* I see in my books? I had the idea that they were crucial for my academic success, though I couldn't have said exactly how or why. In the sixth grade I simply concluded that what gave a book its value was some major idea or theme it contained. If that core essence could be mined and memorized, I would become learned like my teachers. I decided to record in a notebook the themes of the books that I read. After reading *Robinson Crusoe,* I wrote that its theme was "the value of learning to live by oneself." When I completed *Wuthering Heights,* I noted the danger of "letting emotions get out of control." Rereading these brief moralistic appraisals usually left me disheartened. I couldn't believe that they were really the source of reading's values. But for many more years, they constituted the only means I had of describing to myself the educational value of books.

9   In spite of my earnestness, I found reading a pleasurable activity. I came to enjoy the lonely, good company of books. Early on weekday mornings, I'd read in my bed. I'd feel a mysterious comfort then, reading in the dawn quiet—the blue-gray silence interrupted by the occasional churning of the refrigerator motor a few rooms away or the more distant sounds of a city bus beginning its run. On weekends I'd go to the public library to read, surrounded by old men and women. Or, if the weather was fine, I would take my books to the park and read in the shade of a tree. A warm summer evening was my favorite reading time. Neighbors would leave for vacation and I would water their lawns. I would sit through the

twilight on the front porches or in backyards, reading to the cool, whirling sounds of the sprinklers.

10   I also had favorite writers. But often those writers I enjoyed most I was least able to value. When I read William Saroyan's *The Human Comedy,* I was immediately pleased by the narrator's warmth and charm of his story. But as quickly I became suspicious. A book so enjoyable to read couldn't be very "important." Another summer I determined to read all the novels of Dickens. Reading his fat novels, I loved the feeling I got—after the first hundred pages—of being at home in a fictional world where I knew the names of the characters and cared about what was going to happen to them. And it bothered me that I was forced away at the conclusion, when the fiction closed tight, like a fortuneteller's fist—the futures of all the major characters neatly resolved. I never knew how to take such feelings seriously, however. Nor did I suspect that these experiences could be part of a novel's meaning. Still, there were pleasures to sustain me after I'd finish my books. Carrying a volume back to the library, I would be pleased by its weight. I'd run my fingers along the edge of the pages and marvel at the breadth of my achievement. Around my room, growing stacks of paperback books reinforced my assurance.

11   I entered high school having read hundreds of books. My habit of reading made me a confident speaker and writer of English. Reading also enabled me to sense something of the shape, the major concerns, of Western thought. (I was able to say something about Dante and Descartes and Engels and James Baldwin in my high school term papers.) In these various ways, books brought me academic success as I hoped that they would. But I was not a good reader. Merely bookish, I lacked a point of view. I vacuumed books for epigrams, scraps of information, ideas, themes—anything to fill the hollow within me and make me feel educated. When one of my teachers suggested to his drowsy tenth-grade English class that a person could not have a "complicated idea" until he had read at least two thousand books, I heard the remark without detecting either its irony or its very complicated truth. I merely determined to compile a list of all books I had ever read. Harsh with myself, I included only once a title I might have read several times. (How, after all, could one read a book more than once?) And I included only those books over a hundred pages in length. (Could anything shorter be a book?)

12   There was yet another high school list I compiled. One day I came across a newspaper article about the retirement of an English professor at a nearby state college. The article was accompanied by a list of the

"hundred most important books of Western Civilization." "More than any-thing else in my life," the professor told the reporter with finality, "these books have made me all that I am." That was the kind of remark I couldn't ignore. I clipped out the list and kept it for the several months it took me to read all of the titles. Most books, of course, I barely understood. While reading Plato's *Republic*, for instance, I needed to keep looking at the book jacket comments to remind myself what the text was about. Nevertheless, with the special patience and superstition of a scholarship boy, I looked at every word of the text. And by the time I reached the last word, relieved, I convinced myself that I had read *The Republic*. In a ceremony of great pride, I solemnly crossed Plato off my list.

QUESTIONS TO CONSIDER

1. Rodriguez begins and ends this article with a specific event. What is it? What steps does he take to go from being a struggling reader to a vora-cious one? What does Rodriguez come to love so much about books and reading?

2. How does Rodriguez compare his own attitudes towards reading to his parents' attitudes towards reading?

3. Why does Rodriguez claim that, even after his comprehension and fluen-cy improved, he was not a "good" reader? How does Rodriguez seem to ultimately define a "good" reader? By this definition, do you believe you are a "good" reader?

4. Both Frederick Douglass and Richard Rodriguez describe their relation-ships with books and reading. What are some of the most interesting similarities and differences you noticed between these two authors' atti-tudes? These two authors wrote over a century apart from one another, so why do you think reading and the author's relationship to books is a subject with such lasting importance?

5. Do you recall your own attitude towards reading as a child? What do you think was the source of your attitudes towards reading, and how have your attitudes and skills changed over time?

Black and White in Shades of Gray

Reihan Salam

- **AP** Argument and Persuasion
- **CC** Compare and Contrast
- **CD** Classification and Division
- **CE** Cause and Effect
- **IE** Illustration and Exemplification

1   Since the shooting death of Michael Brown in the St. Louis suburb of Ferguson just over a year ago, Americans have been engaged in a spirited dialogue, to put it mildly, about the status of black people in our country. The main result of this dialogue so far appears to have been an alarming rise in what we might call racial pessimism. In August, Gallup released a survey that found that the share of whites satisfied with how African Americans are treated in the United States has fallen from 67 percent in 2013 to 53 percent in 2015, a quite striking decline. The share of blacks who feel the same way, meanwhile, fell from 47 percent to 33 percent over the same period, which is to say from low to dismally low.

2   There has been no similarly dramatic change in the material condition or the legal status of African Americans over this short interval, so what has been the source of this growing dissatisfaction? It is very simple: A rising generation of intellectuals has been offering an unremittingly bleak interpretation of the black experience in American life, and this interpretation has gained a great deal of purchase in the news media. Following the death of Brown, social-media activists, most of them young and black, have been rallying under the banner of #BlackLivesMatter, a Twitter hashtag devised by the activists Patrisse Cullors, Alicia Garza, and Opal Tometi to draw attention to the (alleged) epidemic of police violence against African Americans. Because Black Lives Matter is a diverse, decentralized movement, one hesitates to say that it speaks with a single voice. But I'd say that if there is a preoccupation shared by the leaders of the movement, it's the idea of white supremacy as the chief obstacle to black progress.

3   What is white supremacy, exactly? That is hard to say. The basic idea, as I understand it, is that our public institutions have been created to serve the interests of Americans who are seen by themselves and others as white. This "seen by themselves and others" part might seem silly, but the boundaries of whiteness have long been contested. There was a

time when the Irish didn't count as white, though they certainly do today. What about the son of a Korean-immigrant father and a Czech-immigrant mother? Or the fair-skinned second-generation Iranian American who grew up among *Mayflower* descendants? To the extent that these individuals identify as white and enjoy the benefits of being seen as such, they are white, according to this line of thinking. To be sure, whiteness is not infinitely malleable. The critique of white supremacy maintains that black people are permanently excluded from whiteness, with the rare exception of those who can "pass" as white and choose to do so.

4   The persistence of anti-black racism has indeed disadvantaged African Americans in many ways. The abolition of slavery and the dismantling of Jim Crow laws did not mean the end of exclusionary policies that made it difficult if not impossible for blacks to accumulate wealth. In *When Affirmative Action Was White*, the leftist Columbia University historian and political scientist Ira Katznelson documents the ways in which liberals of the New Deal and Fair Deal eras accommodated the demands of segregationist Democrats, who were quite happy to back generous new social programs as long as blacks weren't allowed to make use of them. Indeed, Katznelson's provocative argument is that the advent of these programs widened the existing gap in economic and educational outcomes between whites and blacks, a development that in his view justifies racial preferences for blacks. Of course, this conclusion doesn't follow if one believes that preferences can actually harm the interests of blacks, but that is a separate matter.

5   Other critics of white supremacy, such as Ta-Nehisi Coates in his much-lauded essay in *The Atlantic* on "the case for reparations," place heavy emphasis on the role of race in shaping American cities. First, these critics argue that racially motivated local land-use regulations, inequitable federal housing subsidies, and selective intimidation helped create hyper-segregated urban neighborhoods. Second, they maintain that a combination of overzealous policing and a racist criminal-justice system have traumatized these heavily black neighborhoods and contributed to family breakdown. There is definitely some truth to the notion that racism played a significant role in the concentration of poverty in black neighborhoods.

6   It is also true, however, that, as Edward Glaeser and Jacob Vigdor found in a 2012 analysis of census data, the share of black Americans living in hyper-segregated ghetto neighborhoods has fallen from 80 percent in 1960 to 20 percent in 2010. Middle-class blacks today lead far more

integrated lives than their parents and grandparents did. But this mass exodus of middle-class blacks from urban ghettos has been a double-edged sword. In *The Truly Disadvantaged*, the renowned African-American sociologist William Julius Wilson argued that the economic and social opportunities created by desegregation led upwardly mobile black families rich in cultural and social capital to depart majority-black communities, leaving these communities in a much-diminished state. What can't be denied is that these opportunities would not have presented themselves had the racism of earlier eras not attenuated to at least some degree. The threat of anti-black racism has historically played a unifying role among African Americans, and its decline has caused the lives of lower-class blacks and their better-off counterparts to sharply diverge.

7   One of the more striking illustrations of the class divide among African Americans is that while in 1978 poor blacks over the age of twelve were only slightly more likely to be the victims of violent crime (45 per 1,000) than better-off blacks (38 per 1,000), poor blacks in 2008 were vastly more likely to be crime victims (75 per 1,000) than better-off blacks (23 per 1,000). Why is it that poor blacks are far more vulnerable today than they were in the late 1970s, while better-off blacks are far less so? In her book *Ghettoside*, the *Los Angeles Times* reporter Jill Leovy argues that while police officers aggressively combat petty offenses in poor black neighborhoods—practicing the "broken-windows policing" that has proven so controversial in recent years—they do an extremely poor job of solving murders and other serious crimes. The disastrous result is that the minority of blacks who reside in hyper-segregated ghetto neighborhoods are more isolated than ever, and many have come to distrust the conventional criminal-justice system, which has proven so ineffective. Instead, residents of these neighborhoods either live in fear or they settle their own scores. In the worst cases, such as the South Los Angeles communities vividly described by Leovy, violent gangs impose their own "shadow law," which competes with the formal law of the police and the courts. Meanwhile, better-off blacks who have been able to exit these neighborhoods are physically much safer, and in a far better position to access economic opportunities, than their counterparts of a generation ago.

8   The failure of our criminal-justice system to liberate ghetto communities from the tyranny of violence is profound. I would argue that this failure amounts to a national crisis. Yet the divergence between poor blacks and better-off blacks suggests that reducing this failure to the

racism of the criminal-justice system is a mistake. James Forman Jr. of Yale Law School has documented the role of black activists in the late 1960s in pushing for more aggressive law enforcement in neighborhoods plagued by violent crime. He details the rise of more-punitive crime policies in black-majority jurisdictions with black-majority police forces, focusing in particular on the District of Columbia. While Forman's work doesn't definitively prove that racism played no role in the incarceration boom, it does remind us that many African Americans embraced tough-on-crime policies as violent-crime rates spiraled out of control, and that white supremacy is at best an incomplete explanation of why incarceration rates soared from the 1960s through the 1990s.

9   The late legal academic William Stuntz insisted that the 14th Amendment guarantee of "equal protection of the laws" ought to be taken literally. To Stuntz, this phrase meant that all citizens, regardless of race or economic status, had the same right to the law's protection. In his view, the systematic under-policing of violent neighborhoods ought to be understood not just as a regrettable policy failure but also as a constitutional violation that governments at all levels should be forced to address. If Leovy and Stuntz are right, one could argue that the real problem with crime-control efforts in violent urban neighborhoods is not that they're overzealous but that they are not zealous enough, or rather that they're not zealous enough about ensuring that violent criminals are brought to justice.

10   What if white supremacy really is as pervasive and powerful a force as many left-of-center intellectuals believe? What would be the implications for those who want African-American communities to flourish?

11   One of the central intellectual tenets of the Black Lives Matter movement has been an emphatic rejection of the "politics of respectability," the notion that black Americans will command respect from the wider society if they embrace bourgeois norms such as persistence, thrift, sobriety, and the value of hard work. Aurin Squire, writing at *Talking Points Memo* in February, elegantly summarized the case against respectability politics, describing it as the view "that systemic oppression can be overcome if we're clean, mild, moderate, and economically successful enough." Last October, Coates offered an equally bracing critique: "Respectability politics is, at its root, the inability to look into the cold dark void of history," he wrote. "For if black people are—as I maintain—no part of the problem, if the problem truly is 100 percent explained by white supremacy, then we are presented with a set of unfortunate facts about our home."

READINGS

12   What the critique of respectability politics obscures is that preaching bourgeois virtues needn't have anything to do with catering to a white audience, or with contempt for the black poor. One could believe that the cultivation of bourgeois norms can be advantageous and, as an entirely separate matter, that dehumanizing treatment at the hands of the police is an outrage regardless of whether one behaves "respectably." Nor must preaching the centrality of self-help entail ignoring or forgiving white supremacy. Rather, accepting the centrality of self-help means rejecting what Amy L. Wax, a law professor at the University of Pennsylvania, has called "remedial idealism." Remedial idealism is the view that "because outsiders, and not blacks themselves, are responsible for present racial inequalities, those outsiders must eliminate them." The trouble is that even if we accept that outsiders ought to eliminate present racial inequalities, it is by no means clear that they will make the sacrifices that this would entail. Most people are self-interested, after all. Demanding that whites forswear their privilege won't suddenly make them do so. If the only route to black progress is a moral reformation among whites, and if white supremacy is here to stay, black people are doomed to lives of poverty, misery, and marginality. If I believed any of that, I'd be a racial pessimist too.

13   Fortunately, there are other ways forward. The divergence in outcomes between poor and better-off blacks demonstrates that black upward mobility is possible, even in a society in which racism persists. It could be that the most effective way to advance black interests is to build up the collective wealth and power of the black community rather than rely on white benevolence. A number of scholars, including Nancy DiTomaso and Daria Roithmayr, have documented how people pass on valuable knowledge, including valuable knowledge about employment and housing opportunities, through their social networks. And these social networks tend to be very racially segregated. While it is a disadvantage not to belong to the most-privileged social networks, less-privileged social networks can make up for this disadvantage to at least some extent by becoming even more tight-knit than the networks of the privileged. This is a strategy that many black migrants from the Deep South pursued in the last century, and it is often employed by immigrants in our own time.

14   Building up wealth and power is of course easier said than done, particularly for people living in neighborhoods and regions plagued by high levels of unemployment and underemployment. Over the past

several decades, there has been a large-scale migration of middle-class blacks from cities in the northern and western United States to dynamic cities in the Old Confederacy, which the Brookings Institution demographer William Frey has dubbed "the New Great Migration." Why would African-American families leave progressive bastions such as New York, San Francisco, and Portland, Ore., for Atlanta, Dallas, and Houston if the former are largely free of anti-black animus while the latter are arguably somewhat less free of it? Are blacks flocking there because those cities have a reputation for providing high-quality social services to African Americans in need, or because their commitment to racial preferences surpasses that of northern metropolises? Hardly.

15   While whites in northern and western cities are generally more "progressive" than those in southern cities, southern cities are more affordable and, as a rule, they offer more job opportunities. This combination means that those who are able to secure full-time employment are also in a better position to save, and therefore to build wealth. Moreover, rising black populations in these fast-growing southern metropolitan areas hold out the promise of rising black political power, which can be wielded to advance communal goals. The New Great Migration might seem unremarkable and bourgeois. But it is in its own way an extraordinary example of communal uplift, and those who want to see racial progress in America ought to celebrate it.

QUESTIONS TO CONSIDER

1. Throughout the essay, Salam critiques the criminal justice system. What are his specific criticisms of the criminal justice system? Do you agree or disagree? Explain.

2. Salam believes upward mobility is possible for middle-class blacks even in a society where racism exists. Do you agree or disagree? Explain.

3. In the text, Salam cites that white supremacy should not be entirely blamed on the conflict in poor black neighborhoods. Do you agree or disagree? Explain.

4. Identify moments of compare/contrast in the essay. What is being compared/contrasted? Do you think this strategy is effective in this instance?

READINGS

Under the Influence

Scott Russell Sanders

- **N** Narration
- **CC** Compare and Contrast
- **DEF** Definition
- **PA** Process Analysis
- **CE** Cause and Effect

1   My father drank. He drank as a gut-punched boxer gasps for breath, as a starving dog gobbles food—compulsively, secretly, in pain and trembling. I use the past tense not because he ever quit drinking but because he quit living. That is how the story ends for my father, age sixty-four, heart bursting, body cooling and forsaken on the linoleum of my brother's trailer. The story continues for my brother, my sister, my mother, and me, and will continue so long as memory holds.

2   In the perennial present of memory, I slip into the garage or barn to see my father tipping back the flat green bottles of wine, the brown cylinders of whiskey, the cans of beer disguised in paper bags. His Adam's apple bobs, the liquid gurgles, he wipes the sandy-haired back of a hand over his lips, and then, his bloodshot gaze bumping into me, he stashes the bottle or can inside his jacket, under the workbench, between two bales of hay, and we both pretend the moment has not occurred.

3   "What's up, buddy?" he says, thick-tongued and edgy.

4   "Sky's up," I answer, playing along.

5   "And don't forget prices," he grumbles. "Prices are always up. And taxes."

6   In memory, his white 1951 Pontiac with the stripes down the hood and the Indian head on the snout lurches to a stop in the driveway; or it is the 1956 Ford station wagon, or the 1963 Rambler shaped like a toad, or the sleek 1969 Bonneville that will do 120 miles per hour on straightaways; or it is the robin's-egg blue pickup, new in 1980, battered in 1981, the year of his death. He climbs out, grinning dangerously, unsteady on his legs, and we children interrupt our game of catch, our building of snow forts, our picking of plums, to watch in silence as he weaves past into the house, where he slumps into his overstuffed chair and falls asleep. Shaking her head, our mother stubs out the cigarette he has left smoldering in the ashtray. All evening, until our bedtimes, we tiptoe past him, as past a snoring dragon. Then we curl fearfully in our sheets, listening. Eventually he wakes with a grunt, Mother slings accusations at him, he snarls back,

she yells, he growls, their voices clashing. Before long, she retreats to their bedroom, sobbing—not from the blows of fists, for he never strikes her, but from the force of his words.

7   Left alone, our father prowls the house, thumping into furniture, rummaging in the kitchen, slamming doors, turning the pages of the newspaper with a savage crackle, muttering back at the late-night drivel from television. The roof might fly off, the walls might buckle from the pressure of his rage. Whatever my brother and sister and mother may be thinking on their own rumpled pillows, I lie there hating him, loving him, fearing him, knowing I have failed him. I tell myself he drinks to ease an ache that gnaws at his belly, an ache I must have caused by disappointing him somehow, a murderous ache I should be able to relieve by doing all my chores, earning A's in school, winning baseball games, fixing the broken washer and the burst pipes, bringing in money to fill his empty wallet. He would not hide the green bottles in his tool box, would not sneak off to the barn with a lump under his coat, would not fall asleep in the daylight, would not roar and fume, would not drink himself to death, if only I were perfect.

8   I am forty-two as I write these words, and I know full well now that my father was an alcoholic, a man consumed by disease rather than by disappointment. What had seemed to me a private grief is in fact a public scourge. In the United States alone, some ten or fifteen million people share his ailment, and behind the doors they slam in fury or disgrace, countless other children tremble. I comfort myself with such knowledge, holding it against the throb of memory like an ice pack against a bruise. There are keener sources of grief: poverty, racism, rape, war. I do not wish to compete for a trophy in suffering. I am only trying to understand the corrosive mixture of helplessness, responsibility, and shame that I learned to feel as the son of an alcoholic. I realize now that l did not cause my father's illness, nor could l have cured it. Yet for all this grown-up knowledge, I am still ten years old, my own son's age, and as that boy I struggle in guilt and confusion to save my father from pain.

9   Consider a few of our synonyms for *drunk*: tipsy, tight, pickled, soused, and plowed; stoned and stewed, lubricated and inebriated, juiced and sluiced; three sheets to the wind, in your cups, out of your mind, under the table; lit up, tanked up, wiped out; besotted, blotto, bombed, and buzzed; plastered, polluted, putrified; loaded or looped, boozy, woozy, fuddled, or smashed; crocked and shit-faced, corked and pissed, snockered and sloshed.

READINGS

10   It is a mostly humorous lexicon, as the lore that deals with drunks—in jokes and cartoons, in plays, films, and television skits—is largely comic. Aunt Matilda nips elderberry wine from the sideboard and burps politely during supper. Uncle Fred slouches to the table glassy-eyed, wearing a lamp shade for a hat and murmuring, "Candy is dandy but liquor is quicker." Inspired by cocktails, Mrs. Somebody recounts the events of her day in a fuzzy dialect, while Mr. Somebody nibbles her ear and croons a bawdy song. On the sofa with Boyfriend, Daughter giggles, licking gin from her lips, and loosens the bows in her hair. Junior knocks back some brews with his chums at the Leopard Lounge and stumbles home to the wrong house, wonders foggily why he cannot locate his pajamas, and crawls naked into bed with the ugliest girl in school. The family dog slurps from a neglected martini and wobbles to the nursery, where he vomits in Baby's shoe.

11   It is all great fun. But if in the audience you notice a few laughing faces turn grim when the drunk lurches on stage, don't be surprised, for these are the children of alcoholics. Over the grinning mask of Dionysus, the leering face of Bacchus, these children cannot help seeing the bloated features of their own parents. Instead of laughing, they wince, they mourn. Instead of celebrating the drunk as one freed from constraints, they pity him as one enslaved. They refuse to believe *in vino veritas,* having seen their befuddled parents skid away from truth toward folly and oblivion. And so these children bite their lips until the lush staggers into the wings.

12   My father, when drunk, was neither funny nor honest; he was pathetic, frightening, deceitful. There seemed to be a leak in him somewhere, and he poured in booze to keep from draining dry. Like a torture victim who refuses to squeal, he would never admit that he had touched a drop, not even in his last year, when he seemed to be dissolving in alcohol before our very eyes. I never knew him to lie about anything, ever, except about this one ruinous fact. Drowsy, clumsy, unable to fix a bicycle tire, throw a baseball, balance a grocery sack, or walk across the room, he was stripped of his true self by drink. In a matter of minutes, the contents of a bottle could transform a brave man into a coward, a buddy into a bully, a gifted athlete and skilled carpenter and shrewd businessman into a bumbler. No dictionary of synonyms for *drunk* would soften the anguish of watching our prince turn into a frog.

13   Father's drinking became the family secret. While growing up, we children never breathed a word of it beyond the four walls of our house.

To this day, my brother and sister rarely mention it, and then only when I press them. I did not confess the ugly, bewildering fact to my wife until his wavering walk and slurred speech forced me to. Recently, on the seventh anniversary of my father's death, I asked my mother if she ever spoke of his drinking to friends. "No, no, never," she replied hastily. "I couldn't bear for anyone to know."

14   The secret bores under the skin, gets in the blood, into the bone, and stays there. Long after you have supposedly been cured of malaria, the fever can flare up, the tremors can shake you. So it is with the fevers of shame. You swallow the bitter quinine of knowledge, and you learn to feel pity and compassion toward the drinker. Yet the shame lingers in your marrow, and, because of the shame, anger.

15   For a long stretch of my childhood we lived on a military reservation in Ohio, an arsenal where bombs were stored underground in bunkers, vintage airplanes burst into flames, and unstable artillery shells boomed nightly at the dump. We had the feeling, as children, that we played in a minefield, where a heedless footfall could trigger an explosion. When Father was drinking, the house, too, became a minefield. The least bump could set off either parent.

16   The more he drank, the more obsessed Mother became with stopping him. She hunted for bottles, counted the cash in his wallet, sniffed at his breath. Without meaning to snoop, we children blundered left and right into damning evidence. On afternoons when he came home from work sober, we flung ourselves at him for hugs, and felt against our ribs the telltale lump in his coat. In the barn we tumbled on the hay and heard beneath our sneakers the crunch of buried glass. We tugged open a drawer in his workbench, looking for screwdrivers or crescent wrenches, and spied a gleaming six-pack among the tools. Playing tag, we darted around the house just in time to see him sway on the rear stoop and heave a finished bottle into the woods. In his good night kiss we smelled the cloying sweetness of Clorets, the mints he chewed to camouflage his dragon's breath.

17   I can summon up that kiss right now by recalling Theodore Roethke's lines about his own father in "My Papa's Waltz":

The whiskey on your breath

Could make a small boy dizzy;

But I hung on like death:

Such waltzing was not easy.

18   Such waltzing was hard, terribly hard, for with a boy's scrawny arms I was trying to hold my tipsy father upright.

 READINGS

19   For years, the chief source of those incriminating bottles and cans was a grimy store a mile from us, a cinder block place called Sly's, with two gas pumps outside and a mangy dog asleep in the window. A strip of flypaper, speckled the year round with black bodies, coiled in the doorway. Inside, on rusty metal shelves or in wheezing coolers, you could find pop and Popsicles, cigarettes, potato chips, canned soup, raunchy postcards, fishing gear, Twinkies, wine, and beer. When Father drove anywhere on errands, Mother would send us kids along as guards, warning us not to let him out of our sight. And so with one or more of us on board, Father would cruise up to Sly's, pump a dollar's worth of gas or plump the tires with air, and then, telling us to wait in the car, he would head for that fly-spangled doorway.

20   Dutiful and panicky, we cried, "Let us go in with you!"

21   "No," he answered. "I'll be back in two shakes."

22   "Please!"

23   "No!" he roared. "Don't you budge, or I'll jerk a knot in your tails!"

24   So we stayed put, kicking the seats, while he ducked inside. Often, when he had parked the car at a careless angle, we gazed in through the window and saw Mr. Sly fetching down from a shelf behind the cash register two green pints of Gallo wine. Father swigged one of them right there at the counter, stuffed the other in his pocket, and then out he came, a bulge in his coat, a flustered look on his reddened face.

25   Because the Mom and Pop who ran the dump were neighbors of ours, living just down the tar-blistered road, I hated them all the more for poisoning my father. I wanted to sneak in their store and smash the bottles and set fire to the place. I also hated the Gallo brothers, Ernest and Julio, whose jovial faces shone from the labels of their wine, labels I would find, torn and curled, when I burned the trash. I noted the Gallo brothers' address, in California, and I studied the road atlas to see how far that was from Ohio, because I meant to go out there and tell Ernest and Julio what they were doing to my father, and then, if they showed no mercy, I would kill them.

26   While growing up on the back roads and in the country schools and cramped Methodist churches of Ohio and Tennessee, I never heard the word *alcoholism*, never happened across it in books or magazines. In the nearby towns, there were no addiction treatment programs, no community mental health centers, no Alcoholics Anonymous chapters, no therapists. Left alone with our grievous secret, we had no way of understanding Father's drinking except as an act of will, a deliberate folly or cruelty, a

moral weakness, a sin. He drank because he chose to, pure and simple. Why our father, so playful and competent and kind when sober, would choose to ruin himself and punish his family, we could not fathom.

27   Our neighborhood was high on the Bible, and the Bible was hard on drunkards. "Woe to those who are heroes at drinking wine, and valiant men in mixing strong drink," wrote Isaiah. "The priest and the prophet reel with strong drink, they are confused with wine, they err in vision, they stumble in giving judgment. For all tables are full of vomit, no place is without filthiness." We children had seen those fouled tables at the local truck stop where the notorious boozers hung out, our father occasionally among them. "Wine and new wine take away the understanding," declared the prophet Hosea. We had also seen evidence of that in our father, who could multiply seven-digit numbers in his head when sober, but when drunk could not help us with fourth-grade math. Proverbs warned: "Do not look at wine when it is red, when it sparkles in the cup and goes down smoothly. At the last it bites like a serpent, and stings like an adder. Your eyes will see strange things, and your mind utter perverse things." Woe, woe.

28   Dismayingly often, these biblical drunkards stirred up trouble for their own kids. Noah made fresh wine after the flood, drank too much of it, fell asleep without any clothes on, and was glimpsed in the buff by his son Ham, whom Noah promptly cursed. In one passage—it was so shocking we had to read it under our blankets with flashlights—the patriarch Lot fell down drunk and slept with his daughters. The sins of the fathers set their children's teeth on edge.

29   Our ministers were fond of quoting St. Paul's pronouncement that drunkards would not inherit the kingdom of God. These grave preachers assured us that the wine referred to during the Last Supper was in fact grape juice. Bible and sermons and hymns combined to give us the impression that Moses should have brought down from the mountain another stone tablet, bearing the Eleventh Commandment: Thou shalt not drink.

30   The scariest and most illuminating Bible story apropos of drunkards was the one about the lunatic and the swine. Matthew, Mark, and Luke each told a version of the tale. We knew it by heart: When Jesus climbed out of his boat one day, this lunatic came charging up from the graveyard, stark naked and filthy, frothing at the mouth, so violent that he broke the strongest chains. Nobody would go near him. Night and day for years this madman had been wailing among the tombs and bruising himself

with stones. Jesus took one look at him and said, "Come out of the man, you unclean spirits!" for he could see that the lunatic was possessed by demons. Meanwhile, some hogs were conveniently rooting nearby. "If we have to come out," begged the demons, "at least let us go into those swine." Jesus agreed. The unclean spirits entered the hogs, and the hogs rushed straight off a cliff and plunged into a lake. Hearing the story in Sunday school, my friends thought mainly of the pigs. (How big a splash did they make? Who paid for the lost pork?) But I thought of the redeemed lunatic, who bathed himself and put on clothes and calmly sat at the feet of Jesus, restored—so the Bible said—to "his right mind."

31   When drunk, our father was clearly in his wrong mind. He became a stranger, as fearful to us as any graveyard lunatic, not quite frothing at the mouth but fierce enough, quick-tempered, explosive; or else he grew maudlin and weepy, which frightened us nearly as much. In my boyhood despair, I reasoned that maybe he wasn't to blame for turning into an ogre. Maybe, like the lunatic, he was possessed by demons. I found support for my theory when I heard liquor referred to as "spirits," when the newspapers reported that somebody had been arrested for "driving under the influence," and when church ladies railed against that "demon drink."

32   If my father was indeed possessed, who would exorcise him? If he was a sinner, who would save him? If he was ill, who would cure him? If he suffered, who would ease his pain? Not ministers or doctors, for we could not bring ourselves to confide in them; not the neighbors, for we pretended they had never seen him drunk; not Mother, who fussed and pleaded but could not budge him; not my brother and sister, who were only kids. That left me. It did not matter that I, too, was only a child, and a bewildered one at that. I could not excuse myself.

33   On first reading a description of delirium tremens—in a book on alcoholism I smuggled from the library—I thought immediately of the frothing lunatic and the frenzied swine. When I read stories or watched films about grisly metamorphoses—Dr. Jekyll becoming Mr. Hyde, the mild husband changing into a werewolf, the kindly neighbor taken over by a brutal alien—I could not help seeing my own father's mutation from sober to drunk. Even today, knowing better, I am attracted by the demonic theory of drink, for when I recall my father's transformation, the emergence of his ugly second self, I find it easy to believe in possession by unclean spirits. We never knew which version of Father would come home from work, the true or the tainted, nor could we guess how far down the slope toward cruelty he would slide.

34   How far a man *could* slide we gauged by observing our back-road neighbors—the out-of-work miners who had dragged their families to our corner of Ohio from the desolate hollows of Appalachia, the tight-fisted farmers, the surly mechanics, the balked and broken men. There was, for example, whiskey-soaked Mr. Jenkins, who beat his wife and kids so hard we could hear their screams from the road. There was Mr. Lava the wino, who fell asleep smoking time and again, until one night his disgusted wife bundled up the children and went outside and left him in his easy chair to burn; he awoke on his own, staggered out coughing into the yard, and pounded her flat while the children looked on and the shack turned to ash. There was the truck driver, Mr. Sampson, who tripped over his son's tricycle one night while drunk and got so mad that he jumped into his semi and drove away, shifting through the dozen gears, and never came back. We saw the bruised children of these fathers clump onto our school bus, we saw the abandoned children huddle in the pews at church, we saw the stunned and battered mothers begging for help at our doors.

35   Our own father never beat us, and I don't think he ever beat Mother, but he threatened often. The Old Testament Yahweh was not more terrible in his wrath. Eyes blazing, voice booming, Father would pull out his belt and swear to give us a whipping, but he never followed through, never needed to, because we could imagine it so vividly. He shoved us, pawed us with the back of his hand, as an irked bear might smack a cub, not to injure, just to clear a space. I can see him grabbing Mother by the hair as she cowers on a chair during a nightly quarrel. He twists her neck back until she gapes up at him, and then he lifts over her skull a glass quart bottle of milk, the milk running down his forearm, and he yells at her, "Say just one more word, one goddamn word, and I'll shut you up!" I fear she will prick him with her sharp tongue, but she is terrified into silence, and so am I, and the leaking bottle quivers in the air, and milk slithers through the red hair of my father's uplifted arm, and the entire scene is there to this moment, the head jerked back, the club raised.

36   When the drink made him weepy, Father would pack a bag and kiss each of us children on the head, and announce from the front door that he was moving out. "Where to?" we demanded, fearful each time that he would leave for good, as Mr. Sampson had roared away for good in his diesel truck. "Someplace where I won't get hounded every minute," Father would answer, his jaw quivering. He stabbed a look at Mother, who might say, "Don't run into the ditch before you get there," or, "Good riddance," and then he would slink away. Mother watched him go with arms crossed

READINGS

over her chest, her face closed like the lid on a box of snakes. We children bawled. Where could he go? To the truck stop, that den of iniquity? To one of those dark, ratty flophouses in town? Would he wind up sleeping under a railroad bridge or on a park bench or in a cardboard box, mummied in rags, like the bums we had seen on our trips to Cleveland and Chicago? We bawled and bawled, wondering if he would ever come back.

37   He always did come back, a day or a week later, but each time there was a sliver less of him.

38   In Kafka's *The Metamorphosis*, which opens famously with Gregor Samsa waking up from uneasy dreams to find himself transformed into an insect, Gregor's family keep reassuring themselves that things will be just fine again, "When he comes back to us." Each time alcohol transformed our father, we held out the same hope, that he would really and truly come back to us, our authentic father, the tender and playful and competent man, and then all things would be fine. We had grounds for such hope. After his weepy departures and chapfallen returns, he would sometimes go weeks, even months without drinking. Those were glad times. Joy banged inside my ribs. Every day without the furtive glint of bottles, every meal without a fight, every bedtime without sobs encouraged us to believe that such bliss might go on forever.

39   Mother was fooled by just such a hope all during the forty odd years she knew this Greeley Ray Sanders. Soon after she met him in a Chicago delicatessen on the eve of World War II, and fell for his butter-melting Mississippi drawl and his wavy red hair, she learned that he drank heavily. But then so did a lot of men. She would soon coax or scold him into breaking the nasty habit. She would point out to him how ugly and foolish it was, this bleary drinking, and then he would quit. He refused to quit during their engagement, however, still refused during the first years of marriage, refused until my sister came along. The shock of fatherhood sobered him, and he remained sober through my birth at the end of the war and right on through until we moved in 1951 to the Ohio arsenal, that paradise of bombs. Like all places that make a business of death, the arsenal had more than its share of alcoholics and drug addicts and other varieties of escape artists. There I turned six and started school and woke into a child's flickering awareness, just in time to see my father begin sneaking swigs in the garage.

40   He sobered up again for most of a year at the height of the Korean War, to celebrate the birth of my brother. But aside from that dry spell, his only breaks from drinking before I graduated from high school were

just long enough to raise and then dash our hopes. Then during the fall of my senior year—the time of the Cuban missile crisis, when it seemed that the nightly explosions at the munitions dump and the nightly rages in our household might spread to engulf the globe—Father collapsed. His liver, kidneys, and heart all conked out. The doctors saved him, but only by a hair. He stayed in the hospital for weeks, going through a withdrawal so terrible that Mother would not let us visit him. If he wanted to kill himself, the doctors solemnly warned him, all he had to do was hit the bottle again. One binge would finish him.

41   Father must have believed them, for he stayed dry the next fifteen years. It was an answer to prayer, Mother said, it was a miracle. I believe it was a reflex of fear, which he sustained over the years through courage and pride. He knew a man could die from drink, for his brother Roscoe had. We children never laid eyes on doomed Uncle Roscoe, but in the stories Mother told us he became a fairy-tale figure, like a boy who took the wrong turning in the woods and was gobbled up by the wolf.

42   The fifteen-year dry spell came to an end with Father's retirement in the spring of 1978. Like many men, he gave up his identity along with his job. One day he was a boss at the factory, with a brass plate on his door and a reputation to uphold; the next day he was a nobody at home. He and Mother were leaving Ontario, the last of the many places to which his job had carried them, and they were moving to a new house in Mississippi, his childhood stomping grounds. As a boy in Mississippi, Father sold Coca-Cola during dances while the moonshiners peddled their brew in the parking lot; as a young blade, he fought in bars and in the ring, seeking a state Golden Gloves championship; he gambled at poker, hunted pheasants, raced motorcycles and cars, played semiprofessional baseball, and, along with all his buddies—in the Black Cat Saloon, behind the cotton gin, in the woods—he drank. It was a perilous youth to dream of recovering.

43   After his final day of work, Mother drove on ahead with a car full of begonias and violets, while Father stayed behind to oversee the packing. When the van was loaded, the sweaty movers broke open a six-pack and offered him a beer.

44   "Let's drink to retirement!" they crowed. "Let's drink to freedom! to fishing! hunting! loafing! Let's drink to a guy who's going home!"

45   At least I imagine some such words, for that is all I can do, imagine, and I see Father's hand trembling in midair as he thinks about the fifteen sober years and about the doctors' warning, and he tells himself

READINGS

Goddamnit, I am a free man, and *Why can't a free man drink one beer after a lifetime of hard work?* and I see his arm reaching, his fingers closing, the can tilting to his lips. I even supply a label for the beer, a swaggering brand that promises on television to deliver the essence of life. I watch the amber liquid pour down his throat, the alcohol steal into his blood, the key turn in his brain.

46   Soon after my parents moved back to Father's treacherous stomping ground, my wife and I visited them in Mississippi with our five-year-old daughter. Mother had been too distraught to warn me about the return of the demons. So when I climbed out of the car that bright July morning and saw my father napping in the hammock, I felt uneasy, for in all his sober years I had never known him to sleep in daylight. Then he lurched upright, blinked his bloodshot eyes, and greeted us in a syrupy voice. I was hurled back helpless into childhood.

47   "What's the matter with Papaw?" our daughter asked.

48   "Nothing," I said. "Nothing!"

49   Like a child again, I pretended not to see him in his stupor, and behind my phony smile I grieved. On that visit and on the few that remained before his death, once again I found bottles in the workbench, bottles in the woods. Again his hand shook too much for him to run a saw, to make his precious miniature furniture, to drive straight down back roads. Again he wound up in the ditch, in the hospital, in jail, in treatment centers. Again he shouted and wept. Again he lied. "I never touched a drop," he swore. "Your mother's making it up."

50   I no longer fancied I could reason with the men whose names I found on the bottles—Jim Beam, Jack Daniels—nor did I hope to save my father by burning down a store. I was able now to press the cold statistics about alcoholism against the ache of memory: ten million victims, fifteen million, twenty. And yet, in spite of my age, I reacted in the same blind way as I had in childhood, ignoring biology, forgetting numbers, vainly seeking to erase through my efforts whatever drove him to drink. I worked on their place twelve and sixteen hours a day, in the swelter of Mississippi summer, digging ditches, running electrical wire, planting trees, mowing grass, building sheds, as though what nagged at him was some list of chores, as though by taking his worries on my shoulders I could redeem him. I was flung back into boyhood, acting as though my father would not drink himself to death if only I were perfect.

51   I failed of perfection; he succeeded in dying. To the end, he considered himself not sick but sinful. "Do you want to kill yourself?" I asked

him. "Why not?" he answered. "Why the hell not? What's there to save?" To the end, he would not speak about his feelings, would not or could not give a name to the beast that was devouring him.

52   In silence, he went rushing off the cliff. Unlike the biblical swine, however, he left behind a few of the demons to haunt his children. Life with him and the loss of him twisted us into shapes that will be familiar to other sons and daughters of alcoholics. My brother became a rebel, my sister retreated into shyness, I played the stalwart and dutiful son who would hold the family together. If my father was unstable, I would be a rock. If he squandered money on drink, I would pinch every penny. If he wept when drunk—and only when drunk—I would not let myself weep at all. If he roared at the Little League umpire for calling my pitches balls, I would throw nothing but strikes. Watching him flounder and rage, I came to dread the loss of control. I would go through life without making anyone mad. I vowed never to put in my mouth or veins any chemical that would banish my everyday self. I would never make a scene, never lash out at the ones I loved, never hurt a soul. Through hard work, relentless work, I would achieve something dazzling—in the classroom, on the basketball floor, in the science lab, in the pages of books—and my achievement would distract the world's eyes from his humiliation. I would become a worthy sacrifice, and the smoke of my burning would please God.

53   It is far easier to recognize these twists in my character than to undo them. Work has become an addiction for me, as drink was an addiction for my father. Knowing this, my daughter gave me a placard for the wall: *workaholic.* The labor is endless and futile, for I can no more redeem myself through work than I could redeem my father. I still panic in the face of other people's anger, because his drunken temper was so terrible. I shrink from causing sadness or disappointment even to strangers, as though I were still concealing the family shame. I still notice every twitch of emotion in the faces around me, having learned as a child to read the weather in faces, and I blame myself for their least pang of unhappiness or anger. In certain moods I blame myself for everything. Guilt burns like acid in my veins.

54   I am moved to write these pages now because my own son, at the age of ten, is taking on himself the griefs of the world, and in particular the griefs of his father. He tells me that when I am gripped by sadness he feels responsible; he feels there must be something he can do to spring me from depression, to fix my life. And that crushing sense of responsibility is exactly what I felt at the age of ten in the face of my father's drinking.

 READINGS

My son wonders if I, too, am possessed. I write, therefore, to drag into the light what eats at me—the fear, the guilt, the shame—so that my own children may be spared.

55   I still shy away from nightclubs, from bars, from parties where the solvent is alcohol. My friends puzzle over this, but it is no more peculiar than for a man to shy away from the lions' den after seeing his father torn apart. I took my own first drink at the age of twenty-one, half a glass of burgundy. I knew the odds of my becoming an alcoholic were four times higher than for the sons of nonalcoholic fathers. So I sipped warily.

56   I still do—once a week, perhaps, a glass of wine, a can of beer, nothing stronger, nothing more. I listen for the turning of a key in my brain.

QUESTIONS TO CONSIDER

1. What does Sanders mean when he says that he does not want to "compete for a trophy in suffering"?

2. Sanders states that he experiences various emotions when it comes to his father's drinking: hate, love, fear, failure. These emotions appear at various points in the essay and help to establish an emotional relationship with the reader. Do you think it is effective?

3. Starting with paragraph 9, Sanders describes the sometimes humorous depiction of drunks in society and pop culture. He then goes on to describe how family members of alcoholics often find this depiction uncomfortable. Why do you think he felt it was necessary to include this section in the essay? Do you think it was effective in relation to the overall tone of the essay?

4. Sanders mentions that his father's drinking was a "family secret." Have you ever had a family secret? What effect did it have on you or the other members of your family?

5. At the end of the essay, Sanders says that he is writing this essay for his ten-year-old son. Why does he do this?

Wonder Woman

Gloria Steinem

- **N** Narration
- **CE** Cause and Effect
- **AP** Argument and Persuasion

1 Wonder Woman is the only female super-hero to be published continuously since comic books began—indeed, she is one of the few to have existed at all or to be anything other than part of a male super-hero group—but this may strike many readers as a difference without much distinction. After all, haven't comic books always been a little disreputable? Something that would never have been assigned in school? The answer to those questions is yes, which is exactly why they are important. Comic books have power—including over the child who still lives within each of us—because they are *not* part of the "serious" grown-up world.

2 I remember hundreds of nights reading comic books under the covers with a flashlight; dozens of car trips while my parents told me I was ruining my eyes and perhaps my mind ("brain-deadeners" was what my mother called them); and countless hours spent hiding in a tree or some other inaccessible spot where I could pore over their pages in sweet freedom. Because my family's traveling meant I didn't go to school regularly until I was about twelve, comic books joined cereal boxes and ketchup labels as the primers that taught me how to read. They were even cheap enough to be the first things I bought on my own—a customer who couldn't see over the countertop but whose dignity was greatly enhanced by making a choice, counting out carefully hoarded coins, and completing a grown-up exchange.

3 I've always wondered if this seemingly innate drive toward independence in children isn't more than just "a movement toward mastery," as psychologists say. After all, each of us is the result of millennia of environment and heredity, a unique combination that could never happen before—or again. Like a seed that contains a plant, a child is already a unique person; an ancient spirit born into a body too small to express itself, or even cope with the world. I remember feeling the greatest love for my parents whenever they allowed me to express my own will, whether that meant wearing an inappropriate hat for days on end, or eating dessert before I had finished dinner.

4   Perhaps it's our memories of past competence and dreams for the future that create the need for super-heroes in the first place. Leaping skyscrapers in a single bound, seeing through walls, and forcing people to tell the truth by encircling them in a magic lasso—all would be satisfying fantasies at any age, but they may be psychological necessities when we have trouble tying our shoes, escaping a worldview composed mainly of belts and knees, and getting grown-ups *to pay attention.*

5   The problem is that the super-heroes who perform magical feats— indeed, even mortal heroes who are merely competent—are almost always men. A female child is left to believe that, even when her body is as big as her spirit, she will still be helping with minor tasks, appreciating the accomplishments of others, and waiting to be rescued. Of course, pleasure is to be found in all these experiences of helping, appreciating, and being rescued; pleasure that should be open to boys, too. Even in comic books, heroes sometimes work in groups or are called upon to protect their own kind, not just helpless females. But the truth is that a male super-hero is more likely to be vulnerable, if only to create suspense, than a female character is to be powerful or independent. For little girls, the only alternative is suppressing a crucial part of ourselves by transplanting our consciousness into a male character—which usually means a white one, thus penalizing girls of color doubly, and boys of color, too. Otherwise, choices remain limited: in the case of girls, to an "ideal" life of sitting around like a Technicolor clotheshorse, getting into jams with villains, and saying things like, "Oh, Superman! I'll always be grateful to you"; in the case of boys of color, to identifying with villains who may be the only ethnic characters with any power; and in the case of girls of color, to making an impossible choice between parts of their identity. It hardly seems worth learning to tie our shoes.

6   I'm happy to say that I was rescued from this dependent fate at the age of seven or so; rescued (Great Hera!) by a woman. Not only did she have the wisdom of Athena and Aphrodite's power to inspire love, she was also faster than Mercury and stronger than Hercules. In her all-woman home on Paradise Island, a refuge of ancient Amazon culture protected from nosy travelers by magnetic thought-fields that created an area known to the world as the Bermuda Triangle, she had come to her many and amazing powers naturally. Together with her Amazon sisters, she had been trained in them from infancy and perfected them in Greek-style contests of dexterity, strength, and speed. The lesson was that each of us might have unknown powers within us, if we only believed and practiced them. (To me, it always seemed boring that Superman had bulletproof

skin, X-ray vision, and the ability to fly. Where was the contest?) Though definitely white, as were all her Amazon sisters, she was tall and strong, with dark hair and eyes—a relief from the weak, bosomy, blonde heroines of the 1940s.

7   Of course, this Amazon did need a few fantastic gadgets to help her once she entered a modern world governed by Ares, God of War, not Aphrodite, Goddess of Love: a magic golden lasso that compelled all within its coils to obey her command, silver bracelets that repelled bullets, and an invisible plane that carried her through time as well as space. But she still had to learn how to throw the lasso with accuracy, be agile enough to deflect bullets from her silver-encased wrists, and navigate an invisible plane.

8   Charles Moulton, whose name appeared on each episode as Wonder Woman's writer and creator, had seen straight into my heart and understood the fears of violence and humiliation hidden there. No longer did I have to pretend to like the "POW!" and "SPLAT!" of boys' comic books, from Captain Marvel to the Green Hornet. No longer did I have nightmares after looking at ghoulish images of torture and murder, bloody scenes made all the more realistic by steel-booted Nazis and fang-toothed Japanese who were caricatures of World War II enemies then marching in every newsreel. (Eventually, the sadism of boys comic books was so extreme that it inspired Congressional hearings, and publishers were asked to limit the number of severed heads and dripping entrails—a reminder that television wasn't the first popular medium selling sadism to boys.) Best of all, I could stop pretending to enjoy the ridicule, bossing-around, and constant endangering of female characters. In these Amazon adventures, only the villains bought the idea that "masculine" meant aggression and "feminine" meant submission. Only the occasional female accomplice said things like "Girls want superior men to boss them around," and even they were usually converted to the joys of self-respect by the story's end.

9   This was an Amazon super-hero who never killed her enemies. Instead, she converted them to a belief in equality and peace, to self-reliance, and respect for the rights of others. If villains destroyed themselves, it was through their own actions or some unbloody accident. Otherwise, they might be conquered by force, but it was a force tempered by love and justice.

10   In short, she was wise, beautiful, brave, and explicitly out to change "a world torn by the hatreds and wars of men."

 READINGS

11   She was Wonder Woman.

12   Only much later, when I was in my thirties and modern feminism had begun to explain the political roots of women's status—instead of accepting some "natural" inferiority decreed by biology, God, or Freud—did I realize how hard Charles Moulton had tried to get an egalitarian worldview into comic book form. From Wonder Woman's birth myth as Princess Diana of Paradise Island, "that enlightened land," to her adventures in America disguised as Diana Prince, a be-spectacled army nurse and intelligence officer (a clear steal from Superman's Clark Kent), this female super-hero was devoted to democracy, peace, justice, and "liberty and freedom for all womankind."

13   One typical story centers on Prudence, a young pioneer in the days of the American Frontier, where Wonder Woman has been transported by the invisible plane that doubles as a time machine. After being rescued from a Perils of Pauline life, Prudence finally realizes her own worth, and also the worth of all women. "From now on," she says proudly to Wonder Woman, "I'll rely on myself, not on a man." Another story ends with Wonder Woman explaining her own long-running romance with Captain Steve Trevor, the American pilot whose crash-landing on Paradise Island was Aphrodite's signal that the strongest and wisest of all the Amazons must answer the call of a war-torn world. As Wonder Woman says of this colleague whom she so often rescues: "I can never love a dominant man."

14   The most consistent villain is Ares, God of War, a kind of meta-villain who considers women "the natural spoils of war" and insists they stay home as the slaves of men. Otherwise, he fears women will spread their antiwar sentiments, create democracy in the world, and leave him dishonored and unemployed. That's why he keeps trying to trick Queen Hippolyte, Princess Diana's mother, into giving up her powers as Queen of the Amazons, thus allowing him to conquer Paradise Island and destroy the last refuge of ancient feminism. It is in memory of a past time when the Amazons did give in to the soldiers of Ares, and were enslaved by them, that Aphrodite requires each Amazon to wear a pair of cufflike bracelets. If captured and bound by them (as Wonder Woman sometimes is in particularly harrowing episodes), an Amazon loses all her power. Wearing them is a reminder of the fragility of female freedom.

15   In America, however, villains are marked not only by their violence, but by their prejudice and lust for money. Thomas Tighe, woman-hating industrialist, is typical. After being rescued by Wonder Woman from accidental imprisonment in his own bank vault, he refuses to give her the

promised reward of a million dollars. Though the money is needed to support Holliday College, the home of the band of college girls who aid Wonder Woman, Tighe insists that its students must first complete impossible tests of strength and daring. Only after Wonder Woman's powers allow them to meet every challenge does Tighe finally admit: "You win, Wonder Woman! I am no longer a woman hater." She replies: "Then you're the real winner, Mr. Tighe! Because when one ceases to hate, he becomes stronger!"

16   Other villains are not so easily converted. Chief among them is Dr. Psycho, perhaps a parody of Sigmund Freud. An "evil genius" who "abhors women," the mad doctor's intentions are summed up in this scene-setting preface to an episode called "Battle for Womanhood": "With weird cunning and dark, forbidden knowledge of the occult, Dr. Psycho prepares to change the independent status of modern American women back to the days of the sultans and slave markets, clanking chains and abject captivity. But sly and subtle Psycho reckons without Wonder Woman!"

17   When I looked into the origins of my proto-feminist super-hero, I discovered that her pseudonymous creator had been a very non-Freudian psychologist named William Moulton Marston. Also a lawyer, businessman, prison reformer, and inventor of the lie-detector test (no doubt the inspiration for Wonder Woman's magic lasso), he had invented Wonder Woman as a heroine for little girls, and also as a conscious alternative to the violence of comic books for boys. In fact, Wonder Woman did attract some boys as readers, but the integrated world of comic book trading revealed her true status: at least three Wonder Woman comic books were necessary to trade for one of Superman. Among the many male super-heroes, only Superman and Batman were to be as long-lived as Wonder Woman, yet she was still a second-class citizen.

18   Of course, it's also true that Marston's message wasn't as feminist as it might have been. Instead of portraying the goal of full humanity for women and men, which is what feminism has in mind, he often got stuck in the subject/object, winner/loser paradigm of "masculine" versus "feminine," and came up with female superiority instead. As he wrote: "Women represent love; men represent force. Man's use of force without love brings evil and unhappiness. Wonder Woman proves that women are superior to men because they have love in addition to force." No wonder I was inspired but confused by the isolationism of Paradise Island: Did women have to live separately in order to be happy and courageous? No wonder even boys who could accept equality might have felt less than

good about themselves in some of these stories: Were there *any* men who could escape the cultural instruction to be violent?

19   Wonder Woman herself sometimes got trapped in this either/or choice. As she muses to herself: "Some girls love to have a man stronger than they are to make them do things. Do I like it? I don't know, it's sort of thrilling. But isn't it more fun to make a man obey?" Even female villains weren't capable of being evil on their own. Instead, they were hyperfeminine followers of men's commands. Consider Priscilla Rich, the upper-class antagonist who metamorphoses into the Cheetah, a dangerous she-animal. "Women have been submissive to men," wrote Marston, "and taken men's psychology [force without love] as their own."

20   In those wartime years, stories could verge on a jingoistic, even racist patriotism. Wonder Woman sometimes forgot her initial shock at America's unjust patriarchal system and confined herself to defeating a sinister foreign threat by proving that women could be just as loyal and brave as men in service of their country. Her costume was a version of the Stars and Stripes. Some of her adversaries were suspiciously short, ugly, fat, or ethnic as a symbol of "un-American" status. In spite of her preaching against violence and for democracy, the good guys were often in uniform, and no country but the United States was seen as a bastion of freedom.

21   But Marston didn't succumb to stereotypes as often as most comic book writers of the 1940s. Though Prudence, his frontier heroine, is threatened by monosyllabic Indians, Prudence's father turns out to be the true villain, who has been cheating the Indians. And the irrepressible Etta Candy, one of Wonder Woman's band of college girls, is surely one of the few fat-girl heroines in comics.

22   There are other unusual rewards. Queen Hippolyte, for instance, is a rare example of a mother who is good, powerful, and a mentor to her daughter. She founds nations, fights to protect Paradise Island, and is a source of strength to Wonder Woman as she battles the forces of evil and inequality. Mother and daughter stay in touch through a sort of telepathic TV set, and the result is a team of equals who are separated only by experience. In the flashback episode in which Queen Hippolyte succumbs to Hercules, she is even seen as a sexual being. How many girl children grew to adulthood with no such example of a strong, sensual mother—except for these slender stories? How many mothers preferred sons, or believed the patriarchal myth that competition is "natural" between mothers and daughters, or tamed their daughters instead of encouraging their wildness and strength? We are just beginning to realize the sense of anger and loss in girls whose mothers had no power to protect them, or forced them

to conform out of fear for their safety, or left them to identify only with their fathers if they had any ambition at all.

23   Finally, there is Wonder Woman's ability to unleash the power of self-respect within the women around her; to help them work together and support each other. This may not seem revolutionary to male readers accustomed to stories that depict men working together, but for females who are usually seen as competing for the favors of men—especially little girls who may just be getting to the age when girlfriends betray each other for the approval of boys—this discovery of sisterhood can be exhilarating indeed. Women get a rare message of independence, of depending on themselves, not even on Wonder Woman. "You saved yourselves," as she says in one of her inevitable morals at story's end. "I only showed you that you could."

24   Whatever the shortcomings of William Marston, his virtues became clear after his death in 1947. Looking back at the post-Marston stories I had missed the first time around—for at twelve or thirteen, I thought I had outgrown Wonder Woman and had abandoned her—I could see how little her later writers understood her spirit. She became sexier-looking and more submissive, violent episodes increased, more of her adversaries were female, and Wonder Woman herself required more help from men in order to triumph. Like so many of her real-life sisters in the postwar era of conservatism and "togetherness" of the 1950s, she had fallen on very hard times.

25   By the 1960s, Wonder Woman had given up her magic lasso, her bullet-deflecting bracelets, her invisible plane, and all her Amazonian powers. Though she still had adventures and even practiced karate, any attractive man could disarm her. She had become a kind of female James Bond, though much more boring because she was denied his sexual freedom. She was Diana Prince, a mortal who walked about in boutique, car-hop clothes and took the advice of a male mastermind named "I Ching."

26   It was in this sad state that I first rediscovered my Amazon super-hero in 1972. *Ms.* magazine had just begun, and we were looking for a cover story for its first regular issue to appear in July. Since Joanne Edgar and other of its founding editors had also been rescued by Wonder Woman in their childhoods, we decided to rescue Wonder Woman in return. Though it wasn't easy to persuade her publishers to let us put her original image on the cover of a new and unknown feminist magazine, or to reprint her 1940s Golden Age episodes inside, we finally succeeded. Wonder Woman appeared on newsstands again in all her original glory, striding through city streets like a colossus, stopping planes and bombs with one hand and rescuing buildings with the other.

READINGS

27   Clearly, there were many nostalgic grown-ups and heroine-starved readers of all ages. The consensus of response seemed to be that if we had all read more about Wonder Woman and less about Dick and Jane, we might have been a lot better off. As for her publishers, they, too, were impressed. Under the direction of Dorothy Woolfolk, the first woman editor of Wonder Woman in all her long history, she was returned to her original Amazon status—golden lasso, bracelets, and all.

28   One day some months after her rebirth, I got a phone call from one of Wonder Woman's tougher male writers. "Okay," he said, "she's got all her Amazon powers back. She talks to the Amazons on Paradise Island. She even has a Black Amazon sister named Nubia. Now will you leave me alone?"

29   I said we would.

30   In the 1970s, Wonder Woman became the star of a television series. As played by Lynda Carter, she was a little blue of eye and large of breast, but she still retained her Amazon powers, her ability to convert instead of kill, and her appeal for many young female viewers. There were some who refused to leave their TV sets on Wonder Woman night. A few young boys even began to dress up as Wonder Woman on Halloween—a true revolution.

31   In the 1980s, Wonder Woman's story line was revamped by DC Comics, which reinvented its male super-heroes Superman and Batman at about the same time. Steve Trevor became a veteran of Vietnam; he remained a friend, but was romantically involved with Etta Candy. Wonder Woman acquired a Katharine Hepburn–Spencer Tracy relationship with a street-smart Boston detective named Ed Indelicato, whose tough-guy attitude played off Wonder Woman's idealism. She also gained a friend and surrogate mother in Julia Kapatelis, a leading archaeologist and professor of Greek culture at Harvard University who can understand the ancient Greek that is Wonder Woman's native tongue, and be a model of a smart, caring, single mother for girl readers. Julia's teenage daughter, Vanessa, is the age of many readers and goes through all of their uncertainties, trials, and tribulations, but has the joy of having a powerful older sister in Wonder Woman. There is even Myndi Mayer, a slick Hollywood public relations agent who turns Wonder Woman into America's hero, and is also in constant danger of betraying Diana's idealistic spirit. In other words, there are many of the currents of society today, from single mothers to the worries of teenage daughters and a commercial culture, instead of the simpler plots of America's dangers in World War II.

32   You will see whether Wonder Woman carries her true Amazon spirit into the present. If not, let her publishers know. She belongs to you.

33   Since Wonder Woman's beginnings more than a half century ago, however, a strange thing has happened: The Amazon myth has been re-thought as archaeological relics have come to light. Though Amazons had been considered figments of the imagination, perhaps the mythological evidence of man's fear of woman, there is a tentative but growing body of evidence to support the theory that some Amazon-like societies did exist. In Europe, graves once thought to contain male skeletons—because they were buried with weapons or were killed by battle wounds—have turned out to hold skeletons of females after all. In the jungles of Brazil, scientists have found caves of what appears to have been an all-female society. The caves are strikingly devoid of the usual phallic design and theme; they feature, instead, the triangular female symbol, and the only cave that does bear male designs is believed to have been the copulatorium, where Amazons mated with males from surrounding tribes, kept only the female children, and returned male infants to the tribe. Such archaeological finds have turned up not only along the Amazon River in Brazil, but at the foot of the Atlas Mountains in northwestern Africa, and on the European and Asiatic sides of the Black Sea.

34   There is still far more controversy than agreement, but a shared supposition of these myths is this: Imposing patriarchy on the gynocracy of pre-history took many centuries and great cruelty. Rather than give up freedom and worship only male gods, some bands of women resisted. They formed all-woman cultures that survived by capturing men from local tribes, mating with them, and raising their girl children to have great skills of body and mind. These bands became warriors and healers who were sometimes employed for their skills by patriarchal cultures around them. As a backlash culture, they were doomed, but they may also have lasted for centuries.

35   Perhaps that's the appeal of Wonder Woman, Paradise Island, and this comic book message. It's not only a child's need for a lost independence, but an adult's need for a lost balance between women and men, between humans and nature. As the new Wonder Woman says to Vanessa, "Remember your power, little sister."

36   However simplified, that is Wonder Woman's message: Remember Our Power.

QUESTIONS TO CONSIDER

1. What pros and cons does Steinem see in the existence of superhero characters?

2. How does Steinem describe Wonder Woman, and how has Wonder Woman changed over time?

3. What does Steinem mean when she describes Wonder Woman as "proto-feminist" but "not as feminist as she could have been"? What are the qualities and abilities that Steinem identifies as "feminist" (in contrast to the qualities and abilities of typical male superheroes)?

4. What does Steinem want her readers to think about women in popular culture?

5. What messages does Steinem seem to believe that media (like comic books) send to readers and viewers?

6. How do Steinem's impressions compare with your own impressions of fictional heroes? What messages do *you* pick up on from the fictional heroes in books, movies, and television?

7. Gloria Steinem has said, "The greatest challenge for all of us, men and women, is not to learn, but to unlearn." What do *you* think people need to unlearn?

Mother Tongue

Amy Tan

- **N** Narration
- **CD** Classification and Division

1   I am not a scholar of English or literature. I cannot give you much more than personal opinions on the English language and its variations in this country or others.

2   I am a writer. And by that definition, I am someone who has always loved language. I am fascinated by language in daily life. I spend a great deal of my time thinking about the power of language—the way it can evoke an emotion, a visual image, a complex idea, or a simple truth. Language is the tool of my trade. And I use them all—all the Englishes I grew up with.

3   Recently, I was made keenly aware of the different Englishes I do use. I was giving a talk to a large group of people, the same talk I had already given to half a dozen other groups. The nature of the talk was about my writing, my life, and my book, *The Joy Luck Club.* The talk was going along well enough, until I remembered one major difference that made the whole talk sound wrong. My mother was in the room. And it was perhaps the first time she had heard me give a lengthy speech, using the kind of English I have never used with her. I was saying things like, "The intersection of memory upon imagination" and "There is an aspect of my fiction that relates to thus- and- thus"—a speech filled with carefully wrought grammatical phrases, burdened, it suddenly seemed to me, with nominalized forms, past perfect tenses, conditional phrases, all the forms of standard English that I had learned in school and through books, the forms of English I did not use at home with my mother.

4   Just last week, I was walking down the street with my mother, and I again found myself conscious of the English I was using, and the English I do use with her. We were talking about the price of new and used furniture and I heard myself saying this: "Not waste money that way." My husband was with us as well, and he didn't notice any switch in my English. And then I realized why. It's because over the twenty years we've been together I've often used that same kind of English with him, and sometimes he

even uses it with me. It has become our language of intimacy, a different sort of English that relates to family talk, the language I grew up with.

5   So you'll have some idea of what this family talk I heard sounds like, I'll quote what my mother said during a recent conversation which I videotaped and then transcribed. During this conversation my mother was talking about a political gangster in Shanghai who had the same last name as her family's, Du, and how the gangster in his early years wanted to be adopted by her family, which was rich by comparison. Later, the gangster became more powerful, far richer than my mother's family, and one day showed up at my mother's wedding to pay his respects. Here's what she said in part:

6   "Du Yusong having business like fruit stand. Like off the street kind. He is Du like Du Zong—but not Tsung-ming Island people. The local people call putong, the river east side, he belong to that side local people. The man want to ask Du Zong father take him in like become own family. Du Zong father wasn't looking down on him, but didn't take seriously, until that man big like become a mafia. Now important person very hard to inviting him. Chinese way, come only to show respect, don't stay for dinner. Respect for making big celebration, he shows up. Mean gives lots of respect. Chinese custom. Chinese social life that way. If too important won't have to stay too long. He come to my wedding. I didn't see. I heard it. I gone to boy's side, they have YMCA dinner. Chinese age I was nineteen."

7   You should know that my mother's expressive command of English belies how much she actually understands. She reads the *Forbes* report, listens to *Wall Street Week*, converses daily with her stockbroker, reads all of Shirley MacLaine's books with ease—all kinds of things I can't begin to understand. Yet some of my friends tell me they understand 50 percent of what my mother says. Some say they understand 80 to 90 percent. Some say they understand none of it, as if she were speaking pure Chinese. But to me, my mother's English is perfectly clear, perfectly natural. It's my mother's tongue. Her language, as I hear it, is vivid, direct, full of observation and imagery. This was the language that helped shape the way I saw things, expressed things, made sense of the world.

8   Lately, I've been giving more thought to the kind of English my mother speaks. Like others, I have described it to people as "broken" or "fractured" English. But I wince when I say that. It has always bothered me that I can think of no way to describe it other than "broken," as if it were damaged and needed to be fixed, as if it lacked a certain wholeness and soundness. I've heard other terms used, "limited English," for example. But they seem just as bad, as if everything is limited, including people's perceptions of the limited English speaker.

9   I know this for a fact, because when I was growing up, my mother's "limited" English limited *my* perception of her. I was ashamed of her English. I believed that her English reflected the quality of what she had to say. That is, because she expressed them imperfectly her thoughts were imperfect. And I had plenty of empirical evidence to support me: the fact that people in department stores, at banks, and at restaurants did not take her seriously, did not give her good service, pretended not to understand her, or even acted as if they did not hear her.

10   My mother has long realized the limitations of her English as well. When I was fifteen, she used to have me call people on the phone to pretend I was she. In this guise, I was forced to ask for information or even complain and yell at people who had been rude to her. One time it was a call to her stockbroker in New York. She had cashed out her small portfolio and it just so happened we were going to go to New York the next week, our very first trip outside California. I had to get on the phone and say in an adolescent voice that was not very convincing, "This is Mrs. Tan."

11   And my mother was standing in the back whispering loudly, "Why he don't send me check, already two weeks late. So mad he lie to me, losing me money."

12   And then I said in perfect English, "Yes, I'm getting rather concerned. You had agreed to send the check two weeks ago, but it hasn't arrived."

13   Then she began to talk more loudly. "What he want, I come to New York tell him front of his boss, you cheating me?" And I was trying to calm her down, make her be quiet, while telling the stockbroker, "I can't tolerate any more excuses. If I don't receive the check immediately I am going to have to speak to your manager when I'm in New York next week." And sure enough, the following week there we were in front of this astonished stockbroker, and I was sitting there red-faced and quiet, and my mother, the real Mrs. Tan, was shouting at his boss in her impeccable broken English.

14   We used a similar routine just five days ago, for a situation that was far less humorous. My mother had gone to the hospital for an appointment, to find out about a benign brain tumor a CAT scan had revealed a month ago. She said she had spoken very good English, her best English, no mistakes. Still, she said, the hospital did not apologize when they said they had lost the CAT scan and she had come for nothing. She said they did not seem to have any sympathy when she told them she was anxious to know the exact diagnosis, since her husband and son had both died of brain tumors. She said they would not give her any more information

until the next time and she would have to make another appointment for that. So she said she would not leave until the doctor called her daughter. She wouldn't budge. And when the doctor finally called her daughter, me, who spoke in perfect English—lo and behold—we had assurances the CAT scan would be found, promises that a conference call on Monday would be held, and apologies for any suffering my mother had gone through for a most regrettable mistake.

15   I think my mother's English almost had an effect on limiting my possibilities in life as well. Sociologists and linguists probably will tell you that a person's developing language skills are more influenced by peers. But I do think that the language spoken in the family, especially in immigrant families which are more insular, plays a large role in shaping the language of the child. And I believe that it affected my results on achievement tests, IQ tests, and the SAT. While my English skills were never judged as poor, compared to math, English could not be considered my strong suit. In grade school I did moderately well, getting perhaps B's, sometimes B-pluses, in English and scoring perhaps in the sixtieth or seventieth percentile on achievement tests. But those scores were not good enough to override the opinion that my true abilities lay in math and science, because in those areas I achieved A's and scored in the ninetieth percentile or higher.

16   This was understandable. Math is precise; there is only one correct answer. Whereas, for me at least, the answers on English tests were always a judgment call, a matter of opinion and personal experience. Those tests were constructed around items like fill-in-the-blank sentence completion, such as "Even though Tom was_____, Mary thought he was_____." And the correct answer always seemed to be the most bland combinations of thoughts, for example, "Even though Tom was shy, Mary thought he was charming," with the grammatical structure "even though" limiting the correct answer to some sort of semantic opposites, so you wouldn't get answers like, "Even though Tom was foolish, Mary thought he was ridiculous." Well, according to my mother, there were very few limitations as to what Tom could have been and what Mary might have thought of him. So I never did well on tests like that.

17   The same was true with word analogies, pairs of words in which you were supposed to find some sort of logical, semantic relationship—for example, "*Sunset* is to *nightfall* as_____is to_____." And here you would be presented with a list of four possible pairs, one of which showed the same kind of relationship: *red* is to *stoplight*, *bus* is to *arrival*, *chills* is to

fever, yawn is to *boring*. Well, I could never think that way. I knew what the tests were asking, but I could not block out of my mind the images already created by the first pair, "*sunset* is to *nightfall*"—and I would see a burst of colors against a darkening sky, the moon rising, the lowering of a curtain of stars. And all the other pairs of words—red, bus, stoplight, boring—just threw up a mass of confusing images, making it impossible for me to sort out something as logical as saying: "A sunset precedes nightfall" is the same as "a chill precedes a fever." The only way I would have gotten that answer right would have been to imagine an associative situation, for example, my being disobedient and staying out past sunset, catching a chill at night, which turns into feverish pneumonia as punishment, which indeed did happen to me.

18   I have been thinking about all this lately, about my mother's English, about achievement tests. Because lately I've been asked, as a writer, why there are not more Asian Americans represented in American literature "Why are there few Asian Americans enrolled in creative writing programs? Why do so many Chinese students go into engineering? Well, these are broad sociological questions I can't begin to answer. But I have noticed in surveys—in fact, just last week—that Asian students, as a whole, always do significantly better on math achievement tests than in English. And this makes me think that there are other Asian-American students whose English spoken in the home might also be described as "broken" or "limited." And perhaps they also have teachers who are steering them away from writing and into math and science, which is what happened to me.

19   Fortunately, I happen to be rebellious in nature and enjoy the challenge of disproving assumptions made about me. I became an English major my first year in college, after being enrolled as pre-med. I started writing nonfiction as a freelancer the week after I was told by my former boss that writing was my worst skill and I should hone my talents toward account management.

20   But it wasn't until 1985 that I finally began to write fiction. And at first I wrote using what I thought to be wittily crafted sentences, sentences that would finally prove I had mastery over the English language. Here's an example from the first draft of a story that later made its way into *The Joy Luck Club,* but without this line: "That was my mental quandary in its nascent state." A terrible line, which I can barely pronounce.

21   Fortunately, for reasons I won't get into today, I later decided I should envision a reader for the stories I would write. And the reader I decided

READINGS

upon was my mother because these were stories about mothers. So with this reader in mind—and in fact she did read my early drafts—I began to write stories using all the Englishes I grew up with: the English I spoke to my mother, which for lack of a better term might be described as "simple"; the English she used with me, which for lack of a better term might be described as "broken"; my translation of her Chinese, which could certainly be described as "watered down"; and what I imagined to be her translation of her Chinese if she could speak in perfect English, her internal language, and for that I sought to preserve the essence, but neither an English nor a Chinese structure. I wanted to capture what language ability tests can never reveal: her intent, her passion, her imagery, the rhythms of her speech and the nature of her thoughts.

22   Apart from what any critic had to say about my writing, I knew I had succeeded where it counted when my mother finished reading my book and gave me her verdict: "So easy to read."

? QUESTIONS TO CONSIDER

1. Tan begins her essay by claiming she is not a scholar of literature. Is this true? Does this fact change by the end of the essay?

2. What does Tan mean by the "language of intimacy"?

3. How does the way you speak change from work to school to home? Does your language change depending on your surroundings?

4. Why does Tan avoid labels like "broken," "fractured," and "limited"? What label does she finally use for her mother's language?

5. Write about a time in your life in which a language misunderstanding caused confusion or even comedy. Use dialogue and describe in detail the characters involved.

Sex, Lies and Conversation: Why Is It So Hard for Men and Women to Talk to Each Other?

Deborah Tannen

- **IE** Illustration and Exemplification
- **CC** Compare and Contrast
- **AP** Argument and Persuasion
- **CE** Cause and Effect

1   I was addressing a small gathering in a suburban Virginia living room—a women's group that had invited men to join them. Throughout the evening, one man had been particularly talkative, frequently offering ideas and anecdotes, while his wife sat silently beside him on the couch. Toward the end of the evening, I commented that women frequently complain that their husbands don't talk to them. This man quickly concurred. He gestured toward his wife and said, "She's the talker in our family." The room burst into laughter; the man looked puzzled and hurt. "It's true," he explained. "When I come home from work I have nothing to say. If she didn't keep the conversation going, we'd spend the whole evening in silence."

2   This episode crystallizes the irony that although American men tend to talk more than women in public situations, they often talk less at home. And this pattern is wreaking havoc with marriage.

3   The pattern was observed by political scientist Andrew Hacker in the late '70s. Sociologist Catherine Kohler Riessman reports in her new book *Divorce Talk* that most of the women she interviewed—but only a few of the men—gave lack of communication as the reason for their divorces. Given the current divorce rate of nearly 50 percent, that amounts to millions of cases in the United States every year—a virtual epidemic of failed conversation.

4   In my own research, complaints from women about their husbands most often focused not on tangible inequities such as having given up the chance for a career to accompany a husband to his, or doing far more than their share of daily life-support work like cleaning, cooking, social arrangements and errands. Instead, they focused on communication: "He doesn't listen to me," "He doesn't talk to me." I found, as Hacker observed years before, that most wives want their husbands to be, first and foremost, conversational partners, but few husbands share this expectation of their wives.

5   In short, the image that best represents the current crisis is the ste-
reotypical cartoon scene of a man sitting at the breakfast table with a
newspaper held up in front of his face, while a woman glares at the back
of it, wanting to talk.

Linguistic Battle of the Sexes

6   How can women and men have such different impressions of communication in marriage? Why the widespread imbalance in their interests and expectations?

7   In the April [1990] issue of *American Psychologist*, Stanford
University's Eleanor Maccoby reports the results of her own and others'
research showing that children's development is most influenced by the
social structure of peer interactions. Boys and girls tend to play with children of their own gender, and their sex-separate groups have different
organizational structures and interactive norms.

8   I believe these systematic differences in childhood socialization make
talk between women and men like cross-cultural communication, heir to
all the attraction and pitfalls of that enticing but difficult enterprise. My
research on men's and women's conversations uncovered patterns similar
to those described for children's groups.

9   For women, as for girls, intimacy is the fabric of relationships, and
talk is the thread from which it is woven. Little girls create and maintain
friendships by exchanging secrets; similarly, women regard conversation
as the cornerstone of friendship. So a woman expects her husband to be
a new and improved version of a best friend. What is important is not
the individual subjects that are discussed but the sense of closeness, of
a life shared, that emerges when people tell their thoughts, feelings, and
impressions.

10   Bonds between boys can be as intense as girls', but they are based less
on talking, more on doing things together. Since they don't assume talk is
the cement that binds a relationship, men don't know what kind of talk
women want, and they don't miss it when it isn't there.

11   Boys' groups are larger, more inclusive, and more hierarchical, so
boys must struggle to avoid the subordinate position in the group. This
may play a role in women's complaints that men don't listen to them.
Some men really don't like to listen, because being the listener makes
them feel one-down, like a child listening to adults or an employee to a
boss.

12   But often when women tell men, "You aren't listening," and the men protest, "I am," the men are right. The impression of not listening results from misalignments in the mechanics of conversation. The misalignment begins as soon as a man and a woman take physical positions. This became clear when I studied videotapes made by psychologist Bruce Dorval of children and adults talking to their same-sex best friends. I found that at every age, the girls and women faced each other directly, their eyes anchored on each other's faces. At every age, the boys and men sat at angles to each other and looked elsewhere in the room, periodically glancing at each other. They were obviously attuned to each other, often mirroring each other's movements. But the tendency of men to face away can give women the impression they aren't listening even when they are. A young woman in college was frustrated: Whenever she told her boyfriend she wanted to talk to him, he would lie down on the floor, close his eyes, and put his arm over his face. This signaled to her, "He's taking a nap." But he insisted he was listening extra hard. Normally, he looks around the room, so he is easily distracted. Lying down and covering his eyes helped him concentrate on what she was saying.

13   Analogous to the physical alignment that women and men take in conversation is their topical alignment. The girls in my study tended to talk at length about one topic, but the boys tended to jump from topic to topic. The second-grade girls exchanged stories about people they knew. The second grade boys teased, told jokes, noticed things in the room and talked about finding games to play. The sixth-grade girls talked about problems with a mutual friend. The sixth-grade boys talked about 55 different topics, none of which extended over more than a few turns.

Listening to Body Language

14   Switching topics is another habit that gives women the impression men aren't listening, especially if they switch to a topic about themselves. But the evidence of the 10th-grade boys in my study indicates otherwise. The 10th-grade boys sprawled across their chairs with bodies parallel and eyes straight ahead, rarely looking at each other. They looked as if they were riding in a car, staring out the windshield. But they were talking about their feelings. One boy was upset because a girl had told him he had a drinking problem, and the other was feeling alienated from all his friends.

15   Now, when a girl told a friend about a problem, the friend responded by asking probing questions and expressing agreement and understanding.

But the boys dismissed each other's problems. Todd assured Richard that his drinking was "no big problem" because "sometimes you're funny when you're off your butt." And when Todd said he felt left out, Richard responded, "Why should you? You know more people than me."

16 Women perceived such responses as belittling and unsupportive. But the boys seemed satisfied with them. Whereas women reassure each other by implying, "You shouldn't feel bad because I've had similar experiences," men do so by implying, "You shouldn't feel bad because your problems aren't so bad."

17 There are even simpler reasons for women's impression that men don't listen. Linguist Lynette Hirschman found that women make more listener noise, such as "mhm," "uhuh," and "yeah," to show "I'm with you." Men, she found, more often give silent attention. Women who expect a stream of listener-noise interpret silent attention as no attention at all.

18 Women's conversational habits are as frustrating to men as men's are to women. Men who expect silent attention interpret a stream of listener-noise as overreaction or impatience. Also, when women talk to each other in a close, comfortable setting, they often overlap, finish each other's sentences and anticipate what the other is about to say. This practice, which I call "participatory listenership," is often perceived by men as interruption, intrusion and lack of attention.

19 A parallel difference caused a man to complain about his wife, "She just wants to talk about her own point of view. If I show her another view, she gets mad at me." When most women talk to each other, they assume a conversationalist's job is to express agreement and support. But many men see their conversational duty as pointing out the other side of an argument. This is heard as disloyalty by women, and refusal to offer the requisite support. It is not that women don't want to see other points of view, but that they prefer them phrased as suggestions and inquiries rather than as direct challenges.

20 In his book *Fighting for Life*, Walter Ong points out that men use "agonistic" or warlike, oppositional formats to do almost anything; thus discussion becomes debate, and conversation a competitive sport. In contrast, women see conversation as a ritual means of establishing rapport. If Jane tells a problem and June says she has a similar one, they walk away feeling closer to each other. But this attempt at establishing rapport can backfire when used with men. Men take too literally women's ritual "troubles talk," just as women mistake men's ritual challenges for real attack.

The Sounds of Silence

21   These differences begin to clarify why women and men have such different expectations about communication in marriage. For women, talk creates intimacy. Marriage is an orgy of closeness: you can tell your feelings and thoughts, and still be loved. Their greatest fear is being pushed away. But men live in a hierarchical world, where talk maintains independence and status. They are on guard to protect themselves from being put down and pushed around.

22   This explains the paradox of the talkative man who said of his silent wife, "She's the talker." In the public setting of a guest lecture, he felt challenged to show his intelligence and display his understanding of the lecture. But at home, where he has nothing to prove and no one to defend against, he is free to remain silent. For his wife, being home means she is free from the worry that something she says might offend someone, or spark disagreement, or appear to be showing off; at home she is free to talk.

23   The communication problems that endanger marriage can't be fixed by mechanical engineering. They require a new conceptual framework about the role of talk in human relationships. Many of the psychological explanations that have become second nature may not be helpful, because they tend to blame either women (for not being assertive enough) or men (for not being in touch with their feelings). A sociolinguistic approach by which male-female conversation is seen as cross-cultural communication allows us to understand the problem and forge solutions without blaming either party.

24   Once the problem is understood, improvement comes naturally, as it did to the young woman and her boyfriend who seemed to go to sleep when she wanted to talk. Previously, she had accused him of not listening, and he had refused to change his behavior, since that would be admitting fault. But then she learned about and explained to him the differences in women's and men's habitual ways of aligning themselves in conversation. The next time she told him she wanted to talk, he began, as usual, by lying down and covering his eyes. When the familiar negative reaction bubbled up, she reassured herself that he really was listening. But then he sat up and looked at her. Thrilled, she asked why. He said, "You like me to look at you when we talk, so I'll try to do it." Once he saw their differences as cross-cultural rather than right and wrong, he independently altered his behavior.

25   Women who feel abandoned and deprived when their husbands won't listen to or report daily news may be happy to discover their husbands trying to adapt once they understand the place of small talk in women's relationships. But if their husbands don't adapt, the women may still be comforted that for men, this is not a failure of intimacy. Accepting the difference, the wives may look to their friends or family for that kind of talk. And husbands who can't provide it shouldn't feel their wives have made unreasonable demands. Some couples will still decide to divorce, but at least their decisions will be based on realistic expectations.

26   In these times of resurgent ethnic conflicts, the world desperately needs cross-cultural understanding. Like charity, successful cross-cultural communication should begin at home.

? QUESTIONS TO CONSIDER

Comprehension

1. What does Deborah Tannen—a professional linguist and expert on gender communication—say is the link between miscommunication in marriages and the high divorce rate?

2. Describe Tannen's use of two of the authorities she mentions in her article concerning the topic of gender communication.

3. What are some of the striking differences in gender communication between men and women that Tannen and her sources note? Are these gender differences valid today?

Rhetoric

1. Who do you think were the likely readers of the original 1990 *Washington Post* article: mostly men or mostly women?

2. Is Tannen gender neutral in her essay—or does she subtly blame men more than women for communication problems?

3. Is Tannen's long, chatty title effective in drawing in general readers?

Writing

1. Using your own experiences, illustrate the differences in the way girls and boys, women and men communicate. Do you think that one way is superior to the other, or is the issue more complex?

2. What other factors in addition to poor communication might significantly affect whether a marriage is successful? Is poor communication also an issue in these other factors?

3. Tannen is talking about the miscommunication in straight couples; do you think that gay couples have similar problems?

Where I Lived, And What I Lived For

Henry David Thoreau

- **N** Narration
- **IE** Illustration and Exemplification
- **CC** Compare and Contrast
- **AP** Argument and Persuasion
- **CE** Cause and Effect

1   At a certain season of our life we are accustomed to consider every spot as the possible site of a house. I have thus surveyed the country on every side within a dozen miles of where I live. In imagination I have bought all the farms in succession, for all were to be bought, and I knew their price. I walked over each farmer's premises, tasted his wild apples, discoursed on husbandry with him, took his farm at his price, at any price, mortgaging it to him in my mind; even put a higher price on it—took everything but a deed of it—took his word for his deed, for I dearly love to talk—cultivated it, and him too to some extent, I trust, and withdrew when I had enjoyed it long enough, leaving him to carry it on. This experience entitled me to be regarded as a sort of real-estate broker by my friends. Wherever I sat, there I might live, and the landscape radiated from me accordingly. What is a house but a sedes, a seat?—better if a country seat. I discovered many a site for a house not likely to be soon improved, which some might have thought too far from the village, but to my eyes the village was too far from it. Well, there I might live, I said; and there I did live, for an hour, a summer and a winter life; saw how I could let the years run off, buffet the winter through, and see the spring come in. The future inhabitants of this region, wherever they may place their houses, may be sure that they have been anticipated. An afternoon sufficed to lay out the land into orchard, wood-lot, and pasture, and to decide what fine oaks or pines should be left to stand before the door, and whence each blasted tree could be seen to the best advantage; and then I let it lie, fallow, perchance, for a man is rich in proportion to the number of things which he can afford to let alone.

2   My imagination carried me so far that I even had the refusal of several farms—the refusal was all I wanted—but I never got my fingers burned by actual possession. The nearest that I came to actual possession was when I bought the Hollowell place, and had begun to sort my seeds, and collected materials with which to make a wheelbarrow to carry it on or

off with; but before the owner gave me a deed of it, his wife—every man has such a wife—changed her mind and wished to keep it, and he offered me ten dollars to release him. Now, to speak the truth, I had but ten cents in the world, and it surpassed my arithmetic to tell, if I was that man who had ten cents, or who had a farm, or ten dollars, or all together. However, I let him keep the ten dollars and the farm too, for I had carried it far enough; or rather, to be generous, I sold him the farm for just what I gave for it, and, as he was not a rich man, made him a present of ten dollars, and still had my ten cents, and seeds, and materials for a wheelbarrow left. I found thus that I had been a rich man without any damage to my poverty. But I retained the landscape, and I have since annually carried off what it yielded without a wheelbarrow. With respect to landscapes,

3   "I am monarch of all I survey, My right there is none to dispute."

4   I have frequently seen a poet withdraw, having enjoyed the most valuable part of a farm, while the crusty farmer supposed that he had got a few wild apples only. Why, the owner does not know it for many years when a poet has put his farm in rhyme, the most admirable kind of invisible fence, has fairly impounded it, milked it, skimmed it, and got all the cream, and left the farmer only the skimmed milk.

5   The real attractions of the Hollowell farm, to me, were: its complete retirement, being, about two miles from the village, half a mile from the nearest neighbor, and separated from the highway by a broad field; its bounding on the river, which the owner said protected it by its fogs from frosts in the spring, though that was nothing to me; the gray color and ruinous state of the house and barn, and the dilapidated fences, which put such an interval between me and the last occupant; the hollow and lichen-covered apple trees, nawed by rabbits, showing what kind of neighbors I should have; but above all, the recollection I had of it from my earliest voyages up the river, when the house was concealed behind a dense grove of red maples, through which I heard the house-dog bark. I was in haste to buy it, before the proprietor finished getting out some rocks, cutting down the hollow apple trees, and grubbing up some young birches which had sprung up in the pasture, or, in short, had made any more of his improvements. To enjoy these advantages I was ready to carry it on; like Atlas, to take the world on my shoulders—I never heard what compensation he received for that—and do all those things which had no other motive or excuse but that I might pay for it and be unmolested in my possession of it; for I knew all the while that it would yield the most abundant crop of the kind I wanted, if I could only afford to let it alone. But it turned out as I have said.

READINGS

6   All that I could say, then, with respect to farming on a large scale—I have always cultivated a garden—was, that I had had my seeds ready. Many think that seeds improve with age. I have no doubt that time discriminates between the good and the bad; and when at last I shall plant, I shall be less likely to be disappointed. But I would say to my fellows, once for all, As long as possible live free and uncommitted. It makes but little difference whether you are committed to a farm or the county jail.

7   Old Cato, whose "De Re Rustica" is my "Cultivator," says—and the only translation I have seen makes sheer nonsense of the passage—"When you think of getting a farm turn it thus in your mind, not to buy greedily; nor spare your pains to look at it, and do not think it enough to go round it once. The oftener you go there the more it will please you, if it is good." I think I shall not buy greedily, but go round and round it as long as I live, and be buried in it first, that it may please me the more at last.

8   The present was my next experiment of this kind, which I purpose to describe more at length, for convenience putting the experience of two years into one. As I have said, I do not propose to write an ode to dejection, but to brag as lustily as chanticleer in the morning, standing on his roost, if only to wake my neighbors up.

9   When first I took up my abode in the woods, that is, began to spend my nights as well as days there, which, by accident, was on Independence Day, or the Fourth of July, 1845, my house was not finished for winter, but was merely a defence against the rain, without plastering or chimney, the walls being of rough, weather-stained boards, with wide chinks, which made it cool at night. The upright white hewn studs and freshly planed door and windowcasings gave it a clean and airy look, especially in the morning, when its timbers were saturated with dew, so that I fancied that by noon some sweet gum would exude from them. To my imagination it retained throughout the day more or less of this auroral character, reminding me of a certain house on a mountain which I had visited a year before. This was an airy and unplastered cabin, fit to entertain a travelling god, and where a goddess might trail her garments. The winds which passed over my dwelling were such as sweep over the ridges of mountains, bearing the broken strains, or celestial parts only, of terrestrial music. The morning wind forever blows, the poem of creation is uninterrupted; but few are the ears that hear it. Olympus is but the outside of the earth everywhere.

10   The only house I had been the owner of before, if I except a boat, was a tent, which I used occasionally when making excursions in the summer,

and this is still rolled up in my garret; but the boat, after passing from hand to hand, has gone down the stream of time. With this more substantial shelter about me, I had made some progress toward settling in the world. This frame, so slightly clad, was a sort of crystallization around me, and reacted on the builder. It was suggestive somewhat as a picture in outlines. I did not need to go outdoors to take the air, for the atmosphere within had lost none of its freshness. It was not so much within doors as behind a door where I sat, even in the rainiest weather. The Harivansa says, "An abode without birds is like a meat without seasoning." Such was not my abode, for I found myself suddenly neighbor to the birds; not by having imprisoned one, but having caged myself near them. I was not only nearer to some of those which commonly frequent the garden and the orchard, but to those smaller and more thrilling songsters of the forest which never, or rarely, serenade a villager—the woodthrush, the veery, the scarlet tanager, the field sparrow, the whip-poor-will, and many others.

11   I was seated by the shore of a small pond, about a mile and a half south of the village of Concord and somewhat higher than it, in the midst of an extensive wood between that town and Lincoln, and about two miles south of that our only field known to fame, Concord Battle Ground; but I was so low in the woods that the opposite shore, half a mile off, like the rest, covered with wood, was my most distant horizon. For the first week, whenever I looked out on the pond it impressed me like a tarn high up on the side of a mountain, its bottom far above the surface of other lakes, and, as the sun arose, I saw it throwing off its nightly clothing of mist, and here and there, by degrees, its soft ripples or its smooth reflecting surface was revealed, while the mists, like ghosts, were stealthily withdrawing in every direction into the woods, as at the breaking up of some nocturnal conventicle. The very dew seemed to hang upon the trees later into the day than usual, as on the sides of mountains.

12   This small lake was of most value as a neighbor in the intervals of a gentle rain-storm in August, when, both air and water being perfectly still, but the sky overcast, mid-afternoon had all the serenity of evening, and the wood thrush sang around, and was heard from shore to shore. A lake like this is never smoother than at such a time; and the clear portion of the air above it being shallow and darkened by clouds, the water, full of light and reflections, becomes a lower heaven itself so much the more important. From a hill-top near by, where the wood had been recently cut off, there was a pleasing vista southward across the pond, through a wide

READINGS

indentation in the hills which form the shore there, where their opposite sides sloping toward each other suggested a stream flowing out in that direction through a wooded valley, but stream there was none. That way I looked between and over the near green hills to some distant and higher ones in the horizon, tinged with blue. Indeed, by standing on tiptoe I could catch a glimpse of some of the peaks of the still bluer and more distant mountain ranges in the northwest, those true-blue coins from heaven's own mint, and also of some portion of the village. But in other directions, even from this point, I could not see over or beyond the woods which surrounded me. It is well to have some water in your neighborhood, to give buoyancy to and float the earth. One value even of the smallest well is, that when you look into it you see that earth is not continent but insular. This is as important as that it keeps butter cool. When I looked across the pond from this peak toward the Sudbury meadows, which in time of flood I distinguished elevated perhaps by a mirage in their seething valley, like a coin in a basin, all the earth beyond the pond appeared like a thin crust insulated and floated even by this small sheer of intervening water, and I was reminded that this on which I dwelt was but dry land.

13   Though the view from my door was still more contracted, I did not feel crowded or confined in the least. There was pasture enough for my imagination. The low shrub oak plateau to which the opposite shore arose stretched away toward the prairies of the West and the steppes of Tartary, affording ample room for all the roving families of men. "There are none happy in the world but beings who enjoy freely a vast horizon"— said Damodara, when his herds required new and larger pastures.

14   Both place and time were changed, and I dwelt nearer to those parts of the universe and to those eras in history which had most attracted me. Where I lived was as far off as many a region viewed nightly by astronomers. We are wont to imagine rare and delectable places in some remote and more celestial corner of the system, behind the constellation of Cassiopeia's Chair, far from noise and disturbance. I discovered that my house actually had its site in such a withdrawn, but forever new and unprofaned, part of the universe. If it were worth the while to settle in those parts near to the Pleiades or the Hyades, to Aldebaran or Altair, then I was really there, or at an equal remoteness from the life which I had left behind, dwindled and twinkling with as fine a ray to my nearest neighbor, and to be seen only in moonless nights by him. Such was that part of creation where I had squatted;

15   "There was a shepherd that did live,
                And held his thoughts as high
             As were the mounts whereon his flocks
                Did hourly feed him by."

16   What should we think of the shepherd's life if his flocks always wandered to higher pastures than his thoughts?

17   Every morning was a cheerful invitation to make my life of equal simplicity, and I may say innocence, with Nature herself. I have been as sincere a worshipper of Aurora as the Greeks. I got up early and bathed in the pond; that was a religious exercise, and one of the best things which I did. They say that characters were engraven on the bathing tub of King Tching-thang to this effect: "Renew thyself completely each day; do it again, and again, and forever again." I can understand that. Morning brings back the heroic ages. I was as much affected by the faint burn of a mosquito making its invisible and unimaginable tour through my apartment at earliest dawn, when I was sailing with door and windows open, as I could be by any trumpet that ever sang of fame. It was Homer's requiem; itself an Iliad and Odyssey in the air, singing its own wrath and wanderings. There was something cosmical about it; a standing advertisement, till forbidden, of the everlasting vigor and fertility of the world. The morning, which is the most memorable season of the day, is the awakening hour. Then there is least somnolence in us; and for an hour, at least, some part of us awakes which slumbers all the rest of the day and night. Little is to be expected of that day, if it can be called a day, to which we are not awakened by our Genius, but by the mechanical nudgings of some servitor, are not awakened by our own newly acquired force and aspirations from within, accompanied by the undulations of celestial music, instead of factory bells, and a fragrance filling the air—to a higher life than we fell asleep from; and thus the darkness bear its fruit, and prove itself to be good, no less than the light. That man who does not believe that each day contains an earlier, more sacred, and auroral hour than he has yet profaned, has despaired of life, and is pursuing a descending and darkening way. After a partial cessation of his sensuous life, the soul of man, or its organs rather, are reinvigorated each day, and his Genius tries again what noble life it can make. All memorable events, I should say, transpire in morning time and in a morning atmosphere. The Vedas say, "All intelligences awake with the morning." Poetry and art, and the faire stand most memorable of the actions of men, date from such an hour. All poets and heroes, like Memnon, are the children of Aurora, and emit their music at

sunrise. To him whose elastic and vigorous thought keeps pace with the sun, the day is a perpetual morning. It matters not what the clocks say or the attitudes and labors of men. Morning is when I am awake and there is a dawn in me. Moral reform is the effort to throw off sleep. Why is it that men give so poor an account of their day if they have not been slumbering? They are not such poor calculators. If they had not been overcome with drowsiness, they would have performed something. The millions are awake enough for physical labor; but only one in a million is awake enough for effective intellectual exertion, only one in a hundred millions to a poetic or divine life. To be awake is to be alive. I have never yet met a man who was quite awake. How could I have looked him in the face?

18   We must learn to reawaken and keep ourselves awake, not by mechanical aids, but by an infinite expectation of the dawn, which does not forsake us in our soundest sleep. I know of no more encouraging fact than the unquestionable ability of man to elevate his life by a conscious endeavor. It is something to be able to paint a particular picture, or to carve a statue, and so to make a few objects beautiful; but it is far more glorious to carve and paint the very atmosphere and medium through which we look, which morally we can do. To affect the quality of the day, that is the highest of arts. Every man is tasked to make his life, even in its details, worthy of the contemplation of his most elevated and critical hour. If we refused, or rather used up, such paltry information as we get, the oracles would distinctly inform us how this might be done.

19   I went to the woods because I wished to live deliberately, to front only the essential facts of life, and see if I could not learn what it had to teach, and not, when I came to die, discover that I had not lived. I did not wish to live what was not life, living is so dear; nor did I wish to practise resignation, unless it was quite necessary. I wanted to live deep and suck out all the marrow of life, to live so sturdily and Spartan-like as to put to rout all that was not life, to cut a broad swath and shave close, to drive life into a corner, and reduce it to its lowest terms, and, if it proved to be mean, why then to get the whole and genuine meanness of it, and publish its meanness to the world; or if it were sublime, to know it by experience, and be able to give a true account of it in my next excursion. For most men, it appears to me, are in a strange uncertainty about it, whether it is of the devil or of God, and have somewhat hastily concluded that it is the chief end of man here to "glorify God and enjoy him forever."

20   Still we live meanly, like ants; though the fable tells us that we were long ago changed into men, like pygmies we fight with cranes, it is error

upon error, clout upon clout, and our best virtue has for its occasion a superfluous and evitable wretchedness. Our life is frittered away by detail. An honest man has hardly need to count more than his ten fingers, or in extreme cases he may add his ten toes, and lump the rest. Simplicity, simplicity, simplicity! I say, let your affairs be as two or three, and not a hundred or a thousand; instead of a million count half a dozen, and keep your accounts on your thumb-nail. In the midst of this chopping sea of civilized life, such are the clouds and storms and quicksands and thousand-and-one items to be allowed for, that a man has to live, if he would not founder and go to the bottom and not make his port at all, by dead reckoning, and he must be a great calculator indeed who succeeds. Simplify, simplify. Instead of three meals a day, if it be necessary eat but one; instead of a hundred dishes, five; and reduce other things in proportion. Our life is like a German Confederacy, made up of petty states, with its boundary forever fluctuating, so that even a German cannot tell you how it is bounded at any moment. The nation itself, with all its so-called internal improvements, which, by the way are all external and superficial, is just such an unwieldy and overgrown establishment, cluttered with furniture and tripped up by its own traps, ruined by luxury and heedless expense, by want of calculation and a worthy aim, as the million households in the land; and the only cure for it, as for them, is in a rigid economy, a stern and more than Spartan simplicity of life and elevation of purpose. It lives too fast. Men think that it is essential that the Nation have commerce, and export ice, and talk through a telegraph, and ride thirty miles an hour, without a doubt, whether they do or not; but whether we should live like baboons or like men, is a little uncertain. If we do not get out sleepers, and forge rails, and devote days and nights to the work, but go to tinkering upon our lives to improve them, who will build railroads? And if railroads are not built, how shall we get to heaven in season? But if we stay at home and mind our business, who will want railroads? We do not ride on the railroad; it rides upon us. Did you ever think what those sleepers are that underlie the railroad? Each one is a man, an Irishman, or a Yankee man. The rails are laid on them, and they are covered with sand, and the cars run smoothly over them. They are sound sleepers, I assure you. And every few years a new lot is laid down and run over; so that, if some have the pleasure of riding on a rail, others have the misfortune to be ridden upon. And when they run over a man that is walking in his sleep, a supernumerary sleeper in the wrong position, and wake him up, they suddenly stop the cars, and make a hue and cry about it, as if this

READINGS

286 READINGS **HENRY DAVID THOREAU**

were an exception. I am glad to know that it takes a gang of men for every five miles to keep the sleepers down and level in their beds as it is, for this is a sign that they may sometime get up again.

21   Why should we live with such hurry and waste of life? We are determined to be starved before we are hungry. Men say that a stitch in time saves nine, and so they take a thousand stitches today to save nine tomorrow. As for work, we haven't any of any consequence. We have the Saint Vitus' dance, and cannot possibly keep our heads still. If I should only give a few pulls at the parish bell-rope, as for a fire, that is, without setting the bell, there is hardly a man on his farm in the outskirts of Concord, notwithstanding that press of engagements which was his excuse so many times this morning, nor a boy, nor a woman, I might almost say, but would forsake all and follow that sound, not mainly to save property from the flames, but, if we will confess the truth, much more to see it burn, since burn it must, and we, be it known, did not set it on fire—or to see it put out, and have a hand in it, if that is done as handsomely; yes, even if it were the parish church itself. Hardly a man takes a half-hour's nap after dinner, but when he wakes he holds up his head and asks, "What's the news?" as if the rest of mankind had stood his sentinels. Some give directions to be waked every half-hour, doubtless for no other purpose; and then, to pay for it, they tell what they have dreamed. After a night's sleep the news is as indispensable as the breakfast. "Pray tell me anything new that has happened to a man anywhere on this globe"—and he reads it over his coffee and rolls, that a man has had his eyes gouged out this morning on the Wachito River; never dreaming the while that he lives in the dark unfathomed mammoth cave of this world, and has but the rudiment of an eye himself.

22   For my part, I could easily do without the post-office. I think that there are very few important communications made through it. To speak critically, I never received more than one or two letters in my life—I wrote this some years ago—that were worth the postage. The penny-post is, commonly, an institution through which you seriously offer a man that penny for his thoughts which is so often safely offered in jest. And I am sure that I never read any memorable news in a newspaper. If we read of one man robbed, or murdered, or killed by accident, or one house burned, or one vessel wrecked, or one steamboat blown up, or one cow run over on the Western Railroad, or one mad dog killed, or one lot of grasshoppers in the winter—we never need read of another. One is enough. If you are acquainted with the principle, what do you care for a myriad instances

and applications? To a philosopher all news, as it is called, is gossip, and they who edit and read it are old women over their tea. Yet not a few are greedy after this gossip. There was such a rush, as I hear, the other day at one of the offices to learn the foreign news by the last arrival, that several large squares of plate glass belonging to the establishment were broken by the pressure—news which I seriously think a ready wit might write a twelve month, or twelve years, beforehand with sufficient accuracy. As for Spain, for instance, if you know how to throw in Don Carlos and the Infanta, and Don Pedro and Seville and Granada, from time to time in the right proportions—they may have changed the names a little since I saw the papers—and serve up a bull-fight when other entertainments fail, it will be true to the letter, and give us as good an idea of the exact state or ruin of things in Spain as the most succinct and lucid reports under this head in the newspapers: and as for England, almost the last significant scrap of news from that quarter was the revolution of 1649; and if you have learned the history of her crops for an average year, you never need attend to that thing again, unless your speculations are of a merely pecuniary character. If one may judge who rarely looks into the newspapers, nothing new does ever happen in foreign parts, a French revolution not excepted.

23   What news! how much more important to know what that is which was never old! "Kieou-he-yu (great dignitary of the state of Wei) sent a man to Khoung-tseu to know his news. Khoung-tseu caused the messenger to be seated near him, and questioned him in these terms: What is your master doing? The messenger answered with respect: My master desires to diminish the number of his faults, but he cannot come to the end of them. The messenger being gone, the philosopher remarked: What a worthy messenger! What a worthy messenger!" The preacher, instead of vexing the ears of drowsy farmers on their day of rest at the end of the week—for Sunday is the fit conclusion of an ill-spent week, and not the fresh and brave beginning of a new one—with this one other draggle-tail of a sermon, should shout with thundering voice, "Pause! Avast! Why so seeming fast, but deadly slow?"

24   Shams and delusions are esteemed for soundest truths, while reality is fabulous. If men would steadily observe realities only, and not allow themselves to be deluded, life, to compare it with such things as we know, would be like a fairy tale and the Arabian Nights' Entertainments. If we respected only what is inevitable and has a right to be, music and poetry would resound along the streets. When we are unhurried and wise, we

READINGS

perceive that only great and worthy things have any permanent and absolute existence, that petty fears and petty pleasures are but the shadow
of the reality. This is always exhilarating and sublime. By closing the eyes
and slumbering, and consenting to be deceived by shows, men establish
and confirm their daily life of routine and habit everywhere, which still
is built on purely illusory foundations. Children, who play life, discern its
true law and relations more clearly than men, who fail to live it worthily,
but who think that they are wiser by experience, that is, by failure. I have
read in a Hindoo book, that "there was a king's son, who, being expelled
in infancy from his native city, was brought up by a forester, and, growing
up to maturity in that state, imagined himself to belong to the barbarous
race with which he lived. One of his father's ministers having discovered
him, revealed to him what he was, and the misconception of his character was removed, and he knew himself to be a prince. So soul," continues
the Hindoo philosopher, "from the circumstances in which it is placed,
mistakes its own character, until the truth is revealed to it by some holy
teacher, and then it knows itself to be *Brahme*." I perceive that we inhabitants of New England live this mean life that we do because our vision
does not penetrate the surface of things. We think that that *is* which
appears to be. If a man should walk through this town and see only the
reality, where, think you, would the "Mill-dam" go to? If he should give us
an account of the realities he beheld there, we should not recognize the
place in his description. Look at a meeting-house, or a court-house, or a
jail, or a shop, or a dwelling-house, and say what that thing really is before
a true gaze, and they would all go to pieces in your account of them. Men
esteem truth remote, in the outskirts of the system, behind the farthest
star, before Adam and after the last man. In eternity there is indeed something true and sublime. But all these times and places and occasions are
now and here. God himself culminates in the present moment, and will
never be more divine in the lapse of all the ages. And we are enabled to
apprehend at all what is sublime and noble only by the perpetual instill-
ing and drenching of the reality that surrounds us. The universe constantly and obediently answers to our conceptions; whether we travel fast or
slow, the track is laid for us. Let us spend our lives in conceiving then. The
poet or the artist never yet had so fair and noble a design but some of his
posterity at least could accomplish it.

25   Let us spend one day as deliberately as Nature, and not be thrown
off the track by every nutshell and mosquito's wing that falls on the rails.
Let us rise early and fast, or break fast, gently and without perturbation;

let company come and let company go, let the bells ring and the children cry—determined to make a day of it. Why should we knock under and go with the stream? Let us not be upset and overwhelmed in that terrible rapid and whirlpool called a dinner, situated in the meridian shallows. Weather this danger and you are safe, for the rest of the way is down hill. With unrelaxed nerves, with morning vigor, sail by it, looking another way, tied to the mast like Ulysses. If the engine whistles, let it whistle till it is hoarse for its pains. If the bell rings, why should we run? We will consider what kind of music they are like. Let us settle ourselves, and work and wedge our feet downward through the mud and slush of opinion, and prejudice, and tradition, and delusion, and appearance, that alluvion which covers the globe, through Paris and London, through New York and Boston and Concord, through Church and State, through poetry and philosophy and religion, till we come to a hard bottom and rocks in place, which we can call reality, and say, This is, and no mistake; and then begin, having a point d'appui, below freshet and frost and fire, a place where you might found a wall or a state, or set a lamp-post safely, or perhaps a gauge, not a Nilometer, but a Realometer, that future ages might know how deep a freshet of shams and appearances had gathered from time to time. If you stand right fronting and face to face to a fact, you will see the sun glimmer on both its surfaces, as if it were a cimeter, and feel its sweet edge dividing you through the heart and marrow, and so you will happily conclude your mortal career. Be it life or death, we crave only reality. If we are really dying, let us hear the rattle in our throats and feel cold in the extremities; if we are alive, let us go about our business.

26   Time is but the stream I go a-fishing in. I drink at it; but while I drink I see the sandy bottom and detect how shallow it is. Its thin current slides away, but eternity remains. I would drink deeper; fish in the sky, whose bottom is pebbly with stars. I cannot count one. I know not the first letter of the alphabet. I have always been regretting that I was not as wise as the day I was born. The intellect is a cleaver; it discerns and rifts its way into the secret of things. I do not wish to be any more busy with my hands than is necessary. My head is hands and feet. I feel all my best faculties concentrated in it. My instinct tells me that my head is an organ for burrowing, as some creatures use their snout and fore paws, and with it I would mine and burrow my way through these hills. I think that the richest vein is somewhere hereabouts; so by the divining-rod and thin rising vapors I judge; and here I will begin to mine.

QUESTIONS TO CONSIDER

1. What does Thoreau mean when he says, "...I wished to live deliberately..."?

2. How are his calls for "simplicity" and his statement "to affect the quality of the day, that is the highest of arts" connected to his intention "to live deliberately"?

3. He views newspapers, railroads, and the post office as antithetical to the quality of life he is seeking. Do you agree that our contemporary equivalents of these prevent us from living "deliberately"?

4. What is the better description of Thoreau's purpose in this selection: an autobiographical account of his experiences living in the woods, or a philosophy of life meant to instruct the reader how to live?

5. To what degree is Thoreau's philosophy dependent upon his observation and approach to nature? To what degree is solitude significant to his ideas and experience?

"This Is the End of the World": The Black Death

Barbara Tuchman

- **N** Narration
- **DES** Description
- **PA** Process Analysis

1   In October 1347, two months after the fall of Calais, Genoese trading ships put into the harbor of Messina in Sicily with dead and dying men at the oars. The ships had come from the Black Sea port of Caffa (now Feodosiya) in the Crimea, where the Genoese maintained a trading post. The diseased sailors showed strange black swellings about the size of an egg or an apple in the armpits and groin. The swellings oozed blood and pus and were followed by spreading boils and black blotches on the skin from internal bleeding. The sick suffered severe pain and died quickly within five days of the first symptoms. As the disease spread, other symptoms of continuous fever and spitting of blood appeared instead of the swellings or buboes. These victims coughed and sweated heavily and died even more quickly, within three days or less, sometimes in 24 hours. In both types everything that issued from the body—breath, sweat, blood from the buboes and lungs, bloody urine, and blood-blackened excrement—smelled foul. Depression and despair accompanied the physical symptoms, and before the end "death is seen seated on the face."

2   The disease was bubonic plague, present in two forms: one that infected the bloodstream, causing the buboes and internal bleeding, and was spread by contact; and a second, more virulent pneumonic type that infected the lungs and was spread by respiratory infection. The presence of both at once caused the high mortality and speed of contagion. So lethal was the disease that cases were known of persons going to bed well and dying before they woke, of doctors catching the illness at a bedside and dying before the patient. So rapidly did it spread from one to another that to a French physician, Simon de Covino, it seemed as if one sick person "could infect the whole world." The malignity of the pestilence appeared more terrible because its victims knew no prevention and no remedy.

3   The physical suffering of the disease and its aspects of evil mystery were expressed in a strange Welsh lament which saw "death coming into

our midst like black smoke, a plague which cuts off the young, a rootless phantom which has no mercy for fair countenance. Woe is me of the shilling in the armpit! It is seething, terrible... a head that gives pain and causes a loud cry... a painful angry knob... Great is its seething like a burning cinder... a grievous thing of ashy color." Its eruption is ugly like the "seeds of black peas, broken fragments of brittle sea-coal... the early ornaments of black death, cinders of the peelings of the cockle weed, a mixed multitude, a black plague like halfpence, like berries..."

4   Rumors of a terrible plague supposedly arising in China and spreading through Tartary (Central Asia) to India and Persia, Mesopotamia, Syria, Egypt, and all of Asia Minor had reached Europe in 1346. They told of a death toll so devastating that all of India was said to be depopulated, whole territories covered by dead bodies, other areas with no one left alive. As added up by Pope Clement VI at Avignon, the total of reported dead reached 23,840,000. In the absence of a concept of contagion, no serious alarm was felt in Europe until the trading ships brought their black burden of pestilence into Messina while other infected ships from the Levant carried it to Genoa and Venice.

5   By January 1348 it penetrated France via Marseille, and North Africa via Tunis. Shipborne along coasts and navigable rivers, it spread westward from Marseille through the ports of Languedoc to Spain and northward up the Rhone to Avignon, where it arrived in March. It reached Narbonne, Montpellier, Carcassonne, and Toulouse between February and May, and at the same time in Italy spread to Rome and Florence and their hinterlands. Between June and August it reached Bordeaux, Lyon, and Paris, spread to Burgundy and Normandy, and crossed the Channel from Normandy into southern England. From Italy during the same summer it crossed the Alps into Switzerland and reached eastward to Hungary.

6   In a given area the plague accomplished its kill within four to six months and then faded, except in the larger cities, where, rooting into the close quartered population, it abated during the winter, only to reappear in spring and rage for another six months.

7   In 1349 it resumed in Paris, spread to Picardy, Flanders, and the Low Countries, and from England to Scotland and Ireland as well as to Norway, where a ghost ship with a cargo of wool and a dead crew drifted offshore until it ran aground near Bergen. From there the plague passed into Sweden, Denmark, Prussia, Iceland, and as far as Greenland. Leaving a strange pocket of immunity in Bohemia, and Russia unattacked until 1351, it had passed from most of Europe by mid-1350. Although the

mortality rate was erratic, ranging from one fifth in some places to nine tenths or almost total elimination in others, the overall estimate of modern demographers has settled—for the area extending from India to Iceland—around the same figure expressed in Froissart's casual words: "a third of the world died." His estimate, the common one at the time, was not an inspired guess but a borrowing of St. John's figure for mortality from plague in Revelation, the favorite guide to human affairs of the Middle Ages.

8   A third of Europe would have meant about 20 million deaths. No one knows in truth how many died. Contemporary reports were an awed impression, not an accurate count. In crowded Avignon, it was said, 400 died daily; 7,000 houses emptied by death were shut up; a single graveyard received 11,000 corpses in six weeks; half the city's inhabitants reportedly died, including 9 cardinals or one third of the total, and 70 lesser prelates. Watching the endlessly passing death carts, chroniclers let normal exaggeration take wings and put the Avignon death toll at 62,000 and even at 120,000, although the city's total population was probably less than 50,000.

9   When graveyards filled up, bodies at Avignon were thrown into the Rhône until mass burial pits were dug for dumping the corpses. In London in such pits corpses piled up in layers until they overflowed. Everywhere reports speak of the sick dying too fast for the living to bury. Corpses were dragged out of homes and left in front of doorways. Morning light revealed new piles of bodies. In Florence the dead were gathered up by the Compagnia della Misericordia—founded in 1244 to care for the sick—whose members wore red robes and hoods masking the face except for the eyes. When their efforts failed, the dead lay putrid in the streets for days at a time. When no coffins were to be had, the bodies were laid on boards, two or three at once, to be carried to graveyards or common pits. Families dumped their own relatives into the pits, or buried them so hastily and thinly "that dogs dragged them forth and devoured their bodies."

10   Amid accumulating death and fear of contagion, people died without last rites and were buried without prayers, a prospect that terrified the last hours of the stricken. A bishop in England gave permission to laymen to make confession to each other as was done by the Apostles, "or if no man is present then even to a woman," and if no priest could be found to administer extreme unction, "then faith must suffice." Clement VI found it necessary to grant remissions of sin to all who died of the plague because so many were unattended by priests. "And no bells tolled," wrote a

chronicler of Siena, "and nobody wept no matter what his loss because almost everyone expected death....And people said and believed, 'This is the end of the world.'"

11   In Paris, where the plague lasted through 1349, the reported death rate was 800 a day, in Pisa 500, in Vienna 500 to 600. The total dead in Paris numbered 50,000 or half the population. Florence, weakened by the famine of 1347, lost three to four fifths of its citizens, Venice two thirds, Hamburg and Bremen, though smaller in size, about the same proportion. Cities, as centers of transportation, were more likely to be affected than villages, although once a village was infected, its death rate was equally high. At Givry, a prosperous village in Burgundy of 1,200 to 1,500 people, the parish register records 615 deaths in the space of fourteen weeks, compared to an average of thirty deaths a year in the previous decade. In three villages of Cambridgeshire, manorial records show a death rate of 47 percent, 57 percent, and in one case 70 percent. When the last survivors, too few to carry on, moved away, a deserted village sank back into the wilderness and disappeared from the map altogether, leaving only a grass-covered ghostly outline to show where mortals once had lived.

12   In enclosed places such as monasteries and prisons, the infection of one person usually meant that of all, as happened in the Franciscan convents of Carcassonne and Marseille, where every inmate without exception died. Of the 140 Dominicans at Montpellier only seven survived. Petrarch's brother Gherardo, member of a Carthusian monastery, buried the prior and 34 fellow monks one by one, sometimes three a day, until he was left alone with his dog and fled to look for a place that would take him in. Watching every comrade die, men in such places could not but wonder whether the strange peril that filled the air had not been sent to exterminate the human race. In Kilkenny, Ireland, Brother John Clyn of the Friars Minor, another monk left alone among dead men, kept a record of what had happened lest "things which should be remembered perish with time and vanish from the memory of those who come after us." Sensing "the whole world, as it were, placed within the grasp of the Evil One," and waiting for death to visit him too, he wrote, "I leave parchment to continue this work, if perchance any man survive and any of the race of Adam escape this pestilence and carry on the work which I have begun." Brother John, as noted by another hand, died of the pestilence, but he foiled oblivion.

13   The largest cities of Europe, with populations of about 100,000, were Paris and Florence, Venice and Genoa. At the next level, with more

than 50,000, were Ghent and Bruges in Flanders, Milan, Bologna, Rome, Naples, and Palermo, and Cologne. London hovered below 50,000, the only city in England except York with more than 10,000. At the level of 20,000 to 50,000 were Bordeaux, Toulouse, Montpellier, Marseille, and Lyon in France, Barcelona, Seville, and Toledo in Spain, Siena, Pisa, and other secondary cities in Italy, and the Hanseatic trading cities of the Empire. The plague raged through them all, killing anywhere from one third to two thirds of their inhabitants. Italy, with a total population of 10 to 11 million, probably suffered the heaviest toll. Following the Florentine bankruptcies, the crop failures and workers' riots of 1346–47, the revolt of Cola di Rienzi that plunged Rome into anarchy, the plague came as the peak of successive calamities. As if the world were indeed in the grasp of the Evil One, its first appearance on the European mainland in January 1348 coincided with a fearsome earthquake that carved a path of wreckage from Naples up to Venice. Houses collapsed, church towers toppled, villages were crushed, and the destruction reached as far as Germany and Greece. Emotional response, dulled by horrors, underwent a kind of atrophy epitomized by the chronicler who wrote, "And in these days was burying without sorrowe and wedding without friendschippe."

14   In Siena, where more than half the inhabitants died of the plague, work was abandoned on the great cathedral, planned to be the largest in the world, and never resumed, owing to loss of workers and master masons and "the melancholy and grief" of the survivors. The cathedral's truncated transept still stands in permanent witness to the sweep of death's scythe. Agnolo di Tura, a chronicler of Siena, recorded the fear of contagion that froze every other instinct. "Father abandoned child, wife husband, one brother another," he wrote, "for this plague seemed to strike through the breath and sight. And so they died. And no one could be found to bury the dead for money or friendship....And I, Agnola di Tura, called the Fat, buried my five children with my own hands, and so did many others likewise."

15   There were many to echo his account of inhumanity and few to balance it, for the plague was not the kind of calamity that inspired mutual help. Its loathsomeness and deadliness did not herd people together in mutual distress, but only prompted their desire to escape each other. "Magistrates and notaries refused to come and make the wills of the dying," reported a Franciscan friar of Piazza in Sicily; what was worse, "even the priests did not come to hear their confessions." A clerk of the Archbishop of Canterbury reported the same of English priests who "turned away from the care of their benefices from fear of death." Cases

READINGS

of parents deserting children and children their parents were reported across Europe from Scotland to Russia. The calamity chilled the hearts of men, wrote Boccaccio in his famous account of the plague in Florence that serves as introduction to the Decameron. "One man shunned another...kinsfolk held aloof, brother was forsaken by brother, oftentimes husband by wife; nay, what is more, and scarcely to be believed, fathers and mothers were found to abandon their own children to their fate, untended, unvisited as if they had been strangers." Exaggeration and literary pessimism were common in the 14th century, but the Pope's physician, Guy de Chauliac, was a sober, careful observer who reported the same phenomenon: "A father did not visit his son, nor the son his father. Charity was dead."

16   Yet not entirely. In Paris, according to the chronicler Jean de Venette, the nuns of the Hotel Dieu or municipal hospital, "having no fear of death, tended the sick with all sweetness and humility." New nuns repeatedly took the places of those who died, until the majority "many times renewed by death now rest in peace with Christ as we may piously believe."

17   When the plague entered northern France in July 1348, it settled first in Normandy and, checked by winter, gave Picardy a deceptive interim until the next summer. Either in mourning or warning, black flags were flown from church towers of the worst-stricken villages of Normandy. "And in that time," wrote a monk of the abbey of Fourcarment, "the mortality was so great among the people of Normandy that those of Picardy mocked them." The same unneighborly reaction was reported of the Scots, separated by a winter's immunity from the English. Delighted to hear of the disease that was scourging the "southrons," they gathered forces for an invasion, "laughing at their enemies." Before they could move, the savage mortality fell upon them too, scattering some in death and the rest in panic to spread the infection as they fled.

18   In Picardy in the summer of 1349 the pestilence penetrated the castle of Coucy to kill Enguerrand's mother, Catherine, and her new husband. Whether her nine-year-old son escaped by chance or was perhaps living elsewhere with one of his guardians is unrecorded. In nearby Amiens, tannery workers, responding quickly to losses in the labor force, combined to bargain for higher wages. In another place villagers were seen dancing to drums and trumpets, and on being asked the reason, answered that, seeing their neighbors die day by day while their village remained immune, they believed that they could keep the plague from entering "by the jollity that is in us. That is why we dance." Further north in Tournai on the border

of Flanders, Gilles li Muisis, Abbot of St. Martin's, kept one of the epidemic's most vivid accounts. The passing bells rang all day and all night, he recorded, because sextons were anxious to obtain their fees while they could. Filled with the sound of mourning, the city became oppressed by fear, so that the authorities forbade the tolling of bells and the wearing of black and restricted funeral services to two mourners. The silencing of funeral bells and of criers' announcements of deaths was ordained by most cities. Siena imposed a fine on the wearing of mourning clothes by all except widows.

19   Flight was the chief recourse of those who could afford it or arrange it. The rich fled to their country places like Boccaccio's young patricians of Florence, who settled in a pastoral palace "removed on every side from the roads" with "wells of cool water and vaults of rare wines." The urban poor died in their burrows, "and only the stench of their bodies informed neighbors of their deaths." That the poor were more heavily afflicted than the rich was clearly remarked at the time, in the north as in the south. A Scottish chronicler, John of Fordun, stated flatly that the pest "attacked especially the meaner sort and common people—seldom the magnates." Simon de Covino of Montpellier made the same observation. He ascribed it to the misery and want and hard lives that made the poor more susceptible, which was half the truth. Close contact and lack of sanitation was the unrecognized other half. It was noticed too that the young died in greater proportion than the old; Simon de Covino compared the disappearance of youth to the withering of flowers in the fields.

20   In the countryside peasants dropped dead on the roads, in the fields, in their houses. Survivors in growing helplessness fell into apathy, leaving ripe wheat uncut and livestock untended. Oxen and asses, sheep and goats, pigs and chickens ran wild and they too, according to local reports, succumbed to the pest. English sheep, bearers of the precious wool, died throughout the country. The chronicler Henry Knighton, canon of Leicester Abbey, reported 5,000 dead in one field alone, "their bodies so corrupted by the plague that neither beast nor bird would touch them," and spreading an appalling stench. In the Austrian Alps wolves came down to prey upon sheep and then, "as if alarmed by some invisible warning, turned and fled back into the wilderness." In remote Dalmatia bolder wolves descended upon a plague-stricken city and attacked human survivors. For want of herdsmen, cattle strayed from place to place and died in hedgerows and ditches. Dogs and cats fell like the rest.

21   The dearth of labor held a fearful prospect because the 14th century lived close to the annual harvest both for food and for next year's seed. "So few servants and laborers were left," wrote Knighton, "that no one knew where to turn for help." The sense of a vanishing future created a kind of dementia of despair. A Bavarian chronicler of Neuberg on the Danube recorded that "Men and women...wandered around as if mad" and let their cattle stray "because no one had any inclination to concern themselves about the future." Fields went uncultivated, spring seed unsown. Second growth with nature's awful energy crept back over cleared land, dikes crumbled, salt water reinvaded and soured the lowlands. With so few hands remaining to restore the work of centuries, people felt, in Walsingham's words, that "the world could never again regain its former prosperity."

22   Though the death rate was higher among the anonymous poor, the known and the great died too. King Alfonso XI of Castile was the only reigning monarch killed by the pest, but his neighbor King Pedro of Aragon lost his wife, Queen Leonora, his daughter Marie, and a niece in the space of six months. John Cantacuzene, Emperor of Byzantium, lost his son. In France the lame Queen Jeanne and her daughter-in-law Bonne de Luxemburg, wife of the Dauphin, both died in 1349 in the same phase that took the life of Enguerrand's mother. Jeanne, Queen of Navarre, daughter of Louis X, was another victim. Edward III's second daughter, Joanna, who was on her way to marry Pedro, the heir of Castile, died in Bordeaux. Women appear to have been more vulnerable than men, perhaps because, being more housebound, they were more exposed to fleas. Boccaccio's mistress Fiammetta, illegitimate daughter of the King of Naples, died, as did Laura, the beloved—whether real or fictional—of Petrarch. Reaching out to us in the future, Petrarch cried, "Oh happy posterity who will not experience such abysmal woe and will look upon our testimony as a fable."

23   In Florence Giovanni Villani, the great historian of his time, died at 68 in the midst of an unfinished sentence: "...e dure questo pistolenza fino a...(in the midst of this pestilence there came to an end...)." Siena's master painters, the brothers Ambrogio and Pietro Lorenzetti, whose names never appear after 1348, presumably perished in the plague, as did Andrea Pisano, architect and sculptor of Florence. William of Ockham and the English mystic Richard Rolle of Hampole both disappear from mention after 1349. Francisco Datini, merchant of Prato, lost both his parents and two siblings. Curious sweeps of mortality afflicted certain bodies of

merchants in London. All eight wardens of the Company of Cutters, all six wardens of the Hatters, and four wardens of the Goldsmiths died before July 1350. Sir John Pulteney, master draper and four times Mayor of London, was a victim, likewise Sir John Montgomery, Governor of Calais.

24   Among the clergy and doctors the mortality was naturally high because of the nature of their professions. Out of 24 physicians in Venice, 20 were said to have lost their lives in the plague, although, according to another account, some were believed to have fled or to have shut themselves up in their houses. At Montpellier, site of the leading medieval medical school, the physician Simon de Covino reported that, despite the great number of doctors, "hardly one of them escaped." In Avignon, Guy de Chauliac confessed that he performed his medical visits only because he dared not stay away for fear of infamy, but "I was in continual fear." He claimed to have contracted the disease but to have cured himself by his own treatment; if so, he was one of the few who recovered.

25   Clerical mortality varied with rank. Although the one-third toll of cardinals reflects the same proportion as the whole, this was probably due to their concentration in Avignon. In England, in strange and almost sinister procession, the Archbishop of Canterbury, John Stratford, died in August 1348, his appointed successor died in May 1349, and the next appointee three months later, all three within a year. Despite such weird vagaries, prelates in general managed to sustain a higher survival rate than the lesser clergy. Among bishops the deaths have been estimated at about one in twenty. The loss of priests, even if many avoided their fearful duty of attending the dying, was about the same as among the population as a whole.

26   Government officials, whose loss contributed to the general chaos, found, on the whole, no special shelter. In Siena four of the nine members of the governing oligarchy died, in France one third of the royal notaries, in Bristol 15 out of the 52 members of the Town Council or almost one third. Tax-collecting obviously suffered, with the result that Philip VI was unable to collect more than a fraction of the subsidy granted him by the Estates in the winter of 1347–48.

27   Lawlessness and debauchery accompanied the plague as they had during the great plague of Athens of 430 B.C., when according to Thucydides, men grew bold in the indulgence of pleasure: "For seeing how the rich died in a moment and those who had nothing immediately inherited their property, they reflected that life and riches were alike transitory and they resolved to enjoy themselves while they could." Human behavior

is timeless. When St. John had his vision of plague in Revelation, he knew from some experience or race memory that those who survived "repented not of the work of their hands....Neither repented they of their murders, nor of their sorceries, nor of their fornication, nor of their thefts."

QUESTIONS TO CONSIDER

1. The essay includes paragraphs that vividly detail the symptoms of the plague (paragraphs 1–3), as well as efforts to tend to the dead (paragraph 9). What is the effect of such detailed imagery?

2. Tuchman frequently intersperses her essay with paragraphs densely packed with statistics concerning the number of deaths, the different places in which the deaths occurred, and names or categories of victims (for example, paragraphs 4 and 5, paragraph 11, etc.). What purposes do these paragraphs serve in terms of the structure of the essay and the value of the information?

3. According to Tuchman, what categories of people were most likely to be struck down by the plague and for what reasons?

4. The plague not only killed people by the thousands but also influenced everything about the lives and culture of the people of the time. What were the changes the plague caused in family life, religious practices, etc?

5. Tuchman incorporates many quotes from people of the time, including the quote she employs as part of the title of the essay. What about these quotes makes this incorporation a good choice on Tuchman's part? Consider the effect on the essay had the quotes not been included.

READINGS

How Computers Change the Way We Think

Sherry Turkle

- ■ **IE** Illustration and Exemplification
- ■ **CC** Compare and Contrast
- ■ **AP** Argument and Persuasion
- ■ **PA** Process Analysis
- ■ **CE** Cause and Effect

1   The tools we use to think change the ways in which we think. The invention of written language brought about a radical shift in how we process, organize, store, and transmit representations of the world. Although writing remains our primary information technology, today when we think about the impact of technology on our habits of mind, we think primarily of the computer.

2   My first encounters with how computers change the way we think came soon after I joined the faculty at the Massachusetts Institute of Technology in the late 1970s, at the end of the era of the slide rule and the beginning of the era of the personal computer. At a lunch for new faculty members, several senior professors in engineering complained that the transition from slide rules to calculators had affected their students' ability to deal with issues of scale. When students used slide rules, they had to insert decimal points themselves. The professors insisted that that required students to maintain a mental sense of scale, whereas those who relied on calculators made frequent errors in orders of magnitude. Additionally, the students with calculators had lost their ability to do "back of the envelope" calculations, and with that, an intuitive feel for the material.

3   That same semester, I taught a course in the history of psychology. There, I experienced the impact of computational objects on students' ideas about their emotional lives. My class had read Freud's essay on slips of the tongue, with its famous first example: The chairman of a parliamentary session opens a meeting by declaring it closed. The students discussed how Freud interpreted such errors as revealing a person's mixed emotions. A computer-science major disagreed with Freud's approach. The mind, she argued, is a computer. And in a computational dictionary—like we have in the human mind—"closed" and "open" are designated by the same symbol, separated by a sign for opposition. "Closed"

equals "minus open." To substitute "closed" for "open" does not require the notion of ambivalence or conflict.

4   "When the chairman made that substitution," she declared, "a bit was dropped; a minus sign was lost. There was a power surge. No problem."

5   The young woman turned a Freudian slip into an information processing error. An explanation in terms of meaning had become an explanation in terms of mechanism.

6   Such encounters turned me to the study of both the instrumental and the subjective sides of the nascent computer culture. As an ethnographer and psychologist, I began to study not only what the computer was doing *for* us, but what it was doing *to* us, including how it was changing the way we see ourselves, our sense of human identity. In the 1980s, I surveyed the psychological effects of computational objects in everyday life—largely the unintended side effects of people's tendency to project thoughts and feelings onto their machines.

7   In the 20 years since, computational objects have become more explicitly designed to have emotional and cognitive effects. And those "effects by design" will become even stronger in the decade to come. Machines are being designed to serve explicitly as companions, pets, and tutors. And they are introduced in school settings for the youngest children.

8   Today, starting in elementary school, students use e-mail, word processing, computer simulations, virtual communities, and PowerPoint software. In the process, they are absorbing more than the content of what appears on their screens. They are learning new ways to think about what it means to know and understand.

9   What follows is a short and certainly not comprehensive list of areas where I see information technology encouraging changes in thinking. There can be no simple way of cataloging whether any particular change is good or bad. That is contested terrain. At every step we have to ask, as educators and citizens, whether current technology is leading us in directions that serve our human purposes. Such questions are not technical; they are social, moral, and political. For me, addressing that subjective side of computation is one of the more significant challenges for the next decade of information technology in higher education. Technology does not determine change, but it encourages us to take certain directions. If we make those directions clear, we can more easily exert human choice.

Thinking about Privacy

10   Today's college students are habituated to a world of online blogging, instant messaging, and Web browsing that leaves electronic traces. Yet they have had little experience with the right to privacy. Unlike past generations of Americans, who grew up with the notion that the privacy of their mail was sacrosanct, our children are accustomed to electronic surveillance as part of their daily lives.

11   I have colleagues who feel that the increased incursions on privacy have put the topic more in the news, and that this is a positive change. But middle-school and high-school students tend to be willing to provide personal information online with no safeguards, and college students seem uninterested in violations of privacy and in increased governmental and commercial surveillance. Professors find that students do not understand that in a democracy, privacy is a right, not merely a privilege. In ten years, ideas about the relationship of privacy and government will require even more active pedagogy. (One might also hope that increased education about the kinds of silent surveillance that technology makes possible may inspire more active political engagement with the issue.)

Avatars or a Self?

12   Chat rooms, role-playing games, and other technological venues offer us many different contexts for presenting ourselves online. Those possibilities are particularly important for adolescents because they offer what Erik Erikson described as a moratorium, a time out or safe space for the personal experimentation that is so crucial for adolescent development. Our dangerous world—with crime, terrorism, drugs, and AIDS— offers little in the way of safe spaces. Online worlds can provide valuable spaces for identity play.

13   But some people who gain fluency in expressing multiple aspects of self may find it harder to develop authentic selves. Some children who write narratives for their screen avatars may grow up with too little experience of how to share their real feelings with other people. For those who are lonely yet afraid of intimacy, information technology has made it possible to have the illusion of companionship without the demands of friendship.

From Powerful Ideas to PowerPoint

14   In the 1970s and early 1980s, some educators wanted to make programming part of the regular curriculum for K–12 education. They argued that because information technology carries ideas, it might as well carry the most powerful ideas that computer science has to offer. It is ironic that in most elementary schools today, the ideas being carried by information technology are not ideas from computer science like procedural thinking, but more likely to be those embedded in productivity tools like PowerPoint presentation software.

15   PowerPoint does more than provide a way of transmitting content. It carries its own way of thinking, its own aesthetic—which not surprisingly shows up in the aesthetic of college freshmen. In that aesthetic, presentation becomes its own powerful idea.

16   To be sure, the software cannot be blamed for lower intellectual standards. Misuse of the former is as much a symptom as a cause of the latter. Indeed, the culture in which our children are raised is increasingly a culture of presentation, a corporate culture in which appearance is often more important than reality. In contemporary political discourse, the bar has also been lowered. Use of rhetorical devices at the expense of cogent argument regularly goes without notice. But it is precisely because standards of intellectual rigor outside the educational sphere have fallen that educators must attend to how we use, and when we introduce, software that has been designed to simplify the organization and processing of information.

17   In "The Cognitive Style of PowerPoint" (Graphics Press, 2003), Edward R. Tufte suggests that PowerPoint equates bulleting with clear thinking. It does not teach students to begin a discussion or construct a narrative. It encourages presentation, not conversation. Of course, in the hands of a master teacher, a PowerPoint presentation with few words and powerful images can serve as the jumping-off point for a brilliant lecture. But in the hands of elementaryschool students, often introduced to PowerPoint in the third grade, and often infatuated with its swooshing sounds, animated icons, and flashing text, a slide show is more likely to close down debate than open it up.

18   Developed to serve the needs of the corporate boardroom, the software is designed to convey absolute authority. Teachers used to tell students that clear exposition depended on clear outlining, but presentation software has fetishized the outline at the expense of the content.

19   Narrative, the exposition of content, takes time. PowerPoint, like so much in the computer culture, speeds up the pace.

Word Processing vs. Thinking

20   The catalog for the Vermont Country Store advertises a manual type-writer, which the advertising copy says "moves at a pace that allows time to compose your thoughts." As many of us know, it is possible to manipulate text on a computer screen and see how it looks faster than we can think about what the words mean.

21   Word processing has its own complex psychology. From a pedagogical point of view, it can make dedicated students into better writers because it allows them to revise text, rearrange paragraphs, and experiment with the tone and shape of an essay. Few professional writers would part with their computers; some claim that they simply cannot think without their hands on the keyboard. Yet the ability to quickly fill the page, to see it before you can think it, can make bad writers even worse.

22   A seventh grader once told me that the typewriter she found in her mother's attic is "cool because you have to type each letter by itself. You have to know what you are doing in advance or it comes out a mess." The idea of thinking ahead has become exotic.

Taking Things at Interface Value

23   We expect software to be easy to use, and we assume that we don't have to know how a computer works. In the early 1980s, most computer users who spoke of transparency meant that, as with any other machine, you could "open the hood" and poke around. But only a few years later, Macintosh users began to use the term when they talked about seeing their documents and programs represented by attractive and easy-to-interpret icons. They were referring to an ability to make things work without needing to go below the screen surface. Paradoxically, it was the screen's opacity that permitted that kind of transparency. Today, when people say that something is transparent, they mean that they can see how to make it work, not that they know how it works. In other words, transparency means epistemic opacity.

24   The people who built or bought the first generation of personal computers understood them down to the bits and bytes. The next generation of operating systems were more complex, but they still invited that old-time reductive understanding. Contemporary information technology encourages different habits of mind. Today's college students are already used to taking things at (inter)face value; their successors in 2014 will be even less accustomed to probing below the surface.

 READINGS

Simulation and Its Discontents

25   Some thinkers argue that the new opacity is empowering, enabling anyone to use the most sophisticated technological tools and to experiment with simulation in complex and creative ways. But it is also true that our tools carry the message that they are beyond our understanding. It is possible that in daily life, epistemic opacity can lead to passivity.

26   I first became aware of that possibility in the early 1990s, when the first generation of complex simulation games were introduced and immediately became popular for home as well as school use. SimLife teaches the principles of evolution by getting children involved in the development of complex ecosystems; in that sense it is an extraordinary learning tool. During one session in which I played SimLife with Tim, a 13-year-old, the screen before us flashed a message: "Your orgot is being eaten up." "What's an orgot?" I asked. Tim didn't know. "I just ignore that," he said confidently. "You don't need to know that kind of stuff to play."

27   For me, that story serves as a cautionary tale. Computer simulations enable their users to think about complex phenomena as dynamic, evolving systems. But they also accustom us to manipulating systems whose core assumptions we may not understand and that may not be true.

28   We live in a culture of simulation. Our games, our economic and political systems, and the ways architects design buildings, chemists envisage molecules, and surgeons perform operations all use simulation technology. In ten years the degree to which simulations are embedded in every area of life will have increased exponentially. We need to develop a new form of media literacy: readership skills for the culture of simulation.

29   We come to written text with habits of readership based on centuries of civilization. At the very least, we have learned to begin with the journalist's traditional questions: who, what, when, where, why, and how. Who wrote these words, what is their message, why were they written, and how are they situated in time and place, politically and socially? A central project for higher education during the next ten years should be creating programs in information-technology literacy, with the goal of teaching students to interrogate simulations in much the same spirit, challenging their built-in assumptions.

30   Despite the ever-increasing complexity of software, most computer environments put users in worlds based on constrained choices. In other words, immersion in programmed worlds puts us in reassuring environments where the rules are clear. For example, when you play a video game, you often go through a series of frightening situations that you escape

by mastering the rules—you experience life as a reassuring dichotomy of scary and safe. Children grow up in a culture of video games, action films, fantasy epics, and computer programs that all rely on that familiar scenario of almost losing but then regaining total mastery: There is danger. It is mastered. A still-more-powerful monster appears. It is subdued. Scary. Safe.

31   Yet in the real world, we have never had a greater need to work our way out of binary assumptions. In the decade ahead, we need to rebuild the culture around information technology. In that new sociotechnical culture, assumptions about the nature of mastery would be less absolute. The new culture would make it easier, not more difficult, to consider life in shades of gray, to see moral dilemmas in terms other than a battle between Good and Evil. For never has our world been more complex, hybridized, and global. Never have we so needed to have many contradictory thoughts and feelings at the same time. Our tools must help us accomplish that, not fight against us.

32   Information technology is identity technology. Embedding it in a culture that supports democracy, freedom of expression, tolerance, diversity, and complexity of opinion is one of the next decade's greatest challenges. We cannot afford to fail.

33   When I first began studying the computer culture, a small breed of highly trained technologists thought of themselves as "computer people." That is no longer the case. If we take the computer as a carrier of a way of knowing, a way of seeing the world and our place in it, we are all computer people now.

QUESTIONS TO CONSIDER

1. Why does Sherry Turkle begin her essay by talking about tools in general? As tools, what do computers have in common with written language?

2. Turkle describes what computers are doing "for us" as well as what computers are doing "to us." What are some examples she gives of each? What are some additional examples that you can think of?

3. What is "computer culture"? What is Turkle's vision of the new type of culture we should develop around information technology? What is your vision of what our culture *should* be using information technology to accomplish?

READINGS

Everyday Use

Alice Walker

- **N** Narration
- **CC** Compare and Contrast
- **DEF** Definition

For Your Grandmama

1   I will wait for her in the yard that Maggie and I made so clean and wavy yesterday afternoon. A yard like this is more comfortable than most people know. It is not just a yard. It is like an extended living room. When the hard clay is swept clean as a floor and the fine sand around the edges lined with tiny, irregular grooves anyone can come and sit and look up into the elm tree and wait for the breezes that never come inside the house.

2   Maggie will be nervous until after her sister goes: she will stand hopelessly in corners homely and ashamed of the burn scars down her arms and legs, eyeing her sister with a mixture of envy and awe. She thinks her sister has held life always in the palm of one hand, that "no" is a word the world never learned to say to her.

3   You've no doubt seen those TV shows where the child who has "made it" is confronted, as a surprise, by her own mother and father, tottering in weakly from backstage. (A pleasant surprise, of course: What would they do if parent and child came on the show only to curse out and insult each other?) On TV mother and child embrace and smile into each other's faces. Sometimes the mother and father weep, the child wraps them in her arms and leans across the table to tell how she would not have made it without their help. I have seen these programs.

4   Sometimes I dream a dream in which Dee and I are suddenly brought together on a TV program of this sort. Out of a dark and soft-seated limousine I am ushered into a bright room filled with many people. There I meet a smiling, gray, sporty man like Johnny Carson who shakes my hand and tells me what a fine girl I have. Then we are on the stage and Dee is embracing me with tears in her eyes. She pins on my dress a large orchid, even though she has told me once that she thinks orchids are tacky flowers.

5   In real life I am a large, big-boned woman with rough, man-working hands. In the winter I wear flannel nightgowns to bed and overalls during the day. I can kill and clean a hog as mercilessly as a man. My fat keeps me hot in zero weather. I can work all day, breaking ice to get water for washing. I can eat pork liver cooked over the open fire minutes after it comes steaming from the hog. One winter I knocked a bull calf straight in the brain between the eyes with a sledge hammer and had the meat hung up to chill before nightfall. But of course all this does not show on television. I am the way my daughter would want me to be: a hundred pounds lighter, my skin like an uncooked barley pancake. My hair glistens in the hot bright lights. Johnny Carson has much to do to keep up with my quick and witty tongue.

6   But that is a mistake. I know even before I wake up. Who ever knew a Johnson with a quick tongue? Who can even imagine me looking a strange white man in the eye? It seems to me I have talked to them always with one foot raised in flight, with my head turned in whichever way is farthest from them. Dee, though. She would always look anyone in the eye. Hesitation was no part of her nature.

7   "How do I look, Mama?" Maggie says, showing just enough of her thin body enveloped in pink skirt and red blouse for me to know she's there, almost hidden by the door.

8   "Come out into the yard," I say.

9   Have you ever seen a lame animal, perhaps a dog run over by some careless person rich enough to own a car, sidle up to someone who is ignorant enough to be kind to him? That is the way my Maggie walks. She has been like this, chin on chest, eyes on ground, feet in shuffle, ever since the fire that burned the other house to the ground.

10   Dee is lighter than Maggie, with nicer hair and a fuller figure. She's a woman now, though sometimes I forget. How long ago was it that the other house burned? Ten, twelve years? Sometimes I can still hear the flames and feel Maggie's arm sticking to me, her hair smoking and her dress falling off her in little black papery flakes. Her eyes seemed stretched open, blazed open by the flames reflected in them. And Dee. I see her standing off under the sweet gum tree she used to dig gum out of; a look of concentration on her face as she watched the last dingy gray board of the house fall in toward the red-hot brick chimney. Why don't you do a dance around the ashes? I'd wanted to ask her. She had hated the house that much.

READINGS

11   I used to think she hated Maggie, too. But that was before we raised the money, the church and me, to send her to Augusta to school. She used to read to us without pity; forcing words, lies, other folks' habits, whole lives upon us two, sitting trapped and ignorant underneath her voice. She washed us in a river of make-believe, burned us with a lot of knowledge we didn't necessarily need to know. Pressed us to her with the serious way she read, to shove us away at just the moment, like dimwits, we seemed about to understand.

12   Dee wanted nice things. A yellow organdy dress to wear to her graduation from high school; black pumps to match a green suit she'd made from an old suit somebody gave me. She was determined to stare down any disaster in her efforts. Her eyelids would not flicker for minutes at a time. Often I fought off the temptation to shake her. At sixteen she had a style of her own: and knew what style was.

13   I never had an education myself. After second grade the school was closed down. Don't ask me why: in 1927 colored asked fewer questions than they do now. Sometimes Maggie reads to me. She stumbles along good-naturedly but can't see well. She knows she is not bright. Like good looks and money, quickness passed her by. She will marry John Thomas (who has mossy teeth in an earnest face) and then I'll be free to sit here and I guess just sing church songs to myself. Although I never was a good singer. Never could carry a tune. I was always better at a man's job. I used to love to milk till I was hoofed in the side in '49. Cows are soothing and slow and don't bother you, unless you try to milk them the wrong way.

14   I have deliberately turned my back on the house. It is three rooms, just like the one that burned, except the roof is tin; they don't make shingle roofs any more. There are no real windows, just some holes cut in the sides, like the portholes in a ship, but not round and not square, with rawhide holding the shutters up on the outside. This house is in a pasture, too, like the other one. No doubt when Dee sees it she will want to tear it down. She wrote me once that no matter where we "choose" to live, she will manage to come see us. But she will never bring her friends. Maggie and I thought about this and Maggie asked me, "Mama, when did Dee ever *have* any friends?"

15   She had a few. Furtive boys in pink shirts hanging about on washday after school. Nervous girls who never laughed. Impressed with her they worshiped the well-turned phrase, the cute shape, the scalding humor that erupted like bubbles in lye. She read to them.

16   When she was courting Jimmy T she didn't have much time to pay to us, but turned all her faultfinding power on him. He *flew* to marry a cheap gal from a family of ignorant flashy people. She hardly had time to recompose herself.

17   When she comes I will meet—but there they are!

18   Maggie attempts to make a dash for the house, in her shuffling way, but I stay her with my hand. "Come back here," I say. And she stops and tries to dig a well in the sand with her toe.

19   It is hard to see them clearly through the strong sun. But even the first glimpse of leg out of the car tells me it is Dee. Her feet were always neat-looking, as if God himself had shaped them with a certain style. From the other side of the car comes a short, stocky man. Hair is all over his head a foot long and hanging from his chin like a kinky mule tail. I hear Maggie suck in her breath. "Uhnnnh," is what it sounds like. Like when you see the wriggling end of a snake just in front of your foot on the road. "Uhnnnh."

20   Dee next. A dress down to the ground, in this hot weather. A dress so loud it hurts my eyes. There are yellows and oranges enough to throw back the light of the sun. I feel my whole face warming from the heat waves it throws out. Earrings, too, gold and hanging down to her shoulders. Bracelets dangling and making noises when she moves her arm up to shake the folds of the dress out of her armpits. The dress is loose and flows, and as she walks closer, I like it. I hear Maggie go "Uhnnnh" again. It is her sister's hair. It stands straight up like the wool on a sheep. It is black as night and around the edges are two long pigtails that rope about like small lizards disappearing behind her ears.

21   "Wa-su-zo-Tean-o!" she says, coming on in that gliding way the dress makes her move. The short stocky fellow with the hair to his navel is all grinning and he follows up with "Asalamalakim, my mother and sister!" He moves to hug Maggie but she falls back, right up against the back of my chair. I feel her trembling there and when I look up I see the perspiration falling off her chin.

22   "Don't get up," says Dee. Since I am stout it takes something of a push. You can see me trying to move a second or two before I make it. She turns, showing white heels through her sandals, and goes back to the car. Out she peeks next with a Polaroid. She stoops down quickly and lines up picture after picture of me sitting there in front of the house with Maggie cowering behind me. She never takes a shot without making sure the house is included. When a cow comes nibbling around the edge of the

yard she snaps it and me and Maggie *and* the house. Then she puts the Polaroid in the back seat of the car, and comes up and kisses me on the forehead.

23   Meanwhile Asalamalakim is going through the motions with Maggie's hand. Maggie's hand is limp as a fish, and probably as cold, despite the sweat, and she keeps trying to pull it back. It looks like Asalamalakim wants to shake hands but wants to do it fancy. Or maybe he don't know how people shake hands. Anyhow, he soon gives up on Maggie.

24   "Well," I say. "Dee."

25   "No, Mama," she says. "Not 'Dee,' Wangero Leewanika Kemanjo!"

26   "What happened to 'Dee'?" I wanted to know.

27   "She's dead," Wangero said. "I couldn't bear it any longer being named after the people who oppress me."

28   "You know as well as me you was named after your aunt Dicie," I said. Dicie is my sister. She named Dee. We called her "Big Dee" after Dee was born.

29   "But who was *she* named after?" asked Wangero.

30   "I guess after Grandma Dee," I said.

31   "And who was she named after?" asked Wangero.

32   "Her mother," I said, and saw Wangero getting tired.

33   "That's about as far back as I can trace it," I said. Though, in fact, I probably could have carried it back beyond the Civil War through the branches.

34   "Well," said Asalamalakim, "there you are."

35   "Uhnnnh," I heard Maggie say.

36   "There I was not," I said, "before 'Dicie' cropped up in our family, so why should I try to trace it that far back?"

37   He just stood there grinning, looking down on me like somebody inspecting a Model A car. Every once in a while he and Wangero sent eye signals over my head.

38   "How do you pronounce this name?" I asked.

39   "You don't have to call me by it if you don't want to," said Wangero.

40   "Why shouldn't I?" I asked. "If that's what you want us to call you, we'll call you."

41   "I know it might sound awkward at first," said Wangero.

42   "I'll get used to it," I said. "Ream it out again."

43   Well, soon we got the name out of the way. Asalamalakim had a name twice as long and three times as hard. After I tripped over it two or three

times he told me to just call him Hakim-a-barber. I wanted to ask him was he a barber, but I didn't really think he was, so I didn't ask.

44   "You must belong to those beef-cattle peoples down the road," I said. They said "Asalamalakim" when they met you, too, but they didn't shake hands. Always too busy: feeding the cattle, fixing the fences, putting up salt-lick shelters, throwing down hay. When the white folks poisoned some of the herd the men stayed up all night with rifles in their hands. I walked a mile and half just to see the sight.

45   Hakim-a-barber said, "I accept some of their doctrines, but farming and raising cattle is not my style." (They didn't tell me, and I didn't ask, whether Wangero [Dee] had really gone and married him.)

46   We sat down to eat and right away he said he didn't eat collards and pork was unclean. Wangero, though, went on through the chitlins and corn bread, the greens and everything else. She talked a blue streak over the sweet potatoes. Everything delighted her. Even the fact that we still used the benches her daddy made for the table when we couldn't afford to buy chairs.

47   "Oh, Mama!" she cried. Then turned to Hakim-a-barber. "I never knew how lovely these benches are. You can feel the rump prints," she said, running her hands underneath her and along the bench. Then she gave a sigh and her hand closed over Grandma Dee's butter dish. "That's it!" she said. "I knew there was something I wanted to ask you if I could have." She jumped up from the table and went over in the corner where the churn stood, the milk in its dabber by now. She looked at the churn and looked at it.

48   "This churn top is what I need," she said. "Didn't Uncle Buddy whittle it out of a tree you all used to have?"

49   "Yes," I said.

50   "Uh huh," she said happily. "And I want the dasher, too."

51   "Uncle Buddy whittle that, too?" asked the barber.

52   Dee (Wangero) looked up at me.

53   "Aunt Dee's first husband whittled the dash," said Maggie so low you almost couldn't hear her. "His name was Henry, but they called him Stash."

54   "Maggie's brain is like an elephant's," Wangero said, laughing. "I can use the churn top as a centerpiece for the alcove table," she said, sliding a plate over the churn, "and I'll think of something artistic to do with the dasher."

55   When she finished wrapping the dasher the handle stuck out. I took it for a moment in my hands. You didn't even have to look close to see

where hands pushing the dasher up and down to make butter had left a kind of sink in the wood. In fact, there were a lot of small sinks; you could see where thumbs and fingers had sunk into the wood. It was beautiful light yellow wood, from a tree that grew in the yard where Big Dee and Stash had lived.

56   After dinner Dee (Wangero) went to the trunk at the foot of my bed and started rifling through it. Maggie hung back in the kitchen over the dishpan. Out came Wangero with two quilts. They had been pieced by Grandma Dee and then Big Dee and me had hung them on the quilt frames on the front porch and quilted them. One was in the Lone Star pattern. The other was Walk Around the Mountain. In both of them were scraps of dresses Grandma Dee had worn fifty and more years ago. Bits and pieces of Grandpa Jarrell's Paisley shirts. And one teeny faded blue piece, about the size of a penny matchbox, that was from Great Grandpa Ezra's uniform that he wore in the Civil War.

57   "Mama," Wangero said sweet as a bird. "Can I have these old quilts?"

58   I heard something fall in the kitchen, and a minute later the kitchen door slammed.

59   "Why don't you take one or two of the others?" I asked.

60   "These old things was just done by me and Big Dee from some tops your grandma pieced before she died."

61   "No," said Wangero. "I don't want those. They are stitched around the borders by machine."

62   "That'll make them last better," I said.

63   "That's not the point," said Wangero. "These are all pieces of dresses Grandma used to wear. She did all this stitching by hand. Imagine!" She held the quilts securely in her arms, stroking them.

64   "Some of the pieces, like those lavender ones, come from old clothes her mother handed down to her," I said, moving up to touch the quilts. Dee (Wangero) moved back just enough so that I couldn't reach the quilts. They already belonged to her.

65   "Imagine!" she breathed again, clutching them closely to her bosom.

66   "The truth is," I said, "I promised to give them quilts to Maggie, for when she marries John Thomas."

67   She gasped like a bee had stung her.

68   "Maggie can't appreciate these quilts!" she said. "She'd probably be backward enough to put them to everyday use."

69   "I reckon she would," I said. "God knows I been saving 'em for long enough with nobody using 'em. I hope she will!" I didn't want to bring up

how I had offered Dee (Wangero) a quilt when she went away to college. Then she had told me they were old fashioned, out of style.

70   "But they're *priceless*!" she was saying now, furiously; for she has a temper. "Maggie would put them on the bed and in five years they'd be in rags. Less than that!"

71   "She can always make some more," I said. "Maggie knows how to quilt."

72   Dee (Wangero) looked at me with hatred. "You just will not understand. The point is these quilts, *these* quilts!"

73   "Well," I said, stumped. "What would *you* do with them?"

74   "Hang them," she said. As if that was the only thing you *could* do with quilts.

75   Maggie by now was standing in the door. I could almost hear the sound her feet made as they scraped over each other.

76   "She can have them, Mama," she said, like somebody used to never winning anything, or having anything reserved for her. "I can 'member Grandma Dee without the quilts."

77   I looked at her hard. She had filled her bottom lip with checkerberry snuff and it gave her face a kind of dopey, hangdog look. It was Grandma Dee and Big Dee who taught her how to quilt herself. She stood there with her scarred hands hidden in the folds of her skirt. She looked at her sister with something like fear but she wasn't mad at her. This was Maggie's portion. This was the way she knew God to work.

78   When I looked at her like that something hit me in the top of my head and ran down to the soles of my feet. Just like when I'm in church and the spirit of God touches me and I get happy and shout. I did something I never had done before: hugged Maggie to me, then dragged her on into the room, snatched the quilts out of Miss Wangero's hands and dumped them into Maggie's lap. Maggie just sat there on my bed with her mouth open.

79   "Take one or two of the others," I said to Dee.

80   But she turned without a word and went out to Hakima-barber.

81   "You just don't understand," she said, as Maggie and I came out to the car.

82   "What don't I understand?" I wanted to know.

83   "Your heritage," she said. And then she turned to Maggie, kissed her and said, "You ought to try to make something of yourself, too, Maggie. It's really a new day for us. But from the way you and Mama still live you'd never know it."

84   She put on some sunglasses that hid everything above the tip of her nose and her chin.

85   Maggie smiled; maybe at the sunglasses. But a real smile, not scared. After we watched the car dust settle I asked Maggie to bring me a dip of snuff. And then the two of us sat there just enjoying, until it was time to go in the house and go to bed.

? QUESTIONS TO CONSIDER

1. "Everyday Use" focuses on a reunion that reveals two contrasting attitudes towards the meaning of family heritage. What are these contrasting attitudes and who are they held by?

2. Why do you think Walker chose to title the story "Everyday Use"? Use examples from the story to back up your opinion.

3. How does Walker describe the differences between the characters and the attitudes they hold? How are Mama and Maggie portrayed in relation to Dee?

4. Walker's story debates whether family heritage is something to be preserved or something to be learned. Which of these sentiments do you agree with? Or do you believe that both sentiments can co-exist?

5. Write an essay exploring the meaning of heritage and what it means to you personally. Does your understanding of heritage differ from that of your family members? From that of your friends or acquaintances?

Once More to the Lake

E. B. White

- **N** Narration
- **DES** Description
- **IE** Illustration and Exemplification
- **CC** Compare and Contrast

1   August 1941

2   One summer, along about 1904, my father rented a camp on a lake in Maine and took us all there for the month of August. We all got ringworm from some kittens and had to rub Pond's Extract on our arms and legs night and morning, and my father rolled over in a canoe with all his clothes on; but outside of that the vacation was a success and from then on none of us ever thought there was any place in the world like that lake in Maine. We returned summer after summer—always on August 1 for one month. I have since become a salt-water man, but sometimes in summer there are days when the restlessness of the tides and the fearful cold of the sea water and the incessant wind that blows across the afternoon and into the evening make me wish for the placidity of a lake in the woods. A few weeks ago this feeling got so strong I bought myself a couple of bass hooks and a spinner and returned to the lake where we used to go, for a week's fishing and to revisit old haunts.

3   I took along my son, who had never had any fresh water up his nose and who had seen lily pads only from train windows. On the journey over to the lake I began to wonder what it would be like. I wondered how time would have marred this unique, this holy spot—the coves and streams, the hills that the sun set behind, the camps and the paths behind the camps. I was sure that the tarred road would have found it out, and I wondered in what other ways it would be desolated. It is strange how much you can remember about places like that once you allow your mind to return into the grooves that lead back. You remember one thing, and that suddenly reminds you of another thing. I guess I remembered clearest of all the early mornings, when the lake was cool and motionless, remembered how the bedroom smelled of the lumber it was made of and of the wet woods whose scent entered through the screen. The partitions in the camp were thin and did not extend clear to the top of the rooms, and as I was always the first up I would dress softly so as not to wake the others,

318 READINGS E. B. WHITE

and sneak out into the sweet outdoors and start out in the canoe, keeping close along the shore in the long shadows of the pines. I remembered being very careful never to rub my paddle against the gunwale for fear of disturbing the stillness of the cathedral.

4   The lake had never been what you would call a wild lake. There were cottages sprinkled around the shores, and it was in farming country although the shores of the lake were quite heavily wooded. Some of the cottages were owned by nearby farmers, and you would live at the shore and eat your meals at the farmhouse. That's what our family did. But although it wasn't wild, it was a fairly large and undisturbed lake and there were places in it that, to a child at least, seemed infinitely remote and primeval.

5   I was right about the tar: it led to within half a mile of the shore. But when I got back there, with my boy, and we settled into a camp near a farmhouse and into the kind of summertime I had known, I could tell that it was going to be pretty much the same as it had been before—I knew it, lying in bed the first morning smelling the bedroom and hearing the boy sneak quietly out and go off along the shore in a boat. I began to sustain the illusion that he was I, and therefore, by simple transposition, that I was my father. This sensation persisted, kept cropping up all the time we were there. It was not an entirely new feeling, but in this setting it grew much stronger. I seemed to be living a dual existence. I would be in the middle of some simple act, I would be picking up a bait box or laying down a table fork, or I would be saying something and suddenly it would be not I but my father who was saying the words or making the gesture. It gave me a creepy sensation.

6   We went fishing the first morning. I felt the same damp moss covering the worms in the bait can, and saw the dragonfly alight on the tip of my rod as it hovered a few inches from the surface of the water. It was the arrival of this fly that convinced me beyond any doubt that everything was as it always had been, that the years were a mirage and that there had been no years. The small waves were the same, chucking the rowboat under the chin as we fished at anchor, and the boat was the same boat, the same color green and the ribs broken in the same places, and under the floorboards the same fresh water leavings and débris—the dead helgramite, the wisps of moss, the rusty discarded fishhook, the dried blood from yesterday's catch. We stared silently at the tips of our rods, at the dragonflies that came and went. I lowered the tip of mine into the water, tentatively, pensively dislodging the fly, which darted two feet away, poised, darted two feet back, and came to rest again a little farther up the

rod. There had been no years between the ducking of this dragonfly and the other one—the one that was part of memory. I looked at the boy, who was silently watching his fly, and it was my hands that held his rod, my eyes watching. I felt dizzy and didn't know which rod I was at the end of.

7   We caught two bass, hauling them in briskly as though they were mackerel, pulling them over the side of the boat in a businesslike manner without any landing net, and stunning them with a blow on the back of the head. When we got back for a swim before lunch, the lake was exactly where we had left it, the same number of inches from the dock, and there was only the merest suggestion of a breeze. This seemed an utterly enchanted sea, this lake you could leave to its own devices for a few hours and come back to, and find that it had not stirred, this constant and trustworthy body of water. In the shallows, the dark, water-soaked sticks and twigs, smooth and old, were undulating in clusters on the bottom against the clean ribbed sand, and the track of the mussel was plain. A school of minnows swam by, each minnow with its small individual shadow, doubling the attendance, so clear and sharp in the sunlight. Some of the other campers were in swimming, along the shore, one of them with a cake of soap, and the water felt thin and clear and unsubstantial. Over the years there had been this person with the cake of soap, this cultist, and here he was. There had been no years.

8   Up to the farmhouse to dinner through the teeming dusty field, the road under our sneakers was only a two-track road. The middle track was missing, the one with the marks of the hooves and the splotches of dried, flaky manure. There had always been three tracks to choose from in choosing which track to walk in; now the choice was narrowed down to two. For a moment I missed terribly the middle alternative. But the way led past the tennis court, and something about the way it lay there in the sun reassured me; the tape had loosened along the backline, the alleys were green with plantains and other weeds, and the net (installed in June and removed in September) sagged in the dry noon, and the whole place steamed with midday heat and hunger and emptiness. There was a choice of pie for dessert, and one was blueberry and one was apple, and the waitresses were the same country girls, there having been no passage of time, only the illusion of it as in a dropped curtain—the waitresses were still fifteen; their hair had been washed, that was the only difference—they had been to the movies and seen the pretty girls with the clean hair.

9   Summertime, oh, summertime, pattern of life indelible with fadeproof lake, the wood unshatterable, the pasture with the sweetfern and

the juniper forever and ever, summer without end; this was the background, and the life along the shore was the design, the cottages with their innocent and tranquil design, their tiny docks with the flagpole and the American flag floating against the white clouds in the blue sky, the little paths over the roots of the trees leading from camp to camp and the paths leading back to the outhouses and the can of lime for sprinkling, and at the souvenir counters at the store the miniature birch-bark canoes and the postcards that showed things looking a little better than they looked. This was the American family at play, escaping the city heat, wondering whether the newcomers in the camp at the head of the cove were "common" or "nice," wondering whether it was true that the people who drove up for Sunday dinner at the farmhouse were turned away because there wasn't enough chicken.

10   It seemed to me, as I kept remembering all this, that those times and those summers had been infinitely precious and worth saving. There had been jollity and peace and goodness. The arriving (at the beginning of August) had been so big a business in itself, at the railway station the farm wagon drawn up, the first smell of the pine-laden air, the first glimpse of the smiling farmer, and the great importance of the trunks and your father's enormous authority in such matters and the feel of the wagon under you for the long ten-mile haul, and at the top of the last long hill catching the first view of the lake after eleven months of not seeing this cherished body of water. The shouts and cries of the other campers when they saw you, and the trunks to be unpacked, to give up their rich burden. (Arriving was less exciting nowadays, when you sneaked up in your car and parked it under a tree near the camp and took out the bags and in five minutes it was all over, no fuss, no loud wonderful fuss about trunks.)

11   Peace and goodness and jollity. The only thing that was wrong now, really, was the sound of the place, an unfamiliar nervous sound of the outboard motors.

12   This was the note that jarred, the one thing that would sometimes break the illusion and set the years moving. In those other summertimes all motors were inboard; and when they were at a little distance, the noise they made was a sedative, an ingredient of summer sleep. They were one-cylinder and two-cylinder engines, and some were make-and-break and some were jumpspark, but they all made a sleepy sound across the lake. The one-lungers throbbed and fluttered, and the twin-cylinder ones purred and purred, and that was a quiet sound, too. But now the campers all had outboards. In the daytime, in the hot mornings, these motors

made a petulant, irritable sound; at night in the still evening when the afterglow lit the water, they whined about one's ears like mosquitoes. My boy loved our rented outboard, and his great desire was to achieve single-handed mastery over it, and authority, and he soon learned the trick of choking it a little (but not too much), and the adjustment of the needle valve. Watching him I would remember the things you could do with the old one-cylinder engine with the heavy flywheel, how you could have it eating out of your hand if you got really close to it spiritually. Motorboats in those days didn't have clutches, and you would make a landing by shutting off the motor at the proper time and coasting in with a dead rudder. But there was a way of reversing them, if you learned the trick, by cutting the switch and putting it on again exactly on the final dying revolution of the flywheel, so that it would kick back against compression and begin reversing. Approaching a dock in a strong following breeze, it was difficult to slow up sufficiently by the ordinary coasting method, and if a boy felt he had complete mastery over his motor, he was tempted to keep it running beyond its time and then reverse it a few feet from the dock. It took a cool nerve, because if you threw the switch a twentieth of a second too soon you would catch the flywheel when it still had speed enough to go up past center, and the boat would leap ahead, charging bull-fashion at the dock.

13   We had a good week at the camp. The bass were biting well and the sun shone endlessly, day after day. We would be tired at night and lie down in the accumulated heat of the little bedrooms after the long hot day and the breeze would stir almost imperceptibly outside and the smell of the swamp drift in through the rusty screens. Sleep would come easily and in the morning the red squirrel would be on the roof, tapping out his gay routine. I kept remembering everything, lying in bed in the mornings—the small steamboat that had a long rounded stern like the lip of a Ubangi, and how quietly she ran on the moonlight sails, when the older boys played their mandolins and the girls sang and we ate doughnuts dipped in sugar, and how sweet the music was on the water in the shining night, and what it had felt like to think about girls then. After breakfast we would go up to the store and the things were in the same place—the minnows in a bottle, the plugs and spinners disarranged and pawed over by the youngsters from the boys' camp, the Fig Newtons and the Beeman's gum. Outside, the road was tarred and cars stood in front of the store. Inside, all was just as it had always been, except there was more Coca-Cola and not so much Moxie and root beer and birch beer

and sarsaparilla. We would walk out with the bottle of pop apiece and sometimes the pop would backfire up our noses and hurt. We explored the streams, quietly, where the turtles slid off the sunny logs and dug their way into the soft bottom; and we lay on the town wharf and fed worms to the tame bass. Everywhere we went I had trouble making out which was I, the one walking at my side, the one walking in my pants.

14　　One afternoon while we were at that lake a thunderstorm came up. It was like the revival of an old melodrama that I had seen long ago with childish awe. The second-act climax of the drama of the electrical disturbance over a lake in America had not changed in any important respect. This was the big scene, still the big scene. The whole thing was so familiar, the first feeling of oppression and heat and a general air around camp of not wanting to go very far away. In midafternoon (it was all the same) a curious darkening of the sky, and a lull in everything that had made life tick; and then the way the boats suddenly swung the other way at their moorings with the coming of a breeze out of the new quarter, and the premonitory rumble. Then the kettle drum, then the snare, then the bass drum and cymbals, then crackling light against the dark, and the gods grinning and licking their chops in the hills. Afterward the calm, the rain steadily rustling in the calm lake, the return of light and hope and spirits, and the campers running out in joy and relief to go swimming in the rain, their bright cries perpetuating the deathless joke about how they were getting simply drenched, and the children screaming with delight at the new sensation of bathing in the rain, and the joke about getting drenched linking the generations in a strong indestructible chain. And the comedian who waded in carrying an umbrella.

15　　When the others went swimming my son said he was going in, too. He pulled his dripping trunks from the line where they had hung all through the shower and wrung them out. Languidly, and with no thought of going in, I watched him, his hard little body, skinny and bare, saw him wince slightly as he pulled up around his vitals the small, soggy, icy garment. As he buckled the swollen belt, suddenly my groin felt the chill of death.

QUESTIONS TO CONSIDER

1. What are the differences between the salt water and the lake water, as described in the first paragraph?

2. What draws the author to the lake water? Why does he take his son to the lake?

3. Did the author have the experiences he expected? Why or why not?

4. In the fifth paragraph the author states that "the years were a mirage and that there had been no years." Explain what the writer means by this.

5. Why does the writer feel "the chill of death" in the end?

Professions for Women

Virginia Woolf

- **AP** Argument and Persuasion
- **A** Analogy

1   When your secretary invited me to come here, she told me that your Society is concerned with the employment of women and she suggested that I might tell you something about my own professional experiences. It is true I am a woman; it is true I am employed; but what professional experiences have I had? It is difficult to say. My profession is literature; and in that profession there are fewer experiences for women than in any other, with the exception of the stage—fewer, I mean, that are peculiar to women. For the road was cut many years ago—by Fanny Burney, by Aphra Behn, by Harriet Martineau, by Jane Austen, by George Eliot—many famous women, and many more unknown and forgotten, have been before me, making the path smooth, and regulating my steps. Thus, when I came to write, there were very few material obstacles in my way. Writing was a reputable and harmless occupation. The family peace was not broken by the scratching of a pen. No demand was made upon the family purse. For ten and sixpence one can buy paper enough to write all the plays of Shakespeare—if one has a mind that way. Pianos and models, Paris, Vienna, and Berlin, masters and mistresses, are not needed by a writer. The cheapness of writing paper is, of course, the reason why women have succeeded as writers before they have succeeded in the other professions.

2   But to tell you my story—it is a simple one. You have only got to figure to yourselves a girl in a bedroom with a pen in her hand. She had only to move that pen from left to right—from ten o'clock to one. Then it occurred to her to do what is simple and cheap enough after all—to slip a few of those pages into an envelope, fix a penny stamp in the corner, and drop the envelope into the red box at the corner. It was thus that I became a journalist; and my effort was rewarded on the first day of the following month—a very glorious day it was for me—by a letter from an editor containing a cheque for one pound ten shillings and sixpence. But to show you how little I deserve to be called a professional woman, how little I know of the struggles and difficulties of such lives, I have to admit

that instead of spending that sum upon bread and butter, rent, shoes and stockings, or butcher's bills, I went out and bought a cat—a beautiful cat, a Persian cat, which very soon involved me in bitter disputes with my neighbors.

3   What could be easier than to write articles and to buy Persian cats with the profits? But wait a moment. Articles have to be about something. Mine, I seem to remember, was about a novel by a famous man. And while I was writing this review, I discovered that if I were going to review books I should need to do battle with a certain phantom. And the phantom was a woman, and when I came to know her better I called her after the heroine of a famous poem. The Angel in the House. It was she who used to come between me and my paper when I was writing reviews. It was she who bothered me and wasted my time and so tormented me that at last I killed her. You who come of a younger and happier generation may not have heard of her—you may not know what I mean by The Angel in the House. I will describe her as shortly as I can. She was intensely sympathetic. She was immensely charming. She was utterly unselfish. She excelled in the difficult arts of family life. She sacrificed herself daily.

4   If there was chicken, she took the leg; if there was a draught she sat in it—in short she was so constituted that she never had a mind or a wish of her own, but preferred to sympathize always with the minds and wishes of others. Above all—I need not say it—she was pure. Her purity was supposed to be her chief beauty—her blushes, her great grace. In those days—the last of Queen Victoria—every house had its Angel. And when I came to write I encountered her with the very first words. The shadow of her wings fell on my page; I heard the rustling of her skirts in the room. Directly, that is to say, I took my pen in my hand to review that novel by a famous man, she slipped behind me and whispered: "My dear, you are a young woman. You are writing about a book that has been written by a man. Be sympathetic; be tender; flatter; deceive; use all the arts and wiles of our sex. Never let anybody guess that you have a mind of your own. Above all, be pure." And she made as if to guide my pen. I now record the one act for which I take some credit to myself, though the credit rightly belongs to some excellent ancestors of mine who left me a certain sum of money—shall we say five hundred pounds a year?—so that it was not necessary for me to depend solely on charm for my living. I turned upon her and caught her by the throat. I did my best to kill her. My excuse if I were to be had up at a court of law, would be that I acted in self-defense. Had I not killed her she would have killed me. She would have plucked the

heart out of my writing. For as I found directly, as I put pen to paper, you cannot review even a novel without having a mind of your own, without expressing what you think to be the truth about human relations, morality, sex. And all these questions, according to the Angel of the House, cannot be dealt with freely and openly by women; they must charm, they must conciliate, they must—to put it bluntly—tell lies if they are to succeed. Thus, whenever I felt the shadow of her wing or the radiance of her halo upon my page, I took up the inkpot and flung it at her. She died hard. Her fictitious nature was of great assistance to her. It is far harder to kill a phantom than a reality. She was always creeping back when I thought I had dispatched her. Though I flatter myself that I killed her in the end, the struggle was severe; it took much time that had better have been spent upon learning Greek grammar; or in roaming the world in search of adventures. But it was a real experience; it was an experience that was bound to befall all women writers at that time. Killing the Angel in the House was part of the occupation of a woman writer.

5   But to continue my story. The Angel was dead; what then remained? You may say that what remained was a simple and common object—a young woman in a bedroom with an inkpot. In other words, now that she had rid herself of falsehood, that young woman had only to be herself. Ah, but what is "herself"? I mean, what is a woman? I assure you, I do not know. I do not believe that you know. I do not believe that anybody can know until she has expressed herself in all the arts and professions open to human skill. That indeed is one of the reasons why I have come here—out of respect for you, who are in process of showing us by your experiments what a woman is, who are in process of providing us, by your failures and successes, with that extremely important piece of information.

6   But to continue the story of my professional experiences. I made one pound ten and six by my first review; and I bought a Persian cat with the proceeds. Then I grew ambitious. A Persian cat is all very well, I said; but a Persian cat is not enough. I must have a motor-car. And it was thus that I became a novelist—for it is a very strange thing that people will give you a motor-car if you will tell them a story. It is a still stranger thing that there is nothing so delightful in the world as telling stories. It is far pleasanter than writing reviews of famous novels. And yet, if I am to obey your secretary and tell you my professional experiences as a novelist, I must tell you about a very strange experience that befell me as a novelist. And to understand it you must try first to imagine a novelist's state of mind. I hope I am not giving away professional secrets if I say that a novelist's chief

desire is to be as unconscious as possible. He has to induce in himself a state of perpetual lethargy. He wants life to proceed with the utmost quiet and regularity. He wants to see the same faces, to read the same books, to do the same things day after day, month after month, while he is writing, so that nothing may break the illusion in which he is living—so that nothing may disturb or disquiet the mysterious nosings about, feelings round, darts, dashes, and sudden discoveries of that very shy and illusive spirit, the imagination. I suspect that this state is the same both for men and women. Be that as it may, I want you to imagine me writing a novel in a state of trance. I want you to figure to yourselves a girl sitting with a pen in her hand, which for minutes, and indeed for hours, she never dips into the inkpot. The image that comes to my mind when I think of this girl is the image of a fisherman lying sunk in dreams on the verge of a deep lake with a rod held out over the water. She was letting her imagination sweep unchecked round every rock and cranny of the world that lies submerged in the depths of our unconscious being. Now came the experience that I believe to be far commoner with women writers than with men. The line raced through the girl's fingers. Her imagination had rushed away. It had sought the pools, the depths, the dark places where the largest fish slumber. And then there was a smash. There was an explosion. There was foam and confusion. The imagination had dashed itself against something hard. The girl was roused from her dream. She was indeed in a state of the most acute and difficult distress. To speak without figure, she had thought of something, something about the body, about the passion, which it was unfitting for her as a woman to say. Men, her reason told her, would be shocked. The consciousness of what men will say of a woman who speaks the truth about her passions had roused her from her artist's state of unconsciousness. She could write no more. The trance was over. Her imagination could work no longer. This I believe to be a very common experience with women writers—they are impeded by the extreme conventionality of the other sex. For though men sensibly allow themselves great freedom in these respects, I doubt that they realize or can control the extreme severity with which they condemn such freedom in women.

7   These then were two very genuine experiences of my own. These were two of the adventures of my professional life. The first—killing the Angel in the House—I think I solved. She died. But the second, telling the truth about my own experiences as a body, I do not think I solved. I doubt that any woman has solved it yet. The obstacles against her are still immensely powerful—and yet they are very difficult to define. Outwardly, what is

simpler than to write books? Outwardly, what obstacles are there for a woman rather than for a man? Inwardly, I think, the case is very different; she has still many ghosts to fight, many prejudices to overcome. Indeed it will be a long time still, I think, before a woman can sit down to write a book without finding a phantom to be slain, a rock to be dashed against. And if this is so in literature, the freest of all professions for women, how is it in the new professions which you are now for the first time entering?

8   Those are the questions that I should like, had I time, to ask you. And indeed, if I have laid stress upon these professional experiences of mine, it is because I believe that they are, though in different forms, yours also. Even when the path is nominally open—when there is nothing to prevent a woman from being a doctor, a lawyer, a civil servant—there are many phantoms and obstacles, as I believe, looming in her way. To discuss and define them is I think of great value and importance; for thus only can the labour be shared, the difficulties be solved. But besides this, it is necessary also to discuss the ends and the aims for which we are fighting, for which we are doing battle with these formidable obstacles. Those aims cannot be taken for granted; they must be perpetually questioned and examined. The whole position, as I see it—here in this hall surrounded by women practising for the first time in history I know not how many different professions—is one of extraordinary interest and importance. You have won rooms of your own in the house hitherto exclusively owned by men. You are able, though not without great labour and effort, to pay the rent. You are earning your five hundred pounds a year. But this freedom is only a beginning; the room is your own, but it is still bare. It has to be furnished; it has to be decorated; it has to be shared. How are you going to furnish it, how are you going to decorate it? With whom are you going to share it, and upon what terms? These, I think are questions of the utmost importance and interest. For the first time in history you are able to ask them; for the first time you are able to decide for yourselves what the answers should be. Willingly would I stay and discuss those questions and answers—but not tonight. My time is up; and I must cease.

? QUESTIONS TO CONSIDER

1. Who is Virginia Woolf's audience for this piece of writing (which she originally gave as a lecture)? Why are they interested in hearing about her experiences as a writer? What does Woolf wish to convey to them?

2. What are some of the benefits that Woolf outlines to having a career? Do you think that Woolf is being genuine when she says, "What could

be easier than to write articles and to buy Persian cats with the profits?" According to Woolf, what is *easy* about being a writer and what is *challenging* about it?

3. What is Woolf referring to when she says that "Even when the path is nominally open—when there is nothing to prevent a woman from being a doctor, a lawyer, a civil servant—there are many phantoms and obstacles, as I believe, looming in her way"?

4. Woolf describes the Angel in the House in the following way: "She was intensely sympathetic. She was immensely charming. She was utterly unselfish. She excelled in the difficult arts of family life. She sacrificed herself daily...in short she was so constituted that she never had a mind or a wish of her own." What does Woolf mean when she says that she had to "kill the Angel in the House" in order to pursue a career as a writer?

Learning to Read

Malcolm X

- **PA** Process Analysis
- **N** Narration
- **IE** Illustration and Exemplification
- **DES** Description

- **CC** Compare and Contrast
- **CE** Cause and Effect

1   It was because of my letters that I happened to stumble upon starting to acquire some kind of a homemade education.

2   I became increasingly frustrated at not being able to express what I wanted to convey in letters that I wrote, especially those to Mr. Elijah Muhammad. In the street, I had been the most articulate hustler out there—I had commanded attention when I said something. But now, trying to write simple English, I not only wasn't articulate, I wasn't even functional. How would I sound writing in slang, the way I would *say* it, something such as "Look, daddy, let me pull your coat about a cat, Elijah Muhammad—"

3   Many who today hear me somewhere in person, or on television, or those who read something I've said, will think I went to school far beyond the eighth grade. This impression is due entirely to my prison studies.

4   It had really begun back in the Charlestown Prison, when Bimbi first made me feel envy of his stock of knowledge. Bimbi had always taken charge of any conversation he was in, and I had tried to emulate him. But every book I picked up had few sentences which didn't contain anywhere from one to nearly all of the words that might as well have been in Chinese. When I just skipped those words, of course, I really ended up with little idea of what the book said. So I had come to the Norfolk Prison Colony still going through only book-reading motions. Pretty soon, I would have quit even these motions, unless I had received the motivation that I did.

5   I saw that the best thing I could do was get hold of a dictionary—to study, to learn some words. I was lucky enough to reason also that I should try to improve my penmanship. It was sad. I couldn't even write in a straight line. It was both ideas together that moved me to request a dictionary along with some tablets and pencils from the Norfolk Prison Colony school.

6   I spent two days just riffling uncertainly through the dictionary's pages. I'd never realized so many words existed! I didn't know *which* words I needed to learn. Finally, just to start some kind of action, I began copying.

7   In my slow, painstaking, ragged handwriting, I copied into my tablet everything printed on that first page, down to the punctuation marks.

8   I believe it took me a day. Then, aloud, I read back, to myself, everything I'd written on the tablet. Over and over, aloud, to myself, I read my own handwriting.

9   I woke up the next morning, thinking about those words—immensely proud to realize that not only had I written so much at one time, but I'd written words that I never knew were in the world. Moreover, with a little effort, I also could remember what many of these words meant. I reviewed the words whose meanings I didn't remember. Funny thing, from the dictionary first page right now, that "aardvark" springs to my mind. The dictionary had a picture of it, a long-tailed, long-eared, burrowing African mammal, which lives off termites caught by sticking out its tongue as an anteater does for ants.

10   I was so fascinated that I went on—I copied the dictionary's next page. And the same experience came when I studied that. With every succeeding page, I also learned of people and places and events from history. Actually the dictionary is like a miniature encyclopedia. Finally the dictionary's A section had filled a whole tablet—and I went on into the B's. That was the way I started copying what eventually became the entire dictionary. It went a lot faster after so much practice helped me to pick up handwriting speed. Between what I wrote in my tablet, and writing letters, during the rest of my time in prison I would guess I wrote a million words.

11   I suppose it was inevitable that as my word-base broadened, I could for the first time pick up a book and read and now begin to understand what the book was saying. Anyone who has read a great deal can imagine the new world that opened. Let me tell you something: from then until I left that prison, in every free moment I had, if I was not reading in the library, I was reading on my bunk. You couldn't have gotten me out of books with a wedge. Between Mr. Muhammad's teachings, my correspondence, my visitors—usually Ella and Reginald—and my reading of books, months passed without my even thinking about being imprisoned. In fact, up to then, I never had been so truly free in my life.

12   The Norfolk Prison Colony's library was in the school building. A variety of classes was taught there by instructors who came from such places

as Harvard and Boston universities. The weekly debates between inmate teams were also held in the school building. You would be astonished to know how worked up convict debaters and audiences would get over subjects like "Should Babies Be Fed Milk?"

13   Available on the prison library's shelves were books on just about every general subject. Much of the big private collection that Parkhurst had willed to the prison was still in crates and boxes in the back of the library—thousands of old books. Some of them looked ancient: covers faded, old-time parchment-looking binding. Parkhurst, I've mentioned, seemed to have been principally interested in history and religion. He had the money and the special interest to have a lot of books that you wouldn't have in general circulation. Any college library would have been lucky to get that collection.

14   As you can imagine, especially in a prison where there was heavy emphasis on rehabilitation, an inmate was smiled upon if he demonstrated an unusually intense interest in books. There was a sizable number of well-read inmates, especially the popular debaters. Some were said by many to be practically walking encyclopedias. They were almost celebrities. No university would ask any student to devour literature as I did when this new world opened to me, of being able to read and *understand*.

15   I read more in my room than in the library itself. An inmate who was known to read a lot could check out more than the permitted maximum number of books. I preferred reading in the total isolation of my own room.

16   When I had progressed to really serious reading, every night at about ten P.M. I would be outraged with the "lights out." It always seemed to catch me right in the middle of something engrossing.

17   Fortunately, right outside my door was a corridor light that cast a glow into my room. The glow was enough to read by, once my eyes adjusted to it. So when "lights out" came, I would sit on the floor where I could continue reading in that glow.

18   At one-hour intervals the night guards paced past every room. Each time I heard the approaching footsteps, I jumped into bed and feigned sleep. And as soon as the guard passed, I got back out of bed onto the floor area of that light-glow, where I would read for another fifty-eight minutes—until the guard approached again. That went on until three or four every morning. Three or four hours of sleep a night was enough for me. Often in the years in the streets I had slept less than that.

19   The teachings of Mr. Muhammad stressed how history had been "whitened"—when white men had written history books, the black man simply had been left out. Mr. Muhammad couldn't have said anything that would have struck me much harder. I had never forgotten how when my class, me and all of those whites, had studied seventh-grade United States history back in Mason, the history of the Negro had been covered in one paragraph, and the teacher had gotten a big laugh with his joke, "Negroes' feet are so big that when they walk, they leave a hole in the ground."

20   This is one reason why Mr. Muhammad's teachings spread so swiftly all over the United States, among *all* Negroes, whether or not they became followers of Mr. Muhammad. The teachings ring true—to every Negro. You can hardly show me a black adult in America—or a white one, for that matter—who knows from the history books anything like the truth about the black man's role. In my own case, once I heard of the "glorious history of the black man," I took special pains to hunt in the library for books that would inform me on details about black history.

21   I can remember accurately the very first set of books that really impressed me. I have since bought that set of books and have it at home for my children to read as they grow up. It's called *Wonders of the World*. It's full of pictures of archeological finds, statues that depict, usually, non-European people.

22   I found books like Will Durant's *Story of Civilization*. I read H. G. Wells' *Outline of History*. *Souls of Black Folk* by W. E. B. Du Bois gave me a glimpse into the black people's history before they came to this country. Carter G. Woodson's *Negro History* opened my eyes about black empires before the black slave was brought to the United States, and the early Negro struggles for freedom.

23   J. A. Rogers' three volumes of *Sex and Race* told about race-mixing before Christ's time; about Aesop being a black man who told fables; about Egypt's Pharaohs; about the great Coptic Christian Empires; about Ethiopia, the earth's oldest continuous black civilization, as China is the oldest continuous civilization.

24   Mr. Muhammad's teaching about how the white man had been created led me to *Findings in Genetics* by Gregor Mendel. (The dictionary's G section was where I had learned what "genetics" meant.) I really studied this book by the Austrian monk. Reading it over and over, especially certain sections, helped me to understand that if you started with a black man, a white man could be produced; but starting with a white man, you never could produce a black man—because the white gene is recessive.

334 READINGS **MALCOLM X**

And since no one disputes that there was but one Original Man, the conclusion is clear.

25   During the last year or so, in the *New York Times*, Arnold Toynbee used the word "bleached" in describing the white man. (His words were: "White (i.e., bleached) human beings of North European origin...") Toynbee also referred to the European geographic area as only a peninsula of Asia. He said there is no such thing as Europe. And if you look at the globe, you will see for yourself that America is only an extension of Asia. (But at the same time Toynbee is among those who have helped to bleach history. He has written that Africa was the only continent that produced no history. He won't write that again. Every day now, the truth is coming to light.)

26   I never will forget how shocked I was when I began reading about slavery's total horror. It made such an impact upon me that it later became one of my favorite subjects when I became a minister of Mr. Muhammad's. The world's most monstrous crime, the sin and the blood on the white man's hands, are almost impossible to believe. Books like the one by Frederick Olmstead opened my eyes to the horrors suffered when the slave was landed in the United States. The European woman, Fannie Kimball, who had married a Southern white slaveowner, described how human beings were degraded. Of course I read *Uncle Tom's Cabin*. In fact, I believe that's the only novel I have ever read since I started serious reading.

27   Parkhurst's collection also contained some bound pamphlets of the Abolitionist Anti-Slavery Society of New England. I read descriptions of atrocities, saw those illustrations of black slave women tied up and flogged with whips; of black mothers watching their babies being dragged off, never to be seen by their mothers again; of dogs after slaves, and of the fugitive slave catchers, evil white men with whips and clubs and chains and guns. I read about the slave preacher Nat Turner, who put the fear of God into the white slavemaster. Nat Turner wasn't going around preaching pie-in-the-sky and "non-violent" freedom for the black man. There in Virginia one night in 1831, Nat and seven other slaves started out at his master's home and through the night they went from one plantation "big house" to the next, killing, until by the next morning 57 white people were dead and Nat had about 70 slaves following him. White people, terrified for their lives, fled from their homes, locked themselves up in public buildings, hid in the woods, and some even left the state. A small army of soldiers took two months to catch and hang Nat Turner. Somewhere I

have read where Nat Turner's example is said to have inspired John Brown to invade Virginia and attack Harper's Ferry nearly thirty years later, with thirteen white men and five Negroes.

28   I read Herodotus, "the father of History," or, rather, I read about him. And I read the histories of various nations, which opened my eyes gradually, then wider and wider, to how the whole world's white men had indeed acted like devils, pillaging and raping and bleeding and draining the whole world's non-white people. I remember, for instance, books such as Will Durant's story of Oriental civilization, and Mahatma Gandhi's accounts of the struggle to drive the British out of India.

29   Book after book showed me how the white man had brought upon the world's black, brown, red, and yellow peoples every variety of the sufferings of exploitation. I saw how since the sixteenth century, the so-called "Christian trader" white man began to ply the seas in his lust for Asian and African empires, and plunder, and power. I read, I saw, how the white man never has gone among the non-white peoples bearing the Cross in the true manner and spirit of Christ's teachings—meek, humble, and Christ-like.

30   I perceived, as I read, how the collective white man had been actually nothing but a piratical opportunist who used Faustian machinations to make his own Christianity his initial wedge in criminal conquests. First, always "religiously," he branded "heathen" and "pagan" labels upon ancient non-white cultures and civilizations. The stage thus set, he then turned upon his non-white victims his weapons of war.

31   I read how, entering India—half a *billion* deeply religious brown people—the British white man, by 1759, through promises, trickery and manipulations, controlled much of India through Great Britain's East India Company. The parasitical British administration kept tentacling out to half of the subcontinent. In 1857, some of the desperate people of India finally mutinied—and, excepting the African slave trade, nowhere has history recorded any more unnecessary bestial and ruthless human carnage than the British suppression of the non-white Indian people.

32   Over 115 million African blacks—close to the 1930s population of the United States—were murdered or enslaved during the slave trade. And I read how when the slave market was glutted, the cannibalistic white powers of Europe next carved up, as their colonies, the richest areas of the black continent. And Europe's chancelleries for the next century played a chess game of naked exploitation and power from Cape Horn to Cairo.

33   Ten guards and the warden couldn't have torn me out of those books. Not even Elijah Muhammad could have been more eloquent than those books were in providing indisputable proof that the collective white man had acted like a devil in virtually every contact he had with the world's collective non-white man. I listen today to the radio, and watch television, and read the headlines about the collective white man's fear and tension concerning China. When the white man professes ignorance about why the Chinese hate him so, my mind can't help flashing back to what I read, there in prison, about how the blood forebears of this same white man raped China at a time when China was trusting and helpless. Those original white "Christian traders" sent into China millions of pounds of opium. By 1839, so many of the Chinese were addicts that China's desperate government destroyed twenty thousand chests of opium. The first Opium War was promptly declared by the white man. Imagine! Declaring *war* upon someone who objects to being narcotized! The Chinese were severely beaten, with Chinese-invented gunpowder.

34   The Treaty of Nanking made China pay the British white man for the destroyed opium; forced open China's major ports to British trade; forced China to abandon Hong Kong; fixed China's import tariffs so low that cheap British articles soon flooded in, maiming China's industrial development.

35   After a second Opium War, the Tientsin Treaties legalized the ravaging opium trade, legalized a British-French-American control of China's customs. China tried delaying that Treaty's ratification; Peking was looted and burned.

36   "Kill the foreign white devils!" was the 1901 Chinese war cry in the Boxer Rebellion. Losing again, this time the Chinese were driven from Peking's choicest areas. The vicious, arrogant white man put up the famous signs, "Chinese and dogs not allowed."

37   Red China after World War II closed its doors to the Western white world. Massive Chinese agricultural, scientific, and industrial efforts are described in a book that *Life* magazine recently published. Some observers inside Red China have reported that the world never has known such a hate-white campaign as is now going on in this non-white country where, present birth-rates continuing, in fifty more years Chinese will be half the earth's population. And it seems that some Chinese chickens will soon come home to roost, with China's recent successful nuclear tests.

38   Let us face reality. We can see in the United Nations a new world order being shaped, along color lines—an alliance among the non-white

nations. America's U.N. Ambassador Adlai Stevenson complained not long ago that in the United Nations "a skin game" was being played. He was right. He was facing reality. A "skin game" *is* being played. But Ambassador Stevenson sounded like Jesse James accusing the marshal of carrying a gun. Because who in the world's history ever has played a worse "skin game" than the white man?

* * *

39   Mr. Muhammad, to whom I was writing daily, had no idea of what a new world had opened up to me through my efforts to document his teachings in books.

40   When I discovered philosophy, I tried to touch all the landmarks of philosophical development. Gradually, I read most of the old philosophers, Occidental and Oriental. The Oriental philosophers were the ones I came to prefer; finally, my impression was that most Occidental philosophy had largely been borrowed from the Oriental thinkers. Socrates, for instance, traveled in Egypt. Some sources even say that Socrates was initiated into some of the Egyptian mysteries. Obviously Socrates got some of his wisdom among the East's wise men.

41   I have often reflected upon the new vistas that reading opened to me. I knew right there in prison that reading had changed forever the course of my life. As I see it today, the ability to read awoke inside me some long dormant craving to be mentally alive. I certainly wasn't seeking any degree, the way a college confers a status symbol upon its students. My homemade education gave me, with every additional book that I read, a little bit more sensitivity to the deafness, dumbness, and blindness that was afflicting the black race in America. Not long ago, an English writer telephoned me from London, asking questions. One was, "What's your alma mater?" I told him, "Books." You will never catch me with a free fifteen minutes in which I'm not studying something I feel might be able to help the black man.

42   Yesterday I spoke in London, and both ways on the plane across the Atlantic I was studying a document about how the United Nations proposes to insure the human rights of the oppressed minorities of the world. The American black man is the world's most shameful case of minority oppression. What makes the black man think of himself as only an internal United States issue is just a catch-phrase, two words, "civil rights." How is the black man going to get "civil rights" before first he wins his *human* rights? If the American black man will start thinking about

 READINGS

his *human* rights, and then start thinking of himself as part of one of the world's great peoples, he will see he has a case for the United Nations.

43   I can't think of a better case! Four hundred years of black blood and sweat invested here in America, and the white man still has the black man begging for what every immigrant fresh off the ship can take for granted the minute he walks down the gangplank.

44   But I'm digressing. I told the Englishman that my alma mater was books, a good library. Every time I catch a plane, I have with me a book that I want to read—and that's a lot of books these days. If I weren't out here every day battling the white man, I could spend the rest of my life reading, just satisfying my curiosity—because you can hardly mention anything I'm not curious about. I don't think anybody ever got more out of going to prison than I did. In fact, prison enabled me to study far more intensively than I would have if my life had gone differently and I had attended some college. I imagine that one of the biggest troubles with colleges is there are too many distractions, too much panty-raiding, fraternities, and boola-boola and all of that. Where else but in a prison could I have attacked my ignorance by being able to study intensely sometimes as much as fifteen hours a day?

QUESTIONS TO CONSIDER

1. Before you read this essay:
    - How important are reading and writing in your life? Explain.
    - Why are you motivated to learn? Explain.
    - What are you most motivated to learn? Why?

2. How far did Malcolm X progress in grade school? Where did he do most of his "book learning"? Why did he begin a program of self-education?

3. How did he learn new words? Would you do this? Why or why not?

4. How would you describe Malcolm X's writing style and level of language? Select several examples of passages from this essay to illustrate your description.

5. Both Richard Rodriguez and Malcom X explain their relationship with books and reading. What are some of the similarities and differences you noticed between the two authors' approach to reading?

6. Do you believe self-education can be just as impactful as academic education? Explain.

Credits

Index of Authors and Titles

A

Adler, Mortimer, "How to Mark a Book," 35–39

"The Allegory of the Cave" (Plato), 198–205

Alvarez, Julia, "I Want to Be Miss America," 40–45

B

"Being Country" (Mason), 160–163

Black and White in Shades of Gray" (Salam), 236–241

C

Carr, Nicholas, "Is Google Making Us Stupid?", 46–56

"The College Dropout Boom" (Leonhardt), 148–159

Coates, Ta-Nehisi, "You Left Out the Part About...," 57–59

D

"The Death of Horatio Alger" (Krugman), 144–147

"Designer Genes" (McKibben), 164–175

Douglass, Frederick, "Learning to Read and Write," 60–65

E

Ehrenreich, Barbara, "Nickel and Dimed: On (Not) Getting By in America," 66–92

Elbow, Peter, "Freewriting," 93–96

"Everyday Use" (Walker), 308–316

F

"Family Values" (Rodriguez), 223–230

"Freewriting" (Elbow), 93–96

G

Gitlin, Todd, "Supersaturation, or, The Media Torrent and Disposable Feeling," 97–103

H

"How Computers Change the Way We Think" (Turkle), 301–307

"How to Mark a Book" (Adler), 35–39

Hughes, Langston, "Salvation," 104–106

I

"Is Google Making Us Stupid?" (Carr), 46–56

"I Want to Be Miss America" (Alvarez), 40–45

J

Jacoby, Susan, "When Bright Girls Decide that Math Is 'a Waste of Time'," 107–110

K

King, Martin Luther, Jr., "Letter from Birmingham Jail," 120–135

King, Stephen, "My Creature from the Black Lagoon," 111–119

Kingsolver, Barbara, "Stone Soup," 136–143

Krugman, Paul, "The Death of Horatio Alger," 144–147

L

"Learning to Read" (Malcolm X), 330–338

"Learning to Read and Write" (Douglass), 60–65

Leonhardt, David, "The College Dropout Boom," 148–159

"Letter from Birmingham Jail" (King Jr.), 120–135

"The Lonely, Good Company of Books" (Rodriguez), 231–235

M

"The Maker's Eye: Revising Your Own Manuscripts" (Murray), 182–187

Mason, Bobbie Ann, "Being Country," 160–163

McKibben, Bill, "Designer Genes," 164–175

Momaday, N. Scott, "The Way to Rainy Mountain," 176–181

"Mother Tongue" (Tan), 265–270

Murray, Donald M., "The Maker's Eye: Revising Your Own Manuscripts," 182–187

"My Creature from the Black Lagoon" (King), 111–119

N

"Nickel and Dimed: On (Not) Getting By in America" (Ehrenreich), 66–92

"A Note to Young Immigrants" (Perkins), 195–197

O

"Once More to the Lake" (White), 317–323

Orwell, George, "Shooting an Elephant," 188–194

P

Perkins, Mitali, "A Note to Young Immigrants," 195–197

Plato, "The Allegory of the Cave," 198–205

"Professions for Women" (Woolf), 324–329

Q

Quindlen, Anna, "Sex Ed," 206–208

R

Reich, Robert B., "Why the Rich Are Getting Richer, and the Poor, Poorer," 209–222

Rodriguez, Richard, "Family Values," 223–230

Rodriguez, Richard, "The Lonely, Good Company of Books," 231–235

S

Salam, Reihan, "Black and White in Shades of Gray," 236–241

"Salvation" (Hughes), 104–106

Sanders, Scott Russell, "Under the Influence," 242–254

"Sex, Lies and Conversation: Why Is It So Hard for Men and Women to Talk to Each Other?" (Tannen), 271–277

"Sex Ed" (Quindlen), 206–208

"Shooting an Elephant" (Orwell), 188–194

Steinem, Gloria, "Wonder Woman," 255–264

"Stone Soup" (Kingsolver), 136–143

"Supersaturation, or, The Media Torrent and Disposable Feeling" (Gitlin), 97–103

T

Tan, Amy, "Mother Tongue," 265–270

Tannen, Deborah, "Sex, Lies and Conversation: Why Is It So Hard for Men and Women to Talk to Each Other?", 271–277

"'This Is the End of the World': The Black Death" (Tuchman), 291–300

Thoreau, Henry David, "Where I Lived, And What I Lived For," 278–290

Tuchman, Barbara, "'This Is the End of the World': The Black Death," 291–300

Turkle, Sherry, "How Computers Change the Way We Think," 301–307

U

"Under the Influence" (Sanders), 242–254

W

Walker, Alice, "Everyday Use," 308–316

"The Way to Rainy Mountain" (Momaday), 176–181

"When Bright Girls Decide that Math Is 'a Waste of Time'" (Jacoby), 107–110

"Where I Lived, And What I Lived For" (Thoreau), 278–290

White, E. B., "Once More to the Lake," 317–323

"Why the Rich Are Getting Richer, and the Poor, Poorer" (Reich), 209–222

"Wonder Woman" (Steinem), 255–264

Woolf, Virginia, "Professions for Women," 324–329

X

X, Malcolm, "Learning to Read," 330–338

Y

"You Left Out the Part About…" (Coates) 57–59